CQ GUIDE TO

CURRENT AMERICAN GOVERNMENT

Spring 1987

Congressional Quarterly Inc.

Congressional Quarterly Inc.

Congressional Quarterly Inc., an editorial research service and publishing company, serves clients in the fields of news, education, business and government. It combines specific coverage of Congress, government and politics by Congressional Quarterly with the more general subject range of an affiliated service, Editorial Research Reports.

Congressional Quarterly publishes the *Congressional Quarterly Weekly Report* and a variety of books, including college political science textbooks under the CQ Press imprint and public affairs paperbacks designed as timely reports to keep journalists, scholars and the public abreast of developing issues and events. CQ also publishes information directories and reference books on the federal government, national elections and politics, including the *Guide to Congress*, the *Guide to the U.S. Supreme Court*, the *Guide to U.S. Elections* and *Politics in America*. The *CQ Almanac*, a compendium of legislation for one session of Congress, is published each year. *Congress and the Nation*, a record of government for a presidential term, is published every four years.

CQ publishes *The Congressional Monitor*, a daily report on current and future activities of congressional committees, and several newsletters including *Congressional Insight*, a weekly analysis of congressional action, and *Campaign Practices Reports*, a semimonthly update on campaign laws.

CQ's online Washington Alert Service provides government affairs specialists with details of congressional action on a continually updated basis.

Printed in the United States of America

Library of Congress Catalog No. 61-16893
International Standard Book No. 0-87187-401-6
International Standard Serial No. 0196-612X

Editor: Amy S. Meyers
Contributors: Andra Armstrong, Bob Benenson, Peter Bragdon, Jacqueline Calmes, Nadine Cohodas, Rhodes Cook, Harrison Donnelly, Philip D. Duncan, Alan Ehrenhalt, John Felton, Jeremy Gaunt, Stephen Gettinger, Rob Gurwitt, Janet Hook, David Rapp, Eileen Shanahan, Pat Towell, Tom Watson, Elizabeth Wehr, Elder Witt
Graphics: Richard A. Pottern, Robert Redding, Kathleen A. Ossenfort, John B. Auldridge
Index: Genevieve Clemens
Production: I. D. Fuller, Maceo Mayo

TABLE OF CONTENTS

THE CQ Guide to Current American Government is prepared twice yearly as an up-to-date handbook for the study of American government. It contains the most useful and instructional of recent Congressional Quarterly news research material, rearranged and edited for students of government and politics.

The Guide is designed to serve two main functions. First, it provides students with current illustrations of the continuing interplay of forces that constitute our political system. It shows not only how the president, Congress and judiciary act and react to one another but how this traditional interplay is tempered and influenced by other vital forces such as politics, changing social pressures, new administrations, current issues and lobbying. A study of the balance of power among the three branches of government, for example, at once raises questions about the current status of that balance — especially between the president and Congress — and likely changes in the balance to come. Illustrations of these forces at work will help the student see and learn from the important differences that exist between theory and operation, between format and function.

Second, the Guide is a starting point for discussion and individual research in the day-to-day operations of government. Such research may be as informal as the careful reading of good newspapers. With reliable news sources, a good library and ample amounts of curiosity and imagination, students can find in daily events — whether in Washington, D.C., their own state capital or hometown — a rich supply of case studies of government and politics in action. In the process, they stand to gain greater sophistication, not only as students, but as citizens.

To facilitate additional research on topical events, a new feature has been added to the Fall 1986 Guide. Citations to related and background articles in the Guide's basic sources of material, the CQ *Weekly Report* and the CQ *Almanac*, have been retained for the benefit of the Guide's users as well. CQ's *Weekly Report* and *Almanac* are available at most school and public libraries.

CQ GUIDE TO

CURRENT AMERICAN
GOVERNMENT

Spring 1987

CONGRESS

Congress Has Broad Authority
To Regulate Fiscal Affairs, Commerce

The authors of the Constitution recognized that the new government needed an executive to carry out the laws and a judiciary to resolve conflicts in them. But Congress would be the heart of the new republic. The House of Representatives was the only part of the federal government originally elected by the people; consequently, Congress was the branch of government expected to respond directly to their needs.

It was thus to the national legislature that the framers entrusted most of the power necessary to govern the new nation. To Congress the Constitution granted "all legislative Powers." These included the power to tax, regulate commerce, declare war, approve treaties and raise and maintain armies.

The framers also gave Congress some authority over the other two branches. Congress was granted the power to establish whatever federal judicial system below the Supreme Court seemed desirable and to impeach and convict the president, federal judges and other federal officers for treason, bribery or other high crimes and misdemeanors. Each chamber has authority to seat and discipline its own members.

The exercise of these powers is subject to some limitation. The Constitution specifically prevents Congress from singling out individuals for punishment and from imposing a direct tax that is unapportioned or an indirect tax that is not uniform. The most significant constitutional limitations may be those added by the First Amendment, prohibiting Congress from interfering with the free exercise of speech, the press, assembly, or religion, and the Fifth Amendment, prohibiting the taking of life, liberty or property without due process of law.

Fiscal Powers

Perhaps the most important of the constitutional prerogatives granted to Congress are the powers to tax and to spend. Congress may use its power to tax both to raise revenue to run the country and as a regulatory device. The power to spend allows Congress to determine policy on almost every matter that affects daily life in the United States.

Taxation

Taxes on the income and profits of individuals and corporations have become the federal government's basic sources of revenue since the 16th Amendment permitting a general income tax was ratified in 1913. In addition, Congress has imposed an excess profits tax on corporations during wartime, levied a variety of excise taxes, authorized estate and gift taxes and imposed payroll taxes to underpin the old-age insurance and unemployment compensation systems.

Tax legislation must, under a constitutional provision, originate in the House of Representatives. Tax and tariff bills are handled there by the Ways and Means Committee. After the House acts, such bills go to the Senate where they are referred to the Finance Committee. Because that committee and the full Senate may amend the House version of a tax bill, the Senate plays an influential role in the consideration and adoption of tax legislation. In a departure from tradition and constitutional dictates, the Senate initiated a major tax bill in 1982. It was enacted, although some House members challenged the constitutionality of the legislation.

In the post-World War II era, initiatives on raising, lowering, or enacting new taxes generally have been taken by the executive branch; it has prepared the initial recommendations and Congress has acted on them. But there is no requirement that the executive initiate tax changes. Congress itself generated a major tax reform bill in 1969 and a wide-ranging tax revision bill in 1976.

Appropriations

Revenue raised through taxation is not available in the Treasury to be disbursed by the executive branch to meet governmental needs simply as agency officials see fit. The Constitution gives to Congress the sole authority to determine how monies collected shall be spent and requires a regular statement of expenditures.

This appropriations procedure works in two steps after the president presents his annual budget requests to Congress. First, the various congressional committees consider the parts of the request that fall under their jurisdictions and report out bills authorizing expenditures and setting a ceiling on the amount of funds that can be spent for the programs. After the authorization becomes law, Congress actually provides (appropriates) the money to fund the programs. The amount of money appropriated often is less than the maximum amount specified in the authorization for the program.

Although the Constitution does not require it, appropriations traditionally originate in the House. Appropriations initially are considered by the relevant subcommittee of the House Appropriations Committee where the bulk of basic spending decisions are made, although both the full committee and the House may amend a bill before it is passed and sent to the Senate. What the Senate does in effect is to review the House action and hear appeals from agencies seeking changes in the allotments accorded them by the House.

Budget Control

Congress, having long treated its taxing and spending powers separately, in 1974 enacted the Congressional Budget and Impoundment Control Act (PL 93-344) to provide a method of setting overall fiscal policy for the federal government, and in some respects constrain congressional committees from acting against the goals espoused in the budget.

The budget law set up House and Senate Budget committees to write annual budgets and keep track of Congress' performance in adhering to them, and it created a Congressional Budget Office to provide technical information about the economy and the budget that previously was available only from the president's budget agency, the Office of Management and Budget.

In December 1985, the perceived failure of the 1974 law to prevent steadily increasing, multibillion-dollar deficits led Congress to make radical changes in budget procedures that presumably would force a balanced budget by October 1990. The new law, known as Gramm-Rudman-Hollings (PL 99-177) for its Senate sponsors, set maximum annual allowable deficits for the years 1986-91, and mandated automatic, across-the-board spending cuts if Congress failed to meet those goals.

Aside from a legal challenge to a key element of the process making the automatic cuts, the law was seen by many observers as a significant political step for a Congress previously unwilling to address huge deficits.

However, legislating under the lash of the 1985 Gramm-Rudman-Hollings anti-deficit law did not turn out quite the way it was advertised when the law was enacted in December 1985.

The first hitch came in early February 1986, when President Reagan submitted a fiscal 1987 budget that, according to the Congressional Budget Office (CBO), exceeded the Gramm-Rudman deficit target of $144 billion by some $16 billion in understated defense spending. Administration officials contested the CBO finding, although months later they acknowledged that fiscal 1986 defense outlays were running at least $5 billion ahead of their February estimate.

The same week as the president's budget request, a special federal court found the key feature of Gramm-Rudman — its automatic spending cut mechanism — to be unconstitutional. The mechanism was to be activated in mid-August each year if deficit re-estimates showed Congress and the president had not managed through conventional legislation to hold deficits below targets set by the statute.

Absent the automatic device, the deficit re-estimates would still be made, but any spending cuts necessitated by those estimates would take effect only if approved by Congress and the president.

The Supreme Court on July 7, 1986, upheld the lower court ruling that the automatic mechanism violated the separation-of-powers doctrine, because it assigned executive-type responsibilities to the General Accounting Office, which the court found to be an entity under the legislative branch.

The ruling brought firm assurances from sponsors of the anti-deficit law that its remaining procedure requiring congressional and presidential approval of spending cuts would work. Yet almost immediately, Sen. Phil Gramm, R-Texas, and his original cosponsors began pushing a revised version of the automatic procedure device which, Gramm said, was needed to eliminate "uncertainty" in deficit cutting.

The Senate July 30 added what became known as Gramm-Rudman-Hollings II, which would allow the Office of Management and Budget to determine the final shape of automatic spending cuts, to legislation (H J Res 668) raising the ceiling on the federal debt.

The debt-limit measure, which became stalled in the Senate by unrelated fights, was passed Aug. 9. But House hostility to the Gramm-Rudman amendment left its future — and that of the debt-limit increase — in considerable doubt.

Meanwhile, the Senate tried unsuccessfully to get the House to swallow a version of the Gramm-Rudman fix as part of a short-term, emergency debt-limit increase, designed to keep the government operating into September. The failed Gramm-Rudman fix would have been in effect for fiscal 1987 only.

Commerce Powers

Nearly as important as the powers to tax and spend is the power to regulate interstate and foreign commerce. Congress' exercise of its virtually exclusive authority in these areas has produced extensive government regulation not only of the actual transport of goods but also of their manufacture, sale and, in many, cases their purity and safety.

The Constitution gave Congress a broad and positive grant of power to regulate interstate and foreign commerce but left interpretation of the extent of the power to precedent and judicial determination. Although the Supreme Court initially gave Congress almost complete control over interstate commerce, the legislative branch seldom exercised its power. But with the passage of the Interstate Commerce Act of 1887, Congress moved decisively into the area of domestic regulation. The act, prompted by the individual states' inability to curb increasing abuses by railroads, ultimately was broadened to include regulation of trucking companies, bus lines, freight forwarders, water carriers, oil pipelines, transportation brokers and express agencies. The act, which established the Interstate Commerce Commission as the first regulatory agency, also led to creation of several other agencies that regulate various aspects of commercial transactions in the United States, as well as entire industries, such as communications and energy.

In 1890 Congress moved into federal regulation of commercial enterprise with enactment of the Sherman Antitrust Act "to protect commerce against unlawful restraints and monopolies." With the turn of the century, Congress began to regulate interstate commerce to protect the health and morals of the general populace. To this end, Congress banned interstate shipment of such items as lottery tickets, impure food and drugs and prostitutes.

Although the Supreme Court sanctioned most of these new uses of the interstate commerce power, it balked occasionally at certain regulations, such as the congressional attempt in 1916 to outlaw child labor by barring the shipment of goods made by children. It was this narrower view of the commerce power that prevailed when the Supreme Court reviewed and declared unconstitutional many of the early New Deal economic recovery programs. The confrontation resulted in the court's recognition of Congress' authority to regulate virtually all aspects of business and manufacture affecting interstate commerce.

Only once since 1937 has the court found an exercise of the commerce clause to be unconstitutional. In that same period it has sanctioned broadened uses of the commerce power. In the Civil Rights Act of 1964, Congress found justification in the commerce clause and the "equal protection" clause of the 14th Amendment for a ban on racial discrimination in most public accommodations. Congress used the commerce clause in 1968 as the basis for legislation making it a federal crime to travel in interstate commerce for the purpose of inciting or participating in a riot. The commerce clause is also the basis for the far-reaching federal clean air and water laws.

Foreign Policy Powers

While the president generally takes the initiative in foreign relations, Congress possesses several constitutionally granted powers that are indispensable to the success of the president's policies. These include the powers to raise taxes (to finance wars), create and maintain an armed force, regulate foreign commerce and ratify treaties. Except for votes on the Vietnam War in the 1970s, and Lebanon and Central America in the 1980s, Congress in the 20th century has chosen to use its powers to support the president in these matters rather than to challenge him.

While the Constitution gives Congress the power to declare war and "provide for the common Defence," both the initiation and conduct of war have come to be almost entirely directed by the president. In November 1973 Congress sought to restore some of its control over war efforts when it enacted, over President Nixon's veto, the War Powers Resolution (PL 93-148). In addition to certain reporting requirements, the measure set a 60-day limit on any presidential commitment of U.S. troops abroad without specific congressional authorization, unless troops were sent to respond to an "attack upon the United States, its territories or possessions or its armed forces." Unauthorized commitments could be terminated prior to the 60-day deadline through congressional passage of a concurrent resolution — a measure that does not require the president's signature to take effect.

Although Congress had never used that "legislative veto" authority to force a president to withdraw troops, the threat of a veto may have forced chief executives to consult more closely with Congress in taking military actions abroad. The Supreme Court's June 1983 ruling that legislative vetoes were unconstitutional dealt a blow to congressional influence over such commitments by nullifying that provision of the War Powers Resolution. In the wake of that ruling Congress wrestled with ways to develop an alternative method of influencing decisions. After the April 14, 1986, bombing of Libya, Congress again addressed the question of presidential prerogative. This time the debate centered on if and when the president should consult Congress in cases involving a U.S. response to terrorism.

Another area in which the Supreme Court's ruling could have a potentially far-reaching impact is congressional control of arms sales. In 1976 Congress enacted the Arms Export Control Act (PL 94-329), substantially expanding its power to veto arms sales to foreign countries through adoption of a concurrent resolution. Again, although most arms sales have raised little controversy, Congress has repeatedly challenged the president's judgment on specific sales to countries, particularly those in the volatile Middle East. As with the War Powers Resolution, Congress never has actually vetoed a proposed arms sale, but the possibility forced Presidents Jimmy Carter and Ronald Reagan to make compromises.

In spite of the Supreme Court's legislative veto ruling, congressional power over some other aspects of foreign policy has increased substantially. Legislative authority over the massive post-World War II foreign aid and military assistance programs is an example. The programs have required specific congressional authorizations and repeated congressional appropriations. Frequently Congress has disagreed with the president over the amounts and allocations for these programs, making its views known either through directives in the authorizing legislation, or by changing funding requests in appropriations bills.

The Constitution gives the president authority to make treaties with other countries if two-thirds of the Senate concur. For years this power served as a cornerstone of American foreign policy. Treaties forged peace agreements with other nations, supported U.S. territorial expansion, established national boundaries, protected U.S. commerce and regulated government affairs with Indian tribes.

Except for rejection of the Versailles Treaty after World War I, Senate action on treaties has not been a major factor in foreign policy. Although the Senate has killed several treaties by inaction, it had by the end of 1985 rejected only 20 treaties since 1789. However, the lengthy debates on the Panama Canal and U.S.-Soviet strategic arms limitation talks (SALT II) treaties in 1978 and 1979, respectively, were seen as Senate moves to expand its power in the foreign policy field.

In recent years the Senate's role has been eroded somewhat by the use of executive agreements instead of treaties with foreign countries; such agreements do not require Senate approval.

Confirmations of Nominations

Under the Constitution the Senate must approve all presidential nominations of federal officers. Most nominations involve promotions of military officers and Senate action is only a formality. But each year several hundred major nominations are subjected to varying degrees of Senate scrutiny. These include nominations to Cabinet and sub-Cabinet positions, independent boards and regulatory agencies, major diplomatic and military posts and the federal judiciary.

The Senate role in Supreme Court appointments has proved particularly important. It may not be able to dictate Supreme Court nominees, but historically the Senate has not been afraid to reject them. Slightly more than one-fifth of all Supreme Court nominations have failed to win Senate confirmation.

Appointments to lower federal courts are another matter. Traditionally the president has used this power — particularly those at the district court level — to please members of both chambers. Generally the president names as district court judge the person recommended by the House member of Congress from that district. These lower court appointments thus provide the president with his important patronage power — the opportunity to win the good will of a member of Congress or a vote on a crucial issue.

The Senate carefully considers nominations of Cabinet officers, but such officers usually are confirmed with little difficulty on the theory that the president should have great leeway in choosing the members of his official "family." There have been exceptions though. President Reagan first nominated Edwin Meese to be attorney general in January 1984. After 13 months — longer than any other Cabinet nominee in recent history — he was confirmed.

Presidential appointments to independent boards and commissions present a somewhat different situation. These agencies are created by Congress and are not subordinate to the executive branch. Congress expects these agencies to implement congressional goals and therefore it plays a large role in the selection process. Contests over these nominations have been frequent, although few nominees actually have been rejected.

Impeachment

Impeachment of federal officers is perhaps the most awesome, though the least used, power of Congress. The Constitution specifies that the House shall impeach (indict) federal officials that it believes guilty of treason, bribery or high crimes and misdemeanors. The charges are drawn up in an impeachment resolution, usually reported by the House Judiciary Committee. If the House adopts the resolution, the Senate holds a trial, with House members acting as prosecutors. If a president is impeached the chief justice presides at the Senate trial. Conviction requires two-thirds approval of the senators present. Punishment is limited to removal from office and disqualification for further federal office. There is no appeal.

The two most famous cases of impeachment resulted in acquittal after sensational trials. They involved President Andrew Johnson, accused of violating the Tenure of Office Act, and Supreme Court Justice Samuel Chase, accused of partisan conduct on the bench. Since 1789 only 14 federal officials have been impeached by the House. Of the 13 cases that went to Senate trial, two were dismissed before trial after the person impeached left office, six resulted in acquittal and five ended in conviction. President Nixon's resignation on Aug. 9, 1974, foreclosed House action on impeachment charges approved by the Judiciary Committee. U.S. District Judge Harry E. Claiborne was removed from office Oct. 9, 1986, for tax fraud. He was the first official to be removed from office in 50 years and the fifth in the history of the nation.

Constitutional Amendments

Congress shares with the states the power to propose amendments to the Constitution. Amendments may be offered by two-thirds of both chambers of Congress or by a convention called by Congress at the request of the legislatures of two-thirds of the states. Amendments must be ratified by the legislatures or conventions of three-fourths of the states. Congress has always specified ratification by the state legislatures, except for the 21st Amendment.

Although these constitutional provisions anticipated a substantial role for the states, Congress has dominated the amendment process. Not once have the states been successful in calling for a convention to propose an amendment to the Constitution. The states fell one short in 1969 when 33 of them called for a convention to write an amendment overturning the Supreme Court's "one person, one vote" decisions. As of 1985 the states were two short of the two-thirds required to call a constitutional convention to draft an amendment requiring a balanced federal budget.

Restrained use of the amendment procedure has enabled the Constitution to remain the fundamental law of the land even though the United States has been trans-

formed beyond recognition since the Constitution was drafted. The states have ratified only 26 amendments. Included among those are the ten amendments comprising the Bill of Rights, extension of the right to vote to blacks and women and the guarantees of equal protection and due process of the law against them.

Altogether, Congress has submitted to the states only 33 amendments. The states failed to ratify seven of these, including a proposal to give the District of Columbia voting representation in Congress. The proposed amendment, approved by Congress in 1978, failed to win ratification by its 1985 deadline.

The Equal Rights Amendment, approved in 1972 by Congress, failed to win ratification by the extended deadline of June 30, 1982. Despite a massive lobby effort, only 35 states had approved the proposal, three short of the necessary 38. The congressionally approved extension and efforts by five states to rescind their ratification raised constitutional questions about the amendment procedure.

Election of the President

Congress under the Constitution has two key responsibilities relating to the election of the president and vice president. First it must receive and in joint session count the electoral votes certified by the states. Second, if no candidate has a majority of the electoral vote, the House must elect the president and the Senate the vice president.

In modern times the formal counting of electoral votes has been largely a ceremonial function. The House actually has chosen the president only twice, in 1801 and 1825. In the course of the nation's history, however, a number of campaigns deliberately have been designed to throw elections into the House. Apprehension over this has nurtured many electoral reform efforts. The most recent attempt came in 1979 when the Senate rejected a proposed constitutional amendment that would have abolished the electoral college system and replaced it with direct popular election of the president.

The 20th and 25th Amendments authorize Congress to settle problems arising from the death of a president-elect or candidate or the disability of a president. The 25th Amendment, ratified in 1967 to cover what its authors assumed would be rare occurrences, was applied twice in 12 months and gave rise to executive leadership unique in the nation's history. The amendment provides that whenever the office of vice president becomes vacant, the president shall appoint a replacement, subject to confirmation by Congress.

Gerald R. Ford was the first vice president to take office under the amendment. He was sworn in Dec. 6, 1973, to replace Spiro T. Agnew, who had resigned after pleading no contest to a charge of federal income tax evasion. Little more than a year later, Nelson A. Rockefeller was sworn in Dec. 19, 1974, to succeed Ford. Ford had become president upon the Aug. 8, 1974, resignation of President Nixon. Thus neither of the nation's two chief officials in 1975 and 1976 was elected by the people.

Congressional Ethics

The Constitution empowers each chamber of Congress to seat, unseat and punish its own members. The House and Senate have the power to determine whether a member fulfills the constitutional requirements for service, to settle contested elections and to censure members for misconduct. Some of these powers come into conflict with the right of voters to decide who will represent them. As a result Congress has been cautious in using its authority. While it has acted often to determine the winner in contested elections, it has rejected the clear choice of the voters, for lack of the requisite qualification, in fewer than 20 cases since 1789.

Censure Proceedings. Congress has shown like restraint in expelling or punishing members for disorderly or improper conduct. Expulsions have numbered 15 in the Senate and four in the House, including the expulsion of Rep. Michael "Ozzie" Myers, D-Pa., in the fall of 1980. Seven senators, 22 representatives and one territorial delegate have been formally censured by their colleagues. In 1979-80 the House censured Charles C. Diggs Jr., a Michigan Democrat who resigned in June 1980, and Charles H. Wilson, D-Calif., both for financial misconduct. In July 1983 Reps. Daniel B. Crane, R-Ill., and Gerry E. Studds, D-Mass., were censured for sexual misconduct with teen-age congressional pages.

One historical reason for the comparatively few instances of congressional punishment of its members had been the difficulty in determining what constitutes conflict of interest and misuse of power. But an increasing incidence of scandals in the 1960s led to creation of ethics committees in both houses to oversee members' conduct.

By the mid-1970s Congress' reputation suffered as a number of current and former members were accused of criminal or unethical behavior. In 1976 Rep. Wayne L. Hays, D-Ohio, was forced to resign under threat of a House probe into charges that he kept a mistress on the public payroll. The same year the House voted to reprimand Robert L. F. Sikes, D-Fla., for financial misconduct.

Shortly after Congress convened in 1977, special committees in both the House and Senate began drawing up new codes of ethics adopted by both chambers in March. The new rules were codified into law and extended to top cials in the executive and legislative branches in 1978.

Still more scandal was unveiled in 1980 through a government undercover investigation of political corruption — known as "Abscam" — in which law enforcement agents, posing as businessmen or wealthy Arabs, attempted to induce some members of Congress and other elected officials to use their influence, for pay, for such things as helping Arabs obtain U.S. residency, get federal grants and arrange real estate transactions.

The expulsion of Ozzie Myers, which resulted from his Abscam conviction, was something of a milestone for a House that had long been the butt of derisive jokes about lax punishment of wayward members. The other congressmen involved in the scandal escaped expulsion. Two of the convicted House members resigned: John W. Jenrette Jr., D-S.C., on Dec. 19, 1980, and Raymond F. Lederer, D-Pa., on May 5, 1981. Three others were defeated for re-election: Richard Kelly, R-Fla., John M. Murphy, D-N.Y., and Frank Thompson Jr., D-N.J.

The lone senator convicted in the Abscam scandal,

Harrison A. Williams Jr., D-N.J., resigned on March 11, 1982, hours before the Senate was expected to vote on his expulsion.

In the wake of the Abscam convictions, both the House and Senate ethics committees considered revising their codes of conduct.

Power of Investigation. The power of Congress to undertake investigations — perhaps its most controversial of legislative branch power — is not specified in the Constitution. It is based instead on tradition and the belief that investigations are indispensable to the legislative process. Yet, the Supreme Court never has questioned the right of Congress to conduct investigations.

No period of American history has been without congressional investigation. The first was held in 1792, to investigate the massacre of U.S. soldiers in Indian territory. Since then, congressional probes have gathered information on the need for possible future legislation, tested the effectiveness of past legislative action, questioned executive branch actions and laid the groundwork for impeachment proceedings. Investigations have elevated comparatively minor political figures to national fame, broken the careers of important public men and women and captured the attention of millions of newspaper readers and television viewers.

Members' Pay

A very ticklish power held by Congress is that of setting members' salaries. Although Congress traditionally has tried to bury its own salary increases in general pay raises for federal workers, increases nevertheless have led to public criticism.

In December 1982, in a break with nearly two centuries of tradition, Congress decided to pay House members more than senators, while the latter could earn unlimited amounts in outside income, including honoraria.

Effective Dec. 18, 1982, House members' salaries were raised to $69,800. Salaries for senators remained at $60,662.50, but they were allowed to earn as much as they chose in outside honoraria. Outside earnings for representatives continued to be limited by the House rules to 30 percent of members' salaries. A limit on outside earned income for senators equal to 15 percent of their congressional salaries, or about $9,100, would have gone into effect Jan. 1, 1983, if the Senate had not acted to change its own rules.

The Senate voted to raise members' salaries to the House level of $69,800 in June 1983. But amid public criticism of senators' outside income, they agreed to place a cap on Senate honoraria effective Jan. 1, 1984, that was equal to the House limit.

In 1985 the annual 3.5 percent pay increase came on top of a 4 percent raise that federal white-collar employees and Congress received in 1984. The 1985 raise boosted the salaries of senators and representatives from $72,600 to $75,100.

Liberal Democrats Adapt to a Hostile Climate

As recently as 1983, Rep. Augustus F. Hawkins, D-Calif., could sponsor and win solid House approval of a $3.5 billion jobs bill, the type of legislation that was once the heart and soul of the liberal agenda.

In 1986, one of the few new programs Hawkins had brought to the House floor was a no-added-cost school improvement bill that would siphon funds from established programs.

Coming from Hawkins, a 12-term veteran schooled in Lyndon Johnson's Great Society tradition of liberalism, that modest education bill was a sign of how hostile the congressional climate had become for creating new social programs.

Liberals have had to resort to such approaches as redirecting existing funds and thinking small in domestic programs, as they have tried to adapt their vision of a government actively involved in solving social problems to an austere, conservative environment.

Although the Reagan era has been difficult for liberals of both parties, it is an especially trying time for Democrats.

Six years of retrenchment have forced liberal Democrats into a seemingly permanent defensive crouch. They have had to accommodate the widespread view that the government cannot afford major new domestic expenditures and that public support is flagging for the kind of government programs that were a key tool of Great Society liberalism.

Broad consensus in Congress about the importance of reducing the federal deficit has blurred somewhat the distinction between liberal and conservative Democrats on fiscal matters: Everyone, it seems, is a fiscal conservative.

But budget constraints remain especially painful for liberals who have known flusher times and continuing social problems observe that they would like the federal government to address.

"It's disappointing and frustrating. We're not doing what we ought to be doing," says Rep. Henry A. Waxman, D-Calif. "The liberal agenda is

Incremental Gains And Damage Control

fighting to keep what we have."

As liberals looked for ways to cope with the inclement political weather, some were lying low, waiting for the storm to pass. Others were trying to adapt their arguments to a conservative era and were looking for new ways to translate their ideals into policy.

Down but Not Out

Although the Senate was in the hands of a GOP majority and the White House occupied by a popular conservative Republican, liberal Democrats still held an important beachhead in the House of Representatives.

The Americans for Democratic Action (ADA), a political group whose ratings of members' votes on key issues have been a standard if disputed measure of how "liberal" they are, gave 140 House Democrats a "passing" liberal grade in 1985. According to ADA, that meant they voted "correctly" on 70 percent or more of the key votes identified by the organization in 1985. Twenty House Democrats got a 100 percent score.

The Senate lost several leading liberals when Republicans took control of the chamber in 1981, but Ann F. Lewis, ADA national director, said she

was encouraged by the number of liberal Democrats who were elected to the Senate in 1984 and the number who ran for the Senate in 1986.

Three of the five Class of '84 Democrats — Tom Harkin of Iowa, Paul Simon of Illinois and John Kerry of Massachusetts — had ADA ratings of at least 85 percent in 1985. Democratic candidates in 1986 included such ADA high-scorers as Reps. Bob Edgar of Pennsylvania and Barbara A. Mikulski of Maryland.

The notion that liberals are a dying breed is "outdated," says Rep. Barney Frank, D-Mass.

"People might have thought that in 1981, but I think people feel a little more aggressive now. Liberals are on the attack" on several fronts, includ-

"It's disappointing and frustrating. We're not doing what we ought to be doing. The liberal agenda is fighting to keep what we have."

—Rep. Henry A. Waxman, D-Calif.

ing arms control and the military budget, Frank says.

Democrats pointed to opinion polls showing that despite President Reagan's personal popularity, public support for liberal positions had not waned on such issues as opposing aid to the "contras" in Nicaragua and supporting anti-poverty programs.

Nonetheless, some members were weathering the conservative climate under another label.

"I don't know anyone who, like me, comes from a marginal district who calls himself a liberal," said Rep. Thomas J. Downey of New York. He describes himself as a "progressive Democrat."

"Liberals have been associated

with unpopular causes, like busing, and mushy thinking. It's unfortunate, but conservatives have done a good job of making it have a pejorative connotation," Downey says.

Many Democrats dispute the notion that a liberal's identity is inherently tied to the "tax and spend" epithet routinely used by Reagan. They emphasize instead the priorities and values that guide their thinking, and argue that the "big spending" label applies just as well to Reagan's defense policies.

Indeed, deficit pressures have cut both ways: The same fiscal pressures that are forcing liberals to abandon hopes of creating new domestic programs are helping them to slow the president's defense buildup.

Damage Control

At a time when some in the Democratic Party have concluded that they should move to the right, the principal job for liberals on Capitol Hill has been damage control — sometimes against measures supported by their fellow Democrats.

That was the role played in 1985 by some House Democrats such as Waxman who were vehemently opposed to the Gramm-Rudman-Hollings anti-deficit law but nonetheless participated in negotiating changes, included in the final version, to protect key health and anti-poverty programs against budget cuts.

"They were able to reshape Gramm-Rudman-Hollings, not that it was a good bill for a liberal end," said David Cohen, co-director of the Advocacy Institute, which counsels public interest groups on lobbying strategy. "But how you negotiate the terms of surrender, how you apply triage, makes a tremendous difference."

Liberals mostly have had their hands full with a supposedly "conservative" chore — guarding key elements of the status quo against a hostile Reagan administration.

They have measured their success in defensive terms: Although domestic spending has been curbed, Congress has blocked administration efforts to abolish dozens of programs and to weaken major regulatory statutes of an earlier era.

"I have to look at stopping the Reagan administration from gutting the Clean Air Act as one of the great successes, and salvaging many of the health programs as an accomplishment," said Waxman, chairman of the Energy and Commerce Subcommittee

---

Background

1983 CQ Almanac: jobs bill, p. 268.

1984 Almanac: Medicaid expansion, p. 148; teacher scholarships, p. 488.

1985 Almanac: Gramm-Rudman-Hollings law, p. 459; MX missile, p. 119.

1986 CQ Weekly Report: school improvement bill, p. 1407; contra aid vote, p. 1443; South Africa sanctions, p. 1384; fiscal 1986 budget reconciliation bill, p. 751; fiscal 1987 budget reconciliation bill, p. 1709; health insurance, p. 1746; House budget resolution adopted, p. 1079; long-term health care, p. 1227.

---

on Health and the Environment.

Strategically placed liberals, including Hawkins and Judiciary Chairman Peter W. Rodino Jr., D-N.J., kept bottled up in committee administration initiatives such as a constitutional amendment to allow prayer in the public schools and proposals to lower the minimum wage for youths.

On foreign policy and defense, where presidents traditionally dominate, liberals have had mixed success.

House Democrats could not prevent production of the MX missile, but they came close several times.

In June 1986, they failed to defeat Reagan's request for $100 million for the "contras" in Nicaragua, but they had blocked military aid to the rebels since mid-1984.

And in an extraordinary slap at Reagan's policies toward South Africa, the House in June approved a total trade embargo on the country proposed by liberal Ronald V. Dellums, D-Calif., rather than milder sanctions backed by Democratic leaders.

Incremental Gains

Liberal Democrats' accomplishments have not been solely defensive. Occasionally, in sometimes-obscure legislative corners, they have been able to achieve incremental gains by choosing their targets carefully, building coalitions with moderates and seizing opportune moments.

For example, in both 1984 and 1985, Waxman helped win modest expansions of Medicaid eligibility for poor children and pregnant women — an effort to reduce infant mortality through the federal-state health pro-

---

gram for the poor.

The moves pale in comparison with predecessor $2 billion child health legislation that died after passing the House in 1979. But even a modest expansion was considered a coup at a time when Congress was looking for ways to cut, not increase, Medicaid and other social programs.

The Medicaid initiatives have been buried in annual budget "reconciliation" bills that are supposed to reduce spending. Using reconciliation as the vehicle for proposals to boost spending has been an increasingly popular legislative strategy, despite complaints from some Republicans.

Changed Packaging

In select areas like the infant mortality initiative, some liberal Democrats say they have been finding it easier recently to win moderate and conservative support for anti-poverty programs than in the past. New packaging has helped.

Because the programs were described as liberal, says one lobbyist, moderates and conservatives paid little attention to them.

But during debate on the fiscal 1987 budget resolution (S Con Res 120), conservative Democrats such as Marvin Leath of Texas joined moderates like Buddy MacKay, D-Fla., and liberals on the House Budget Committee in support of spending increases for selected anti-poverty programs targeted on children.

Carefully packaged as a "children's initiative," the plan called for increases of $1.8 billion over three years for a handful of existing health and education programs with well-established track records. Some of the programs included Head Start for poor preschool children; compensatory education for the poor; and nutrition programs for women, infants and children (WIC).

Backers of these programs say conservatives are increasingly receptive to arguments that education and health spending on children is an investment that pays off in the future.

"For a while we couldn't be heard, and our arguments weren't cogent enough to turn the onslaught of the Reagan forces," said Rep. George Miller, D-Calif., a member of the Budget Committee and chairman of the Select Committee on Children, Youth and Families. "That's now changed. I've gone from begging people to give me a few dollars for WIC to having it be part of the Republican budget."

Pushing the Private Sector

Faced with little immediate prospect of significant growth in the domestic budget, members who see new horizons for social activism — like curbing high-school dropout rates or helping the elderly pay for nursing home care — are under pressure to find solutions that do not involve large federal expenditures.

Some see this as part of a healthy rethinking of liberal strategies for domestic problem solving.

"Where liberalism was at fault in preceding decades is that we got into the habit of assuming that the federal solution worked for every issue," said Lewis of the ADA. "The legislation of the 1930s and 1960s is not going to solve the problems of the '80s."

Rather than launch major new federal initiatives, liberals increasingly have looked to the states or pushed the private sector to do jobs that, in the past, they might have assigned to the federal government.

For example, the old liberal dream of national health insurance has been all but abandoned. But Rep. Fortney H. "Pete" Stark, D-Calif., has pushed incremental measures to fill in the gaps of private health insurance coverage.

The fiscal 1986 reconciliation bill (PL 99-272) included provisions, drawn largely from legislation introduced by Stark and Sen. Edward M. Kennedy, D-Mass., penalizing hospitals that failed to provide emergency treatment to the indigent. The bill also required employers to continue offering health insurance coverage at group rates to laid-off workers and spouses of deceased employees.

In the reconciliation bill approved in July by the House Ways and Means Committee, Stark backed a provision designed to encourage states to set up insurance risk pools, to make affordable group health coverage available to all regardless of their health status.

In another health area, Rep. Ron Wyden, D-Ore., a leading advocate for the elderly, has pushed measures to encourage private insurance companies to offer policies to cover nursing home care for the elderly — expenditures not generally covered by Medicare. Such measures provide a pragmatic backstop to more ambitious proposals calling for increased federal spending for long-term health care.

'Think Small'

Wyden is an able practitioner of the "think small" approach to domestic policy.

"I'm as frustrated about the imbalance of priorities as anybody, but I think this has forced Democrats to do some rethinking, and look at new approaches," Wyden said. "You have to be very focused. You have to be willing to scale back your efforts."

For example, at a time when demands for better schools far outstripped the federal government's resources and role in education, Wyden authored a modest program of scholarships to encourage bright students to go into teaching. "It's small, but it's going to prove a point," he said.

dent, but in constraining people's vision and aspirations. We don't consider whether something is a good idea. The only question is what something costs."

Awaiting Pendulum's Swing

Hawkins has not lost heart. He expects the political pendulum eventually to swing back in his direction.

"There's a season for conservatism, a season for liberalism," Hawkins said. "I've seen it so many times over my 50 years in politics. I recognize when you can move a jobs bill and when you can't."

His school improvement bill would earmark modest funds from existing programs to implement research about what makes schools effective. Hawkins sees it as a seed that could flower in a more liberal future. "At least you have the principle there."

"Where liberalism was at fault in preceding decades is that we got into the habit of assuming that the federal solution worked for every issue. The legislation of the 1930s and 1960s is not going to solve the problems of the '80s."

—Ann F. Lewis,
national director, ADA

Sen. Simon agreed that lawmakers have to be pragmatic about budget constraints but argued that it is important occasionally to think on a grander scale. For example, Simon said in 1986 he that he was thinking of introducing a jobs bill that would go nowhere.

"I know in this atmosphere it isn't going to pass this year, but unless we start talking about these things, they'll never happen," said Simon. "The danger is we all start fighting for the status quo, when in fact there is no such thing as the status quo — you're either making progress or slipping back."

One Democratic aide to the House Education and Labor Committee lamented: "The president has been successful not just in making Congress pru-

Some liberals saw signs that the clouds of conservatism already were starting to lift. They eagerly await the the post-Reagan era, anticipating that the conservative agenda will lose its steam without an extraordinarily popular president to push it.

Even then, few assume that an ebbing of the conservative tide will mean a robust recovery of Great Society liberalism. However, it is not quite clear what might take its place.

"We're too inchoate to be labeled, but something will emerge," said Rep. Charles E. Schumer, D-N.Y. "The idea that government should be helping people that need help, that government is a necessary force for good — that will be the core. The government-bashing that's taken place in the last 10 to 12 years I think will recede." ∎

The Plight of a Permanent Minority

What's a House Republican to do, when his party has been in the minority for more than 30 years, has little prospect of gaining control of the chamber and faces an increasingly unified Democratic majority?

"Do your homework, know more about the issue than anyone else, arrive early and stay late."

That is the prescription of Texan Steve Bartlett, who has been remarkably successful at leaving his imprint on important legislation even though he is one of the most conservative Republicans in an overwhelmingly Democratic House.

In June 1986, Bartlett won House approval of an amendment making a fundamental shift in federal housing policy, channeling hundreds of millions of dollars into renovation rather than construction of new dwellings for the poor.

At a time when House Republicans have suffered party-line defeats and complained about being "shut out" of the legislative process on such high-visibility issues as the budget, taxes and trade, Bartlett's housing policy coup was a striking reminder that there is legislative life in the minority party.

For members in the minority party, it is not always a comfortable life, and victories often go unnoticed. But, says Henry J. Hyde, R-Ill., "if you come to understand your role is to be a gadfly, a conscience factor, and try to work some influence in committee ... if that's enough and you don't need to be chairman of a committee or subcommittee or see your name on a bill, this can be very rewarding."

Bartlett says that Republicans trap themselves when they "think like a minority and then give up before the legislative battle begins."

Yet the battlefield is unquestionably sloped against them, and House Republicans sometimes find the only way they can assert themselves is through dramatic floor tactics — such as those deployed in April to derail a vote on aid to anti-government rebels in Nicaragua or in the 1985 walkout to protest a contested election in Indiana's 8th District.

This minority "bomb-throwing" instinct is less in evidence in the Senate, but Senate Democrats and House Republicans face the same basic fact of political life: As members of the minority party, they can neither set the legislative agenda nor prevail in a partisan showdown. *(1986 CQ Weekly Report, p. 1394)*

Minority Status Quo

In June 1986, Republicans were at a 70-seat disadvantage in the House, which the Democrats controlled 252-182. (One seat is vacant.) On powerful committees such as Ways and Means and Rules, GOP representation was even less than in the House as a whole.

"If we have a united Democratic position, Republicans are irrelevant," says Henry A. Waxman, D-Calif.

More discouraging to many Republicans is the seeming permanence of their status as the minority. The last time the GOP held a majority in the House was 1954, before any Republican now serving was elected.

"I haven't chaired a subcommittee or full committee in my 30 years in Congress," says Minority Leader Robert H. Michel of Illinois. "It's a pretty doggone discouraging and debilitating thing."

Michel says the lack of any immediate prospect for GOP control has contributed to some Republicans' decisions to leave the House.

"The only difference between a freshman Republican and a ranking Republican is that the ranking Republican gets to ask questions first" at hearings, says John McCain, R-Ariz., who quit the House to run for the Senate in 1986.

To add insult to injury, Republicans complain of mistreatment by House Democrats on such matters as committee ratios and staffing. They argue that the Democrats have been in the majority for so long that they have become arrogant in the use of power, riding roughshod over the minority.

"Democrats have run the House for so long, they have lost the capacity to be embarrassed by any partisan act," says Bill Frenzel, R-Minn.

"If you come to understand your role is to be a gadfly, a conscience factor, and try to work some influence in committee ... this can be very rewarding."
—Rep. Henry J. Hyde, R-Ill.

"I haven't chaired a subcommittee or full committee in my 30 years in Congress. It's a pretty doggone discouraging and debilitating thing."
—Minority Leader
Robert H. Michel, R-Ill.

Senate Rules, Closeness of GOP Margin . . .

House Republicans, vastly outnumbered by Democrats and constrained by rigid institutional procedures, looked with envy in 1986 at the powers enjoyed by members of the minority party in the Senate.

"I don't think there is such a thing as minority status in the U.S. Senate," said Rep. Edward R. Madigan, R-Ill., noting that Senate rules give every member, regardless of party, extraordinary opportunities to wield influence.

"The ability of a senator to put a 'hold' on a bill is power that exceeds the power of committee chairmen in the House," said Madigan, referring to the Senate's custom of allowing a single member to delay consideration of bills otherwise ready for floor action.

But for all their institutional advantages, Senate Democrats — like House Republicans — suffered certain inescapable handicaps simply because they are in the minority, 53-47. *(1986 CQ Weekly Report, p. 1393)*

When they lost control of the Senate after the 1980 elections, Democrats were stripped of the power to choose the subjects of hearings and investigations, set committee schedules and decide what will be the business of the day on the Senate floor. With the White House in GOP hands as well, they found themselves completely eclipsed.

"Many of us felt neutered, totally powerless, like fifth wheels around this place," said Sen. J. Bennett Johnston, D-La., who challenged Robert C. Byrd of West Virginia for the job of Senate Democratic leader in the 100th Congress. *(1986 Weekly Report p. 1316)*

With Republicans calling the shots, Senate Democrats were thrown on the defensive on issues such as school prayer and balanced-budget constitutional amendments that would have been much harder to bring up if Democrats were in charge.

Democrats hoped to recapture control of the Senate in the 1986 elections. While House Republicans had little immediate prospect of gaining majority status, Senate Democrats had a chance to do so in 1986.

"We have never adopted a mindset that ours is a permanent minority," said Byrd.

Tools of the Minority Trade

Democrats benefited from rules and customs of the Senate that protect minority rights and give far more deference to individual lawmakers than is possible in the 435-member House.

"It's like the difference between being a spectator and being a player," said Sen. Thad Cochran, R-Miss., who served in the House from 1973 until his election to the Senate in 1978.

Any senator, for example, can delay floor action for days by filibustering a bill; just the threat of "extended debate" gives members powerful leverage.

When rumblings of a Democratic filibuster in May 1986 led GOP leaders to put off a key vote on President Reagan's proposed sale of arms to Saudi Arabia, Barry Goldwater, R-Ariz., snapped, "I think we ought to vote tonight, frankly. That is what the majority party is for. We are supposed to run this place, but I am beginning to think we do not."

Senate rules permitting members to offer non-germane amendments to most legislation allow senators to bypass committee consideration and force a floor vote on pet proposals. In May, for example, Howard M. Metzenbaum, D-Ohio, won Senate approval of stiffer infant-formula standards as an amendment to another bill (HR 1848), although he had been unable to get even a hearing on his proposal in the Labor and Human Resources Committee. *(1986 Weekly Report p. 1106)*

In the House, by contrast, Tom Tauke, R-Iowa, has been stymied for years in trying to move broadcast deregulation legislation — even though his bill in the last Congress was cosponsored by more than half of the House.

House members' ability to offer amendments on the floor is strictly limited by germaneness rules and by the power of the Rules Committee, which is essentially an arm of the majority leadership.

The Precarious Balance of Power

In addition to their institutional advantages, Senate Democrats benefit from the comparatively narrow margin of GOP control. Unless Republicans exercise extraordinarily tight party discipline — as they did on key issues in the first two years of the Reagan administration — Democratic votes are needed to pass legislation.

The balance of power is even more precarious in certain committees, where Republicans hold only one- or two-seat majorities. If Democrats on those panels stick together, they can often pick up enough GOP votes to prevail on a given issue.

Through just such a coalition, the Judiciary Committee in the 99th Congress rejected Reagan's nomination of William Bradford Reynolds to the No. 3 Justice Department post and of Jefferson B. Sessions III to a federal judgeship in Alabama.

A similar coalition on the Labor and Human Resources Committee consistently blocked the president's proposal for a subminimum wage for teenagers. And on

---

Without more frequent changes in party control, says former Rep. Barber B. Conable Jr., R-N.Y. (1965-85), "there is a tendency for the majority to become flabby, the minority to become irresponsible and demoralized."

Democrats insist that they treat Republicans fairly. They say the House GOP has a "minority mental-

ity" that is uncompromising, obstructionist and unwilling to share in the responsibilities of governing.

Tony Coelho, Calif., chairman of the Democratic Congressional Campaign Committee, says House Democrats have a good idea of what it means to be in the minority: They are one themselves, in a broader sense,

because the House is the only arm of the federal government that they control. What's more, Democratic leaders got a bitter taste in 1981-82 of what it is like to lose control of the House floor and the political agenda.

A Taste of Power

Those first two years of President

. . . Keep Democrats Influential in Minority

June 18, 1986, a bipartisan majority rejected Reagan's nomination of Texas lawyer Robert E. Rader Jr. to a review panel within the Labor Department's Occupational Safety and Health Administration. *(1986 Weekly Report, p. 1392)*

The 1986 budget debate reflected not only the differing balance of power in the House and Senate, but also the Senate's greater tradition of bipartisanship. While the House version of the budget was drafted exclusively by Budget Committee Democrats and passed by a party-line vote, the Senate budget resolution (S Con Res 120) bore the shared imprint of Budget Committee Chairman Pete V. Domenici, R-N.M., and ranking Democrat Lawton Chiles, Fla. It drew more votes from Democrats than from Republicans.

And while tax overhaul legislation (HR 3838) was initially blocked by angry House Republicans who claimed they had been cut out of the process, debate over the Senate version was a bipartisan love feast. Finance Chairman Bob Packwood, R-Ore., publicly praised the contributions of key Democrats.

Some argue that the degree of bipartisanship in the Senate has put increased pressure on House Democrats to cast issues in partisan terms. "The only place where Democratic Party interests are fully protected is in the House — if Democrats in the House behave like Democrats," says Rep. Henry A. Waxman, D-Calif.

The Democratic Difference

One aide to the House Democratic leadership complains that Senate Democrats, by cooperating with Republicans on key issues rather than staking out alternatives, undercut the party's message about what Democrats would offer if they took control of the Senate.

But Byrd argues that a Democratic-controlled Senate could pull the legislative agenda away from "administration extremes" in such areas as defense spending.

And other senators say Democrats would pursue more aggressive trade policies and would pose a major new obstacle to the confirmation of controversial Reagan nominees to the federal courts and other key posts.

In certain areas, however, the legislative bottom line probably would not differ much under the Democrats — especially if their margin of control were narrow. In light of how closely Domenici and Chiles worked on the 1986 budget, for instance, some senators say that the budget might look much the same if Chiles were chairman instead of Domenici. *(1986 Weekly Report, p. 1397)*

Changes would be "more at the margins," predicts Thomas F. Eagleton, D-Mo., who retired after the 1986

Senate Minority Leader Robert C. Byrd, D-W.Va., right, hoped to change roles with Majority Leader Robert Dole, R-Kan., after November's elections. "We have never adopted a mind-set that ours is a permanent minority," says Byrd.

session. A Democratic majority, he says, would be constrained by continuing high federal deficits and the threat of a Reagan veto. "You would not see a raft of new programs."

Learning How the Other Half Lives

Some observers argue that it has been good for the Senate to have had a change of party control. "It cleared away a ton of deadwood," said one Republican aide.

The switch gave members of both parties a chance to see how the other half lived in the 26 years prior to 1981 during which Democrats were in the majority.

"Some Republican senators had been in the minority for so long, they didn't understand the responsibilities of governing," said Johnston. "It's useful for them to see that side."

"If you want to see a silver lining in this dark cloud, we'll have been able to see what the Republicans had gone through for 26 years," said Wendell H. Ford, D-Ky. "Maybe when we do take the majority, we'll do things differently from what they've done, what we've done in the past."

Reagan's tenure were heady times for House Republicans, who put together a working majority on key tax and spending issues by holding their own troops in line and picking off votes of "Boll Weevil" conservative Democrats.

That period came to an end after the 1982 elections gave Democrats a net gain of 26 seats. The Democratic

leadership later took steps to keep the Boll Weevils from defecting, and Republicans themselves became less willing to march in lock step behind increasingly unpopular Reagan policies.

"We had more success and greater activity in the 97th Congress than we'd had in 30 years," says an aide to Michel. "We just got a horrible stom-

ach punch in 1982, which set everybody and everything back."

Now, the aide adds, GOP leaders are trying to "pull out of the doldrums" with aggressive floor tactics.

Among the more eye-catching maneuvers of recent months was a procedural sneak attack in April 1986 that scuttled Democratic plans to attach a compromise package of aid to Nicaraguan rebels to a supplemental appropriations bill (HR 4515) opposed by Reagan. In another surprise move, House Republicans in late 1985 initially blocked consideration of the House's tax overhaul bill (HR 3838).

But Democrats charge that such tactics win Republicans nothing but attention. The "contra" aid maneuver, they say, only delayed action on the president's request for aid.

Predicting in May that the Democrats will widen their House majority in this November's elections, Coelho said, "Republicans will continue to be non-players in the legislative arena."

Making a Difference

Those are fighting words to the likes of Steve Bartlett.

"There are a fair number of irrelevant Democrats as well as irrelevant Republicans in the House," says Bartlett. "Party affiliation has very little to do with one's effectiveness."

Opportunities for Republicans to shape legislation vary by committee, subject and personality. But Tom Tauke, R-Iowa, says, "On most issues around here, Republicans can play a role. There are only a few issues on which Democrats decide to stake out a party position and ram it through."

Edward R. Madigan, R-Ill., identified by Republicans and Democrats alike as a skilled legislative player on the Agriculture and Energy and Commerce committees, argues that some of his GOP colleagues underestimate how much Democrats need their cooperation and votes.

Madigan himself often works on health legislation with Waxman, who is chairman of the Energy Subcommittee on Health and the Environment. Madigan's endorsement tends to bring along moderate and conservative votes that the liberal Waxman might otherwise lose. Madigan's price for cooperation is often lower authorization levels — sometimes even lower than those approved by the Republican-controlled Senate.

Madigan says that on an array of issues that divide Democrats on the Energy and Commerce Committee, such as toxic-waste cleanup and acid rain legislation, Republicans do not have to wait until they are in the majority to have influence.

"The terrible shock for them will be on the day they are in the majority and realize they need Democrats in order to get things done," says Madigan. "Perhaps if more realized that

now, they would be more involved in the process than they are now."

GOP 'Sore Thumbs'

Wielding Madigan's kind of influence requires a willingness to compromise that comes easiest for legislators who are not rigidly ideological.

Other House Republicans are just as happy to play defense.

"I don't have time to sit around feeling frustrated. I'm too busy trying to stop [Democrats'] bills," says Dick Armey, R-Texas, a staunch conservative who calls himself the "resident sore thumb" on the liberal Education and Labor Committee. "I'd rather be alone and be right than be part of a compromise on legislation I so totally disagree with."

The confrontational style of minority politics has been the hallmark of "Young Turk" Republicans in the

---

Background

1986 CQ Weekly Report: Housing bill, p. 1299; trade bill, p. 1154; Senate tax overhaul bill, p. 1375; House budget resolution, p. 1079; Senate budget resolution, p. 955; aid to Nicaraguan rebels, p. 835; "Boll Weevils," p. 909.

1985 CQ Almanac: House tax overhaul bill, p. 480; contested Indiana election, p. 28.

1984 Almanac: Conservative Opportunity Society and partisan skirmishing, p. 206.

Conservative Opportunity Society (COS), a dozen-member group that made its biggest splash in the 98th Congress. More interested in partisan combat than in making incremental changes in Democrats' legislation, COS members used parliamentary maneuvers and "special order" speeches to promote conservative causes.

The faction has quieted down somewhat since then, in part because its leaders are busy with "other agendas," said COS leader Vin Weber, R-Minn., who was himself preoccupied with a tough race for re-election in a district mired in the farm crisis.

Weber says that the group's guerrilla floor tactics may no longer be appropriate in what he called a more "complex political environment."

"In 1984, Reagan was in a strong position, Democrats were on the defensive and could be made more on

the defensive," Weber says. "That's not the environment of 1986."

Weber and others say there is less need for COS activism now, in part because they think the GOP leadership itself has been more willing to confront House Democrats.

COS founder Newt Gingrich, R-Ga., said the group nonetheless prepared a fresh cycle of special order speeches in summer 1986 to call attention to a new set of issues, such as cocaine trafficking and welfare reform.

White House: Boon or Burden?

House Republicans have some additional leverage in shaping legislation now that the White House is in GOP hands. Although they cannot block or pass legislation without Democratic help, they do have enough votes to sustain a presidential veto.

Although having a Republican in the White House is mostly a boon, some GOP House members say it can also be a burden when they are called upon to support administration positions they dislike.

For example, House Republicans opposed to the Ways and Means Committee's tax overhaul bill found themselves at odds with the White House, which wanted to pass the bill to keep Reagan's top domestic priority alive.

And a number of Republicans distanced themselves from the White House on the 1986 omnibus trade bill, which garnered some 59 GOP votes despite a Reagan veto threat.

Forget the Credit

Many House Republicans say it takes a certain tolerance for anonymity to enjoy life in the minority. Tauke cites a maxim he attributes to Gen. Douglas MacArthur: "It's amazing how much you can get done if you don't care who gets the credit."

But junior Democrats, too, have problems getting attention, which tends to flow to subcommittee chairmen and others in conspicuous leadership positions. Indeed, it could be argued that many of the frustrations House Republicans feel are not peculiar to being in the minority.

"There is a certain amount of frustration built into the collective decision-making process," said Conable before he left the House. "A lot of folks who come here who think they are going to change the world overnight wind up very quickly frustrated because there are 534 other people who think they're going to change the world overnight, too."

Media, Power Shifts Marked O'Neill's House

When he went home to Massachusetts in January 1987, Thomas P. O'Neill Jr. turned over to his successor a House of Representatives far different from the one whose gavel he assumed a decade ago.

The extent of the change may not be obvious to those who think of the past 10 years as a time of relative stability in the House, compared with the period that preceded it. In the 10 years before O'Neill became Speaker, the institution underwent a surge of democracy, with the seniority system successfully challenged and power made available to the most junior members.

Nothing that dramatic happened in the O'Neill years. The changes were more gradual and more subtle. But a combination of forces — the Speaker himself, the Reagan administration, the budget process and economic austerity — created an institution that the proverbial traveler, returning after a 10-year absence, might find difficult to comprehend.

It is an institution in which media and public opinion have become a common preoccupation both of the leadership and of much of the rank and file in both parties. At the same time, it is one in which real legislative power is quietly concentrating itself in a relatively small number of hands.

It is a place where Democrats and Republicans argue noisily against each other on the floor, and minor issues quickly become politicized beyond either side's apparent control. But it is a place where, beneath the veneer of partisanship, the two parties are co-operating more than at any point in recent times.

Media Show

One small, symbolic way to start measuring the change might be to visit one of the Speaker's press conferences, conducted just before the opening of each House session.

Ten years ago, Speaker Carl Albert of Oklahoma met quietly with a handful of reporters prior to the session each day, answering a few perfunctory questions about the upcoming schedule. Few things that he said were printed or broadcast anywhere; none of them was calculated to influence the media.

An O'Neill press conference was a media event, not only because dozens of print and broadcast reporters crowded his office to hear him, but because much of what he said was designed for their benefit.

O'Neill often began with a prepared statement challenging one or another aspect of Reagan administration policy, drafted for him by press secretary Christopher J. Matthews, a glib wordsmith and specialist in one-liners. Often, O'Neill's comments were repeated on the evening news that night; even more often, they were printed in *The New York Times* and *The Washington Post* the next day.

A decade ago, and for most of its history before that, the House was a relatively insular place outside the circle of national publicity and attention. Its members responded to each other, and to their constituents.

In 1986, with Republicans in control of the presidency and the Senate, the House was the one visible outpost of Democratic strength. The words of its leaders took on an importance far beyond the walls of the Capitol; they helped shape public opinion on all the important issues of the day. And they were uttered for that purpose.

"Ten years ago, nobody paid any attention to us," said Tony Coelho of California, who was favored to become

Speaker Thomas P. (Tip) O'Neill, Jr., D-Mass., presiding over the House.

After Ups and Downs of Reagan and Carter Years . . .

Colleagues had a right to feel some apprehension when Thomas P. O'Neill Jr. took over in 1977 as the 47th Speaker of the House. After 12 terms, he was a familiar and popular member, but one without any real reputation as a legislator. He had been a compromise choice for Democratic whip in 1971, acceptable to liberals because of his anti-war record, and he had simply moved up the ladder after that.

Even during the previous four years, as majority leader under Speaker Carl Albert of Oklahoma, O'Neill had worked a short week in Washington, continuing to focus on life and politics in Boston and playing little role in the day-to-day management of the House. Some of O'Neill's contemporaries knew that he had been Speaker of the Massachusetts House in the late 1940s, and that he had been considered a strong one. But there was nothing in his easygoing congressional career to suggest much of an appetite for leadership.

The first few months seemed to bear out contentions that O'Neill as Speaker would be like the man who had run the Massachusetts House, not the one who had coasted through 12 terms in Washington. "Power is when people assume you have power," he told a reporter in 1977. O'Neill began his speakership by convincing people that he had it.

Confronted with the challenge of enacting President Carter's energy package, he came up with a novel and successful idea, appointing an ad hoc committee to take up the bills on an emergency basis and thus bypass the parochial jealousies of the existing committee structure. Carter unveiled his proposals in April; by Aug. 5, O'Neill had moved them through the House.

By the fall of 1977, there were stories claiming that O'Neill was the strongest congressional leader since Sam Rayburn. That early reputation was crucial, because he had to live off its capital for a long time. It was five years before O'Neill was able to win as impressively as he did the summer he took office.

By 1978, the perceived failures of the Carter administration had taken their toll on the Democratic Party in Congress, and given O'Neill a Democratic majority that was increasingly reluctant to follow him. In November of that year, the midterm election brought in a belligerent

Speaker Thomas P. O'Neill Jr., D-Mass., standing before a portrait of a predecessor, Sam Rayburn, D-Texas.

crop of youthful Republicans, sensitive to the public relations potential of the House floor, and skillful at linking the Democratic leadership to the Carter White House and to overall economic decline.

The last two years of Carter's presidency marked the low point in O'Neill's personal management of the House.

House majority whip, the third-ranking Democratic leader, in the 100th Congress. "The Reagan years have forced the House into the spotlight. The question is whether we can go back anymore. I don't think the press is going to let the House go back to where it was. It's a goldfish bowl."

'Back-Room Operator'

In the center of the bowl swam the largest and unlikeliest goldfish, the 74-year-old Speaker who spent a quarter-century in the House not only failing to attract media attention but actively avoiding it.

"I'm a back-room operator, no question about it," O'Neill told a television interviewer from the Cable-Satellite Public Affairs Network (C-SPAN) in August, and his long career left little room for doubt about the issue.

Before he took over as Speaker, O'Neill had few dealings with the national press and virtually none with network television. He was a rank-and-file Massachusetts Democrat who arrived in Washington on Tuesday mornings, returned home on Thursday afternoons, and conducted his congressional business over poker, golf

and dinner at Duke Zeibert's restaurant at Connecticut Avenue and L Street in downtown Washington.

Even in 1986, as a national figure, O'Neill consistently avoided the Sunday TV interview programs, insisting that his Sabbath was reserved for church, golf and family.

Nevertheless, in the glare of attention the House has commanded during the Reagan years, it was O'Neill who became the first media celebrity in the history of the speakership. None of his recent predecessors was the subject of endless cartoon caricature in newspapers across the coun-

... Speaker O'Neill's Stature Is on the Ascendancy

The leadership was embarrassed on issue after issue — energy, budget, foreign policy — by a coalition of Republicans and nervous conservative Democrats who thought it prudent to keep their distance from O'Neill as well as Carter.

"I've got a lot of good friends out there," the Speaker said one frustrating night in 1980, "who won't even give me a vote to adjourn."

Those frustrations, however, proved to be only a mild foreshadowing of what took place a year later, with President Reagan in the White House. Given Reagan's popularity and the Republican gain of 33 House seats in the fall of 1980, there may never have been much chance for O'Neill's Democrats to derail the president's economic program.

But O'Neill's handling of the 1981 economic debate did not particularly reinforce his image as a leader.

In April, while other Democrats were struggling to stave off a Reagan budget victory, the Speaker took his usual springtime foreign tour, this one to Australia. On his return, he announced that Reagan could not be beaten, an observation that struck some Democratic colleagues as an abdication of responsibility.

A few months later, he seemed to switch to the other extreme, fighting aggressively to win passage of a Democratic tax bill that had been laced with special interest concessions in an effort to hold Southern Democratic votes. Reagan won easily on the tax issue; the simple fact was that the Democratic leadership did not have control of the chamber.

Had O'Neill chosen to retire in 1982, his speakership would have had an aura of failure about it. But he opted to stay on, and his last five years in office brought a gradual revival, not only in his public reputation but in his ability to lead.

By early 1982, recession had ended the Southern Democratic infatuation with Reagan policies, and there were no more Republican victories on major economic policy issues. That fall, GOP candidates throughout the country campaigned by attacking the Speaker as an obsolete hack, and they failed spectacularly. With national unemployment cresting above 10 percent on Election Day, Democrats regained 26 of the seats they had lost in 1980, reclaiming political control of the House in addition to the nominal control they never lost.

The two Congresses since then witnessed no landmark legislative initiatives from the Democratic side. But they established O'Neill as a Speaker who nearly always had the votes to prevail when he wanted to.

The key committees are packed with enough leadership loyalists to make most key votes predictable. Budget resolutions drafted in large part by the leadership win wide approval on the House floor, with Republicans offering only halfhearted opposition.

The Republican strategy of making O'Neill their national campaign villain was a failure for the second time in 1984, and polls have shown the Speaker's popularity rising among the American people in the closing months of his career.

> *"I don't know the depth of every piece of legislation that goes around here.... The important stuff, I understand it."*
>
> —Speaker Thomas P. O'Neill Jr.

Tip O'Neill will not be remembered as a great legislator — his casual attitude toward detail is too well documented for that. "I don't know the depth of every piece of legislation that goes around here," he told a television interviewer in August. "The important stuff, I understand it."

But like the Republican president who was his antagonist for five years, O'Neill has persuaded skeptics that there are elements of leadership that go beyond the mastery of facts.

"Tip is not a man who is interested in substance," says John D. Dingell, the veteran Michigan Democrat. "But he has the ability to reduce complicated issues down to a few simple, easily understood points. That's not a weakness. It's an unbelievable political strength."

try, and none provided material for monologues on late-night TV talk shows.

Some House Democrats, acknowledging this ironic development, take pains to point out that little of it was O'Neill's doing. The media needed a symbol for the Democratic Party, and the Republicans helped out by choosing O'Neill as the symbol of what they hoped to portray as an obsolete political generation.

For the future of the House, though, what is important is that the speakership has worked its way out of its historic low profile, and nearly all members seem to agree with Coelho that it will not return there.

"Sam Rayburn could have walked down the streets of Spokane, Wash., without anybody noticing him," says Majority Whip Thomas S. Foley of Washington, who will become majority leader in January.

"Tip O'Neill couldn't do that," Foley said. "And it is very unlikely that any future Speaker will be anonymous to the country. The Speaker is going to join the vice president, the chief justice and a few Cabinet members in the forefront of public recognition."

Winning the Nation at Large

The implications of this change bore down heavily on Jim Wright of Texas, the current majority leader and unopposed front-runner for Speaker in the 100th Congress. An accomplished orator, but a less-than-commanding TV performer and a man who has tended to be wary of the press in general, Wright had an adjustment ahead, and knew it.

"I don't think you can turn the clock back," he conceded in a recent interview. "We live in an electronic age — the public gains its knowledge from the ever-present tube. I don't shrink from it. I think it's an opportunity." It is an opportunity he has no choice but to confront.

Still, if the only impact of the past few years of media coverage were to give future Speakers a familiar face and more quotes in *The New York Times*, the significance for life in the House would be limited.

In reality, something more has been going on. The media are not only using House leaders as a political symbol and source of news — House leaders are coming to use the media to accomplish their legislative goals.

A decade ago, nearly all influential House members would have said that legislative arguments are won on the floor, by the tireless personal cultivation of colleagues.

Nowadays, many of them say that sort of work is only part of the story. Increasingly, they believe, floor fights are won by orchestrating a campaign aimed over the heads of the members, at the country at large.

"The idea is growing more and more," says a leadership aide, "that you have to have a media strategy to win an important vote."

The passage of President Reagan's 1981 economic program convinced leading House Democrats that an important legislative battle is a media engagement, not just a lobbying effort.

When Reagan used national television to promote his budget-reduction plan in May 1981, O'Neill found himself unable to hold the support of nervous Democrats whose constituents liked the president's speech.

"Am I lobbying?" O'Neill said at one point. "The answer is yes. Am I getting commitments? The answer is no." He said Reagan had done "the

greatest selling job I've ever seen."

From that day on, House leaders have operated on the assumption that traditional inside tactics are no longer enough. "Sometimes to pass a bill," Foley says, "you have to change the attitude of the country."

For the past few years, nearly any showdown on a major issue — a budget resolution, an arms control proposal, aid to the Nicaraguan anti-government "contras" — has been preceded by a House leadership media effort orchestrated to match whatever campaign the administration is waging. That means, among other things, floor speeches by Democratic members meant for inclusion on TV news programs, and op-ed articles in national newspapers by senior members of key committees.

Taking the Pulse

In the current Congress, developing a media and public opinion strategy has moved beyond the ad hoc stage and become a year-round element of leadership thinking.

At least twice a week, a core group of House Democrats led by Californian Don Edwards meets over breakfast to talk about using media to help them win on the floor. "When you don't put public pressure on your colleagues," says Edwards, "just enough of them succumb to the other side for you to lose. That's what happened to us on the contras."

Earlier in 1986, Edwards and the Democratic leadership fell narrowly short (221-209) in their bid to block Reagan from sending $100 million in U.S. aid to the contra forces fighting Nicaragua's leftist regime.

Members of the media group reg-

ularly call producers of TV talk shows to suggest House Democrats as guests. On Sundays, if a national newspaper has not given space to the Democratic response to the president's Saturday radio address, they call one of its editors to complain.

Edwards himself has a far more ambitious plan for building a public relations apparatus in the post-O'Neill era. He wanted to persuade Wright to abandon the current Tuesday-through-Thursday schedule of House action, arguing that it afforded Reagan and the Republicans three days of uncontested media exposure on days when the one Democratic organ of government is off for the weekend.

"We die on weekends in the media," Edwards complained. "Meanwhile, there's the president smiling and getting into his plane and waving at everybody."

What Edwards has in mind is a seven-days-a-week, 365-days-a-year plan of action that would include not only a full schedule of Monday-through-Friday committee hearings chaired by Democrats, but also a regular press conference each Saturday by the Speaker or one of his top allies.

Moreover, he wants Wright to become a more familiar media personality than his TV-shy predecessor. "We've got to polish Jim Wright up," he says. "We want an important, persuasive national figure."

The Edwards plan may or may not be adopted. It remained to be seen how many key Democrats would be willing to devote their weekends to promoting their party on television, as opposed to promoting themselves in their districts. What was clear, though, was the direction in which

"Sam Rayburn could have walked down the streets ... without anybody noticing him," says Rep. Thomas S. Foley, D-Wash., left. "Tip O'Neill couldn't do that.... The Speaker is going to join the vice president, the chief justice and a few Cabinet members in the forefront of public recognition."

things were moving. In the O'Neill years, media strategy became indispensable to House leadership, and it was going to remain that way.

Competing for Prime Time

But House leaders are not the only ones who have turned the House into a media-minded institution. In fact, they are several steps behind some of their more enterprising rank-and-file colleagues.

The House of 1986 — as opposed to the one of 1976 — was a place where literally any member who wanted to publicize his issues or himself could do it with relatively little effort.

This does not mean that the average U.S. representative is a television star. It remains true that the average member has virtually no continuing name recognition outside his district. But it is also true that the opportunity for coverage exists on a day-to-day basis, and even the most junior members realize it and think about ways to take advantage of it.

Some months ago, Democrats Thomas J. Downey of New York and Edward J. Markey of Massachusetts used up spare time on the House floor by ranking the value of television exposure readily available to them.

In first place, they decided, was coverage on all three network news programs on the same night. That constituted "hitting for the cycle." An appearance on the Public Broadcasting System's "MacNeil-Lehrer Newshour" was less of a coup, but still very valuable. Farther down the list were other PBS public-affairs programs, such as the now-defunct "Lawmakers" or its successor, "Capitol Journal." Below those was an appearance on network radio, which, they agreed, any member can obtain simply by calling up and asking for it.

"If you want to reach your colleagues," Downey explained later, "sometimes the best way is to let them see you on TV or read your name in the paper. If you say something pithy or clever, you can find yourself on the national news in a matter of hours. . . . News management by members through the electronic media is a more viable option than it ever was."

Few House members in either party are as media-minded as Downey or Markey. But nearly all recognize the opportunities that have surfaced for them in the past 10 years.

To start with, there is C-SPAN. Since the cable network began televis-

"There's a certain amount of resentment among members who thought they had achieved power and find it's a blind alley. They are presiding over the dissolution of the empire."
—Rep. Vic Fazio, D-Calif.

ing House proceedings in 1979, the number of people able to receive the broadcasts has grown to 25 million. Only a tiny fraction of those people are watching the House at a given moment, of course, but nearly every member returns home on weekend trips to find at least a few constituents who saw him perform recently on the House floor.

One day-to-day consequence of C-SPAN has been the thinning out of House floor attendance. Members who used to spend part of each afternoon on the floor to follow debate now do the same thing by watching TV in their offices. In a broader way, though, C-SPAN has sensitized members to the importance of TV in their work. There is always the chance that something they say in debate might turn up on a news program — or even in the campaign commercials of their opponents many months down the road.

C-SPAN is only the beginning. Cable News Network went on the air in 1980; its non-stop broadcasting gives members of Congress who want to be interviewed a 24-hour target to shoot at. Three years later, MacNeil-

Lehrer expanded its nightly public affairs program from 30 minutes to a full hour. Instead of dealing with one subject each evening, it now tackles as many as four, and its need for credible spokesmen on major issues neatly matches the entrepreneurship of articulate members of the House.

"You have members talking on the floor all the time about how they are using the media," says Democrat Dan Glickman of Kansas, a 10-year House veteran. "And the media encourage us to do that — especially the electronic media. The media have found Congress to be a lot more interesting than they used to."

'Great Television'

There is no evidence that either newspapers or TV are focusing more on how the House works as an institution than they used to. *The Washington Post*, which maintained a full-time reporter for routine institutional House coverage until about 1980, has since then used a series of people to perform that job more selectively.

But at the same time, there is unprecedented opportunity for individual members to present themselves as analysts, commentators, polemicists and specialists in quick reaction to events around the world.

Some of the more traditional members find this disturbing. "You've got a bunch of verbalizers who have a smattering of the jargon and who have natural media ability," says Illinois Republican Henry J. Hyde. "A lot of them have been touched by the aphrodisiac of seeing their name in the papers or going on the evening news. It's a heady experience for them."

Matthews, O'Neill's press secretary, is just as critical. "You ask these guys why they want to be on TV," he says, "and it's like asking a moth why he likes a light bulb. It's why they're there."

But not all of them seem to be in it simply for self-gratification. New York Democrat Charles E. Schumer, elected in 1980, has made himself a significant force on a variety of issues with a media offensive that has been relentless and brilliant in its understanding of media needs.

A typical year for Schumer almost always includes op-ed articles in *The Washington Post*, *The New York Times* and *The Wall Street Journal*, and so many MacNeil-Lehrer appearances that it is sometimes hard to tell whether he is a guest or a host.

The Foreign Affairs Committee

has become a media gold mine for newly elected members. Some have attracted national news coverage remarkably soon after their arrival.

Robert G. Torricelli of New Jersey, elected as a Democrat in 1982, was on national news programs a few months later when he traveled to El Salvador and returned with the body of an American journalist murdered there. Later that year, he drew publicity for arranging a papal audience for a 97-year-old constituent. "Great television," he called the latter episode.

The Foreign Affairs Committee is worth dwelling on for a moment as a clue to the ways the House changed in the O'Neill years.

It is not primarily a legislative committee. Its only regular legislative responsibility is an annual foreign aid authorization, which in most years does not clear both chambers and become law, if it passes the House at all. The Foreign Affairs Committee is a debating society.

And yet, it has evolved in the past decade from a backwater committee with a lackluster membership to a prize assignment that draws some of the best legislative talent arriving in any given year.

What the Foreign Affairs Committee offers its members is the unparalleled chance to talk, and to be listened to, not only by colleagues but by the media and the public.

The freedom to talk is precious in the House, and it is growing more important all the time. That is because the freedom to legislate, for many of the members, is disappearing.

"If I had been free to choose a time in the last 25 years to become Speaker," Jim Wright says, "I wouldn't have chosen this moment. I'm coming to the office at a time when Congress is circumscribed."

Power Shifts

It is not hard to figure out what Wright means. The combination of $200 billion deficits and an anti-government Republican president makes it all but futile for House members to think about launching new programs to solve society's social problems.

This is the work that has been drawing Democratic members of Congress to Washington since Franklin D. Roosevelt's time. Blocked from performing it in the past few years, many of them have gradually come to the conclusion that there is little for them to do in the House.

Democrats are not alone in this feeling. Even the conservative Republicans who used to fight to scale back programs acquire a sense of irrelevance when there are no new programs even to argue about. "Some of the younger members," says GOP leader Robert H. Michel of Illinois, "don't really know what it's like to be in the position of working on legislation with the thought that it might become law someday."

It would be foolish to describe the current Congress as an unimportant one. Any Congress that overhauls the entire U.S. tax code and mandates a balanced federal budget is passing landmark laws.

But tax revision and the Gramm-Rudman-Hollings budget law are only two pieces of legislation, and a relatively small number of House members worked on them. The rest, unable to create programs and spend money the way they used to, have been on the sidelines.

"When major changes are made," admits Henry A. Waxman, D-Calif., one of the most effective current legislators, "they are made with limited input."

Many members like to refer to the current legislative process in the House as the "four bill" system. What they mean is that in the average year, there may be only four important domestic legislative vehicles — the budget resolution, continuing appropriations, supplemental appropriations, and the reconciliation package of spending cuts that the budget dictates. Sometimes legislation to raise the federal debt limit is another.

"The only way to get things done in recent years," says Leon E. Panetta, a California Democrat, "has been to attach them to bills the Senate and the president cannot refuse."

Return to Oligarchy

Those who are in a position to influence one of the "must pass" bills can count on being important players in the process. Those who are not can count on being spectators.

As a result, one of the most common clichés about the modern House — its open, democratic character — is ceasing to be accurate. The current House is democratic in the sense that all members, even the most junior ones, are part of the debate. But when it comes to making decisions, democracy is the wrong word to use.

"The natural tendency of this institution is toward oligarchy," says

Democrat Philip R. Sharp of Indiana, a six-term veteran. "What we have now is a technique for returning to a closed system where a few people make all the decisions."

This frustrates members not only in Washington but at home. Two decades ago, most of them could return to their districts and explain that the restrictions of the seniority system made it difficult to accomplish what they wanted to do. These days that explanation will not do, at least among sophisticated constituents.

In the mid-1980s, an honest explanation of why something cannot be accomplished is likely to involve parliamentary distinctions and power relationships so complex that few members want to attempt it.

The return to oligarchy tends to escape notice because it bears so little resemblance to the form of oligarchy that prevailed before the reform wave of the early 1970s.

In the old days, power was vested in seniority; committee chairmen were the oligarchs. The current system concentrates power not in the chairmen of many committees, as before, but in virtually all the members of a few elite committees.

Granting Favors

Appropriations is a power committee largely because it writes the continuing resolution, which funds all programs for which regular appropriation bills have not cleared Congress when the new fiscal year begins Oct. 1.

In recent years, that has meant virtually every bill, so the continuing resolution has been a budget unto itself, all but certain of presidential approval and so massive that there is little chance to question any item someone from the Appropriations Committee is able to place in it.

Increasingly, the continuing resolution is moving beyond the funding process to authorize programs on its own. Given the budget-cutting mentality of the Reagan administration, dozens of federal programs, from legal services for the poor to environmental protection grants, could not be reauthorized by Congress and avoid a presidential veto.

But the Appropriations Committee can continue to fund them, and even, in the past couple of years, to make decisions about the way the programs should be structured.

There is still a significant difference in legislative influence between the Appropriations chairman, Jamie

L. Whitten, a Democrat from Mississippi, and those at the bottom of Whitten's committee. But there is even more difference between anybody on Appropriations and most of the other members of the House.

When the fiscal 1987 Transportation Department appropriations bill passed the House in late July, it specifically included money for two projects in the district represented by one of the panel's lowest-ranking members, Democrat Robert J. Mrazek of New York. Projects like those are supposed to be authorized by the Public Works and Transportation Committee, but these days, Appropriations more often than not simply does that work on its own.

Even the most senior member of Public Works would have found it difficult to accomplish what Mrazek could do simply by having a seat at the Appropriations table.

The result of this situation is that members of the less fortunate committees spend much of their time trying to persuade those on the more fortunate committees to help them out.

"What you do," says Democrat Thomas A. Daschle of South Dakota, a member of the Agriculture Committee, "is you find a couple of people on Appropriations that you can rely on, and they are willing to do their homework for you."

Taxes and Spending

The Ways and Means Committee remains powerful not only because it writes tax bills but because of its role in reconciliation. Ways and Means has jurisdiction over hundreds of billions of dollars in spending for health, Social Security and a variety of other social needs.

It therefore has leverage over reductions made in these areas, and in making its cuts, it has the ability to reshape the programs themselves in important ways.

Democrat Fortney H. "Pete" Stark of California has become a major player on numerous issues largely because he chairs the Ways and Means Health Subcommittee. When budget priorities call for massive cuts in health spending, as happens nearly every year, Stark can help structure the cuts, and quietly change the programs themselves at the same time.

In 1986, when the LTV Corp. faced bankruptcy and refused to pay health benefits to the workers who lost their jobs, House members representing those workers struggled for a way

"Partisanship is a game that's being played for media and the campaign committees.... We have reached a sort of modus vivendi in which each side knows it can't score any real political victories."
—Rep. Philip R. Sharp, D-Ind.

to force payment of the benefits. As it turned out, there was one way: Approach Stark and persuade him to add language requiring such benefit payments to an upcoming reconciliation bill. Stark obliged.

The Energy and Commerce Committee possesses similar leverage, partly because so much spending is under its control, and partly because of the legislative skills of its most influential members, led by Chairman John D. Dingell of Michigan and by Waxman, the Health Subcommittee chairman.

Waxman, unsuccessful in 1980 in his effort to enact a new child health entitlement program, has since managed to slip nearly all its provisions into law through the reconciliation process.

Reconciliation is such an important legislative outlet these days that even those members who are not well-positioned to take advantage of it are reluctant to place limits on its use. In 1986, when Budget Chairman William H. Gray III, D-Pa., considered changing the rules to make it harder to attach new legislative language to reconciliation bills, a cross-section of

members lobbied Speaker O'Neill to tell Gray to drop the idea, which Gray did.

At a time when there are only a handful of legislative trains leaving the station, few want to see any of them derailed.

'Irrelevant' Players

With a few important exceptions, the committees mentioned above pretty much delineate the power structure of the House in the important areas of domestic policy. And the people on the inside know it.

"The budget system has made many of the committees irrelevant," says Matthew F. McHugh, D-N.Y., who has been on Appropriations since 1978. "Over a period of time, it distorts the legislative process in a way that creates tension and frustration.... Some of the members don't have anything to do. So they have to look for ways to express themselves."

"In the retrenchment of the state, power is being concentrated," agrees Vic Fazio, D-Calif., an Appropriations colleague. "There's a certain amount of resentment among members who thought they had achieved power and find it's a blind alley. They are presiding over the dissolution of the empire."

Where Budget fits on the ranking of committee power is open to debate. There is no doubt that it is a glamour committee of the 1980s. Seats on it are prestigious and hard to get, and members have an advantage in visibility over most of their colleagues.

On the other hand, the rank-and-file Budget Committee Democrats do not necessarily have much control over the resolution that is approved (Republicans have none), and the resolution itself often bears little resemblance to the spending that eventually takes place under its supposed guidelines. There is a substantial bloc in the House that believes the Budget Committee belongs to the talk-and-media region of current House life, not the region of legislative power.

"I've never taken the budget process very seriously," says David E. Bonior, D-Mich., who studies the whole system from his Rules Committee perch. "You go through the whole long process of passing the resolution and the numbers get changed later anyway. It's a mathematical game. The Budget Committee is a talker's shop."

Some of those who have served there say similar things, if less bluntly. "The Budget Committee has been put here to be a debating forum," says

Fazio. "It's become symbolic to a lot of people, and less important. . . . Being on the Budget Committee is a source of external power. People think you're important, so they listen to you. The media wants to hear from members of the Budget Committee."

A top House leader, asked if he wanted to challenge that assertion, instead supported it. "There's a feeling among an increasing number of members," he said, "that the entire budget process is a waste of time."

Tight Reins at Rules

As recently as five years ago, a House member who felt shut out of the important action in committee could count on virtually absolute freedom to make his case on the floor. That is changing.

The O'Neill years have seen the floor evolve into a much more efficient legislative machine, with most major bills brought there under procedures barring more than a handful of amendments.

In 1983, a nuclear-freeze bill generated dozens of amendments and 40 hours of debate over a two-month period, and created an embarrassing atmosphere of chaos for the Democratic majority. Since then, House leaders and the Rules Committee have kept the terms of debate and amendment under tight control. Rarely does discussion of even the most controversial bill take more than a couple of days. Few sessions last past 7 p.m.

In 1978, thanks to a profusion of floor amendments, there were 834 roll calls on the House floor. By 1984, the figure was down to 408. In September 1986, with about one month of legislating to go, there had been more than 330. In 1979, there were 30 amendments to the budget resolution, and debate stretched on for more than two weeks. In 1986, there were three amendments, and consideration of the entire issue was finished in 24 hours.

One result of the change is a feeling of pride among some members that their institution, unlike the disorganized and haphazard Senate, now does its work in a competent, orderly way that does not embarrass them when people see it on television. "This place operates like a Swiss watch compared with 10 years ago," says Downey, who arrived in 1975.

At the same time, though, the new efficiency is a further obstacle to members who do not have a place on the power committees and would like some freedom to legislate on the floor.

In the aftermath of the Chernobyl nuclear power plant disaster in the Soviet Union, Glickman decided that it would be useful — and politically feasible — to offer a floor amendment adding funds for the Nuclear Regulatory Commission.

"Seven years ago," he says, "I would have gone right down to the floor to add some money. Now you don't do that any more. If you are an activist member, it is a frustrating experience. It makes a member seem impotent at home when a bill comes to the floor and he can't offer an amendment."

Partisanship

One common perception about floor debate — and about the House in general in the O'Neill years — is that it has become considerably more partisan.

Background

1977 CQ Almanac: Carter's energy package, p. 708; House TV coverage, p. 826.

1981 Almanac: Tax bill, p. 91; budget, p. 247.

1985 Almanac: Gramm-Rudman, p. 459; tax overhaul, p. 480.

1986 CQ Weekly Report: Labor-HHS appropriation, p. 1936; Transportation appropriation, p. 1951; continuing resolution, p. 2059; Nicaraguan "contras," p. 1443.

Beneath the surface, though, the situation is different. All the talk about the 1980s as a time of rampant partisanship is badly misplaced.

The key bills that keep government operating each year have been passing with a minimum of partisan controversy. Reconciliation, continuing resolutions and most appropriation bills move through the House with relative ease. When they come up for debate, the main argument seems to be between the House itself and the Reagan administration.

"To the extent we have been able to work out our differences in a bipartisan way," says Fazio, "it's because of Reagan. Reagan has cut off our running room in Congress to the point where we are driven together."

On this point, leaders of both parties seem to be in agreement. "The Congress is not riven with disputes about basic policies," says Foley. "Be-

cause we are so restrained in our spending," says Michel, "we all have to talk the same tune around here."

A decade ago, any major appropriations bill generated serious Republican alternatives calling for substantially less spending. These would be discussed at length and would draw roughly as many votes as there were Republicans in the House. Nowadays, bipartisan consensus moves these bills through to final passage with a minimum of dissent.

Michel had that lesson reinforced for him in 1986 when he tried to scale back the appropriations for labor, health and human services and education.

The bill as offered on the floor increased funds for the National Institutes of Health by about 15 percent. Michel offered an amendment to cut that figure. There were 12 members on the floor, and he lost on an 8-4 vote. There was no roll call. Later, Michel was decisively beaten on a proposal to cut the entire bill by $2.7 billion. Then the bill passed by a vote of 328-86.

Nearly all of the significant legislative changes enacted through reconciliation in the past two Congresses — such as approval of Waxman's child health program and decisions about the use of oil revenue from the Outer Continental Shelf — have provoked no real partisan dispute.

Some major legislation does produce Republican amendments closely tied to media efforts being promoted by the party campaign committee. But even this is more difficult than it used to be — it now requires a complicated parliamentary maneuver for a member to add language to an appropriations bill placing limits on the ways its money can be used.

More and more, members regard the periodic flashes of House partisanship as a kind of show that obscures the working cooperation that governs the real institution in the closing months of the O'Neill era.

"Partisanship is a game that's being played for media and the campaign committees," says Sharp. "We have reached a sort of *modus vivendi* in which each side knows it can't score any real political victories."

"You look at issues," says Panetta, "and you try to play them for political effect. But on the major bills, everyone knows they have to pass. Nobody is willing to throw themselves in front of these trains. What they want is to get on board.

"On stage, they are throwing

things at each other, and sword fights are going on. But behind the curtain there's basic cooperation. Otherwise, there would be a huge embarrassment to all incumbents. Incumbency still drives this place."

The Next Speaker

During the O'Neill years, the House was evolving into two parallel institutions, one focused on talk and offering most members a reasonably equal chance to participate, and the other focusing on crucial economic decisions and involving only a few.

It will be Jim Wright's job to run both of these institutions. He will be the spokesman and media symbol of his party and the House, and he will be the manager of a lopsided legislative process likely to grow more frustrating in the coming years.

Neither job will be easy. As a polished orator, Wright has obvious assets to bring to the task of making his party's case to the public. He also has liabilities. He can be long-winded when people want him to be brief, and defensive when challenged even on a small point. Some of his closest Democratic allies wonder whether he will ever develop the sort of affable style that made O'Neill, despite his tangled syntax, a reporters' favorite.

"Jim Wright gets a few people together and he acts like he's addressing a national convention," says a leadership Democrat. "He views a press conference as a duel of words." Accomplishing the public relations transition is certain to preoccupy Wright for his first few months in office.

More subtle is the task of managing the inequitable legislative system. Wright is not by nature a man who loves playing with procedure. He wants to leave his imprint as a Speaker who made policy for the country. "I'd like to be free to focus on legislation," he says, "not on internal rules changes. Those are distractions right now. I hope we don't use our time tinkering with the machinery."

Others feel the machinery is becoming so defective that people are going to be demanding repair before long. "Members are at a terrible disadvantage," says Wisconsin Democrat David R. Obey, "when they can't explain the system to their people back home. Democracy requires that things be simple enough for you to be able to explain them to the people who are the ultimate judges. The next Speaker has to find a way to simplify the system." ■

Sam Nunn: The Careful Exercise of Power

When Sam Nunn, as a newly elected Democratic senator, first won a spot on the influential Armed Services Committee, some political observers back home in Georgia were dubious.

"The immediate concern, which Nunn obviously shares to some extent," a local newspaper reported, "is that the seemingly attractive committee assignment will turn out to be something of a political albatross which will earn the young senator few friends and make him a lot of enemies."

By 1986 — thirteen years and many political battles later — Nunn had earned a different kind of assessment from the committee's crusty chairman, Barry Goldwater, an Arizona Republican.

"We better come up with somebody," Goldwater said of the GOP, "or I'm going to support this guy for president. He's terrific."

Such praise, coming as the Senate approved Goldwater's pet project of reorganizing the Pentagon, is typical of his blunt hyperbole. But it also reflects the esteem in which most senators hold Nunn — now Armed Services' senior Democrat. In an era of cosmetically tailored politicians, Nunn — with his light brown hair combed straight across a bald spot and his flat drawl — has become a power by the simple expedient of knowing what he is talking about.

Nothing testifies more eloquently to the 47-year-old Georgian's personal dominance of Senate defense debates than the frustration of those critics — typically to his political left — whose loudest complaint is that he has not taken up their particular cause.

Some want him to lead a center-left coalition that would reshape President Reagan's defense program, which Nunn has attacked for lacking strategic coherence.

On a partisan level, although Nunn supports Reagan more consistently than almost any other Senate Democrat, some party leaders see Nunn's prestige as an important political asset that could erase their party's image as being "weak" on defense.

But as Congress has become disaf-fected with Reagan's military buildup, some Capitol Hill aides and lobbyists complain that Nunn has been too hesitant to take on the tough ones. He has the talents of a brilliant legislative technician, they say, but has not shown the will to be a national political leader.

A New Role?

Some of these critics thought Nunn would be forced to take a tougher stance as the Senate took up

"You don't just go and change 100 percent of the opinion" in the Pentagon. "You've got to find a fertile field to plant the seed in."

—Sen. Sam Nunn, D-Ga.

Reagan's $5.4 billion budget request for research on an anti-missile defense — the strategic defense initiative (SDI).

Nunn repeatedly has brushed aside as a fantasy Reagan's conception of SDI as a nationwide shield. Moreover, in 1987, a year of severe budget austerity, funds spent on SDI meant less money for the improvements in conventional military forces that

Nunn has emphasized over the years.

On top of that, one influential critic thinks Nunn finally is showing the kind of national political ambition that will make him susceptible to pressure from more liberal Democrats.

In a wide-ranging interview early in June 1986, Nunn said he would speak out "more forcefully" on SDI. He did not tip his hand, but he rejected the position taken in June by 46 senators — including some prominent centrists — who signed a letter calling for a $2 billion reduction in Reagan's request.

"I can agree with many things said in the letter," Nunn said, "but I cannot agree with the bottom line." It was incumbent on the critics to propose a coherent alternative to Reagan's program, Nunn insisted. "Just to cut $2 billion off of it or go to a 3 percent growth rate is not enough."

Some liberal arms control advocates disagreed with Nunn's belief that SDI has some value as "arms control leverage" — an incentive for hefty Soviet concessions in the Geneva arms talks in return for restraint of SDI. As a rule, liberal arms control advocates have rejected using weapons as bargaining chips.

The issue highlights a fundamental obstacle to any facile coalition between Nunn and more liberal Democratic leaders: On some of the most politically charged defense issues, Nunn simply does not agree with them.

Knowing His Stuff

The key to Nunn's influence is knowledge.

"He knows more about the subject he talks about than anybody else by the time he starts talking about it," said Armed Services member Carl Levin, D-Mich.

Tales of Nunn's capacity for homework — more significantly, of his demand for prodigious amounts of it — are legion, a point of pride among his staff and of envy among aides to other senators. "Nunn wants to make sure he understands the issue the best he can," said a committee aide. "It isn't until he's comfortable that he's ready to move."

One example of many: Late in May, Nunn took home one weekend a ring binder more than two inches thick containing detailed analyses of issues that might arise in the Armed Services Committee's forthcoming markup of the fiscal 1987 defense authorization bill. He returned the book to aides the following Tuesday, extensively underlined and annotated with his characteristic marginal notes.

Aides tell of him routinely digesting 30-page memos on complex issues. "He'll ask for a lot more information than we could possibly send to any other senator," said one.

By all accounts, he is an omnivorous reader, has an extraordinarily talented staff and maintains a wide circle of expert contacts within the defense community. *(Box, this page)*

But he also is an omnivorous reader and maintains a wide circle of contacts in the defense community.

"He knows a good idea when he hears it and he knows whom he ought to be talking to when he's looking for advice," commented James F. McGovern, staff director for the Armed Services Committee's GOP majority.

For all the help, it is Nunn's reputation for personal mastery of issues that makes the difference. Said one aide, in what may be the highest accolade a staffer can give to a member of Congress, "You never worry about him going to a meeting by himself."

Picking His Shots

Another component of Nunn's reputation for legislative success is that his proposals usually sound reassuringly moderate.

They are shaped by what his colleague Levin calls "the practicalities of power" on Capitol Hill: that a member can only work so many issues at one time with any competence; that he can go to his colleagues for a tough vote only so many times and can ask them to move only so far from their earlier positions; and that he can push a massive bureaucracy only so far.

"He not only reaches conclusions about what's right, but about what's achievable," said Levin.

In addition to knowing what to go for, Nunn gets high marks for knowing when to go for it. "His real genius is to . . . wait for the right moment to come up with a solution after allowing the sides to play themselves out," said Armed Services member William S. Cohen, R-Maine.

At the same time, he sees limits in how far he can push the executive branch. "You don't just go and change 100 percent of the opinion" in the Pentagon, Nunn says. "You've got to find a fertile field to plant the seed in."

For change to take hold, Nunn contends, a substantial part of the military bureaucracy must see its military merit. "It's like the board of directors of a company," said one Senate

aide. "You've got to focus the attention of management."

However, to some of his critics, Nunn's caution goes to the point of timidity. One Democratic aide derided his record of arriving at a position "so firmly in the center that it must have been fashioned by a compass."

And a GOP observer contrasted Nunn's careful, incremental approach with the sweeping deficit-reduction legislation driven through the Senate in 1985 by Texas freshman Phil Gramm, R. The comparison is difficult to evaluate: None of Nunn's issues engages sentiments similar to Congress' fever to slice deficits.

Courting His Colleagues

A third facet of Nunn's method is a velvet touch in dealing with his colleagues: "When you come out of a battle with Sam Nunn — which he usually wins — there's no animosity," comments J. James Exon, D-Neb., another Armed Services member.

"I listen to people and I hear what they're saying," says Nunn. But more importantly, people believe Nunn is willing to change his mind based on the merits of an argument. "He is seen as capable of listening to the evidence and coming up with a new conclusion," said one Pentagon official.

Moreover, he gains points for not using his expertise to demolish less knowledgeable political foes in debate.

"I think he feels that in the long term, its better to consider other peoples' arguments, feelings and positions before he dominates an argument," said Levin.

Another senator put the point less diplomatically: Nunn treats his colleagues' viewpoints with respect, "no matter how asinine they might be."

Nunn also has a reputation for scrupulous observance of his commitments: "You can take an IOU from Sam Nunn and carry it to the bank," says Senate Sergeant-at-Arms Ernest E. Garcia, the Pentagon's chief of Senate liaison in 1981-85.

Other Hats

Nunn sometimes expresses frustration that his reputation as a defense specialist obscures his work on the Governmental Affairs Permanent Subcommittee on Investigations. As chairman in 1979-80, and senior Democrat since, Nunn has probed organized crime, drug traffic, labor racketeering and the government's control of secret information.

Nunn's investigations led directly

Help From Some Savvy Specialists

As ranking Democrat on the Senate Armed Services Committee, Sam Nunn draws on a staff that includes several highly regarded technical specialists, some of them with unusually strong credentials.

Among those cited by several observers:

● Robert G. Bell, a strategic weapons specialist formerly with the Congressional Research Service of the Library of Congress and then arms control specialist for the Senate Foreign Relations Committee.

● John J. Hamre, specializing in budget analysis. He formerly served as deputy chief of the Congressional Budget Office's national security division.

● William E. Hoehn Jr., a strategic arms specialist who was a vice president of RAND Corp., 1973-82, and a deputy assistant secretary of defense, 1982-84.

● David S. Lyles, specializing in manpower and combat readiness issues, who served previously on the staff of the Senate Appropriations Subcommittee on Defense.

● Jeffrey H. Smith, who was an assistant legal adviser in the Department of State — a position equivalent to deputy assistant secretary.

The more usual career path for smart and ambitious technical specialists is from a Senate committee staff to a job as deputy assistant secretary, not the reverse. But the prospect of working for Nunn has its own compensations: "He's having an impact. These people know that," said a committee source.

to legislation cracking down on criminal abuse of the workers' compensation program for longshoremen, and increasing penalties for union officials found guilty of corruption.

He also pushed for creation of a conservation "soil bank" to encourage farmers to remove from crop production easily eroded land.

Nevertheless, it is his work on defense that gives Nunn his clout.

Getting Started

Even before his election in November 1972, Nunn had gotten Senate Democratic leaders to agree to assign him a seat on Armed Services, partly through the intercession of his great-uncle Rep. Carl Vinson, D-Ga. (1914-65), a former chairman of the House Armed Services Committee.

Late in September 1973, Nunn took his first step into the policy arena that would make his reputation: NATO strategy.

The Senate was restive over the number of U.S. troops deployed in Europe, partly because the U.S. balance of payments was hurt by the day-to-day living expenses on the continent of more than 300,000 American soldiers and their dependents. By only six votes, the body turned down an amendment to the annual defense authorization bill by Majority Leader Mike Mansfield, D-Mont., that would have slashed the number of U.S. troops stationed in Europe.

In hopes of co-opting some of the sentiment behind Mansfield's move, Nunn and Henry M. Jackson, D-Wash., then proposed an amendment — adopted overwhelmingly — directing the president to seek reimbursement by the allies for a greater share of the cost of stationing U.S. troops in Europe. *(1973 CQ Almanac p. 925)*

In February 1974, Nunn took his first trip to Europe at the request of Armed Services Chairman John C. Stennis, D-Miss., partly in preparation for another showdown with Mansfield. According to Nunn, that trip laid the foundation of his thinking on the alliance. It also set the pattern for his workaholic approach to boning up on an issue. He and committee aide Francis J. Sullivan "probably spent a hundred hours talking to every expert within reach of Washington," according to Nunn.

The trip produced a report documenting the Armed Services panel's brief for preserving the status quo regarding deployments to Europe. But Nunn also used the report to challenge key elements of NATO military policy in central Europe. He charged that:

● NATO was planning on an unrealistically long warning time to get ready for a Soviet attack, and therefore had many of its troops too far back from the East German frontier.

● The alliance was getting too little combat power out of the troops it deployed, partly because too few were assigned to combat jobs and partly because its combat units had too little ammunition stockpiled for wartime.

● Because of the deficiencies in its non-nuclear military posture, the alliance would be driven to an early decision to use nuclear weapons in case of a Soviet attack.

When the Senate took up the annual defense bill that July, Nunn first led the battle against Mansfield's new troop withdrawal amendment, beating it 44-46.

He then offered successfully his own package of NATO amendments intended to goad the Pentagon to: shift personnel into combat roles; develop a coherent policy on the deploy-

ment of short-range nuclear weapons; and increase the efficiency of NATO's collective defense effort by standardizing more of its equipment. *(1974 Almanac p. 580)*

In the 12 years since his first NATO report, those themes have remained high on Nunn's agenda.

"That's one of the good things about NATO," Nunn quipped early in June while recalling his early inquiries. "Once you learn the defects, you can be reasonably sure that that knowledge is not going to become outmoded any time soon."

In 1976, Nunn returned to Europe with Armed Services Republican Dewey F. Bartlett, R-Okla. (1973-79). The resulting report underscored Nunn's earlier critique and publicized a fear held by some military officers and analysts: That newly improved Soviet forces might carry out a blitzkrieg attack before NATO could mobilize its defenses. Several observers credit Nunn's focus on the problem with stimulating a raft of changes in U.S. and NATO planning.

Other Campaigns

Nunn has ranged over other defense issues. Among his major thrusts:

Manpower. As chairman of the Armed Services Subcommittee on Manpower and Personnel, Nunn subjected the all-volunteer Army to withering scrutiny in the late-1970s.

He opposed the all-volunteer force on philosophical grounds: It was dangerous to insulate middle-class youth from the obligation to serve.

But he also contended that the all-volunteer policy simply was not working. The services were plagued with recruits who were undisciplined and very difficult to train.

In 1980, Nunn threatened to cut

the Army's manpower on grounds that it could not recruit enough qualified men. Cohen and Levin fended off that effort, but the committee approved (and Congress enacted) stiff limits on the number of recruits who could be accepted without a high school diploma. *(1980 Almanac p. 57)*

The combination of the higher recruiting standards, pay hikes pushed by Nunn and John W. Warner, R-Va., and a 1980 recession produced a dramatic turnaround in the Pentagon's manpower problems. Says one participant in the battle, "It was Nunn's criticism that strengthened the all-volunteer force and made it viable."

Nuclear Strategy. Nunn had begun in the mid-1970s to study nuclear arms issues, focusing on the "survivability" of the U.S. forces as a key to the stability of the nuclear balance.

Nunn had supported the Carter administration plan to shuffle MX missiles at random among dozens of armored underground launch sites as a means of forestalling a Soviet attack.

When Reagan dropped that approach, Nunn and Cohen blocked his alternatives on grounds that none of them would ensure the survival of the missiles as well as the rejected Carter scheme. *(1981 Almanac p. 323)*

Early in 1983, with Reagan's request for MX funding under fire, Nunn, Cohen, and Foreign Relations Committee Chairman Charles H. Percy, R-Ill. (1967-85), and a group of centrist House Democrats used MX as a bargaining lever on Reagan.

Though Reagan planned to deploy the new missile in existing launch silos that were vulnerable to a Soviet attack, Nunn and his allies supported MX production in return for Reagan's adoption of both a strategic weapons program and an arms control agenda that — in Nunn's view — promoted strategic arms stability. *(1983 Almanac p. 195)*

NATO Planning. NATO returned to the top of Nunn's agenda in 1984. He was unhappy that NATO was dawdling on certain improvements in combat readiness.

So he offered an amendment to the fiscal 1985 defense authorization bill that would have trimmed U.S. troops in Europe by up to 90,000 over three years unless NATO began meeting its force improvement goals.

The amendment was rejected 55-41 after the administration lobbied intensely against it. One Nunn skeptic cites the amendment as an instance of political opportunism. But Nunn's

boosters — including some of the Reagan officials who fought him — insist that the amendment was meant to goad the administration and the allies into action, and that it succeeded. *(1984 Almanac p. 50)*

Pentagon Reorganization. Early in 1984, in one of his first statements as the Armed Services panel's senior Democrat, Nunn announced the crusade that led to his most recent legislative triumph. "We will not be able to get the most effective fighting force possible until we begin to make some fundamental changes in the structure of the Defense Department," he declared.

Several studies had proposed changes along the same lines: shifting power from the separate military services to the chairman of the Joint Chiefs of Staff, the combat commanders in chief, and other institutions intended to coordinate the services.

But then-chairman John Tower, R-Texas, blocked any such moves and Nunn bided his time until Tower retired at the end of 1984. Tower's successor, Goldwater, saw eye-to-eye with Nunn on the issue and the two began a long legislative campaign.

Despite numerous compromises with other committee members, the two insist that the core of their idea — shifting significant power to the cross-service institutions — survived intact. Over vehement opposition from the Navy and some other quarters in the Pentagon, the Senate adopted the bill May 7. *(CQ Weekly Report p. 1030)*

What's the Beef?

Nunn's critics concede that he brings to bear on the issues an unrivaled expertise and political savvy. Given all that clout, they contend, his net impact on policy is too marginal.

Some complain that Nunn focuses on technical questions of secondary importance while skirting broader national issues.

One experienced arms control lobbyist cited his focus on Pentagon reorganization as an example. "I don't find that to be an issue of ethical or moral importance," she declared.

As an example of dodging a big one, on the other hand, the critics cite Nunn's refusal to join any of the efforts to slice SDI funds during Senate floor debate on the fiscal 1986 defense authorization bill.

Nunn had scathingly dismissed Reagan's goal of a nationwide defense that would render nuclear missiles "impotent and obsolete."

When the bill came to the Senate floor, SDI critics believed they had a shot at cutting the program from the $3 billion recommended by Senate Armed Services to $1.9 billion, if only Nunn would help.

Nunn did not actively oppose the amendment, but he voted against it and the cutback was defeated handily. *(1985 Almanac p. 150)*

What looks like a question of will from one angle, however, may seem a difference of view from another. Nunn sees Pentagon reorganization as the precondition to solving a raft of problems — for instance, devising a rational defense program that fits whatever budget level Congress will provide.

Nunn declares that timing was an important consideration in the 1985 SDI battle; he was giving priority to ending the MX battle with a cap on the number of deployed missiles. "I felt last year was the time to put the MX debate to bed; And I didn't think the time was right for a major debate on SDI," Nunn said.

A Democratic aide cited another factor: Nunn and other SDI skeptics felt obligated not to oppose the committee's stance on the program. "Nunn wasn't down there in the well defending the committee's position," said the source, "but he felt committed."

Another complaint is that Nunn too readily compromises for the sake of increasing an already adequate majority — what one Democratic aide called "the 78-vote syndrome."

The focus of this criticism was Nunn's negotiation with the White House in 1985 to cap the number of MX missiles deployed in vulnerable silos at 50 instead of 40.

Sources on both sides of the battle contend that the White House had exhausted its political capital in earlier MX fights and that Nunn could have prevailed at the lower figure, winning a majority of fewer than 60 votes, comprising Democrats and a handful of liberal Republicans. *(1985 Almanac p. 119)*

Nunn rejects that analysis. The highest priority was to end the MX debate, he insists. If a narrow and largely Democratic Senate majority had forced a 40-missile cap on the White House, he said, "we would have been fighting again this year."

But one Pentagon official saw a broader reason for Nunn's conciliatory conduct. "He knew he had us," said the source, adding: "He values the fact that he's respected from all quarters. He doesn't need to make an enemy."

Is He 'Democratic' Enough?

Nunn's position to the right of the Democratic mainstream shows up when senators are rated on their voting records. During 1985, by *Congressional Quarterly*'s analysis, he supported Reagan on contested issues more often than any other Democrat and he tied for first place with Howell Heflin, Ala., in the frequency with which he supported conservative positions. *(Weekly Report pp. 68, 75)*

"I don't think there is anyone who has as much respect on an issue and is as out of line with his party," said one liberal activist.

He heads the national security policy group within the Senate Democratic Conference. But one Democratic defense aide complained that he is trying to get the members to focus on complex technical questions rather than questions of political strategy.

"It shouldn't be a seminar," the exasperated aide said. "It should be a political action group.... He's not trying to appeal to Democrats on hot issues. He's trying to re-create them in his own image, and it won't work."

To this charge, Nunn responds, "We have to have as little as possible of partisan politics in national security. There's always going to be some, but the purpose of leadership is to minimize that."

Coming from almost any other public figure, such a statement would be summarily dismissed. But there seems to be a remarkably broad consensus that Nunn really believes it. "I can't fault him for that," says Levin. "He just doesn't believe that there's a 'Democratic' defense policy."

Levin also sees Nunn as an important party asset in spite of the fact that he frequently differs with a majority of his fellow Democrats on issues. "He's done more than anyone else to improve the Democratic image on defense," Levin said, by demonstrating "that there's no difference between the two parties in their commitment to defense."

But that contribution to the party's image does not satisfy critics' complaint that Nunn does not stand with his party's majority on politically key questions. "Nunn is recognized as the leading spokesman for his party on national defense," said one of the critics. "To fulfill that kind of role over an extended period, you cannot do it from the standpoint of being one of eight or 10 Democratic votes" aligned with Republicans on a hot issue.

Nunn's Democratic affiliation has been virtually irrelevant to his rise to power in the Senate. But some who wish he would move toward the party's center of gravity think that may

have changed, citing his newly demonstrated interest in partywide affairs.

In 1985, he joined then-Virginia Gov. Charles S. Robb and Rep. Richard A. Gephardt, Mo., to form the Democratic Leadership Council (DLC) with the avowed intention of moving the party toward the political mainstream.

At the same time, some Democratic operatives began touting Nunn as a potential vice presidential — perhaps even a presidential — nominee.

Nunn does not disclaim interest in a future party nomination. But he insists that he is not seeking it at this time and would not jeopardize his various legislative campaigns to move

> ***"** He knows more about the subject he talks about than anybody else by the time he starts talking about it. **"***
>
> —Sen. Carl Levin,
> D-Mich.

into the broader arena.

He does not want to go "sputtering around the country, spending two days a week in the Senate, seeing a lot of the things I'm working on come to nothing," he said.

"If someone told me right now that I'd have to start running for president next month or not in the rest of my life," he would pass. "I'll take another look after the November election," he said, but not with any expectation of deciding to jump into the race.

His investment in the DLC would fit well with long-term goals other than laying the groundwork for a Nunn presidential bid. ∎

In Conference: New Hurdles, Hard Bargaining

Only a few hundred feet separate the House and Senate chambers, but most members rarely venture to the opposite side of the Capitol.

The traffic between chambers became thicker, however, after Congress reconvened Sept. 8, 1986, because members increasingly were drawn into the House-Senate conference committees that always proliferate around that time of year.

While the spotlight tends to focus on floor action, crucial decisions are made in conferences — the least visible stage of the legislative process.

"Conference committees are the ultimate high for legislators," said Rep. Dennis E. Eckart, D-Ohio. "They are the Supreme Court of legislation. If you don't get it here, there's no other place to go."

That's heady stuff, but institutional and political factors in recent years have complicated conference committees' job of reconciling differences between House and Senate versions of major legislation.

In an era of budget austerity, negotiators rarely can afford to hammer out agreements with a tool once freely wielded: spending more money to buy off competing interests.

"In the old days, it was not a zero-sum game," said John E. Dean, who until 1985 was an aide to the House Education and Labor Committee. "You could come up with a package that gave the House and Senate everything they wanted."

Lawmakers also have had to adapt to growing complexity in the negotiating process itself. The proliferation of wide-ranging omnibus bills has spawned some conferences of almost unmanageable size, spanning the jurisdictions of several committees. In other cases, however, sweeping bills are negotiated by a handful of people.

A testament to such variety is the contrast between budget-related conferences of the Reagan era that have involved hundreds of members and the extraordinary chairman-to-chairman private negotiations between Rep. Dan Rostenkowski, D-Ill., and Sen. Bob Packwood, R-Ore., that produced the tax overhaul bill (HR 3838).

"Here in a short span we've seen the political process stretch its way from one extreme to the other, from a concentration of decision-making power to the other extreme of almost chaos," said Jeff Drumtra, director of the Tax Reform Research Group, an affiliate of Ralph Nader's Public Citizen group.

Few but Important

Conference committees are so critical to the legislative process that they are sometimes referred to as the "third house" of Congress. Although conferences are convened on a relatively small number of measures, these generally include the most important bills before Congress.

According to a study by Ilona B.

> *"Conference committees are the ultimate high for legislators. They are the Supreme Court of legislation. If you don't get it here, there's no other place to go."*
>
> **—Rep. Dennis E. Eckart, D-Ohio.**

Nickels of the Congressional Research Service, only 8 percent of the public laws enacted in the 98th Congress were the product of conference committees. But these included such major legislation as an overhaul of the Social Security system (PL 98-21) and all appropriations bills.

Most other laws cleared when one chamber accepted the other's amendments, or when an identical bill was passed by both chambers.

In the fall, conference committees were scheduled to be at work on such issues as appropriations, financing the "superfund" toxic-waste cleanup program, the defense budget, hydroelectric power, higher education programs, reorganizing the Pentagon and correcting the constitutional flaws of the Gramm-Rudman-Hollings anti-deficit law (PL 99-177).

A Modicum of Openness

House and Senate rules changes since the mid-1970s have broken down the barriers of secrecy and seniority that previously denied the public and junior members access to conference committee proceedings.

In 1964, when the House and Senate Armed Services committees were headed by Rep. Carl Vinson and Sen. Richard B. Russell, both Georgia Democrats, a junior member gave a succinct description of the conference that produced the annual military authorization bill.

The process, said then-Rep. Otis G. Pike, D-N.Y., involved "two gentlemen from Georgia talking, arguing, laughing and whispering in each other's ears."

Almost all conference committees then met in private. But in 1975, both chambers adopted rules changes requiring open conferences unless a majority of either side's conferees voted publicly to close the session. The House went a step further in 1977, voting to require open meetings unless the House itself voted to close them.

Even with those reforms, the conference remains the least accessible part of the legislative process. Transcripts are not always kept of proceedings, and meetings frequently are held in tiny rooms that cannot accommodate all who want to attend.

Typically, conferees are senior members of the committees with jurisdiction over the legislation at issue. But increasingly in recent years, more junior lawmakers have been named if they are members of the relevant subcommittee, sponsors of important amendments or have special expertise.

The composition of conference committees is so critical that for legislation as monumental as the 1986 tax overhaul bill, the selection of conferees was itself a moment of high drama.

Usually the Speaker of the House and presiding officer of the Senate appoint conferees selected by the relevant committee chairmen. But occasionally, congressional leaders play a more active role.

For example, Speaker Thomas P. O'Neill Jr., D-Mass., made critical decisions about whom to appoint as negotiators on the Gramm-Rudman-Hollings measure, because that proposal had never been considered by any House committee. Instead, it was attached by the Senate as an amendment to a bill raising the debt ceiling.

And before Rostenkowski chose conferees on the tax overhaul bill, sources said, O'Neill made it clear he wanted one of them to be Rep. Richard A. Gephardt, D-Mo., an early Democratic proponent of tax reform.

House-Senate Differences

As one of the few congressional institutions that is a creature of both chambers, a conference is a prime arena for institutional rivalries.

A legendary House-Senate staredown came in 1962, when appropriations action was stalled by a feud between House and Senate committee chairmen over, among other things, whether the conferences would meet on the House or Senate side of the Capitol. That particular issue was later defused with the construction of a meeting room exactly halfway between the chambers.

House members sometimes have an advantage in conferences, because they serve on fewer committees than senators and thus tend to specialize more. House members may know the details of a bill, while senators rely on staffers for such information.

"You find yourself arguing with Senate staff," said Rep. Tom Tauke, R-Iowa. "For a House member, that's a frustrating experience."

With more committee assignments and other demands on their time, busy senators also often leave negotiations to one or two senators who know conference issues best.

In a summer 1986 conference on a major higher education bill (S 1965), Robert T. Stafford, R-Vt., at one point found himself the sole Senate conferee. After receiving a House proposal, he quipped, "I'm caucusing with myself. Can you give me a couple minutes to complete the arguments?"

Sometimes intramural rivalry between House and Senate is overshadowed by divisions within a chamber's own delegation. For example, during a grueling six-month conference on key elements of the superfund bill (HR 2005) in 1986, there were frequently more bitter splits among House Democrats than between the two chambers. Senate conferees, too, were divided on many issues.

"There was not much traditional us-vs.-them," said Eckart, a House conferee. "There were lots of us-es and lots of thems."

Toeing the Line

The power of conference committees derives in large part from the great deference given to conference reports, which are rarely' rejected and cannot be amended on the floor under ordinary procedures.

Although few rules bind negotiators, the conference report generally has to remain within the scope of what the House and Senate passed. Conferees are expected to defend their own chamber's provisions even if they dis-

agree with them. Those who wander too far from their chamber's position do so at their peril.

In 1985, for example, House Armed Services Chairman Les Aspin, D-Wis., was bitterly castigated by some colleagues after a conference on the annual defense authorization bill in which critics, predominantly liberals, said that House conferees yielded too much to the pro-Pentagon Senate. That is one of the complaints now being aired by some House Democrats who are seeking to oust Aspin from his committee chairmanship after this session of Congress.

The Few Bargain for the Many

The private chairman-to-chairman talks that wrapped up the tax conference flew in the face of the last decade's drive to reduce secrecy and reliance on seniority in conferences.

Although they were unlikely to herald a wholesale reversion to closed sessions, the private negotiations did continue a pattern of recent years in which tax writers increasingly have conducted business behind closed doors. Conferees can circumvent "sunshine" requirements for open proceedings by meeting separately in House and Senate caucuses with staff shuttling between them, then ratifying decisions in the full conference.

"It's something of a reversion to the old way of doing things," said Drumtra. "Yet we have to admit the only way to pass good tax reform now is behind closed doors out of the glare of tax lobbyists. We [who supported sunshine rules] were hoisted on our own petard on that."

There have been other important occasions on major legislation when

Traditional full-scale conferences, like the one on the 1986 higher education reauthorization bill, sometimes give way to private, chairman-to-chairman negotiations.

conferees have been willing to leave deal-making to their two chairmen or a small group of senior members.

More than once, for instance, a budget deadlock has been broken by marathon private negotiations among the chairmen and ranking minority members of the House and Senate Budget committees.

"Attitudes have changed in the last few years," said Rep. Leon E. Panetta, D-Calif. "There's a willingness to accept whatever it takes to resolve" tough issues.

During the second of two conferences on the Gramm-Rudman law, a 66-member affair, many of the key compromises were made by a group of six House and Senate leaders.

"When a conference is huge, it's not where the bill is written," said Lynn Martin, R-Ill., a senior Budget Committee member.

But contemporary back-room dealers are much more likely than their predecessors to be solicitous of their rank and file. "It's like a good marriage," said Martin. "If there are good communications, they say go ahead."

The Problem With Packages

Congress' increasing tendency to legislate in omnibus packages has introduced new complications in the final stages of the legislative process.

Some conferences are so large, or their subjects so complex, that they have to break into sub-conferences, task forces and the like. The super-fund conference, for example, drew negotiators from six House committees and three Senate committees. Much of the work was done by small subgroups that were more manageable and focused than the full conference.

A conference with such broad jurisdictional spread was once quite rare. Former Rep. John N. Erlenborn, R-Ill. (1965-85), said it was considered extraordinary in 1974 when a conference on pension legislation drew negotiators from four committees.

Background

Appropriations stalemate in 1962, CQ's Congress and the Nation Vol. I, p. 378.

House, Senate open conference rules, 1975 CQ Almanac p. 930.

House conference rule revised, 1977 Almanac p. 8

Fiscal 1982 budget reconciliation bill, 1981 Alamanac p. 256.

Omnibus crime bill, 1984 Almanac p. 215.

Gramm-Rudman-Hollings law, 1985 Alamanac p. 459; fiscal 1986 defense authorization, p. 138; fiscal 1986 continuing resolution, p. 360.

Tax bills in closed sessions, 1985 CQ Weekly Report p. 1706; fiscal 1986 continuing resolution conference, p. 2651.

Tax overhaul conference, 1986 Weekly Report pp. 1947, 1601; higher education conference, p. 2036; "superfund" conference, pp. 1595, 1774; defense authorization conference, p. 2307; continuing resolution history, p. 2059; fiscal 1986 budget reconciliation bill, p. 751.

That pales in comparison with the scope of conferences now convened almost routinely to handle annual budget "reconciliation" bills. These bills tie together measures drafted by virtually all committees to bring programs under their jurisidiction into compliance with savings targets mandated by the budget resolution.

In 1981, the reconciliation law (PL 97-35) that was a critical part of President Reagan's first-year legislative program was handled by the largest conference on record: 280 members meeting in more than 50 subgroups.

The second largest conference, which brought together 242 conferees in 31 subgroups, met on the fiscal 1986

reconciliation bill (PL 99-272).

But on other omnibus bills, a relatively small group of members may handle a wide range of issues.

It is now common for supplemental appropriations bills and continuing appropriations resolutions to become unwieldy packages, laden with measures that may fall outside the jurisdiction of the Appropriations committees that traditionally provide conferees for those measures.

One of the most extreme examples was in 1984, when a huge omnibus crime bill was attached to the annual continuing resolution (PL 98-473). Members of the Judiciary committees were not named as conferees on the measure, although they were called in for consultation.

Conferences on continuing resolutions make decisions about financing large chunks of the government's operations in a single measure. They have generally tended to be dominated by senior members of the Appropriations committees, while junior members generally are more involved in conferences on regular appropriations bills.

But in 1985, junior members of the House Appropriations Committee secured several seats on the conference on the fiscal 1986 continuing resolution (PL 99-190), following a drive led by Norman D. Dicks, D-Wash.

Dicks, a member of the Defense Subcommittee and a conferee on that portion of the resolution, said the presence of junior members was crucial to retaining a House provision to ban testing of anti-satellite (ASAT) weapons.

"The conference would have never gotten that if we hadn't been there fighting for it," remarked Dicks. "In the old days, the chairman and ranking members, maybe four people, were deciding the entire defense budget.

"Let's face it, the conference committee is where it all happens." ∎

GOP Leader Dole: Determined to Do It All

Just before the Labor Day recess, as senators were plodding through yet another late-night session, some weary reporters in the Senate press room momentarily ignored the proceedings to watch a television game show.

At one point, three contestants were asked to identify President Gerald R. Ford's running mate in 1976. One wrongly answered Nelson Rockefeller. The others did not even guess.

The reporters snickered. The correct name belonged not to some figure from politics past, but to the man running the show just yards away — Senate Republican leader Robert Dole of Kansas.

A decade after the 1976 campaign, Dole was laboring to become so well-known, and liked, that by 1988 he would once again be on the national Republican ticket — this time as the presidential nominee. To that end, he may have been glad if voters had largely forgotten his role in the 1976 loss, one that tarred him long afterward as a "hatchet man."

Dole's role as the Senate's leader in the 99th Congress, which put him center stage once proceedings were televised live nationwide, was the one he hoped would carry him into the White House.

But it was a role of multiple, sometimes conflicting, personas. Dole had to be the statesmanlike head of Congress' upper chamber, yet a partisan promoter of fellow Republicans seeking re-election. He had to protect the institutional rights of the legislative branch, yet serve as chief Capitol Hill lobbyist for a Republican president.

All the while, Dole had to advance his own interests and identity if he were to rise above the crowd competing for his party's 1988 nomination.

Conflicting Ambitions?

As the 1986 elections approached Dole was expected to ask Senate Republicans to re-elect him as their leader for the 100th Congress. Since that Congress will last from January 1987 through 1988, the question of whether Dole could be both leader and presidential candidate loomed larger than

Seeking Presidency From Senate Pinnacle

it did in 1984, when Dole beat four rivals for the leadership job.

His predecessor, Republican Howard H. Baker Jr. of Tennessee, said it couldn't be done. Dole's closest contender for leader in 1984, Ted Stevens of Alaska, said it shouldn't be.

"His ambition is to be president; my only ambition is to be the Republican leader," Stevens said, explaining why he might challenge Dole again.

But after 20 months as leader, Dole had stilled most colleagues' doubts. With a thin 53-47 Republican majority, he had averted major losses and engineered severals significant victories. Among the latter were a comprehensive overhaul of the tax code, a law relaxing gun controls, approval of a long-stalled genocide treaty, which Jewish groups had wanted, and of President Reagan's Saudi arms sale that they opposed, and passage of military aid to Nicaraguan rebels.

"Bob Dole has performed way beyond what even his supporters expected," said Pete V. Domenici of New Mexico, another Republican who had sought the leadership.

"He's turned out to be the best leader we could have," said Minnesota Republican Dave Durenberger.

There were critics. "You can't do the two jobs," said Connecticut Republican Lowell P. Weicker Jr. "It is very difficult to run for president and [also] be the catalyst around which all points of view come together in the majority party."

Weicker saw "a clear-cut choosing of being Bob Dole the candidate, not the catalyst." One result, he said was "unabated contentiousness on the Senate floor. Everybody is at each other's throat all the time."

"It's just chaos," said a Senate Republican who asked to be unnamed. "You hear more and more the idea of, 'When is he going to decide what he is going to be? Is he going to be a presidential candidate, or the president's man, or the Senate's man?'"

"I think he's done pretty well," said James A. McClure, an Idaho Republican who ran for leader against Dole. But McClure also worried about Dole's ability to balance his "individual and collective roles."

"It has the potential to change the agenda of the Senate," he added. "Just recognizing that potential for distortion is of some concern to me."

Democrat Gary Hart of Colorado chose to retire rather than run again for his party's presidential nomination while serving in the Senate. "It's hard enough to be a senator and a national candidate," he said. "I can't imagine myself being majority leader *and* a national candidate."

But Ohio Democrat Howard M. Metzenbaum was certain Dole could do both: "Every single day the majority leader is on television. That gives him an exposure that's invaluable. If he acquits himself well — and Dole usually looks well — it's an incalculable advantage."

Dole, of course, saw no problems. His various roles, he said "all run together.... First I want to be a good senator. Then I want to be a good majority leader. If you can fulfill those two things, the other things just fall into place."

Retaining Senate Control

For his wit, intelligence, command and hustle, Dole is by all accounts one of the Senate's most effective members. And apart from the questions about his ability to be both leader and presidential candidate, criticisms of his leadership have been few.

Some committee chairmen said Dole would hold matters too close to his vest; while Baker held weekly meetings with them, Dole called the chairmen together infrequently.

Several Republicans agreed with Durenberger, who said, "Dole is not a good vote counter.... That's a repeated problem."

In explaining the lapses, these members said Republicans often weren't forced to commit to how they would vote, and Dole lacked his predecessor's sources in Democrats' ranks. "Howard Baker could get a feel for the Democratic side that I know Dole does not have," said one source.

Dole's defenders disputed the contention. "What has he lost?" asked Rudy Boschwitz, a Minnesota Republican. "He wins."

"The acid test is performance and he's had some close calls, but he hasn't dropped one yet," said Charles McC. Mathias Jr., R-Md.

Whether Dole's success as a senator and leader could translate into a winning presidential campaign depended in part on the fall elections.

Dole first had to win re-election for a fourth term as Kansas senator, which was considered certain. But the same could not be said of Republicans' odds of holding other Senate seats, and a net loss of just four seats on Nov. 4 would have put the Democrats in power. Dole, at best, would have been demoted to minority leader.

That, said Kentucky Democrat Wendell H. Ford, would be a less visible post from which to run for president, particularly against Vice President George Bush, the GOP frontrunner.

Stevens argued that Dole, as minority leader, would find it harder to juggle campaign travels and Senate GOP business since he would no longer control the Senate schedule.

But Nancy Landon Kassebaum, Dole's Republican colleague from Kansas, said, "I've always thought he would be better off as minority leader, because then he could criticize [Democrats' failures] and have more time to be away from the Senate."

McClure agreed. But he added, "One of the things he must have in the back of his mind is, if we lose the majority, does he want to be a minority leader?"

Dole was struggling to make that a moot question. As a *Republican* leader in an election year, colleagues expected him to orchestrate floor action in ways that would advance the candidacies of the 18 other Republican senators seeking re-election.

"Dole is always looking at the political consequences to our incumbents," said Thomas C. Griscom, executive director of the National Republican Senatorial Committee. "That's important when we're fighting for our political survival."

Democrats, predictably, chafed. "You can't say it's never been done before, but he's using the Senate for Republican re-election campaigns, and it's being done more frequently and blatantly than ever before," charged George J. Mitchell of Maine, chairman of the Democratic Senatorial Campaign Committee.

In 1986, when the Senate debated a measure (H J Res 668) to raise the federal debt limit, Dole accommodated numerous requests from Republican colleagues wanting to offer unrelated amendments that could help their re-election bids.

Oil-state member Don Nickles of Oklahoma won adoption of his pro-

"Bob Dole has performed way beyond what even his supporters expected."

—Sen. Pete V. Domenici, R-N.M.

posal to repeal the so-called windfall profits tax on petroleum. Paula Hawkins of Florida, home to many retirees, passed an amendment to ensure cost-of-living hikes for Social Security even if inflation remains low.

In April, Dole helped Charles E. Grassley, up for re-election in Iowa, with a rare gambit that allowed a floor vote on Grassley's bill (S 1774) making labor violence subject to federal anti-extortion penalties, though the bill had lost in committee. It was defeated as expected, but the attempt was important to business groups.

Dole's political antennae reach beyond the floor. When the Finance Committee voted in July to raise tobacco taxes to reduce the deficit, Dole lobbied panelists to reverse the decision, which imperiled tobacco-state Republican James T. Broyhill of North Carolina. He failed, narrowly.

As the Senate impresario, Dole

could use the floor for televised tributes to fellow Republicans. For instance, it was Dole who won Senate passage July 22, 1986, of a measure forcing the Reagan administration to let the Soviet Union buy subsidized U.S. grain. But he publicly gave credit to James Abdnor of South Dakota, whose Democratic rival, Rep. Thomas A. Daschle, was sponsor of a similar House bill promoting farm exports.

As the grain flap showed, sometimes Dole's efforts for Republicans could mean bucking their president.

Another example is the issue of sanctions aimed at South Africa's white-minority government. After loyally blocking action in 1985 on a bill Reagan opposed, in 1986 Dole expedited passage of an even tougher one (HR 4868). He rebuffed veto threats and, in an angry session at the White House, reportedly said the matter had

"You can't do the two jobs. It is very difficult to run for president and [also] be the catalyst around which all points of view come together in the majority party."

—Sen. Lowell P. Weicker Jr., R-Conn.

become "a domestic civil rights issue."

Dole was also trying to alleviate the political damage that Reagan's free-trade policies had caused Republicans in states that had lost businesses and jobs to foreign competition. He has declared trade legislation a priority for 1986 and cosponsored a bill (S 1860) to boost exports.

On weekends, Dole continued his work for Republicans, making campaign appearances that raised their identity and his own. He taped political ads; in one he vouched for Hawkins' claim to be "the Senate's general in the war on drugs."

What the Democrats Think

Dole's partisanship is no surprise to Democrats. He is, after all, the man who charged in the 1976 campaign that the country's four armed conflicts in this century were "Democrat wars."

"Dole is considerably more parti-

san than Baker," Mitchell says. "But I don't state that as a criticism. Our system contemplates that."

Members of both parties say the Senate itself became a more partisan place while Dole was leader. Democrats had only recently overcome the 1980 shock of losing their longtime majority and were emboldened, Boschwitz said, "by the sweet smell of control in their nostrils."

Domenici likened the floor to an arena, where both sides seek political advantage: "Very rarely have you had an occasion where that was so controlling. It's in that atmosphere that Dole has to run this place."

The tension was exposed Aug. 5, 1986, in an extraordinary argument between Dole and Democratic leader Robert C. Byrd of West Virginia.

The exchange climaxed a two-week standoff between Democrats and Dole, who insisted that a vote on aid for Nicaraguan rebels, which most Democrats opposed, be linked to a vote for South Africa sanctions, which had bipartisan support.

What sparked Byrd's attack was Dole's charge that Byrd tried to "sneak" a South Africa amendment onto a pending defense bill. Byrd snapped that he had offered the amendment openly, and only after Dole tried to choke off debate on the bill in a way that would bar a South Africa amendment.

Then Byrd vented other complaints: "I have had enough of this business of having the majority leader stand here and act as a traffic cop on this floor.... He determines who will call up an amendment, when they will call up an amendment, and what will be in the amendment."

"... While a senator may today be in a position to choke off the rights of

another senator, the time will come when the worm will turn."

Dole defended his actions, and told Byrd, "I did not become the majority leader to lose."

Byrd subsequently declined to be interviewed about Dole, while Dole dismissed the incident as "nothing in the scheme of things."

That aside, Democrats generally praised Dole and, like Mitchell, excused some of his partisanship as part of the game.

"I think he's a good leader; I think he's effective. I have no difficulty working with him, because he respects my point of view," Metzenbaum said. "There are times when I've had to stand up against him and it rarely gets personal. Oh, there have been a few times when he's lost his cool. But don't we all?"

"Bob Dole has been fair and never broken his word to me," said Nebraska Democrat J. James Exon. "For a man with that many balls up in the air, all of which could come down any time, I think he's done a good job."

The Manion Fight

The Democrats say their side had no big complaints about Dole — until the fight in 1986 to confirm Daniel A. Manion, Reagan's nominee to be a federal appeals court judge.

"I think the handling of the Manion thing was deplorable," Mitchell said. "What it displayed about him was that he'll do just about anything to win."

Democrats called Manion unqualified, while Republicans said the conservative was being harassed on ideological grounds. He was finally confirmed July 23 when the Senate voted 49-50 against reconsidering an earlier, disputed 48-46 vote in Manion's favor.

Democrats had sought the first vote, calling Dole's bluff after he taunted them for stalling. He was taken by surprise. But in complicated maneuvering, the votes of three Manion opponents were "paired" by Dole with those of three absent Republicans who Dole said were for Manion, although he had not spoken with them. In effect, this canceled the "no" votes and produced a 47-47 tie.

Byrd then switched his vote to "yea" to avert Bush's tie-breaker and to be able to demand a second vote, as only those on the winning side can do. As it turned out, two of the three absent Republicans, Barry Goldwater of Arizona and Bob Packwood of Oregon, had not yet decided how to vote.

"It was poorly handled," said Kassebaum, a Manion foe who paired with Goldwater. "The one thing that was troubling in the whole issue was the pairing of votes. It bothered Goldwater. In the past, you always had to get the senator's approval."

Kassebaum did not blame either Dole or Dan Quayle, R-Ind., who pressed her to pair with Goldwater. But she was critical that Senate leaders did not do a better job of counting votes, and were caught off guard.

Dole, in his defense, noted it was Quayle who arranged the Kassebaum-Goldwater pair and that Democrats waived his offer to contact Packwood, assuming Packwood would have voted for Manion.

On the second vote, Goldwater again was absent but allowed his vote to be paired with a Manion opponent. Packwood voted to reconsider the original approval of the nominee, indicating his opposition to Manion.

Metzenbaum, although a leading Manion opponent, said Dole "was just doing his job. I feel certain he did not intentionally misrepresent the facts."

But a Republican senator, a Dole admirer, said the Manion incident illustrates that Dole's political intuitiveness, usually a great asset, could backfire. "Manion is the best example there's been of Bob Dole flying by the seat of his pants," the senator said.

White House Lobbyist

The fact is, Manion was confirmed. So along with blame, Dole also got the credit for scoring a major victory for the president. It was only the latest example of Dole's effectively performing the role of White House lobbyist, and at a time when both Republicans and Democrats were increasingly inclined to snub the president despite his popularity.

When Dole was elected leader, one Senate Republican hailed the result as a "declaration of independence" from the White House. Still, pushing the president's program is part of the job when the leader is of the same party.

"While Dole clearly ran on the position that he was leader of the Senate first, and the president's man second, you have to recognize the reality of dealing with a very popular president like Reagan," Domenici says.

In his first days on the job, Dole sacrificed home-state interests to oppose a farm relief bill that Reagan later vetoed. A widely published photo

showed protesting farmers with a banner reading, "We're from Kansas. Bob Dole doesn't work for us, either."

"Sometimes I just have to marvel," Exon said. "How he in good conscience subscribes to these anti-agriculture policies of this administration and gets by with it in a farm state is a tribute to his agility."

Dole moved ingeniously in 1985 to block the earlier South Africa bill, averting a major slap at Reagan's foreign policy for the time. When opponents insisted on the bill's passage, after Dole had persuaded the president to order sanctions on his own, Dole had the bill taken from the Senate and locked in a safe.

Perhaps Dole's most frustrating work on Reagan's behalf involved the budget. In both 1985 and 1986, he shelved the Senate Budget Commit-

"I did not become the majority leader to lose."

—Sen. Robert Dole, R-Kan.

tee's budget resolutions so he could forge changes acceptable to Reagan.

That contrasts with the defiance Dole voiced on his first day as leader. On Jan. 3, 1985, he declared deficit reduction as Senate Republicans' top priority. They would break with tradition, he said then, and draft a budget without waiting for a Reagan package that was sure to be rejected.

But Dole was unable to craft a budget, and the Budget Committee's subsequent package had more funding for domestic programs and less for defense than Reagan would support.

Dole then brokered a compromise. With Reagan's approval and Bush's

tie-breaking vote, on May 10 the Senate voted 50-49 for a fiscal 1986 budget freezing Social Security, holding defense to an inflation increase and killing 13 domestic programs.

Dole not only had Bush there for the 2 a.m. vote; he had California Republican Pete Wilson brought from a hospital by ambulance and gurney.

"He has a certain flare which he uses to pull the chestnuts out of the fire," Mathias said of Dole.

But later, after a meeting of Dole, Reagan and House Speaker Thomas P. O'Neill Jr., D-Mass., Reagan reneged on his backing for a Social Security freeze when O'Neill agreed to support higher defense spending.

Until then, said North Dakota Republican Mark Andrews, "Bob was making an honest, good-faith effort to get the White House to move." But as a party to the Reagan-O'Neill swap, "he left a lot of his troops hanging" with the politically dangerous vote on Social Security.

In 1986, the Budget Committee produced a bipartisan fiscal 1987 budget that again defied the president on defense, taxes and domestic cuts. Dole scrapped it, too, partly in deference to the president but mostly because a majority of Republicans would not support it on the floor.

In 1985, Reagan's abandonment of the Senate's budget freezing Social Security was the first big setback for Dole's goal of being the leader who presided over significant deficit reduction. "A lot of people just sort of gave up after that," he said.

And in 1986, the president's goal — overhaul of the tax code — took over. "I hope we haven't backed off the budget," Dole said. "We haven't tried to do that."

For a long time, Dole was a reluctant shepherd for Reagan's tax initiative, agreeing with most Republican senators that budget cutting was more important. But the historic result, which cleared Congress Sept. 27, promised to rank as a major achievement of his leadership.

Unlike any predecessor, Dole was subject to administration pressure even at home — his wife is Transportation Secretary Elizabeth Dole. The link was obvious in 1986 when the Senate, to the vexation of many members, spent two weeks on a bill (S 638) allowing her department to sell Conrail, the federal freight railroad. It passed, only to die in the House. But overall, Republicans were content with the balance Dole had struck.

"He is less the president's man than Howard Baker was," Stafford says. "Baker considered himself the president's spokesman in the Senate. Dole considers himself the Senate's spokesman to the president."

"I'm obviously loyal to the president," Dole said, citing a Congressional Quarterly study rating his 1985 presidential support at 92 percent, the Senate's highest score. "And that's how it should be. But on the other hand, my constituency is the Republican senators and not the White House. And they didn't elect me to try to run over the senators in favor of the White House or anybody else."

Wooing the Right

If managing Reagan's legislative portfolio was sometimes a problem, it also boosted Dole's stock among the pro-Reagan conservatives who would determine the party's nominee.

But his approaches to that group went beyond loyal service to Reagan, members said. "I don't think there's any doubt he's making a deliberate play to the right," Metzenbaum said.

"I don't know that he is reaching out to the conservatives, at least not gratuitously," said Republican Sen. Jesse Helms of North Carolina, a leader of the right. "I think that Bob is basically a conservative. . . . I don't see that there is any political adjustment to be made on Bob Dole's part."

That Dole's conservative credentials were questioned was a sign of the GOP's rightward tilt since 1976, when Ford tapped him partly to pacify Reagan's backers. Reagan reportedly cleared the choice.

Moreover, Dole was no recent convert to causes dear to conservative groups. A theme of his 1974 Senate campaign was support for a constitutional ban on abortions. Since 1961, his first year in Congress, Dole's voting record annually ranked high in conservative groups' ratings and at the bottom of liberal groups' lists.

"He has a legitimate claim on conservatives' support," Stafford said. "But some of them might not agree."

The most-often cited evidence of Dole's courtship of the conservative doubters were his forays into foreign policy, an area in which he had not been notably active before.

After Reagan ordered an attack on Libya in April 1986 to retaliate for alleged terrorism, leaders in both parties proposed designating members with whom the president should consult before future military actions.

But Dole joined conservatives in sponsoring a bill (S 2335) freeing the president from existing restrictions on his war powers in cases of terrorism.

In 1986 Dole also pressured the administration for covert aid to rebels fighting leftist Angola. He led conservatives in urging Reagan to disown the 1979 strategic arms limitation treaty, SALT II, charging the Soviet Union with "blatantly violating" its limits.

Dole has been a tireless advocate of Reagan's requests for aid to rebels battling the Marxist Nicaraguan government, calling them by Reagan's term — "freedom fighters."

On domestic issues, Dole pushed votes for a balanced budget, school prayer and presidential power to veto items in appropriations bills. Though unsuccessful, conservatives applauded

Background

Majority leader election, 1984 CQ Almanac p. 3.

For 1985 action, see 1985 Almanac on fiscal 1986 budget, p. 441; farm-credit action, p. 542; and South Africa, p. 90.

Also, 1986 CQ Weekly Report on fiscal 1987 budget, p. 955; labor-violence bill, p. 846; cigarette tax, p. 1727; trade, p. 1543; grain sales, p. 1730; South Africa, p. 1969; debt-limit amendments, p. 1723; Manion confirmation, p. 1685; proposed War Powers Act changes, p. 1021; Angola aid, p. 457; SALT II, p. 1218; Conrail, p. 1974; Stevens' challenge, p. 1611; and Byrd-Dole argument, p. 1784.

the effort.

But among anti-tax, supply-side conservatives, Dole remained suspect for his achievements as Finance Committee chairman, prior to becoming leader. When deficits climbed after 1981, he was instrumental in passing the largest peacetime tax increase in U.S. history in 1982 and, in 1984, another $50 billion tax bill. Dole was damned as "the tax collector for the welfare state" by conservative House Republican Newt Gingrich of Georgia.

Subsequently, Dole as leader privately lobbied for budgets that did not raise taxes significantly. Once in 1985, a Democratic Senate source said, he reminded a budget group of Gingrich's censure. "He talked of taking the heat once and said he didn't want to do it again," this source recalled.

Several senators said Dole's actions that were perceived as self-promotions to the right often were a leader's attempts to represent his members. Dole dismissed talk that he was moving to the right to curry conservative favor for a presidential bid.

"I've been voting here for 20-some years. I don't think I've changed any," he said.

Durenberger noticed a rightward shift. But, he added, "Bob Dole is not going to sell himself out just to be president of the United States."

What Lies Ahead?

Dole's strategy of using the Senate leadership as a springboard to the presidency was a gamble that tested voters' recent bias against Washington insiders. Former governors Ronald Reagan and Jimmy Carter both parlayed that bias into victory, and Reagan still rails against the government he now heads.

In contrast, Dole boasted a quarter-century in both chambers of Congress and a wife who headed a federal agency. "We're going back to the real world," he joked after the right-dominated 1984 GOP convention. "It's called Washington."

Stafford thought Dole could succeed. Though he said he would support Baker if Baker mounted a serious campaign for the 1988 Republican presidential nomination, he added, "I think, very frankly, that Baker made a mistake when he left the Senate. He lost a major launching pad."

Baker said that he did not regret his decision to retire after 1984 to free himself for a possible presidential bid. Even so, he conceded that his old leadership job could well launch his successor Dole to the very goal Baker seeks.

"I think Bob will profit from the leadership role, as indeed he has already," Baker said in a July 31, 1986, speech in Washington, D.C. "He's done an extraordinary job as majority leadership job could launch his successor Dole to the very goal Baker seeks.

For his part, Dole said the dual roles were manageable. "If you're willing to give up your time, you can make it work," he said. But, he added, "if it really got to be where I really had a good shot at the nomination, then I think I'd have to revisit the leadership question."

Meanwhile, "I don't know why you'd give up something unless you know you're going to have something else." ∎

Senate's Romance With TV Ends in Marriage

The Senate, in an anticlimactic yet historic ending to a two-month experiment with live television, voted overwhelmingly July 29, 1986, to keep the cameras rolling permanently.

The 78-21 vote came at the end of a typical Senate day, the kind opponents formerly cited as argument against televising floor proceedings: There was little action, a dozen time-consuming quorum calls, and in this case, no suspense about the outcome.

And as usual, the most important debates went on behind closed doors. Disputes over the budget, defense and foreign policy in Central America and South Africa had hardened into a legislative knot that blocked action on any of those major issues, and the leadership struggled to negotiate a way out. *(1986 CQ Weekly Report, pp. 1723, 1767, 1731)*

Even in the back rooms, however, TV may have intruded. One Republican aide, for example, expressed hope that the prospect of vacant TV screens would encourage adversaries to compromise on procedures for floor debate, preventing inaction and protracted filibusters.

While that would please members who hoped that TV would quicken the Senate's pace, foes of live broadcasts bemoaned to the end what they foresaw as the demise of their body's historic role as the slower, more deliberative chamber of Congress.

Some members feared television would end a revered tradition of deliberation, including frequent filibusters and time-delaying quorum calls. The TV audience sees only a printed message about what the Senate is doing at such moments, as it did repeatedly for short periods during action on a higher-education bill (S 1965), the first to be debated on live TV. *(1986 CQ Weekly Report, p. 1275)*

"My fundamental objection to television is rooted in my deep concern that television in the Senate will result in an increase in political expediency at the expense of statesmanship," said Russell B. Long, D-La., on July 29. No one had fought TV in the Senate longer or harder than Long.

Albert Gore Jr., D-Tenn., sought to allay such fears with release of a Library of Congress study concluding, "Television coverage has changed the patterns of Senate floor activity very little."

The study, which surveyed 20 types of floor activity, found that the only change clearly traceable to TV was a 250 percent increase in the number of "special orders," or speeches that senators make on a variety of subjects, before the start of regular business.

"Television has not disrupted the institution of the Senate," Gore said. "If anything, television has helped to keep the Senate on its toes."

nent. The test started May 1 with closed-circuit transmissions to legislative offices and, on June 2, public broadcasts began. Cameras were to be turned off for two weeks before the final vote, so senators could assess the results, but the Senate voted July 15 to reduce the blackout to three days. *(1986 CQ Weekly Report pp. 1611, 1274, 1216, 520)*

In the end, opposition to TV crossed party and generational lines. Foes included Republican Dan Quayle of Indiana, 39, a telegenic freshman, and 84-year-old Democrat John C. Stennis of Mississippi, the Senate's longest-serving member.

"Television has not disrupted the institution of the Senate. If anything, television has helped to keep the Senate on its toes."

—Sen. Albert Gore Jr., D-Tenn.

A Long Time Coming

The vote to continue live radio and TV broadcasts of the Senate was the "final step of a long journey," said Charles McC. Mathias Jr., R-Md.

Sen. Claude Pepper, D-Fla. (1936-51), now a House member, first proposed broadcasting proceedings of Congress 39 years ago. But the successful 1986 drive dates to an effort begun by Majority Leader Howard H. Baker Jr., R-Tenn. (1967-85), in 1981, two years after the House had begun broadcasting live. *(1981 CQ Almanac p. 391)*

The Senate on Feb. 27, 1986, approved a resolution (S Res 28) allowing broadcasting. The vote was 67-21. But the resolution required a two-step test and a second vote July 29 before TV coverage could become perma-

Opponents also included two Republicans who had supported TV as an experiment — Jake Garn of Utah and Alan K. Simpson of Wyoming, the assistant majority leader.

In a pre-vote survey by the Cable-Satellite Public Affairs Network (C-SPAN), which airs gavel-to-gavel coverage of House and Senate proceedings, Garn complained of a slower pace and too much grandstanding since broadcasts began. But Simpson was listed in favor of TV.

"He feels as though the Senate needs more rules changes to prevent posturing before the TV cameras," a Simpson aide said.

Those changes, she said, include limits on filibusters and on the addition of non-germane amendments to legislation.

Among supporters were three Republicans who had opposed TV in February — Mitch McConnell, Ky.; Rudy Boschwitz, Minn.; and Robert T. Stafford, Vt.

Before the vote, Majority Leader Robert Dole, R-Kan., reiterated his hope that any changes would make the Senate more efficient, speeding up roll-call votes and minimizing delays. He hailed radio and TV as "an electronic bridge to the American people."

Both the House and Senate control what is broadcast and make it available to public and commercial stations. Most use excerpts on newscasts, but C-SPAN provides live satellite signals to its cable TV affiliates. Though 25.5 million homes can watch House proceedings, the potential Senate audience is one-third that size, mainly because many cable stations lack extra channel space.

More Rules Changes Ahead?

In the weeks before the final vote, the Rules and Administration Committee reviewed members' comments to consider possible modifications.

No major changes were proposed for Senate rules, despite earlier predications from many, including Dole, that the test would prove a need to sharpen and speed debate. However, by giving final approval to S Res 28, the Senate made permanent several rules changes tentatively adopted in February. The major one reduced to 30 hours, from 100, the time allowed for debate after senators have voted to break off a filibuster.

Rules Committee hearings elicited few major complaints. Wendell H. Ford, Ky., the panel's ranking Democrat who compiled comments from fellow Democrats, said July 16 that his only problem with Senate TV "is that not many in our state are carrying the Senate show."

Perhaps the most serious wrinkle during the test period involved the question of senators' and outsiders' use of TV tapes and satellite signals.

The Rules Committee, by voice vote July 16, approved a resolution (S Res 447) banning political and commercial use of Senate TV coverage. Mathias, the committee chairman, said that resolution would have to be voted on separately in the Senate, because S Res 28 could not be amended on the floor.

The ban provided by S Res 447 is

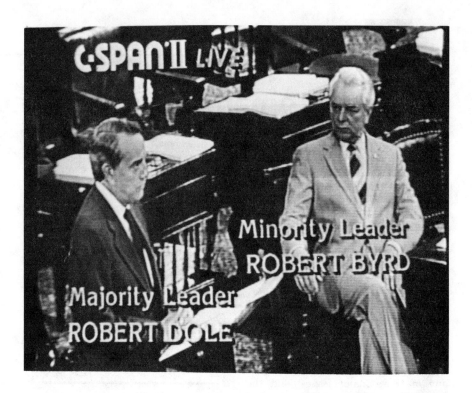

identical to one that Rules originally had written in its TV resolution, but the wording was changed on the floor in February to bar rebroadcasts "for any purpose outside the Senate."

Senators said that a strict reading of that broader ban would mean TV networks are in violation for using tapes on their newscasts, and so are senators who send tapes or satellite "TV press releases" to their home-state commercial stations.

About 30 senators, many from states that do not receive C-SPAN, have sent broadcasts to local stations. Ted Stevens, R-Alaska, wrote the Select Committee on Ethics seeking advice.

Ethics turned to the Rules Committee, which responded that its proposed ban on commercial and political uses should remedy the problem. But as panel members noted repeatedly, the definition of such uses is unclear.

The subject received little attention during floor debate July 29. TV foe Warren B. Rudman, R-N.H., complained that senators' transmission of satellite signals to home-state stations "is going to be the greatest use of television in the Senate, by a body that is obviously occupied by people who run for elective office."

Among other recommendations from Rules was one approved July 25

that would allow transfer of tapes to the Library of Congress and National Archives after 30 days. Mathias said the proposal would be offered on the floor as an amendment to S Res 447.

In action that does not require the full Senate's approval, Rules voted July 25 to buy the equipment now being leased, to add a seventh camera and a new audio system, and to equip a permanent control room. The panel rejected Architect of the Capitol George M. White's initial request for an added $1.5 million to buy "the best there is." Mathias said the scaled-down acquisition plans would not exceed the original $3.5 million first-year budget for TV and radio.

The committee limited floor displays of charts and other graphics to 24-by-30-inch flats. Each senator could display two graphics pertinent to the debate. A signal light is to be installed so the presiding officer knows when he or she is on camera.

Rules sent some complaints about decorum to the sergeant-at-arms, including requests to limit staff near a senator being televised. Among "cosmetic changes" to be made, Dole said, is a new color for Senate walls. Senators televised against that backdrop now "look like they're standing in split-pea soup," he said. ▮

Bill Gray Builds a Political Career on Paradox

In his eight years in Congress, Pennsylvania Democrat William H. Gray III has built an auspicious career by confounding expectations.

Gray came to Congress in 1979 as a minister with no experience in party politics or public office. He quickly maneuvered his way onto some of the most sought-after House committees.

In 1984, while more experienced members wrestled to become chairman of the Budget Committee, Gray slipped in from behind to win the leadership post — without stepping on any toes.

Though he is a black urban liberal at a time when that combination is out of political fashion, Gray has won the enthusiastic support of conservative Southerners for his running of the committee.

In 1986, Gray faced the straitjacket of the Gramm-Rudman-Hollings law, which he opposed. But he shepherded a budget resolution through the House that went Gramm-Rudman one better, promising to bring deficits almost $7 billion below the law's $144 billion target.

Thriving on apparent paradox makes Gray hard to pin down. He is popular with his colleagues, but they do not seem able to define or predict him. In interviews with dozens of members and staff, none could name an enemy he had made — but none offered a revealing anecdote, either.

"Bill is a very sophisticated dancer," admired Mickey Leland, D-Texas. Said a House leadership aide, "He's a very complex guy."

Gray operates with a deft style that leaves no fingerprints. He loves to preach but hates to tell others exactly what to do. With the press, he is informal but not informative. He avoids confrontation, yet chairs one of the most partisan committees in Congress. Some Republicans see him as a puppet of the Democratic leadership, but Democrats say he has often tugged the leadership along behind him.

An ambitious man who focuses intently on the task at hand, Gray still leaves Washington frequently to tend to the affairs of his Baptist church in Philadelphia.

'Sophisticated Dancer' Skirts Budget Traps

Gray himself sees no incongruity in all of this. "I decided my career would be preaching and teaching," he said. "After all, every sermon isn't delivered from the pulpit." *(Gray at a glance, box, next page)*

As Budget Committee chairman since 1985, Gray has won the thanks of party leaders. "I think he's doing very well," said Majority Whip Thomas S. Foley, D-Wash. "The percentage by which this budget was adopted among Democrats was truly extraordinary."

Interviewed in August 1986, Foley was referring to the fiscal 1987 budget resolution (H Con Res 337) adopted May 15 by a 245-179 vote. Democrats voted for the plan 228-19.

In the 12-year history of the budget process, the only greater margin occurred in Gray's first year as chairman, when Democrats voted 234-15 in favor of the House budget.

The Democratic leadership is intensely concerned about defections on the budget, since it sees the document as a fundamental statement of political priorities. Under Gray's predecessors, Democrats frequently failed to support the budget. Leaders recall 1977 and 1982 with particular bitterness; in those years, the Budget Committee's resolutions were defeated on the floor due to massive Democratic defections. In 1981 and 1982, conservative Democrats united with Republicans to pass budgets geared to Ronald Reagan's priorities.

The hallmark of Gray's tenure, according to committee members and others, is his ability to forge consensus.

"Bill has a capacity for conciliation," said Majority Leader Jim Wright, D-Texas. "He has almost infi-

Cleric and legislator: House Budget Chairman William H. Gray III has found congregations in his Philadelphia church and on Capitol Hill: "After all, every sermon isn't delivered from the pulpit."

Gray at a Glance

Born: Aug. 20, 1941, Baton Rouge, La.
Education: Franklin and Marshall College, B.A. 1963; Drew Theological Seminary, M.Div. 1966; Princeton Theological Seminary, Th.M. 1970.
Occupation: Clergyman.
Family: Wife, Andrea Dash; three children.
Religion: Baptist.
Political Career: Sought Democratic nomination for House, 1976. Elected to House, 1978.

Committees

Budget (chairman)

Appropriations
(27th of 35 Democrats)
Subcommittees: Foreign Operations; Transportation.

District of Columbia
(4th of 7 Democrats)
Subcommittees: Fiscal Affairs and Health; Government Operations and Metropolitan Affairs.

CQ Vote Studies

Year	Presidential Support S	O	Party Unity S	O	Conservative Coalition S	O
1985	15	78	82	3	13	73
1984	19	73	90	3	7	86
1983	11	78	93	1	2	93
1982	21	65	80	5	8	84
1981	29	59	87	2	4	88
1980	65	21	80	5	5	83
1979	79	14	94	2	2	92

S = Support   O = Opposition

Elections

1984 General
Gray (D) 200,484 91%
Ronald Sharper (R) 18,224 8

1984 Primary
Gray (D) 64,754 84
Susan Bowen (D) 12,112 16

1982 General
Gray (D) 120,744 76
Milton Street (I) 35,205 22

Prior Winning Percentages
1980 96%   1978 82%

Interest Group Ratings

Year	ADA	ACA	AFL-CIO	CCUS
1985	95	*	93	15
1984	90	5	92	38
1983	85	0	100	21
1982	85	0	100	26
1981	90	0	93	6
1980	72	19	95	62
1979	100	0	100	0

* Not yet available.

nite patience — a willingness to sit for long tedious hours while others extrude for the airwaves the ecstatics of their positions."

Contrast With Jones

Gray's style as Budget chairman is in marked contrast with his predecessor, James R. Jones, D-Okla.

A relatively conservative Democrat with a strong independent streak, Jones frequently clashed with leaders and with the liberal wing of his party.

"Jones' problem was real obvious: Jones never had the trust of his own committee," said Lynn Martin, R-Ill., who served under both chairmen. "Jones had to keep proving that he was a liberal. Bill Gray doesn't have to prove that he's a liberal."

In the House, the Budget Committee has always divided sharply along partisan lines, while the Senate Budget Committee has frequently searched for bipartisan agreement. House Democrats meet in closed caucuses to hammer out a budget draft before allowing Republicans to see it.

Especially in his first years as chairman (1981-82), Jones would consult with a few trusted colleagues and aides, develop his own budget proposals, and then sell hard his "chairman's mark" to his committee. Later, Democratic leaders gave Jones more direction to keep their members from rebelling.

Gray's approach is different. He walks into the first sessions not with a chairman's mark but with a blank

sheet of paper. He shuts the door and keeps Democrats meeting together for long hours, days and weeks until they iron out their differences and produce their own budget.

"It makes them work, makes them understand that if they fund this, they've got to cut that," said Gray.

Talk, Talk and More Talk

Building a Democratic consensus on the budget in 1986 was not easy.

"I couldn't be Budget chairman. I don't have the patience," said Wright.

Several Democrats said they were occasionally frustrated by Gray's refusal to provide guidance when the committee seemed stuck. "We finally reached the point where no one wanted to talk," said panel member Buddy MacKay, D-Fla. "I would have speeded it up. But maybe letting us get to the point of being worn out was part of his psychology."

Gray exhibited remarkable skill at avoiding and managing conflict, several members said. Gray's approach "is that of a lover, not a fighter," said Vic Fazio, D-Calif., a member of Budget.

"He's careful not to leave people personally threatened by the fact that they're on the losing side of an argument," said MacKay. One technique Gray used, MacKay said, was to stop an argument and move to another issue when it became clear that a member was going to have to back down. When the panel resumed deliberations the next day, the decision was treated as if it had already been made.

When the panel's Democrats finally did come together on a plan, it was one in which they had pride of authorship, and one they went out and enthusiastically sold to a somewhat reluctant party leadership.

After it was over, members said they could point to almost no area of the budget that had Gray's personal stamp on it, but they suspected that the final document was what Gray wanted all along.

"He knows the direction he wants to go and very gently and subtly gets there with the members thinking they arrived at it themselves," said committee member Charles E. Schumer, D-N.Y.

Conservative Support

Some of Gray's most enthusiastic fans come from the conservative wing of his party.

Charles W. Stenholm, a Texas

Democrat who is not on the Budget Committee but who helped lead the 1981 revolt against the party leadership in favor of Reagan's economic program, said: "I can't think of anybody we could have elected as Budget chairman who could have done better — and I think I can speak for the conservative wing of Democrats."

Marvin Leath, D-Texas, a conservative who has played an important role on the committee in brokering agreement on defense spending, said Gray won his support because he was fair. The House resolution included $285 billion for defense, compared with the Senate's $301 billion and the administration's request for $320 billion. Leath said that cuts in domestic programs were equally deep.

"He's willing to lay his personal priorities on the deck and chop them along with others he thinks ought to be chopped," said Leath.

In 1985, at the start of his chairmanship, party leaders helped Gray's cause by adding Leath and other conservatives to the committee to broaden its base and make it better reflect the Democratic Caucus.

Preaching and Teaching

Watching Gray preach on a steamy summer Sunday in Philadelphia is like watching a man unchained, in comparison with his demeanor on the air-conditioned House floor.

He alternately shouts and whispers, quotes spirituals and modern theologians, shifts topics effortlessly from South Africa to the Bible. The arms of his black gown wave freely as he raises his hands to make a point.

Gray builds to a crescendo, then stands back and mops his brow as the congregation sends up a volley of "amens."

Many members interviewed for this story said the key to Gray was his background and continuing role as a minister. He preaches at Bright Hope Baptist Church two to three times a month, does most weddings and funerals there, and actively takes care of church affairs.

Bob Edgar, D-Pa., whose district adjoins Gray's, is a Methodist minister who entered Drew Theological Seminary two years after Gray. Edgar said that seminary training in preaching and counseling helped develop Gray's techniques.

"He has the ability to read body language, to speak clearly, and to compromise with people of different phi-

Background

House Budget Committee adoption, 1986 CQ Weekly Report p. 1061; House passage, p. 1079; reconciliation, p. 1725.

Earlier budget action: 1985 CQ Almanac p. 441; 1984 Almanac p. 155; 1983 Almanac p. 435; 1982 Almanac p. 186; 1981 Almanac pp. 247, 267; 1980 Almanac pp. 108, 119; 1979 Almanac p. 163; 1978 Almanac p. 49; 1977 Almanac p. 189.

Gramm-Rudman-Hollings (PL 99-177): 1985 Almanac p. 459; Weekly Report pp. 1559, 1680.

Budget chairmanship fight, 1985 Almanac p. 5.

losophies," Edgar said.

Edgar and Gray said that the politics of running a large Baptist church, where the minister is expected to be a strong leader yet is hired by the congregation, are no simpler than those of Congress.

Family Traditions

Gray was born in 1941 into a family where politics provided a constant undercurrent to religion. His grandfather founded Bright Hope Church in 1925. He was succeeded as pastor after his death by Gray's father, who had a doctorate from the University of Pennsylvania and had been president of two black universities in Florida.

Gray's father was active in Democratic reform politics in Philadelphia and in the civil rights movement. Gray recalls that the Rev. Dr. Martin Luther King Jr. was a frequent house guest, sometimes staying for weeks at a time.

Gray showed no particular interest in the ministry until late in college, when he decided he would go on to the seminary. His father, he says, "was quite pleased but quite shocked." Gray earned degrees from Drew and then from Princeton Theological Seminary. In 1972, he was recently married, teaching at a Catholic college and running a Baptist church in Montclair, N.J., when his father died, and he returned to take over the family church.

Ministering to an urban area brought him into direct contact with secular politics, and in 1976 Gray challenged the incumbent 2nd District congressman, Robert N. C. Nix (1958-79) in the Democratic primary. Nix was a member of the old-line black

political hierarchy and one of the first blacks to chair a House committee (Post Office and Civil Service). Charging that Nix had lost touch with the district, Gray lost by only 339 votes. Two years later, Gray ran again and won by almost 12,000 out of 63,000 votes cast.

That election left some resentment in Philadelphia among those in the local party organization who had been patiently waiting for Nix to retire to run for his seat.

But Gray has taken firm control of his district. His only significant challenge came in the 1982 primary from Milton Street, a tough-talking community activist and state senator. Gray won with 76 percent of the vote. In 1986, he faced opposition only in the May primary, and won 96.6 percent of the vote. He was unopposed in the general election in November.

Off to a Fast Start

Even though he had never held a political office, Gray jumped quickly into House politics. He made friends with power brokers such as John P. Murtha, D-Pa., and won a coveted seat on the Democratic Steering and Policy Committee, which makes committee assignments.

Showing a precocious ability at behind-the-scenes dealing, Gray announced that he would not oppose any other freshman for a committee seat, and stood aside so someone else could take an opening he wanted on Banking, Finance and Urban Affairs. When time came to select members for the Budget Committee, he spoke in favor of other freshmen — then sat back while other members of Steering and Policy put him on the panel.

In his other committee assignment, Foreign Affairs, Gray won establishment of a new African development program, a remarkable success for a freshman. He also became one of the leaders of the drive to impose sanctions on South Africa.

In 1981, Gray gave up his seats on Budget and Foreign Affairs to take a position on Appropriations, but two years later came back to Budget as a representative of the spending panel.

His campaign for the committee's chairmanship in 1984 was a model of quiet political acumen. Under House rules, members are allowed only six years on the committee, with an extra two possible for a chairman elected in his last term. At the end of 1984, Chairman Jones lost his eligibility, but and announced that he would seek a

"Here's a black, urban progressive doing good at the worst time in history for black, urban progressives."
—Rep. Bob Edgar, D-Pa.

"Because he feels he's open and fair, there is also an air of moral superiority . . . that rankles [Republicans]."
—Rep. Vin Weber, R-Minn.

rules change to permit him to keep the job. Jones was challenged by another committee member, Leon E. Panetta, D-Calif. But Panetta had himself served the full six years and needed a rules change to be able to serve as chairman.

While attention was focused on the Jones-Panetta race and the rules changes they sought, Gray used the Pennsylvania delegation and the Congressional Black Caucus to explore his chances for a dark-horse challenge. He went to members asking for their support in case the rules were not changed. The rules change was narrowly defeated in December, and when other Democrats — chiefly Martin Frost of Texas — attempted to mount a last-minute campaign for chairman, they found that Gray had sewn up the votes.

When Gray was sworn in as Budget chairman, 2,000 constituents flooded the Capitol for the brief ceremony in an unusual show of support. The trip was organized by his church.

The congregation "is the root of my life," said Gray. "It is my family."

GOP Praise, Skepticism

House Republicans are left out of most budget maneuvers. They are kept to a committee ratio (20-13) that understates their overall numbers in the House, and they are not invited to help write the House budget.

The Republicans complain bitterly about this system, but they do not, by and large, blame Gray for it.

"On my side, I haven't heard a word spoken in anger about Bill Gray, and I've heard a lot of good things," said Bill Gradison, R-Ohio, a member of the Budget Committee.

Although their economic ideas could hardly be more different, Gray has joined forces with Jack F. Kemp,

R-N.Y., on several issues such as tax-free "enterprise zones" for urban areas.

"I think he's very open to ideas," said Kemp. "He's one of the fastest-rising stars of the party."

While not giving Republicans much opportunity to affect the budget, Gray made friends with small personal gestures. When panel member Bobbi Fiedler, R-Calif., was indicted on a charge that she had attempted to bribe a rival in a Senate race, Gray won her gratitude by praising her committee work.

When asked why he voted in favor of the budget resolution in the committee, becoming the only Republican to break ranks, Vin Weber, R-Minn., said that in addition to finding the budget minimally acceptable, he also remembered that Gray had chaired a hearing on farm problems the previous year in Weber's district.

Independence Questioned

While they may like him personally, Republicans see the Budget chairman as something of a leadership puppet.

"He is controlled by the Caucus," said Delbert L. Latta of Ohio, ranking Republican on Gray's committee. "I think he would prefer a little longer leash."

But Democrats on the committee said that in 1986, at least, Gray was more in the position of leading the leadership than vice versa. They pointed particularly to the tax issue. House Speaker Thomas P. O'Neill Jr., D-Mass., wanted no part of anything that could be labeled a tax increase so long as Reagan threatened to veto it.

Senate conferees, meanwhile, had insisted that some sort of new tax initiative was essential.

Gray was able to convince O'Neill

to go along with conditional "reserve funds" involving new taxes in both the House resolution and the conference report. And the final compromise, which would allow a revenue increase for defense and other "critical needs," raised the possibility of forcing Reagan to choose between defense spending and taxes.

The conditional nature of the deal was reminiscent of one of Gray's first major budget actions, in 1983. Negotiations on the fiscal 1984 budget had foundered until Gray, a junior member of the committee, came forward with a reserve fund to provide money for 10 new initiatives, including farm relief and employment programs, if they were enacted by Congress. The idea broke a logjam and the budget was adopted. Few of the programs ever were enacted.

Rhetoric

One area of Gray's style that comes in for mild criticism is his rhetoric. While he is accessible and friendly, in dealings with reporters and colleagues he often relies on a few outworn metaphors: the deficit as a "sea of red ink" and Reagan's ".44-magnum veto gun" aimed at any bill increasing taxes. Sometimes solid information on where Gray stands is hard to come by.

"I still don't know to this day whether Bill Gray supports [additional] revenues or not," Panetta said.

Some find that Gray's rhetoric can grate. "Gray places a high priority on being open and fair," said Weber. "But because he feels he's open and fair, there is also an air of moral superiority. I think that rankles [Republican] members."

A House leadership aide admitted that Gray's rhetorical style sometimes left members uncertain. But he said that no one had ever complained that Gray misled a member.

From the viewpoint of the Senate, however, sources close to the conference on the budget said that at several points in negotiations, Gray agreed to a compromise from which he later backed away, apparently because of objections from chairmen of House authorizing committees.

Senate Budget Committee Chairman Pete V. Domenici, R-N.M., said that Gray was hemmed in by the short tenure of the Budget chairmanship, which gives him little independence.

"That's not anything new," he said. "It's the result of the way they do business over there."

Some members also criticize Gray for playing virtually no role in the 1985 conference that established the final form of Gramm-Rudman. It is incongruous, they said, that the Budget chairman played no part in the most important budgetary law of the decade.

Gray says he stayed out of the Gramm-Rudman conference because, "I don't want to have responsibility for carrying the ball on something I don't support."

Others note that Gray also had to watch his relations with other committee chairmen. "He didn't think it was particularly seemly for him to be involved in aggrandizing the powers of the Budget Committee, as somebody might see it," said Foley.

Once Gramm-Rudman was enacted, Gray resisted several attempts by authorizing committee chairmen to circumvent it. In late July, for instance, he helped convince the House Rules Committee not to allow the House Public Works and Transportation Committee to offer an amendment that would protect transportation trust funds from budget-cutting.

An Eye on the Future

The Budget chairmanship is considered a House leadership position, and as the first black member to have such a post, Gray is often referred to as "the most powerful black member of Congress."

Said Edgar, "Here's a black, urban progressive doing good at the worst time in history for black, urban progressives."

It is not clear how much real power Gray exercises, or whether his popularity among his colleagues will

"Bill Gray wants to be the first black president or vice president of the United States. . . . He has the people skills to do so. But the budget track demands some discipline and other skills that we have to see."
—Rep. Lynn Martin, R-Ill.

last. "It's still pretty early in his career," observed a leadership aide.

But, the aide went on, "the bottom line is completing the budgets and not alienating people in the process." On that score, he said, Gray is two-for-two.

At the time Gray was elected Budget chairman, some Democrats feared that putting a black Northeastern liberal in a key post was the wrong signal for a party that, in the wake of its 1984 electoral rout, needed to appeal more to white voters in the South and West.

But today, members agree that Gray has been able to overcome both stereotypes and limitations imposed by his race in a way that will help his future career — in the House or beyond it.

"It's important for people in the South to understand that he's making it on his own merit," said MacKay. "He's not part of 1970s tokenism."

Gray's success has provoked some criticism within the Black Caucus

from members who are uncomfortable with the ease with which Gray drops his personal concerns. They cite the fact that Gray voted "present" on the last two substitute budgets offered by the Black Caucus.

But Leland, chairman of the caucus, defended Gray. "He has been in a wrenching and dangerous position," Leland said. "I've seen him agonize over those decisions."

Gray resents being characterized as a "black committee chairman," but he acknowledges that his race affects others' perceptions of his performance.

"Every black person carries a burden of limitations, no matter how high they go," Gray says. "I have had more opportunities than the overwhelming majority, but that doesn't mean that I have broken through the limitations."

His challenge, Gray says, is to push the limits farther so race will be less of a factor when other black members seek powerful positions in Congress.

In 1986, rumors circulated that Gray was thinking of challenging Foley for majority leader of the next Congress. But Gray denied any interest in such a long-shot race.

Nevertheless, House members are quite aware that Gray has only two more years to serve as Budget chairman. They assume he will not be satisfied by merely going back to the Appropriations Committee, where there are 26 Democrats ahead of him in seniority.

"I see Bill Gray in a broader picture than the next step," said MacKay. "One of the things we need [in the Democratic Party] is a black who is clearly not subject to the charge that he is an Uncle Tom but who is able to succeed in a white-dominated party. And he is doing it. There may come a time when Bill Gray could do very well in national elections."

Martin was more blunt. "Bill Gray wants to be the first black president or vice president of the United States," she said. "He has the people skills to do so. But the budget track demands some discipline and other skills that we have to see."

Gray himself is coy when the subject of his future is raised. "I play one game at a time," he says. "And right now that's the budget. I'll start to think about other things in a year or so." ∎

PRESIDENCY/EXECUTIVE

Powers of the President

The place of the executive branch in the new plan of government greatly troubled the framers of the Constitution. A longstanding fear of authority, arising from experience with England's monarchy, led them to consider first a plan in which the executive deferred to the national legislature. The final draft of the Constitution, however, provided for a more balanced system in which some powers were to be shared between the president and Congress. Explicit congressional powers were enumerated at length, but Article II on the presidency was short and somewhat vague.

The looseness of the constitutional grant of power to the president allowed strong 19th century chief executives such as Thomas Jefferson, Andrew Jackson and Abraham Lincoln to establish precedents that steadily enhanced the position. Laws that provided them special powers in emergencies further strengthened presidents' authority.

Presidential power grew rapidly in the 20th century, spurred by a major economic depression and two world wars, until it posed a threat to the viability of Congress as a coequal branch of government. As the volume and complexity of federal business increased, legislative initiative shifted from the Capitol to the White House. Congress with its antiquated procedures found that it often was no match for the tremendous resources of the executive branch.

The result was repeated clashes between Congress and the president, particularly over the spending, war and treaty powers, as legislators resisted executive usurpation of the powers assigned to them by the Constitution.

Authorities for Powers

Constitutional Grant of Power

In sharp contrast to the explicit power granted the legislative branch (almost half the words of the Constitution are devoted to the functions of Congress), Article II of the Constitution describes only briefly the powers of the president. It begins with the ambiguous sentence: "The executive Power shall be vested in a President of the United States of America." But the nature of the president's authority has evolved only through practice.

The only authority for what has become presidential dominance in foreign affairs is contained in Section 2. In addition to appointing ambassadors and making treaties, the Constitution provides that "The President shall be Commander in Chief of the Army and Navy of the United States and of the Militia of the several states." Even those powers, however, were to be shared with the legislative branch; the Constitution gave Congress power to "provide for the common Defence," declare war, raise and support armies, ratify presidential treaties and confirm presidential nominations. Conversely, the Constitution requires Congress to share its legislative function by authorizing the president to provide Congress with certain information and to propose legislation.

The president's legislative role always has been important, but the complexity of running today's government has put the chief executive at the center of the legislative process. Political scientist Lawrence H. Chamberlain has observed that "When so much of the life of the individual is influenced by federal legislation, the attitude of the President toward this legislation and his skill in gaining legislative approval of his proposals are matters of practical interest to millions of people. . . ."

While the Constitution vests "all legislative powers" in Congress, it also directs the president to "give to the Congress Information of the State of the Union and recommend to their Consideration such Measures as he shall judge necessary and expedient." Congress has broadened this function to direct the president to present to Congress each year, in addition to the State of the Union message, two other general statements of presidential aims — an economic report including proposals directed to the maintenance of maximum employment, and a budget message outlining spending and revenue proposals. During a typical session, the president transmits to Congress scores of other legislative proposals, some initiated by the White House and others in conformity with various statutes. The president's responsibility for proposing legislation has become so important that one measure of his effectiveness is how successful he is in persuading Congress to adopt those proposals.

Article I of the Constitution gives the president an additional legislative power, that of the veto. Congress must submit every bill and joint resolution (except those joint resolutions proposing constitutional amendments) to the president, who may approve the measure, let it become law without his signature, or veto it and return it to Congress within 10 days. If a president disapproves a bill, Congress can override the veto only by a two-thirds vote of both houses. Because presidents usually find it relatively easy to muster the support of at least one-third plus one member of either the House or Senate, the veto has been used with deadly effect; fewer than 6 percent of all vetoes have been overridden.

In addition to the regular veto, the Constitution gives the president the special power of the pocket veto, which he may use at the end of a congressional session. Under this procedure the president, presented with a bill 10 days or less (Sundays excepted) prior to the adjournment of Congress, can merely ignore or "pocket" it, depriving Congress of an opportunity to override the veto.

Court decisions in 1974 and 1976 specified that a president's power to use the pocket veto was restricted to final adjournments of Congress and not to holiday recesses. This provision was reaffirmed in 1984 when a federal appeals court ruled that President Ronald Reagan had acted unconstitutionally when he pocket vetoed a bill between two sessions of the same Congress in November 1983.

The first American presidents conceived of the veto as a device to be used rarely and then only against legislative encroachment on the prerogatives of another branch of government. Presidents increased use of the veto in the 19th century, often to prevent Congress from passing private bills benefiting specific individuals. In the 20th century presidents began to use the threat of a veto as a powerful tool of persuasion.

Another major power the Constitution granted to the president is the power to make appointments. Article II, Section 2 empowers the president to appoint, besides ambassadors, "other public Ministers and Consuls, Judges of the Supreme Court, and all other Officers of the United States," subject to Senate confirmation. In the case of high offices such as Supreme Court justices and Cabinet officers, the president is able to pick persons of his own philosophy who presumably will aid his program.

The president's patronage power — gained through making appointments to increase political strength — derives from the constitutional authority to appoint lower court judges and other federal officials.

Despite the chance to reward a friend or political ally, many members of Congress bemoan their task of recommending patronage recipients to the president. The late Sen. Patrick McCarran, D-Nev. (1933-54) once said of judicial appointments, "It's the lousiest duty in the world because what you end up with is 100 enemies and one ingrate."

Powers Authorized by Congress

A number of the president's powers have been conferred by Congress. It was common at one time for Congress to grant special powers during emergencies. During World War I, for example, President Woodrow Wilson acquired sweeping control of the economy in what political scientist Rexford G. Tugwell has called "the most fantastic expansion of the executive known to the American experience." The numerous powers granted to him by Congress included prohibition of exports, takeover of the railroads and requisition of food and fuel for public use.

Statutes passed during World War I were still in effect as the United States prepared to enter World War II. In 1941 there were approximately 250 different laws delegating discretionary authority to the president and other executive officials. Congress also had given the executive emergency powers to deal with economic crises, most notably in the case of Franklin Delano Roosevelt and the Great Depression. Scholars theorized that an activist president probably could find some legislative grant for any action he deemed appropriate in an emergency.

In 1976 Congress moved to reassert its authority in this area by subjecting to congressional review all states of national emergency declared by the president. The measure also terminated, as of Sept. 14, 1978, all existing powers of the president and federal employees that were based on national emergency declarations in effect in 1976. Four such states of emergency, dating back to 1933, were in effect when the legislation was approved.

Modern laws authorizing the president to assign federal contract awards and to choose the location of government installations have given the president the powerful weapon of preferment. Preferment makes it possible for the president to reward or punish members of Congress quite spectacularly. It became particularly important after World War II as federal budgets skyrocketed. Members of the powerful committees and subcommittees dealing with defense, for example, frequently received defense installations in their districts in return for their support for military requests.

Powers From Precedent

Certain presidential powers are considered part of the office today simply because they were assumed by strong presidents and then carried on by their successors. Executive orders, by which the president can alter legislation, fall into this category. There is no legislative or constitutional basis for such orders. An example of an executive order with far-reaching effect was President Ronald Reagan's decontrol of crude oil, gasoline and propane prices issued on Jan. 28, 1981, for which no concurring act of Congress was necessary.

The president also holds certain powers simply because of the prestige of his office and the respect with which it is generally approached. This gives the president the ability to shape public opinion through his command of television, radio and the press. Such techniques as live televised news conferences, introduced by John F. Kennedy, and televised addresses before Congress have enabled presidents to gain public support for their legislative programs. President Reagan used television to his advantage in gathering support for his Economic Recovery Program in 1981.

The prestige of the president's office also helps him in persuading members of Congress to go along with his programs. Breakfast at the White House, a walk in the Rose Garden or a publicity picture taken with the president all are flattering to members of Congress and useful in their re-election campaigns.

War Powers

Probably the most fateful of the president's powers is the authority to act as commander in chief in times of war. The president's war powers are ambiguously stated in the Constitution but, in presenting the new charter to the nation, the authors of *The Federalist Papers* — James Madison, Alexander Hamilton and John Jay — made it clear that they construed the president's war powers narrowly.

Richard B. Morris, professor emeritus of history at Columbia University, told the Senate Foreign Relations Committee in 1971 that the Constitution's authors intended the presidential war powers to be "little more than the power to defend against imminent invasion when Congress was not in session."

Historically, however, the president has exercised much more than a defensive war-making power. Successive presidents — following the precedent of Lincoln's administration perhaps — have interpreted their authority in this realm broadly and dynamically. The list of specific actions

Presidency/Executive

taken by the White House under the authority of this constitutional provision is almost endless.

Throughout its history, the United States has been involved in more than 125 instances in which American troops have been sent into areas of conflict under presidential authority and without specific congressional approval. For example, in 1846 President James K. Polk unquestionably provoked Mexico into war when he ordered the army to occupy disputed territory along the Rio Grande River.

Recent years have seen increasingly frequent examples of presidential moves that involved the country in armed conflicts without the prior authorization of Congress. In 1950 President Harry S Truman ordered American armed forces in the Pacific to resist North Korea's aggressive drives into South Korea, thereby involving the United States in one of the most prolonged and expensive undeclared wars in its history. Beginning with President Dwight D. Eisenhower, a succession of chief executives expanded America's military commitments to the government of South Vietnam, thereby in time virtually guaranteeing massive American involvement in the conflict between North and South Vietnam.

Until it became clear that the war in Vietnam would not be easily or quickly won, most members of Congress thought that modern diplomatic and military conditions required that the president be free to conduct foreign policy and defend the nation. But as opposition to the war grew both among the public and on Capitol Hill, a number of members of Congress began to question the authority of the Lyndon B. Johnson administration to involve the United States so heavily in Vietnam. Many Americans came to equate White House reliance upon the armed forces to achieve diplomatic objectives — often with little or no consultation with Congress — as a symbol of the "imperial presidency."

In response, Congress sought to assume some of the responsibility for determining whether the United States should engage in armed conflict. On Nov. 7, 1973, Congress enacted, over President Richard Nixon's veto, the War Powers Resolution (PL 93-148). Intended to restrict the president's war-making powers, the measure set a 60-day limit on the president's authority to wage undeclared war and required him to report within 48 hours to House and Senate officers on any commitment of U.S. combat forces abroad. It also required the president to consult with Congress "in every possible instance" in advance of a troop commitment overseas.

Presidents Gerald R. Ford, Jimmy Carter and Reagan submitted reports to Congress under the War Powers Resolution in sending troops to Southeast Asia and the Middle East, but Congress never has tried to use its veto power to force a withdrawal of troops.

Moreover, that power was called into question by the Supreme Court's June 23, 1983, decision nullifying so-called "legislative veto" provisions in legislation.

The possibility of a confrontation between the White House and Congress loomed over the American presence in Lebanon. As U.S. Marines were drawn into the hostilities in 1983, some members of Congress began questioning their presence in the country and the president's power to keep U.S. forces in hostile situations without congressional approval. Shortly after Congress reluctantly approved a resolution in September authorizing the Marines to remain for another 18 months, 241 servicemen were killed in an explosion at their headquarters. Faced with the likelihood of a congressional resolution calling for removal of the troops,

President Ronald Reagan withdrew the Marines in February 1984 to offshore ships, and ended all U.S. participation within a few weeks.

Spending Power

For the first 134 years of the republic, Congress held undisputed sway over the government's purse strings, except for scattered incidents of executive impoundment, where the president refuses to spend money Congress has appropriated. But the increasing complexity of both the economy and government led to fragmentation of congressional control over the budget and an expanded role for the executive. In 1921 Congress itself ceded coordination over government spending and revenue estimates to the executive branch, and the next half-century was marked by further erosion of the congressional budget-making power. Nonetheless, Congress clung jealously to its taxing and appropriating powers specifically granted by the Constitution.

Then in the late 1960s and 1970s an intense dispute between Congress and the Nixon administration over impoundment prompted Congress to try to reclaim some of its control over fiscal policy and spending priorities.

Although the Constitution gave Congress complete authority to appropriate federal funds, it left vague whether a president was required to spend the appropriated money or whether he could make independent judgment on the timing and need for outlays. The issue had been a nettlesome one throughout the nation's history; precedent for such impoundments apparently went back to the administration of Thomas Jefferson. But impoundments became a major dispute only when President Nixon refused to spend appropriated funds running into the billions of dollars.

Nixon argued that he was withholding funds to combat inflation, but opposition Democrats contended that Nixon was using impoundment primarily to assert his own spending priorities.

This conflict prompted Congress to enact the Congressional Budget and Impoundment Control Act of 1974 (PL 93-344) to reassert control over the federal budget. In full operation for the first time in 1976, the measure streamlined congressional procedures for handling spending and tax legislation and created a mechanism for congressional disapproval of presidential impoundments. The legislation called for the president, when deciding to withhold funds, to submit a report to Congress. If the withholding was intended to be temporary (a deferral), either chamber could disapprove it at any time. The funds then would have to be released for obligation by the agencies. If the withholding was intended to be permanent (a rescission), the president would have to obtain the support of both houses within 45 days of continuous session. Otherwise, the funds would have to be released.

Congress lost some of this control over spending with the Supreme Court's 1983 decision striking down the legislative veto. The ruling nullified Congress' power to halt deferrals without the president's consent. It did not affect rescissions.

As part of the budget process, Congress could direct its authorizing and appropriating committees to enact a single omnibus bill reconciling the spending and revenue requirements with the levels set out in the budget resolutions. It was the reconciliation tool that the White House and Republican strategists seized upon in 1981 to achieve the Reagan administration's desired budget cuts.

44

Senate Clears Massive Tax Overhaul Measure

The big tax overhaul bill (HR 3838), hit a final snag the week of Sept. 29, 1986.

But there appeared to be no possibility — political or technical — that the latest problem could kill the bill. The final version, as written in the House-Senate conference committee, had been passed by the House Sept. 25, by a 292-136 vote and was passed by the Senate 74-23, Sept. 27. *(Vote 296, 1986 CQ Weekly Report p. 2373; evolution of tax bill, p. 2348; final provisions, p. 2350; House action, p. 2255)*

Correcting Errors

A battle over what were supposed to be only corrections of errors in the bill caused a delay in sending it to the White House.

After two weeks' delay, Senate leaders had nearly abandoned hope of getting agreement on the resolution (H Con Res 395) making "corrections" in the tax overhaul bill (HR 3838) and took the first procedural step toward sending the bill to the White House.

There was, however, no doubt that President Reagan would sign HR 3838, even if it reached his desk full of typographical errors and without the long list of substantive changes that would be made by H Con Res 395, which the House had approved and many senators wnated to lengthen. *(1986 Weekly Report p. 2344)*

Technical corrections measures, in the form of concurrent resolutions, are routinely passed following action on major pieces of legislation, and their contents are incorporated in the bill before it goes to the White House.

The move made by the Senate to get the uncorrected bill on its way to the White House consisted simply of physically sending the bill back to the House for processing before it was presented to the president for his signature. In fact, the processing had already taken place and the House clerk had had the 879-page bill printed — from an unofficial copy — on the required simulated parchment.

In this case, however, the concurrent resolution (H Con Res 395) approved by the House when it passed

Technical Corrections Pose Minor Hang-up

the tax bill did more than "correct technical errors in the enrollment of the bill," as House Ways and Means Committee Chairman Dan Rostenkowski, D-Ill., described it — and that caused two problems.

The first is that some senators did not like some of the provisions the House approved, including one terminating, as of 1990, the tax-free status of per diem payments to members of state legislatures.

Second, a large number of senators, seeing the substantive changes the House included in the concurrent resolution, decided they wanted to

---

> *This is "less tax reform and more a continuation of the philosophy of Ronald Reagan that government has no role to play in meeting the needs of the American people."*
> **—Christopher J. Dodd, D-Conn.**

---

add changes of their own.

Finance Committee Chairman Bob Packwood, R-Ore., wanted to expand a provision of HR 3838 to give all insurance companies, not just the 15 large ones named in the bill, a special tax benefit on certain bond transactions. It was an issue on which many senators lobbied heavily.

Other senators asked for a variety of new provisions, among them one that amounts to outright repeal of a provision in HR 3838 that takes a tax advantage away from recipients of government pensions.

The biggest obstacle was said to be Sen. John Melcher, D-Mont., who wanted to reinstate income averaging for farmers, which was repealed by the bill.

Rostenkowski had informed Sen-

ate leaders that the House would refuse to pass the resolution if it came back with this provision.

Howard M. Metzenbaum, D-Ohio, continuing a fight he began when the Senate first passed the tax bill and resumed on the conference agreement, opposed many of the provisions in the concurrent resolution that affect just one or a small group of beneficiaries. He served notice that he would object on the Senate floor if they were not eliminated.

To add to the difficulties, the Finance Committee staff, which was trying to work the whole thing out with the senators involved, was put on notice by Ways and Means Committee staff that the House would not pass the concurrent resolution if, should it come back for approval of Senate changes, it contained any provisions that were not in the House version.

As one member of the Ways and Means staff explained the problem, "We have to be able to tell our members, 'Everything that's in here is something you voted on before.'"

The pressures to change countless provisions of the tax bill before it was even signed were illustrated in a separate action by the Senate, in the early hours of Oct. 3.

J. Bennett Johnston, D-La., got an amendment put on the continuing appropriations resolution (H J Res 738), postponing the effective date of a provision of the tax bill that disallowed interest deductions on certain loans against life insurance policies in excess of $50,000. *(1986 Weekly Report, p. 2332)*

When asked by Mack Mattingly, R-Ga., how he could change a law that was not yet a law, Johnston replied, "It's difficult but not impossible."

The Final Senate Debate

The Senate's vote on HR 3838, at 4 p.m. Saturday, Sept. 27, ended two days of debate, a large portion of which was taken up with angry exchanges between Packwood and Metzenbaum over the one-beneficiary provisions known as "transition rules."

On the broader provisions of the bill, the chief opponent was John C.

Evolution of Proposals to Overhaul the Tax Code . . .

	Existing Law	Reagan Plan [1]
Individual tax rates	11-50 percent (14 brackets)	15, 25 and 35 percent
Corporate tax rates	15-40 percent on first $100,000 of income; 46 percent thereafter	15-25 percent up to $75,000; 33 percent above $75,000
Capital gains	60 percent exclusion; top effective rate of 20 percent	50 percent exclusion; top effective rate of 17.5 percent, but limits on eligible assets
Minimum tax	20 percent "alternative" minimum tax imposed on individuals who greatly limit their tax liability through tax breaks; 15 percent "add-on" minimum tax for corporations that use tax breaks to reduce their liability greatly	Revise the way of computing the individual minimum tax to include more taxpayers; redesign the corporate minimum tax as an "alternative" to tax the value of some so-called preferences, but not depreciation
Personal exemption	$1,080 (1986)	$2,000
State and local taxes	Deductible	Deduction eliminated
Charitable donations	Deductible	Full deductions for itemizers; none for non-itemizers
Interest deductions	Deductions for home mortgage and non-business interest	Unlimited deduction for mortgages on primary residences; additional interest deductions capped at $5,000
Retirement benefits	Tax-deductible Individual Retirement Account (IRA) contributions of $2,000 for each worker and $200 for each non-working spouse; employer-sponsored 401(k) tax-exempt savings plans with maximum contributions of $30,000 annually	Allow non-working spouse IRA contributions of $2,000; limit 401(k) contributions to $8,000 annually, less amounts contributed to IRAs
Investment tax credit	6-10 percent	Repealed
Depreciation	Recovery periods of 3-19 years with accelerated write-off	More generous write-off over 4-28 years; value adjusted for inflation
Business expenses	Deductible	Deduction for entertainment repealed; limit on meals
Tax-exempt bonds	Bonds earning tax-free interest allowed for governmental and many non-governmental purposes, such as sports arenas and mortgages	Effectively eliminate use of bonds for non-governmental purposes

SOURCES: Treasury Department, House Ways and Means Committee, Senate Finance Committee, Joint Committee on Taxation

. . . From Existing Law Through HR 3838 as Cleared

House Bill [2]	Senate Bill [3]	HR 3838 [4]
15, 25, 35 and 38 percent	15 and 27 percent (lower rate phased out for high-income taxpayers)	15 and 28 percent (lower rate phased out for high-income taxpayers)
15-30 percent up to $75,000; 36 percent above $75,000	15-30 percent up to $75,000; 33 percent above $75,000	15-30 percent up to $75,000; 34 percent above $75,000
42 percent exclusion; top effective rate of 22 percent	Special exclusion repealed; taxed at same rates as regular income	Special exclusion repealed; taxed at same rates as regular income
Increase the rate on the individual and corporate minimum tax to 25 percent and revise it to tax more so-called preferences	Retain the individual minimum tax rate of 20 percent but revise it to tax more so-called preferences; retain the 20 percent corporate minimum tax but redesign it to include more preferences, basing the tax on "book income" in order to include many corporations that escape taxation	Increase the rate on the individual minimum tax to 21 percent and revise it to tax more so-called preferences; retain the 20 percent corporate minimum tax and redesign it to include more preferences, basing the tax on "book income" to include many firms that escape taxation
$2,000 for non-itemizers; $1,500 for itemizers	$2,000 for low- and middle-income taxpayers (exemption phased out for high-income taxpayers)	$2,000 by 1989 for most taxpayers (exemption phased out for high-income taxpayers)
No change from existing law	Income, real estate and personal property taxes deductible; sales tax deduction limited to 60 percent of the amount in excess of state income taxes	Income, real estate and personal property taxes deductible; sales taxes not deductible
Full deduction for itemizers; non-itemizers could deduct amount above $100; appreciated value of charitable gifts subject to minimum tax	Full deductions for itemizers; none for non-itemizers	Full deductions for itemizers; none for non-itemizers; appreciated value of charitable gifts subject to minimum tax
Unlimited deduction for mortgages on first and second residences; additional deduction of $10,000 ($20,000 for joint returns) plus the value of a taxpayer's investment income	Unlimited deduction for mortgages on first and second residences; no consumer interest deduction; interest paid on borrowing to produce investment income deductible equal to the value of the investment earnings	Unlimited deduction for mortgages on first and second residences; limits on mortgage borrowing for unrelated purposes; no consumer interest deduction; interest paid on borrowing to produce investment income deductible equal to the value of the earnings
Continue existing law on tax-exempt IRA contributions; restrict 401(k) contributions to $7,000 annually; limit to $2,000 the total exemption for contributions by an individual to both an IRA and a 401(k) plan, to encourage 401(k) and discourage IRA contributions	Limit tax-exempt IRA contributions to persons not covered by pension plans; restrict 401(k) contributions to $7,000 annually; make sweeping changes in private pension plans to improve coverage and restrict benefits for high-income persons	Limit tax-exempt IRA contributions to persons not covered by pension plans or those below specified income levels; restrict 401(k) contributions to $7,000 annually; make sweeping changes in private pensions to improve coverage and restrict benefits for high-income persons
Repealed	Repealed retroactively to Jan. 1, 1986	Repealed retroactively to Jan. 1, 1986
Recovery periods of 3-30 years; partially indexed for inflation	Retain existing system of rapid write-offs, permitting larger write-offs for most property over longer periods	Retain system of rapid write-offs similar to existing law; permit larger write-offs for most property, but over longer periods
Deduction of 80 percent of business meals and 80 percent of entertainment costs	Similar to House for meals and entertainment; most miscellaneous deductions eliminated	Deduction of 80 percent of business meals and entertainment costs; miscellaneous employee business expenses limited
Cap use of non-governmental bonds; reserve a portion for charitable organizations; some interest subject to minimum tax	Cap use of non-governmental bonds, exclude multifamily rental housing and charitable organizations from the cap	Cap use of non-governmental bonds, exclude charitable organizations from the cap; some interest subject to minimum tax

[1] *Proposed May 28, 1985*   [2] *Passed Dec. 17, 1985*   [3] *Passed June 24, 1986*   [4] *Cleared Sept. 27, 1986*

Danforth, R-Mo., who had been a part of the core group of seven Finance Committee members who wrote the original Senate bill.

But the conference committee, Danforth said, in its determination to keep the tax rates in the final version as close as possible to those in the Senate bill, "was willing to dump more and more taxes on our industrial sector, on research and development, on education, in order to placate this god of low rates."

As a result, he said, although the conferees increased the top tax rates only 1 percentage point from those in the Senate bill — to 28 percent for individuals and 34 percent for corporations — "I defected."

Danforth said he knew he could not defeat the bill but was making his lengthy speech so that senators would know the dangers he saw in it.

The final 3-to-1 vote on the bill displayed a curious collection of Democrats and Republicans, liberals, moderates and conservatives, on both sides.

Despite the bad-tempered exchanges over transition rules, the debate in the Senate was considerably less emotional than the House debate earlier in the week, presumably because there was never any question that the Senate would approve the bill by a big margin.

Nonetheless, as in the House, there were many expressions of doubt about the impact on the economy of such a wide-ranging and complicated piece of legislation.

Typical of liberal critics was Christopher J. Dodd, D-Conn., who said there was no economist or member of the Senate who could say where the bill would lead the economy.

Dodd added his own view was that the bill "has the real potential to push this nation into a recession."

Dodd also denounced the bill as "less tax reform and more a continuation of the philosophy of Ronald Reagan that government has no role to play in meeting the needs of the American people."

Among the many supporters who confessed uncertainties was Budget Committee Chairman Pete V. Domenici, R-N.M., who noted that he had long been concerned, and remained so, over the budget implications of the bill. He warned his colleagues that the revenue losses resulting from the bill for fiscal 1988, estimated at $16.7 billion, "will come back to haunt us. . . .

"I used to wonder," he continued, "if this was the right time to pass this bill. I have concluded there will never be a right time if we wait around for economists to say we are ready. . . . I conclude it is absolutely the right time because we are ready and the people are ready."

Questions about the impact on the economy were mentioned again and again, by both opponents and supporters.

Packwood, himself, in his final speech just before the vote, admitted that "the basic decisions on this bill have to be subjective decisions. Will this bill help the economy or hurt the economy? There is not a person in this room" — he paused to name half a dozen who had been prominent in the debate — "who can tell you for sure.

"But taxes are about more than money, they are about more than economics. They are about fairness — and this bill is fair."

The vote made plain that a 3-1 majority of the Senate agreed with the Finance chairman. ∎

Court Strikes Down Core of Gramm-Rudman

More than most laws, Gramm-Rudman-Hollings raised doubts from the beginning. Its goal of a balanced budget in five years was so ambitious and its method — automatic, across-the-board spending cuts — so novel that skepticism tempered hope when the law was enacted in December 1985.

Doubts multiplied July 7, 1986, when the Supreme Court declared the automatic spending-cut procedure unconstitutional. The device was the linchpin in Gramm-Rudman's scheme for forcing $200 billion deficits down to zero by fiscal 1991. *(Court ruling, box, this story; text excerpts, 1986 CQ Weekly Report p. 1581)*

The beauty of the invalidated procedure — its "hands off" approach to politically painful spending cuts — was also its fatal flaw, according to the court. Under the law (PL 99-177), Congress and the president were to aim for a specified annual deficit target through the normal legislative process. If they failed to reach it, the Congressional Budget Office (CBO) and the Office of Management and Budget (OMB) were to calculate across-the-board spending reductions needed to bring the deficit down to the target.

The comptroller general, head of the General Accounting Office (GAO), was to review, reconcile as needed and transmit to the president the reductions proposed by the other two agencies. The president was required to issue an order making those spending cuts, without change.

The court said that because Congress can initiate removal of the comptroller general by a joint resolution, he is subservient to Congress. And an agent of Congress, in the court's view, may not exercise executive powers of the type given the comptroller general under Gramm-Rudman.

Without the automatic device, the reductions must come in what Rep. Leon E. Panetta, D-Calif., calls "the old-fashioned way — by voting for them."

Because members had doubts from the beginning about the constitutionality of the automatic cuts, Gramm-Rudman provided an alterna-

Repair Try Likely But Outlook Unclear

tive procedure. It followed much the same steps, but the "sequester" order for spending cuts would be imposed only if approved by Congress and the president. *(Box, this story)*

Whether members would actually adopt the indiscriminate cuts if they could not reach the deficit targets any other way was the critical question.

The law's three original sponsors, Sens. Phil Gramm, R-Texas, Ernest F. Hollings, D-S.C., and Warren B. Rud-

man, R-N.H., minimized the damage done by the court decision and insisted the statute still could force Congress to meet the targets.

Gramm declared, "I don't have any doubt that that secondary trigger will work." Yet he was foremost among those wanting to restore the automatic process because, he said, "I want certainty."

Others thought it was unlikely that Congress would vote for, or the president accept, the sequester cuts.

"The reason Gramm-Rudman was so jerry-built is that people *didn't* want to make the vote they would now have to make" under the alternative procedure, according to Charles E. Schumer, D-N.Y., a member of the House Budget Committee.

A Win for Synar, Reagan

The Supreme Court decision was

an important victory for Rep. Mike Synar, D-Okla., who in fall 1985 insisted on amending Gramm-Rudman to ensure an early test of its constitutionality. Hours after the measure was signed into law Dec. 12, Synar filed the successful legal challenge to Gramm-Rudman. His suit was later joined by 11 other members of Congress and consolidated with a suit filed by the National Treasury Employees Union. The union's retired members lost a scheduled cost-of-living adjustment in their pensions as a result of Gramm-Rudman's fiscal 1986 cuts.

Synar contends that budget decisions must be made by elected officials accountable to the voters.

"Gramm-Rudman tried to insulate Congress from the hard choices our Founding Fathers gave us and expected us to make. We argued this was wrong, and the court agreed."

—Rep. Mike Synar, D-Okla.

"Gramm-Rudman tried to insulate Congress from the hard choices our Founding Fathers gave us and expected us to make," Synar said after the decision. "We argued this was wrong, and the court agreed."

The court decision was also a triumph for President Reagan. He had questioned the GAO role at the time he signed Gramm-Rudman into law.

More importantly, with the automatic procedure scuttled, the president was spared the inexorable pressure for a budget compromise that the device might have exerted.

The automatic scheme was meant to put Reagan in the same tight box as Congress. Advocates hoped that if Reagan faced deep, automatic cuts in his defense buildup, he would finally abandon his longstanding objections to tax increases as a partial solution to the deficit.

Court Sees Fatal Gramm-Rudman Flaw . . .

The Supreme Court July 7, 1986, took the federal budget off its crash diet, ruling 7-2 that a key provision of the new Gramm-Rudman-Hollings balanced-budget law is unconstitutional.

The decision upheld a lower court ruling issued exactly five months earlier, on Feb. 7. It invalidated the law's procedure for automatic, across-the-board spending cuts when Congress and the president fail to meet specified annual deficit targets through the normal legislative process.

The ruling left intact the remainder of the Gramm-Rudman law (PL 99-177), including a fallback mechanism inserted for just such a contingency. But it was not immediately clear whether Congress would use that alternative procedure.

Separated Powers

The court said Gramm-Rudman violated the separation of powers among the legislative, executive and judicial branches by granting to the comptroller general, an official who can be removed only at the initiative of

"The threat to separation of powers conjured up by the majority is wholly chimerical."

—Justice Byron R. White

Congress, the power to tell the president what fixed-percentage cuts he must make in federal spending.

"By placing the responsibility for execution of the Balanced Budget and Emergency Deficit Control Act in the hands of an officer who is subject to removal only by itself, Congress in effect has retained control over the execution of the act and has intruded into the executive function," wrote Chief Justice Warren E. Burger in his last major opinion as chief justice. "The Constitution does not permit such intrusion."

Only Justices Byron R. White and Harry A. Blackmun dissented in *Bowsher v. Synar, United States Senate v. Synar, O'Neill v. Synar.* They argued that the constitutional flaw paled in significance alongside the budget-cutting mechanism it doomed.

The decision was the court's second major separation-of-powers ruling in three years. In 1983, in the case of *Immigration and Naturalization Service v. Chadha,* the justices by a similar 7-2 vote declared the legislative veto unconstitutional. *(Separation of powers, 1986 CQ Weekly Report p. 873; legislative veto, 1983 CQ Almanac p. 565)*

Burger, who wrote both opinions, quoted from the legislative veto decision in explaining why the court struck down the core provision of Gramm-Rudman:

"No one can doubt that Congress and the president are confronted with fiscal and economic problems of unprecedented magnitude," Burger said, but " 'the fact that a given law or procedure is efficient, convenient, and useful in facilitating functions of government . . . will not save it if it is contrary to the Constitution. Convenience and efficiency are not the primary objectives — or the hallmarks — of democratic government.' "

Although Congress had not removed a comptroller general in the 65 years it has had such power, the mere existence of that removal authority was sufficient to doom the law.

"The Constitution does not contemplate an active role for Congress in the supervision of officers charged with the execution of the laws it enacts," wrote Burger. "To permit an officer controlled by Congress to execute the laws would be, in essence, to permit a congressional veto," he added.

Responding to Justice White's argument that it was unlikely that Congress would ever remove a comptroller general, Burger warned that "the separated powers of our government can not be permitted to turn on judicial assessment of whether an officer exercising executive power is on good terms with Congress."

"The Framers recognized that, in the long run, structural protections against abuse of power were critical to preserving liberty. In constitutional terms, the removal powers over the comptroller general's office dictate that he will be subservient to Congress," the chief justice concluded.

Delegated Powers

Justices John Paul Stevens and Thurgood Marshall agreed that the Gramm-Rudman mechanism for automatic budget cuts was unconstitutional, but for different reasons. They said that Congress could not delegate its power to set national policy to one of its chambers, committees or officers.

"When Congress legislates, when it makes binding policy," wrote Stevens, "it must follow the procedures prescribed in Article I," that is, passage by both chambers and submission to the president for his signature or veto.

"Neither the unquestioned urgency of the national budget crisis nor the comptroller general's proud record of professionalism and dedication provides a justification for allowing a congressional agent to set policy that binds the nation," Stevens concluded.

Dissenting Views

White criticized the court's "willingness to interpose its distressingly formalistic view of separation of powers" to strike down "one of the most novel and far-reaching legislative responses to a national crisis since the New Deal."

He said it was "eminently reasonable and proper for Congress to vest the budget-cutting authority in an officer who is to the greatest degree possible non-partisan and independent of the president and his political agenda, and who therefore may be relied upon not to allow his

. . . In Power Given to Comptroller General

calculations to be colored by political considerations."

White emphasized that the president had to concur in any joint resolution passed by Congress to remove the comptroller general. That, he argued, "reduces to utter insignificance the possibility that the threat of removal will induce subservience to the Congress."

"Realistic consideration of the nature of the comptroller general's relation to Congress . . . reveals that the threat to separation of powers conjured up by the majority is wholly chimerical," he concluded.

Justice Blackmun, who also dissented, argued that the court should have struck down the removal provision, which is part of the 1921 Budget and Accounting Act, not the Gramm-Rudman mechanism.

"However wise or foolish it may be," he wrote, the latter statute "unquestionably ranks among the most important federal enactments of the past several decades.

"I cannot see the sense of invalidating legislation of this magnitude in order to preserve a cumbersome, 65-year-old removal power that has never been exercised and appears to have been all but forgotten until this litigation," Blackmun continued.

"I do not claim that the 1921 removal provision is a piece of statutory deadwood utterly without contemporary significance. But it comes close. Rarely if ever invoked even for symbolic purposes, the removal provision certainly pales in importance beside the legislative scheme the court strikes down today. . . . The constitutional defect found by the court cannot justify the remedy it has imposed," he concluded.

Independent Agencies

Although President Reagan had signed Gramm-Rudman into law, he noted at the time his concern about the role of the comptroller general. The Justice Department urged the Supreme Court to strike down the disputed provision of the law because of this concern.

In the administration's brief, Solicitor General Charles Fried took the opportunity to suggest, obliquely, that the court also review the status of independent agencies such as the Federal Trade Commission and the Federal Reserve Board. Members of these commissions and boards typically are appointed by the president for fixed terms and can be removed only for specified causes. In 1935, the court in the case of *Humphrey's Executor v. United States* endorsed these limits on the president's removal power in light of what it termed the "quasi-legislative" and "quasi-judicial" powers of those agencies.

In his Gramm-Rudman brief, Fried suggested in a footnote that various legal and political developments of the past half century have "cast a shadow" upon the premises of the 1935 decision. *(Background, 1986 Weekly Report p. 879)*

But the court saw no such shadow. It disposed of the matter in a footnote of its own, stating tersely that "no issues involving such agencies are presented here."

Competition in Contracting Case.

The court's Gramm-Rudman decision did call into question at least one other function that the comptroller

general performs. For decades, the General Accounting Office (GAO), which the comptroller general heads, has adjudicated protests by unsuccessful bidders for federal contracts who believed that they were wronged.

In a 1984 deficit-reduction law (PL 98-369), Congress strengthened GAO's hand in this role, authorizing it to suspend the award of a federal contract until such challenges are resolved. *(1984 Almanac pp. 143, 198)*

The administration first refused to comply with this law, the Competition in Contracting Act, and then challenged it in court.

"To permit an officer controlled by Congress to execute the laws would be, in essence, to permit a congressional veto."
—Chief Justice Warren E. Burger

Making arguments similar to those it used against GAO's role in the Gramm-Rudman process, the government contends that the comptroller general is an officer of the legislative branch and cannot exercise contracting functions that are executive in nature.

Two district courts rejected that claim, as did the 3rd U.S. Circuit Court of Appeals. *(Background, 1986 Weekly Report p. 298)*

Ruling in the case of *Ameron Inc. v. U.S. Army Corps of Engineers,* that appeals court agreed that adjudicating bids was an executive function, but it rejected the argument that the comptroller general was an officer of the legislative branch just because Congress could fire him.

"The power of removal does not determine to which branch the comptroller general belongs," wrote the appeals court. Indeed, its opinion concluded, he "appears to be one of the most independent officers in the whole of the federal government, and one whose functions are drawn from each of the branches."

The GAO, the court added, "is best viewed a part of a headless 'fourth branch' of government consisting of independent agencies having significant duties in both the legislative and executive branches but residing not entirely within either."

The government, anticipating the Gramm-Rudman ruling, asked the appeals court to rehear the case. The government was expected to cite the new decision in reiterating its challenge to the contracting competition law.

(The deficit problem has resolved itself into three parts: domestic spending, which Reagan wants cut and Congress does not; rapid defense growth, which Reagan wants and which Congress resists; and new revenues, which Reagan opposes but many members consider essential.)

Without the automatic device, Congress appeared at a loss to force the president to share in the proverbial "hard choices" of the budget. In fact, Reagan greeted the court decision with a prompt declaration that "now Congress must make the difficult choices."

Like Reagan, most who commented on the court's ruling ignored the dual thrust of the automatic device. The common theme was that an irresponsible Congress had tried to escape its constitutional duty with the automatic scheme but now must face the music.

The court decision, said Senate Majority Leader Robert Dole, R-Kan., "doesn't change a thing. Congress had the responsibility of reducing the deficit before Gramm-Rudman. We have it now. And we'll have it 10 years from now."

The invalidated automatic procedure was already used once, producing the fiscal 1986 sequester order that cut $11.7 billion from defense and non-defense programs on March 1.

Fixing the Law

Gramm, Rudman and Senate Budget Committee Chairman Pete V. Domenici, R-N.M., wanted to fix the automatic mechanism by eliminating from the 1921 Budget and Accounting Act the provision that makes the comptroller general subject to removal by a joint resolution originating in Congress.

A first draft of this "Gramm-Rudman-Hollings II" amendment would allow a president to remove the comptroller general from office, but only for specified causes. Members of the Federal Trade Commission and certain other independent agencies are now subject to such qualified presidential removal authority, which has been exercised only once in 60 years, according to a Rudman aide.

But the influential chairman of the Government Operations Committee, Jack Brooks, D-Texas, vehemently opposed the amendment. Brooks pointed out that GAO conducts extensive auditing of the executive branch for Congress. He said he would resist any change that would make the comptroller general more beholden to the branch that he investigates.

"I am absolutely opposed to amending the manner in which the comptroller general can be removed from office," Brooks said. Current law "provides the comptroller general with vitally needed independence."

What's Left of Gramm-Rudman

Even without the automatic-cut process, Gramm-Rudman still offered meaningful deficit-fighting tools, including its annual deficit targets, which decline to zero by October 1990. Also left untouched by the high court's decision were assorted procedural levers, primarily points of order, intended to to curb over-budget legislation.

Many members believe the annual deficit targets themselves have considerable political force. The targets provide, for the first time, a simple yardstick for measuring budget success or failure.

Budget-cutting has been a confusing chase after multiple moving targets. "Savings" were calculated as reductions in projected rates of growth, which changed constantly in response to economic and legislative variables. Moreover, the broad spending targets set by budget resolutions mesh poorly with program-specific legislation.

Another form of discipline imposed by the law was its requirement that individual fiscal decisions be "deficit-neutral," meaning any proposed spending increase must be matched by an equivalent boost in revenues or cut in spending for some other purpose. This provision was credited with helping fend off revenue-losing amendments to historic tax-overhaul legislation (HR 3838) cleared by Congress Sept. 27, 1986. *(Senate Clears Massive Tax Overhaul Measure, p. 45)*

"It's a zero-sum process," said Rudman. "It forces people to look at the deficit consequences of what they do." ∎

Hill Overrides Veto of South Africa Sanctions

Elbowing aside a president uncharacteristically resistant to compromise, the Senate on Oct. 2, 1986, overrode Ronald Reagan's veto of a measure (HR 4868) imposing economic sanctions against South Africa.

The 78-21 vote enacting the bill into law (PL 99-440) marked the most serious defeat Reagan has suffered on a foreign issue and one of the most stunning blows of his presidency.

The House had acted on Sept. 29, voting to override Reagan's veto 313-83. Reagan had vetoed the bill Sept. 26, but his aides did not lobby House members on the issue and made only limited efforts to block action in the Republican-controlled Senate. *(Senate vote 311, 1986 CQ Weekly Report p. 2377; House vote 390, p. 2374)*

Although fundamentally altering a major U.S. policy, the veto override was not expected to have a long-term effect on Reagan's ability to handle foreign affairs. There was widespread agreement on Capitol Hill that South Africa represented a special case in which Reagan was so out of step with the American public that Congress had no choice but to intervene.

"We believe the president was not being heard loud and clear" in his opposition to South Africa's apartheid system of racial discrimination, said Richard G. Lugar, R-Ind., chairman of the Senate Foreign Relations Committee. With passage of the bill, he said, "We're going to make sure we are all heard with one voice."

Reagan readily accepted the congressional action and promised to implement the law. In a statement issued by the White House after the vote, Reagan said the debate between himself and Congress "was not whether to oppose apartheid but, instead, how best to oppose it and how best to bring freedom to that troubled country."

Nevertheless, Reagan insisted he had been correct in opposing sanctions because "they hurt the very people they are intended to help."

Not surprisingly, the white minority government of South Africa was not so receptive to the message from Capitol Hill. Foreign Minister Pik Botha said the United States and other countries should "leave us alone." Congress acted "regardless of our reform program, and no reason or argument could stop this emotional wave," he said.

The Senate Vote

The Senate originally had passed the sanctions bill Aug. 15 by an 84-14 vote, so Reagan needed to pick up 20 votes to prevent an override by the required two-thirds majority. On the day of the vote, one senator who said he supported Reagan — Jake Garn, R-Utah — was at home recuperating from surgery; even so, Reagan still needed 34 votes to sustain the veto.

The Senate debated the issue for four hours on Oct. 1, and again for about two hours just before the vote the next day.

As the roll call began, the Senate chamber was extraordinarily quiet, as if to signify the import of the event. In the gallery were several civil rights leaders who had backed the bill, including Coretta Scott King, comedian Dick Gregory and Randall Robinson, head of the TransAfrica lobby group.

Adhering to a normally ignored rule, most senators voted from their seats. When his turn came to vote, Lugar rose to his feet and quietly said "aye," formally breaking with the president he had unswervingly supported on other foreign issues.

Democrats voted unanimously to support the veto override — including southerners who usually support the president on crucial votes. As Republican after Republican voted "aye" for the override, it became clear the outcome would not even be close.

Only six of the Republicans who originally had voted for the bill switched and supported the veto: Thad Cochran, Miss.; Robert Dole, Kan., the majority leader; Orrin G. Hatch, Utah; Don Nickles, Okla.; Alan K. Simpson, Wyo., the assistant majority leader; and Ted Stevens, Alaska. Barry Goldwater, R-Ariz., who had been absent on the first vote, also backed Reagan on the veto, raising the total to 21.

Thirty-one Republicans supported the override. Among them were six senators who agreed to support the veto if the vote was close, a White House lobbyist said. When it became clear that Reagan would lose, the White House decided not to press any

---

The Next Step: Sanctions Take Effect

Most provisions of the South Africa sanctions bill (HR 4868 — PL 99-440) took effect immediately when the bill was enacted into law on Oct. 2, 1986.

Among the major immediate provisions were bans on imports of South African iron, steel, sugar and other agricultural products, and a prohibition on exports to South Africa of petroleum products. Several other major provisions were to be phased in: A ban on new U.S. investments in South Africa takes effect 45 days after enactment and a ban on imports of South African uranium, coal and textiles 90 days after the law was passed. *(Full provisions, 1986 CQ Weekly Report p. 1982)*

The Transportation Department 10 days after enactment was to issue orders barring direct air travel between South Africa and the United States. The main effect would be to stop flights by South Africa Airways, the state-owned airlines. No U.S. carriers now fly directly to South Africa.

The bill threatens further sanctions in 1987 if South Africa fails to take major steps toward dismantling apartheid. Among the contemplated steps are a ban on imports of South African strategic minerals and a cutoff of military aid to any country found to be violating a United Nations arms embargo against South Africa.

'Less Than Brilliant' Administration Role . . .

Throughout his presidency, Ronald Reagan's successes in Congress have come in large part because of his ability and willingness to strike a deal at the right moment, even on issues that involved his fundamental principles.

But on South Africa, Reagan staked out a position early in his presidency and steadfastly refused to make anything other than minor changes in it. He ignored or missed several opportunities to shape the course of political sentiment in the United States toward South Africa.

"To put it in the mildest terms," Robert H. Michel, R-Ill., the House minority leader said Sept. 29, 1986, "the administration has been less than brilliant in handling this issue."

In the early years of his presidency, Reagan himself seemed to ignore South Africa, leaving policy making to the State Department's Africa bureau, headed by Assistant Secretary Chester Crocker. Reagan devoted no speeches to and made no comments about South Africa until late 1984, when the movement toward sanctions was beginning to build.

Crocker in 1981 drafted and got Reagan's approval for a policy described as "constructive engagement." As envisioned by Crocker, the policy was to apply to all of southern Africa, and was to include friendly persuasion not only toward racial reform in South Africa but also toward settlement of longstanding disputes involving South Africa and the neighboring countries of Angola, Mozambique and Namibia.

In spite of Crocker's diplomatic success in negotiating limited agreements, the phrase "constructive engagement" was widely interpreted both in the United States and in South Africa as a policy of sympathy for the government in Pretoria. That interpretation was reinforced by some of Reagan's earliest actions toward South Africa — the easing of embargoes that President Carter had imposed on sales of computers and other items to security forces in Pretoria.

Liberals and blacks in the United States condemned

constructive engagement from the start, but it took several years for South Africa and Reagan's policy to become a major issue in the United States.

The key event was a demonstration at the South African Embassy in Washington on Thanksgiving Day, 1984. Del. Walter E. Fauntroy, D-D.C., TransAfrica director Randall Robinson and other civil rights leaders demonstrated at the embassy, deliberately getting themselves arrested.

In the following weeks, more than 20 members of Congress — including one senator, Lowell P. Weicker Jr., R-Conn. — joined the hundreds stepping from the embassy picket line into police patrol wagons. Charges were not pressed against any of those arrested, but the demonstrations helped make South Africa a public issue.

Americans also were impressed by the eloquence of Anglican bishop Desmond Tutu, a black South African awarded the Nobel Peace Prize in December 1984.

Anti-apartheid groups in South Africa stepped up demonstrations early in 1985, provoking a cycle of crackdowns by security forces and more protests. Unrest in South Africa became daily news in the United States, forcing politicians to focus on the substance and results of Reagan's policy toward that country.

Sensing growing concern, many Republicans in Congress — especially those who had been involved in the civil rights struggles of the 1960s — urged Reagan to step up his pressure on South Africa. In December 1984, 35 House conservatives wrote the South African ambassador, Bernardus G. Fourie, threatening to support some economic sanctions unless Pretoria moved to dismantle apartheid.

The House in June 1985 overwhelmingly passed a bill (HR 1460) imposing modest sanctions on South Africa, such as banning bank loans to the government and businesses, barring new business investment there and prohibiting importation of South African gold coins called Krugerrands. The Senate followed suit in July with an **even** more limited version (S 995) banning bank loans to the Pretoria government and prohibiting most nuclear and computer sales to South Africa, among other things.

A House-Senate conference on July 31, 1985, focused on the Krugerrand issue. Foreign Relations Committee Chairman Richard G. Lugar, Ind., pressed by the House and facing defections by other Senate Republicans, reluctantly agreed to the import ban on those coins.

The August recess interrupted congressional action on the conference bill and gave Reagan time to act on his own. On Sept. 9, 1985, Reagan issued an executive order imposing many of the sanctions in the bill, including the Krugerrand ban.

Giving Reagan credit for acting, Lugar and Majority Leader Robert Dole, R-Kan., supported a Senate filibuster of the conference bill. Several attempts to stop the filibuster failed; to ensure the bill's death Dole and Lugar took the official copy from the Senate chamber

ESCALATING STRIFE: Many died in violence, black-against-black and white-against-black, that stemmed from protests against apartheid.

. . . Contributed to Momentum for Sanctions

and locked it in the Foreign Relations Committee safe. *(1985 CQ Almanac p. 83)*

Lugar and other Republicans said they hoped Reagan would follow up his executive order with new diplomatic pressure on South Africa for real changes in apartheid. Those hopes were dashed, however, by Reagan's willingness to accept assertions by South Africa's president, P. W. Botha, that his government was moving as quickly as possible.

Sanctions Drive Gathers Speed

Racial violence continued in South Africa in 1986, adding fuel to the pro-sanctions movement in the United States. In June, anticipating demonstrations marking the 10th anniversary of the 1976 black riots in Soweto, Pretoria imposed strict press censorship and a sweeping state of emergency. The press rules — effectively banning any reporting not sanctioned by the government — got Washington's attention as have few other events in South Africa, causing members of Congress to question why Reagan appeared blind to that dictatorship while he was willing to castigate others.

The House in June took up a bill (HR 4868) strengthening the sanctions Reagan had ordered and adding new ones, such as a ban on new business investment in South Africa. In a calculated gamble, Republicans stepped aside and allowed the House to pass an amendment sponsored by Ronald V. Dellums, D-Calif., suspending virtually all trade with South Africa and forcing U.S. businesses to leave that country within six months.

The Republicans thought the Dellums measure was so extreme that its passage by the House would kill any chance for sanctions legislation in the Senate. They were wrong. Instead, the House action shifted the entire political balance on South Africa, establishing a new set of limits for what Congress could consider and making any other set of sanctions seem moderate by comparison. As Dellums said later, the House had moved back the political "fear barrier" for members.

Reagan apparently failed to recognize the changed circumstances. The turning point came on July 22, when Reagan made a nationally televised speech from the Oval Office intended to quell sanctions fervor in the Senate. The speech was timed specifically to affect action by the

BISHOP TUTU: Eloquent anti-apartheid appeals by this Nobel Prize-winner impressed Americans.

SECURITY CRACKDOWN: Police confrontations and the ongoing unrest forced U.S. politicians to rethink President Reagan's policy.

Foreign Relations Committee, which had scheduled hearings on South Africa to start on July 23.

The day before the president's speech, Lugar and Sen. Nancy Landon Kassebaum, R-Kan., went to the White House and tried to urge Reagan to make a strong anti-apartheid speech.

Reagan did come out against apartheid, but that message was lost in his condemnation of sanctions and his sharp attack on the African National Congress. The speech was a political and public relations disaster; rather than calming the furor in Congress, it generated more controversy by seeming to show that the president was unyielding on his policy and more sympathetic toward the Botha government than toward South African blacks.

Dismayed, Lugar immediately set about to forge a consensus for a "moderate" bill. He introduced his own proposal, including several export bans and a prohibition on new business investment in South Africa. In committee, and again on the floor, Lugar accepted strengthening amendments by Democrats as the price for getting a bill passed with broad bipartisan support. But he fought off amendments that might have jeopardized GOP votes.

Hours before leaving for its recess on Aug. 15, the Senate passed the sanctions bill 84-14. Lugar immediately began putting pressure on the House to bypass a conference committee and accept the Senate bill, saying only such a course would prevent a filibuster from killing the bill. In private talks with House leaders, Lugar offered another incentive: If the House accepted the Senate bill, Lugar promised to stand by it, even in the face of an almost certain veto by the president.

The House reluctantly gave in to Lugar's pressure, and on Sept. 12 sent the Senate bill to Reagan by a 308-77 vote. *(Vote 351, 1986 Weekly Report p. 2236)*

Lugar, Kassebaum and others tried but failed to persuade the president to accept it. Reagan vetoed the bill on Sept. 26 — the last of 10 days he had to consider it, saying it would impose "sweeping punitive sanctions that would injure most the very people we seek to help. . . ."

"The thrust of this legislation is to bring about violence and revolutionary change and, after that, everlasting tyranny."
—Sen. Jesse Helms, R-N.C.

"We're not destroying that government; that government is self-destructing. . . . We are saying: 'Wake up.' "
—Sen. Richard G. Lugar, R-Ind.

of those senators for their votes.

In spite of the seriousness of the issue, the administration never pulled out all the stops to support the veto in the Senate. Reagan telephoned and met with several senators, and the State Department dispatched its senior black official — Alan L. Keyes, assistant secretary of state for international organizations — to the Capitol.

Reagan also took two steps to demonstrate his concern about South Africa: On Sept. 29 he sent congressional leaders a letter promising to sign an executive order with limited sanctions if the veto was sustained, and the next day he named Edward Perkins, a senior black Foreign Service officer, as the new U.S. ambassador to Pretoria. Perkins replaces Herman W. Nickel, who has served in South Africa since 1982. *(Reagan texts, 1986 Weekly Report pp. 2370, 2372)*

In spite of those symbolic steps, one lobbyist said the vote was "never winnable" for the president, and so the administration decided not to use up valuable political capital on it.

The administration also made only feeble efforts to link the vote to Reagan's "pre-summit" meeting in Iceland with Soviet leader Mikhail S. Gorbachev. Talking to undecided Republicans on Sept. 30, Secretary of State George P. Shultz noted that Reagan would need congressional support for his sessions in Iceland. But most senators said the surprise announcement of the Iceland meeting had little effect on the vote because South Africa would not be on the superpower agenda. *(Pre-summit, 1986 Weekly Report p. 2359)*

Perhaps the most telling indication of the administration's willingness to accept the veto override was

the proffered executive order. Its suggested sanctions were substantially weaker than draft proposals that White House lobbyists had floated on Capitol Hill in advance of the veto.

Reagan also got little productive help from his allies on Capitol Hill. While supporting the veto, Dole made only a faint stab at winning the vote. And Lugar, the man to whom most senators would turn for advice on foreign affairs, actively opposed Reagan.

The two senators who spent the most time supporting the veto carried little political clout with their colleagues: Jesse Helms, R-N.C., and Larry Pressler, R-S.D.

In repeated speeches, they warned that sanctions would not force change in South Africa's racial policies and would instead strengthen the hand of radical black groups.

"The thrust of this legislation is to bring about violence and revolutionary change and, after that, everlasting tyranny," Helms said.

Pressler had supported sanctions in 1985 but changed his mind after traveling to South Africa in 1986. He said Congress was ignoring "fundamental reforms" the Pretoria government had made in apartheid.

A Historic Vote

The vote was the first override of a presidential veto on a major foreign policy issue since 1973, when Congress enacted into law the War Powers resolution (PL 93-148), giving it the right to withdraw troops from combat situations. *(1973 CQ Almanac p. 905)*

Congress in the mid-1970s forced President Ford to accept modified versions of two major foreign policy bills after he exercised vetoes: an embargo on arms sales to Turkey in 1974 (PL 93-448) and a bill (PL 94-329) in

1976 giving Congress the right to veto foreign arms sales. *(1974 Almanac p. 547; 1976 Almanac p. 213)*

Congress has modified or stalled Reagan's policies on several foreign issues, most often involving Central America. In 1984 and 1985, Congress refused Reagan's requests for military aid to the Nicaraguan "contra" rebels. Political pressure also has forced Reagan to abandon seemingly fixed positions, as in 1984 when he responded to congressional demands and withdrew U.S. Marines from Lebanon.

But until the veto override, Congress had never repudiated Reagan so decisively. The rebuke was so complete, in fact, that Dole suggested Congress had taken control of the South Africa issue. "It's going to be our policy; it's going to be the policy the Congress establishes, and then we'll be responsible," Dole told his colleagues minutes before the vote. "Who's going to direct that policy from the Congress of the United States?"

The common theme binding all of Congress' foreign policy battles with Reagan was public sentiment. Although an enormously popular president, Reagan has implemented a number of policies that appeared to have little backing among the voters. In those cases, Congress responded by devising alternatives and then seeking to negotiate with Reagan.

The difference in the South Africa case was that Reagan refused to budge. In 1985 he reluctantly imposed his own sanctions in response to congressional demands. But in 1986 Reagan stood fast in the face of mounting pressure. *(Box, this story)*

Domestic Politics

Some senators and White House officials said the Senate's vote was determined by the calendar: It came just a month before the Nov. 4 elections that would decide which party controls the Senate in the 100th Congress.

Democrats were eager to exploit Reagan's political weakness on the issue, and some attempted to portray his attitude toward South Africa as a Republican policy.

Nervous Republicans did not want to risk antagonizing black voters for whom South Africa is especially important. House Minority Whip Trent Lott, R-Miss., said: "It's right before an election, and there are a lot of districts with a heavy black population, and members don't want to take a chance of offending them."

Dole for months had contended that South Africa was a "domestic civil rights issue" as much as a foreign policy matter. Concluding Senate debate, Dole derisively said his colleagues were about to cast a "feel-good vote" for a "feel-good foreign policy."

Several Republican senators who had voted for the bill in August also feared the repercussions of changing their minds on such a highly-publicized matter.

Some sanctions supporters readily acknowledged the domestic implications, but insisted they were positive ones arising out of the civil rights struggles of the 1960s. South Africa, they said, is important for the United States precisely because of the recent history of racism here.

"The vote matters not because of what it says about South Africa," said Rep. Lynn Martin, R-Ill., when the House acted. "It matters more because of what it says about America."

Lugar's Role

The key actor in the Senate was Lugar, normally one of Reagan's most loyal and effective supporters. Lugar was the main architect of the Senate bill, and in early September he promised House leaders that he would stand by it — even in the face of a veto — if they would adopt it.

Lugar was joined by Nancy Landon Kassebaum, R-Kan., chairman of the African affairs subcommittee, who long had questioned whether sanctions would lead to changes the United States seeks in South Africa. But in recent months she supported the sanctions bill as a way of demonstrating U.S. leadership on the issue.

Together, they appealed to Reagan to sign the bill. When he refused, they said Congress should move ahead on its own because Reagan had missed his chance to demonstrate leadership.

Lugar lamented that Reagan "didn't take my advice the first, second, third or even fourth time."

For his stand, Lugar came under harsh attack from some fellow conservatives, including White House Communications Director Patrick J. Buchanan. At a rally on Sept. 29, Buchanan said Lugar held his chairmanship only because of Reagan's popularity. Quoting from Shakespeare's "King Lear," Buchanan said of Lugar: "How sharper than a serpent's tooth, to have a thankless child."

Helms, the second ranking Republican on Foreign Relations, got in his own jabs. "Dick Lugar and Ted Kennedy" would be responsible for turning South Africa over to "militant blacks" and ultimately the Soviet Union, he told reporters.

As the Senate's debate got under way, Lugar aides sent to the press gallery a list based on Congressional Quarterly figures showing that, from 1981-85, he had voted with Reagan more than any other senator.

In an impassioned speech highlighting Senate debate, Lugar said Congress was acting because there was "a small window of opportunity . . . in which hope could be given to blacks in South Africa that we care, that the world cares. The fact is that people are being killed and harmed there now."

Responding to charges by his fellow conservatives that the sanctions bill attacked South Africa and ignored worse human rights violations in the Soviet Union, Lugar said the United States must oppose dictatorships of both the left and the right. "We are against tyranny, and tyranny is in South Africa, and we must be vigorous in that fight," he said.

Lugar offered no assurances that sanctions will bring an end to apartheid, because U.S. influence over South Africa is limited. "Our influence may be so limited that the government of South Africa will pursue headlong a course bound to destruction of that government," Lugar said. "We're not destroying that government; that government is self-destructing. At this late point, as a friend of that government, we are saying: 'Wake up.' That's what sanctions are about."

Botha's Lobbying

The night before the vote, Lugar and Helms exchanged charges about Helms' involvement in the lobbying of two farm-state senators by South African Foreign Minister Botha.

Lugar learned the afternoon of Oct. 1 that Botha had told Sens. Edward Zorinsky, D-Neb., and Charles E. Grassley, R-Iowa, that South Africa would retaliate against sanctions by refusing to buy U.S. farm goods and by barring shipment of those products to neighboring black states whose transportation links are controlled by Pretoria. Lugar also said Botha had promised increased South African grain purchases from the United States if Reagan's veto was sustained.

Botha had telephoned Helms at the Senate Republican cloakroom; Helms then invited Zorinsky and Grassley to the telephone.

One provision of the sanctions bill barred U.S. imports of agricultural products from South Africa. Lugar and other senators long had warned that the provision likely would provoke retaliation by South Africa.

Lugar angrily charged that Botha's calls were "despicable" and amounted to "foreign bribery and intimidation to change the votes of members of the United States Senate. It is an affront to the decency of the American people." Further, Lugar said, Helms' involvement in the Botha lobbying effort was "inappropriate."

Helms immediately defended his actions and those of Botha, who he said had been a friend for 10 years.

"Methinks Mr. Lugar doth protest too much," Helms said. "I think Ed Zorinsky was entitled to know that the farmers of America will be shot in the foot by Dick Lugar and Ted Kennedy and the others."

Helms later suggested that he might consider challenging Lugar for the Foreign Relations Committee chairmanship "if there are any more outbursts" such as Lugar's charges against him. Questioned about the seriousness of that comment, Helms then contended his suggestion was "flip." Helms in 1984 gave up his claim to the committee chairmanship so he could take the leadership of the Agriculture Committee instead.

Botha defended his lobbying and called "absolutely laughable" Lugar's complaints. He told reporters in Johannesburg: "If you rob us of our markets, we have to look out after the interests of our farmers."

After the Senate voted, Dole and others discounted the effect of Botha's lobbying, noting that Zorinsky and Grassley supported the veto override. "I don't think it made much of a difference," Dole said. "It's no big deal."∎

In the Wake of the Summit: Proposals, Politics

A weekend summit meeting of President Reagan and Soviet leader Mikhail S. Gorbachev, held on short notice at Reykjavik, Iceland, broke up Oct. 12, 1986, over the issue of anti-missile defenses.

Immediate congressional reactions were clear-cut and predictable. On the one hand, proponents of the strategic defense initiative (SDI) — Reagan's plan to develop anti-missile defenses — were heartened by his adamant refusal to defer for 10 years field tests of SDI components, even in return for Soviet agreement to sweeping nuclear arms cuts.

For their part, many of the arms control advocates who oppose SDI were relieved that they had agreed Oct. 10 to have the House put aside its effort to force Reagan to adopt certain arms control policies. Now, these sources contended, Reagan could not blame his liberal critics for his inability to reach an agreement with Gorbachev.

For the longer term, the Iceland episode raised further the already high political profile of SDI, but the consequences were less clear. Reagan made support for the program a prominent theme of campaign appearances on behalf of Republican Senate candidates in Maryland and North Dakota. He told a Baltimore audience on Oct. 15 that it would be a tragedy "if those on Capitol Hill opposed to SDI are allowed to hand over to the Soviet Union free of charge what we refused to hand over across the bargaining table."

However, some key members contended that Reagan's performance in Reykjavik may increase SDI's political difficulties in Congress. House Armed Services Committee Chairman Les Aspin, D-Wis., for one, argued that SDI heretofore has been supported by two kinds of members: "true believers in SDI plus the people who will vote for it because it's a bargaining chip," with which to extract the very kind of Soviet concessions Reagan apparently had turned down.

Loss of the second group of backers would put SDI in serious political trouble, Aspin maintained.

The First Offer

In the weeks before the Iceland meeting was unexpectedly announced on Sept. 30, there were widespread press reports of progress toward agreement on limiting "intermediate-range nuclear forces" (INF) — basically, missiles based in or aimed at Europe.

But in the days before the meeting began, administration officials repeatedly told reporters not to expect any substantive agreement from the session. What was hoped for, officials said, was an "impulse" from the two leaders that would accelerate the conculsion of formal agreements in the ongoing Geneva arms reduction talks.

Instead, the two leaders and a handful of their top national security aides apparently agreed on major elements of sweeping arms reduction proposals. According to an Oct. 13

President Reagan and Mikhail S. Gorbachev in Iceland: A sudden meeting, new offers, an abrupt finish.

press briefing by Vice Admiral John M. Poindexter, Reagan's national security adviser, discussions between U.S. and Soviet aides on the night of Oct. 11 and the morning of Oct. 12 came to the following tentative conclusions:

● The total number of intercontinental ballistic missiles and bombers would be cut to 1,600 for each country. The total number of missile warheads and bomber-dropped nuclear bombs carried by this fleet would be reduced to 6,000. An important dispute remained over how large a reduction was required in each type of weapon. U.S. officials continued their longstanding policy of insisting that intercontinental ballistic missiles (ICBMs), which account for the bulk of the Soviet nuclear firepower, be reduced in proportion to other kinds of strategic launchers. The Soviets rejected the idea of "sublimits" on different kinds of launchers within the overall limit of 1,600. However, they said they were willing to consider "significant" reductions in the force of very large Soviet ICBMs that Reagan officials deem especially suited for a surprise attack.

● The total number of INF warheads would be cut to 100 for each country: 100 U.S. Pershing IIs and cruise missiles, each of which carries one warhead, and 33 of the triple-warhead Soviet SS-20s. None of the allowed U.S. missiles would be stationed in Western Europe and none of the allowed Soviet missiles would be based within striking distance of Western Europe. Officials previously had suggested that, in the event of such a pact, the U.S. missiles might be based in Alaska, where they would be within range of Soviet territory and thus serve as a political counterweight to the Soviet missiles stationed within reach of Japan and China.

Since this would require a reduction of almost 90 percent in the total number of Soviet INF warheads, Reagan administration officials have been particularly insistent that any agreement include far-reaching procedures for verifying mutual compliance with the pact, including the presence of observers to witness the dismantling of existing weapons.

• Talks would begin toward the eventual banning of nuclear weapons tests. Initially, the two sides would negotiate improved verification techniques for two treaties negotiated in the 1970s, but never ratified; those pacts would limit nuclear tests to the explosive force of 150 kilotons — more than 10 times the size of the Hiroshima bomb. Once those amendments were agreed to, the negotiators would seek further limitations on nuclear testing with the ultimate goal of a ban on all nuclear weapons tests.

Here, too, important disagreements remained. The Soviets wanted these talks characterized as comprehensive test ban talks, while the U.S. side insisted that an absolute end to nuclear testing would have to coincide with the abolition of nuclear weapons. But in his briefing Poindexter speculated that agreement on modification of the two existing treaties would have been possible regardless of the farther-reaching issues.

Anti-missile Treaty

Gorbachev was adamant that all those tentative agreements could be made final only if Reagan took two steps with regard to the 1972 U.S.-Soviet treaty limiting anti-ballistic missile (ABM) weapons:

• A pledge not to exercise for 10 years the provision of the 1972 treaty that allows either party to withdraw from the pact on six months' notice. No militarily significant anti-missile system could be deployed without withdrawing from the pact.

• An amendment to the 1972 treaty that would restrict SDI research to work conducted within a laboratory.

The Reagan administration contended that all SDI testing planned for the next several years — including several tests in space — would be consistent with the treaty. Many arms control advocates disputed that claim, charging that the administration was torturing legal logic to claim that the treaty would allow highly realistic tests of components of an anti-missile system.

The Soviet position transcended this debate, requiring a flat prohibition on all SDI-related testing outside the four walls of a laboratory.

The Second Round

With the SDI issue blocking the package of detailed agreements, the

U.S. side offered a second proposal on the afternoon of the second day of meetings:

• Neither side would withdraw from the ABM treaty for five years.

• ICBMs and long-range bombers (and their warheads) would be reduced by 50 percent.

• At the end of that five-year period, both sides would renew the five-year pledge not to withdraw from the ABM treaty. Concurrently, they would begin a five-year process of dismantling all remaining offensive ballistic missiles, including ICBMs, INF ballistic missiles and shorter-range nuclear missiles.

• During the entire 10-year period, both sides would be free to conduct ABM research, development and testing as currently permitted by the 1972 treaty. At the end of that period, both sides would be free to deploy anti-missile weapons.

Gorbachev quickly rejected the second U.S. package unless it incorporated a ban on SDI testing outside the laboratory. Reagan refused, and the talks ended.

Spokesmen for both sides later insisted that all proposals made during the two-day meeting remained on the table, to be pursued in ongoing negotiations in Geneva or in other forums. But, after some initial confusion, the Soviets made it clear they regarded the various offers as valid only as components of a comprehensive package that included the stringent limits on SDI testing.

Dodging the Bullet

Under intense political pressure from Reagan to close ranks behind him on the eve of the Iceland meeting, the House Democratic leadership had agreed Oct. 10 to drop efforts to mandate several arms control policies.

At issue were House-passed amendments to the annual defense authorization bill (S 2638) that would have barred all but the smallest nuclear test explosions and would have mandated continued compliance with

the unratified 1979 U.S.-Soviet strategic arms limitation treaty (SALT II).

In announcing the decision to back off on the nuclear testing and SALT II issues, House Speaker Thomas P. O'Neill Jr., Mass., and other Democratic leaders stressed their desire to present a united front to the Soviet leader.

But many of these members — and some leading arms control lobbyists, such as Common Cause President Fred Wertheimer, also told reporters that they supported the decision because it would deny Reagan a scapegoat if the Iceland talks went sour.

By Oct. 15, when the compromise version of the defense bill came to the House floor, some members, including

> *It would be a tragedy "if those on Capitol Hill opposed to SDI are allowed to hand over to the Soviet Union free of charge what we refused to hand over across the bargaining table."*
>
> **—President Reagan**

Patricia Schroeder, D-Colo., and arms control lobby groups charged that the arms control issues should be reopened in light of Reagan's rejection of sweeping arms cuts for the sake of saving SDI. If members felt bound by the earlier agreement on the defense bill, these critics argued, they should vote against enactment of an omnibus fiscal 1987 continuing appropriations resolution (H J Res 783) so that tough arms control provisions could be added to that measure.

But Democratic leaders and several key arms control advocates strongly opposed this effort, partly because — as usually happens in a period of international tension — public opinion appeared to be solidly behind Reagan.

"Our time will come at the beginning of next year," Wertheimer told a reporter. "The president has had his clear shot and has opened up a tremendous number of questions."

The House adopted the defense authorization conference report 283-128 on Oct. 15. Democrats voted "aye" by a ratio of 2-to-1 and Northern Democrats — the bulwark of arms control in the House — opposed the measure by only 70-77.

Later that day, despite calls by Schroeder and others, the House adopted the continuing resolution. ∎

SUPREME COURT

Power to Rule Legislation
Unconstitutional Exerts Deterrent Effect

Under the United States' system of checks and balances, the Supreme Court stands at the pinnacle of the federal judicial structure as the final reviewing authority of congressional legislation and executive action.

However, as is implicit in a checks-and-balance system of government, the high court and the lower federal judiciary do not function with complete independence. On the one hand, the size, salaries and jurisdiction of the judicial branch are determined by the legislative branch. On the other hand, the membership of the judicial branch is selected by the executive branch.

Federal and State Courts

Two types of judicial systems, state and federal, provide forums for the resolution of disputes. The state judicial systems are composed of the state supreme court, or state court of appeals, intermediate appellate courts and trial courts with general jurisdiction over disputes where most cases of a serious nature begin. In addition, states usually have a group of lower courts, such as municipal, police and justice-of-the-peace courts, which are the lowest courts in the judicial hierarchy and have limited jurisdiction in both civil and criminal cases. The federal system forms a tri-level pyramid, comprised of district courts at the bottom, circuit courts of appeals in the middle, and the Supreme Court at the top. *(Chart, p. 66)*

Provision for a federal judiciary was made by Article III, Section 1, of the Constitution, which stated: "The judicial power of the United States shall be vested in one supreme court, and in such inferior courts as the Congress may from time to time ordain and establish." Thus, aside from the required "supreme court," the structure of the lower federal judicial system was left entirely to the discretion of Congress.

Congress and Federal Courts

The Judiciary Act of 1789 established the Supreme Court; 13 district courts, each with a single judge; and, above the district courts, three circuit courts, each presided over by one district and two Supreme Court judges. Thereafter, as the nation grew and the federal judiciary's workload increased, Congress established additional circuit and district courts. In 1985 there were 12 circuit courts of appeals, 89 district courts and three territorial courts. Supreme Court justices no longer presided over federal circuit courts; each level of courts had its own judges.

The influence of Congress over the federal judiciary goes beyond the creation of courts. Although the power to appoint federal judges resides with the president, by and with the Senate's advice and consent, the power to create judgeships to which appointments can be made resides with Congress. It is in this area that politics historically plays its most critical role in the federal judicial system. For example, in 1801 the Federalist Congress created additional circuit court judgeships to be filled by a Federalist president. However, in 1802, when the Jeffersonian Republicans came into power, the new posts were abolished.

As federal judges are appointed to serve during good behavior, the power of Congress to abolish judgeships is limited to providing that when one becomes vacant, it cannot be filled. The history of the Supreme Court's size provides the best illustration of the earlier habit of creating and abolishing judgeships. Originally, the Supreme Court was composed of six justices. Subsequently, however, its membership varied: seven justices, 1807-37; nine justices, 1837-63; 10 justices, 1863-66; seven justices, 1866-69; and nine justices since 1869.

Jurisdiction of Federal Courts

Article III, Section 2, of the Constitution vests in the Supreme Court original jurisdiction — the power to hear a case argued for the first time — over only a few kinds of cases. The most important of these are suits between two states, which might concern such issues as water rights or offshore lands. Article III, Section 2, also extends to the court "judicial power" over all cases arising under the Constitution, federal laws and treaties. This jurisdiction, however, is appellate (i.e., limited to review of decisions from lower courts) and is subject to "such exceptions and ... regulations as Congress shall make."

Most of the high court's present jurisdiction is defined by the Judiciary Act of 1925, largely drafted by the court itself under Chief Justice William Howard Taft.

The Judiciary Act of 1925 made exercise of the court's appellate jurisdiction largely discretionary, giving the justices more leeway to refuse to review cases.

Except for certain limited types of cases in which the court is still "obligated" to take appeals, the court is allowed to decide whether the decisions from the lower courts present questions or conflicts important enough or of such a constitutional nature as to warrant the court's consideration on review.

But only in this way is the court able to control the

issues with which it deals. Its power is limited by the fact that it cannot reach out to bring issues before it, but must wait until they are properly presented in a case which has made its way through the lower courts.

In the relationship between federal and state judicial systems, federal courts have jurisdiction over cases relating to federal rights or actions in which the parties are citizens of different states. The state courts, on the other hand, are concerned with cases generally involving citizens of that state and their own state laws. There is some overlap of jurisdiction. The state courts are empowered to hear litigation concerning some federal rights, and federal constitutional rights often form the basis of decisions in state court cases. In the federal courts, where jurisdiction is based on a "diversity of citizenship" (i.e., the litigants are from different states), the court is obliged to find and apply the pertinent law of the state in which the court is sitting. In state court cases, similarly, in those few instances where a "federal question" might be resolved, the court is obliged to disregard its own precedents and apply appropriate federal law.

The Power of Judicial Review

The Supreme Court exerts a strong restraining influence upon Congress through its power to declare that certain of its legislative acts are unconstitutional and invalid. Although the Constitution does not expressly authorize the court to strike down acts it deems unconstitutional, the court assumed that important authority in 1803 through its own broad interpretation of its vested powers. Without this process, known as judicial review, there would be no assurance (not even in the president's veto) against domination of the entire government by runaway congressional majorities.

The court has been restrained in its exercise of this power; only a few more than 100 acts of Congress have been declared unconstitutional. Of those invalidated, many were relatively unimportant and others, such as the measures prohibiting the spread of slavery and those carrying out parts of Franklin D. Roosevelt's New Deal program, were replaced by legislation revised so as to pass muster with the Supreme Court.

Most constitutional scholars find the real significance of the Supreme Court's power of judicial review in the awareness of Congress that all of its acts are subject to a final veto by the Supreme Court.

With a few exceptions, the court has interpreted the legislature's power to enact specific laws as broadly as it has viewed its own authority to sit in review of the statutes.

The court's traditional approach to its duty of judicial review was outlined in 1827 by one of its first members — Justice Bushrod Washington. Justice Washington observed that "it is but a decent respect due to the wisdom, the integrity and the patriotism of the legislative body, by which any law is passed, to presume in favor of its validity until its violation of the Constitution is proved beyond all reasonable doubt." Justices on almost every court since Justice Washington's day have reaffirmed that attitude.

Changes in Court's Philosophy

Because Supreme Court justices are appointed for life terms, changes in the court's philosophy occur less frequently than in the other two branches of the federal government.

For its first 150 years, the court served primarily as a bulwark against encroachment on property rights. Even in the 1930s, with the passage of precedent-shattering legislation aimed at the nation's economic crisis, the court struck down 11 New Deal statutes — the heart of the recovery program. After his reelection in 1936, President Roosevelt threatened to "pack" the court with six additional justices who presumably would favor his program. However, before Congress had turned to his proposal, a judicial about-face was under way. On March 29, 1937, the court upheld Washington State's minimum wage law. Implicit in *West Coast Hotel v. Parrish* was the willingness of a majority of the justices to accept government authority to protect the general welfare and to discard the court's role as censor of economic legislation. On the same day, the court also upheld two New Deal statutes.

This shift of doctrine was completed during the term of Chief Justice Earl Warren (1954-1969), when the court promulgated a series of sweeping decisions in support of individual rights.

But with Warren's retirement, the pendulum began to swing back. The membership of the court changed. By 1985 only three Warren court justices remained. The court's rulings in the 1970s were less protective of individual rights, making clear that they were rarely absolute.

Moreover, in 1976 the court for the first time in 40 years held that Congress exceeded its authority to regulate commerce when it extended the coverage of federal wages and hours legislation to state and local government employees. The action was reminiscent of the court's actions overturning New Deal legislation applying to the private sector of the economy and raised questions about whether the justices in future years would place additional limits on the power of Congress to control the actions of state and local governments.

Whatever the court's philosophy, it has always had its share of congressional critics quick to accuse it of usurping undue powers. The early Anti-Federalists (later known as Democratic-Republicans and finally as Democrats) thought the court nullified the Constitution by a series of rulings strengthening federal power at the expense of individuals and the states. New Deal Democrats thought the court was attempting to seize the pre-eminent role in government by voiding much of their legislative program. In the 1950s and 1960s, Republicans and Southern Democrats were driven virtually to despair by the Warren court's decisions on school desegregation, criminal law, and voter representation. In the 1970s, as the court became more conservative, criticism came again from liberal observers who worried that the court unduly favored the state at the expense of the individual.

Such criticism of the court has led to a number of proposals to curb the tribunal's powers. Among the proposals have been a requirement of more than a majority vote to render a statute unconstitutional, removal of justices upon concurrence of the president and both houses of Congress, and restriction of the court's appellate jurisdiction to exclude certain types of cases in which the court has made decisions not to the liking of some members of Congress. Although certain of these proposals have attracted wide support, only one — in 1868 — has ever been enacted into law. The only sanctions effectively wielded by Congress have been the Senate's refusal to confirm court nominees and the reversal or modification of court rulings through legislation. The court's critics have blocked 27 of 139 court nominations submitted by successive presidents. Eleven of the 27 nominations were rejected outright, and the others were withdrawn or allowed to lapse in the face of Senate opposition.

Sources of Court's Power

Unlike the rebels who framed the Declaration of Independence, the men who met at Philadelphia in 1787 to shape the U.S. Constitution represented conservative financial interests. These interests had suffered heavily during the period of national confederation following the Revolution, when state legislatures, controlled mostly by agrarian interests, made repeated assaults on vested rights.

While the framers of the Constitution deprecated the excesses of the legislatures, they held a high respect for the courts, which gave judgments in favor of creditors and sent delinquent debtors to jail. As political scientist Charles A. Beard, a leading constitutional scholar, once put it in his book *The Supreme Court and the Constitution:* "The conservative interests, made desperate by the imbecilities of the Confederation and harried by the state legislatures, roused themselves from their lethargy, drew together in a mighty effort to establish a government that would be strong enough to pay the national debt, regulate interstate and foreign commerce, provide for national defense, prevent fluctuations in the currency created by paper emissions, and control the propensities of legislative majorities to attack private rights."

At the time the framers met, judicial review had not yet been instituted in any country in the world. And despite considerable discussion of some means to check the excesses of Congress, the matter of a judicial veto never came up for a direct vote. The closest the convention got to considering such a scheme was when it rejected the Virginia Plan of government. That plan contained a section establishing a Council of Revision, consisting of Supreme Court justices and the president, to consider the constitutionality of proposed acts prior to final congressional passage. As submitted to the state conventions for ratification, the Constitution did not designate a final arbiter of constitutional disputes. Wilfred E. Binkley and Malcolm C. Moos have pointed out in their book *A Grammar of American Politics* that there were matters the delegates "dared not baldly assert in the Constitution without imperiling its ratification, but they doubtless hoped that implications would eventually be interpreted to supply the thing desired." Judicial review appeared to be one of those things. Most other constitutional scholars have supported this view.

In *The Federalist,* a series of essays written to promote adoption of the Constitution, Alexander Hamilton made clear that the framers expected the judiciary to rule on constitutional issues. In Number 78 of *The Federalist,* Hamilton wrote: "The complete independence of the courts of justice is peculiarly essential in a limited constitution. By a limited constitution, I understand one which contains certain specified exceptions to the legislative authority, such for instance, as that it shall pass no bills of attainder, no ex post facto laws, and the like. Limitations of this kind can be preserved in practice no other way than through the courts of justice, whose duty it must be to declare all acts contrary to the manifest tenor of the Constitution void. Without this, all the reservations of particular rights or privileges would amount to nothing."

The court itself set out the doctrine of judicial review in the famous case of *Marbury v. Madison* (5 U.S. (1 Cranch) 137) in 1803.

The Judiciary Act of 1789, among other provisions, empowered the court to issue writs of mandamus compelling federal officials to perform their duties. Citing this authority, William Marbury, named by outgoing President John Adams as justice of the peace for the District of Columbia, asked the court to order James Madison, secretary of state to the new president, Thomas Jefferson, to deliver to Marbury his commission. Upon taking office, Jefferson had ordered all such commissions withheld.

Chief Justice John Marshall wrote that Marbury was entitled to his commission, but that the Supreme Court did not have the power to issue the requested writ, because Congress in attempting to give the court this power had acted unconstitutionally to expand its original jurisdiction. Therefore, held the court, that portion of the Judiciary Act was unconstitutional and invalid.

Judicial review thus became firmly established as part of the American system of government. Binkley and Moos asserted: "Whether or not the Supreme Court 'usurped' the practice of judicial review is now purely an academic question. So completely has the practice been woven into the warp and woof of our constitutional fabric that the garment could now scarcely endure its elimination."

Court-Curbing Proposals

Intermittently throughout American history, congressional critics of judicial power have sought to impose restrictions on the Supreme Court. The methods have ranged from proposed curbs on the court's authority to the Senate's rejection of court nominees.

Early Proposals

Charles Warren details the circumstances of the first move against the court in his study *The Supreme Court.* In 1802 the newly elected Congress dominated by Jeffersonian Republicans abolished the additional federal circuit courts set up the year before by the old Congress and staffed with 16 Federalist judges (the "midnight judges") appointed by President Adams on the eve of his departure from office. To delay a decision in the *Marbury* and other controversial cases, Congress also enacted legislation postponing the Supreme Court's term for 14 months, until February 1803. In 1805 Rep. John Randolph, a Virginia Republican, proposed a constitutional amendment providing for removal of Supreme Court justices by the president upon the approval of both houses of Congress. However, Randolph's proposal attracted little support and was dropped.

Alarmed by a series of Supreme Court decisions strengthening federal power at the expense of the states, states' rights advocates in Congress introduced a variety of other court-curbing proposals. In 1807 Republicans proposed a constitutional amendment providing for a limited tenure of office for federal judges and for their removal by the president upon a two-thirds vote of each house.

Warren also points out other attempts in the early years of the Republic to limit the court. In 1831 congressional Democrats (the old Jeffersonian Republican Party) launched a determined effort to repeal Section 25 of the Judiciary Act of 1789, which authorized writs of error to the Supreme Court to review state court judgments. (A writ of error is a process under which an appellate court may bring up a case from a lower court to examine the trial record as to questions of law but not of fact.) On Jan. 29, 1831, the House rejected this proposal by a wide margin. Later that year, Democrats introduced another proposal directing the House Judiciary Committee to study the feasibility of amending the Constitution to limit the tenure of federal judges. That proposal was also overwhelmingly rejected.

In a later study, *Congress, The Constitution and Supreme Court,* Warren discusses another series of attacks on the court launched in the early 1900s by critics of the court's decisions protecting property rights. In 1923 Sen. William E. Borah, R-Idaho, introduced a bill to require concurrence by seven of the nine justices to invalidate an act of Congress. The following year Sen. Robert M. La Follette, R-Wis., proposed a constitutional amendment providing that a statute once struck down by the Supreme Court could be declared constitutional and immune from further court consideration by a two-thirds majority of both houses of Congress. Neither the Borah nor the La Follette proposal received serious consideration.

After Congress rejected the Roosevelt court-packing plan in 1937, the Supreme Court experienced a period of relatively placid relations with Congress until the Warren court launched on its course of judicial activism in the mid-1950s. The only proposed curb on the court that attracted much support from the mid-1930s to the early 1950s was a 1953 proposal to amend the Constitution to make retirement mandatory for all federal judges at age 75. The resolution proposing the amendment, suggested by the American Bar Association, was adopted by the Senate in 1954 but was shelved by the House.

Attacks on the Warren Court

Congressional attacks on the Warren court began in 1954, the year of the court's famous school desegregation decision. On May 17, 1954, the court had declared in the case of *Brown v. Board of Education of Topeka, Kansas* that racial segregation in public schools was inherently discriminatory and therefore in contravention of the equal protection clause of the Fourteenth Amendment. The period of the next four years was a time of unusual anti-court activity in Congress, spurred at first by Southern members. Some 19 senators and 74 representatives from the South signed a "Declaration of Constitutional Principles" — the so-called Southern Manifesto — on March 12, 1956, protesting the "decision of the Supreme Court in the school cases as a clear abuse of judicial power." The Southerners were joined in time by colleagues from other sections who were dismayed by the court's decisions in such matters as federal-state relations, communist activities, and contempt of Congress.

From 1955 through 1962 proposals were introduced in Congress to curb the Supreme Court's power to strike down state laws as pre-empted by federal laws. Under Article VI, Section 2, of the Constitution, making federal law the "supreme law of the land," the courts had invalidated state laws in cases where: (1) Congress had stated an intention to take over ("pre-empt") a given field of legislation; (2) there was a direct conflict between a federal law and a state law; or (3) congressional intention to pre-empt a field of legislation could be inferred, even though it had not been specified by Congress (the doctrine of "pre-emption by implication"). In 1958 a broad anti-pre-emption bill was passed overwhelmingly by the House and was defeated in the Senate by only one vote.

The other major threat to the court's jurisdiction during this period was the Jenner-Butler bill (for Republican Sens. William E. Jenner of Indiana and John Marshall Butler of Maryland). It would have deprived the Supreme Court of authority to review several types of cases, including those concerning contempt of Congress, the federal loyalty-security program, state anti-subversive statutes and admission to the practice of law in any state. After lengthy committee hearings and bitter floor debate, the Senate tabled the Jenner-Butler bill by a vote of 49 to 41 on Aug. 20, 1985.

Attacks on the Supreme Court came not only from Congress but also from the judiciary itself. Three days after the Jenner-Butler bill was shelved by the Senate, the Conference of State Chief Justices approved a statement asserting that the court "too often has tended to adopt the role of policy-maker without proper judicial restraint." The statement added: "We are not alone in our view that the Court, in many cases ... has assumed what seems to us primarily legislative powers."

Senate Republican Leader Everett McKinley Dirksen, Ill., was the leader of congressional efforts to modify the Supreme Court's "one man, one vote" doctrine on legislative apportionment set out in a series of decisions during the early 1960s. The House passed a bill in 1964 to deny federal courts jurisdiction over apportionment of state legislatures, but it was blocked in the Senate. At this juncture, court foes proposed a constitutional amendment to permit states to apportion one house of their legislatures on some basis other than population. The proposal came to a vote in the Senate in 1965 and again in 1966 — each time failing by seven votes to achieve a two-thirds majority.

A new move to restrict the jurisdiction of the Supreme Court emerged in the early 1980s. Angered by years of decisions by a "liberal" Supreme Court establishing a woman's right to an abortion, affirming the need to continue the effort to desegregate public schools, and refusing to condone official prayer in schools, Congress proposed to strip the court of jurisdiction to hear cases involving these issues. Republican Senator Jesse Helms of North Carolina proposed one such amendment in 1982 that would have barred federal courts, including the Supreme Court, from hearing "voluntary" school prayer cases. After a prolonged filibuster, the amendment was dropped.

Several measures designed to relieve the increased workload of the court were introduced during the 97th Congress. One proposed to eliminate the court's "mandatory" jurisdiction, that is, certain types of cases that the court must hear. Among the cases now guaranteed review are those involving the invalidation of an act of Congress or the unconstitutionality of a state law.

Congressional Reversals of Rulings

Of all its methods of influencing the Supreme Court, Congress has had the most success in reversing individual rulings either through adoption of a constitutional amendment or passage of legislation.

Four of the 26 amendments to the Constitution were adopted specifically to overrule the Supreme Court's interpretation of that document. The amendments reversed the court's rulings on the ability of citizens of one state to bring suit against another state, the status of blacks as citizens, the income tax and the 18-year-old vote.

But it is difficult and time-consuming to amend the Constitution. Each chamber of Congress must approve the proposed amendment by a two-thirds vote and it must then be ratified by three-fourths of all the states. Moreover, there is longstanding and deeply held sentiment that amendments to the Constitution should not be adopted every time there is a significant disagreement with a Supreme Court ruling. As a result, most proposals for such constitutional amendments never emerge from Congress.

Despite these acknowledged difficulties three issues — school prayer, abortion and busing — have provoked determined efforts in Congress during the last two decades to curb or undo Supreme Court rulings through constitutional amendments.

The court in 1962 ruled unconstitutional the use of a 22-word prayer in New York state public schools. Justice Hugo L. Black, speaking for the court in the case of *Engel v. Vitale*, said the prayer requirement violated the First Amendment's clause forbidding laws "respecting the establishment of religion." Soon afterward, Senate Republican leader Dirksen championed a proposed constitutional amendment to legalize voluntary student participation in prayers in public schools. Four years later, the proposal came to a vote in the Senate and fell nine votes short of receiving the necessary two-thirds majority. In 1971 and 1984 Congress defeated similar constitutional amendments permitting prayer in public schools.

Early in 1973 the court limited the power of states to ban abortions in the case of *Roe v. Wade*, allowing such prohibitions only in the last months of pregnancy. In 1975 a Senate subcommittee rejected several amendments intended to reverse that ruling and in 1976 the Senate refused to debate such an amendment. Renewed efforts in 1982 to pass anti-abortion legislation again came to a halt in the Senate after members voted to lay aside a proposal to ban virtually all abortions.

In a 1983 case, *Akron v. Akron Center for Reproductive Health*, the court reaffirmed its 1973 ruling. The decision reversed many local restrictions on access to abortions that had been established in the aftermath of the 1973 ruling.

In several rulings, the Supreme Court upheld the use of court-ordered busing to desegregate public school systems. The proposed anti-busing constitutional amendments before Congress would have denied lower federal courts the power to issue such orders. In mid-1979 the House soundly rejected an anti-busing amendment.

The more frequent — and successful — way of reversing the Supreme Court is for Congress to repass the offending statute after modifying it to meet the court's objections. This kind of reversal through simple legislation is easily accomplished if the court has interpreted a statute contrary to the construction intended by Congress. The House and Senate may then pass new legislation explicitly setting forth their intention. In many cases of this type, the court in its opinion will suggest the course the legislation should take to achieve its original purpose.

Reversal is not so easily accomplished when the court and Congress are at political or philosophical odds. Twice in the early 1900s Congress passed legislation to end child labor, for example, and twice the Supreme Court ruled that such legislation was not within Congress' power to enact. That its interpretation was based on philosophical differences rather than constitutional considerations was evident when the court reversed these two decisions several years later. In the mid-1930s it appeared that a similar confrontation would develop over New Deal legislation, but the court's re-examination of its position on congressional authority to regulate economic matters eased the crisis.

Three recent congressional reversals of Supreme Court decisions concerned pregnant women, news organizations and bankruptcy. Congress in 1978 required employers to include benefits for pregnancy, childbirth and related medical conditions in their health insurance and temporary

disability plans. This measure overturned a 1976 court ruling that pregnancy did not have to be covered by such plans.

In 1980 Congress required law enforcement officers to subpoena news organizations and newsmen for information they sought, instead of obtaining a search warrant and searching a news organization's office. This law overturned a 1978 decision upholding police power to conduct such searches.

In February 1984, the court ruled that federal law allowed companies attempting to organize their affairs under the bankruptcy code to unilaterally repudiate their labor contracts. Four months later Congress overturned the decision by requiring companies in financial straits to seek court approval to break their labor contracts. Prior to filing the application the company would have to make a proposal to the union to alter the contract and seek to negotiate changes.

Not all attempts at congressional reversal are successful. In June 1984, the House approved legislation to overturn a court ruling on Title IX of the 1972 Education Amendments. On Feb. 28, 1984, the court stated that Title IX's general ban on sex discrimination does not apply to all school activities, but only to the particular program receiving funds. The legislation, however, failed to be approved by the Senate before adjournment of the 98th Congress.

Court Nominees

Congress exerts influence over the judiciary in another major way — through the Senate's prerogative to "advise and consent" in the president's selection of candidates for judicial offices, including not only Supreme Court justices but also other federal court judges.

Patronage

The power to name members of the federal judiciary — to well-paid, prestigious, lifetime posts — is perhaps the strongest patronage lever possessed by an incumbent president. As a result federal judgeships traditionally go to persons of the president's political party, despite the stated intention of almost every chief executive to make nonpartisan judicial appointments.

In apparent contradiction of the American ideal of an independent non-partisan judiciary, the process of selecting federal judges is pure politics. No constitutional guidelines exist beyond the provision that the president "shall nominate, and by and with the advice and consent of the Senate, shall appoint . . . judges of the Supreme Court, and all other officers of the United States. . . ."

Only custom dictates that the president nominate and the Senate confirm federal judges below the Supreme Court level.

Only tradition requires that federal judges reside in their districts or that they be attorneys.

The president has complete independence in selecting his Supreme Court nominees, but since 1840 tradition has awarded to senators of the president's party the prerogative of selecting persons for vacant or newly-created federal judgeships within their states. If there are no senators of the appropriate party from that state, the White House usually looks to its party organization in the state for suggested nominees.

Senatorial recommendations carry less weight in the

choice of persons for seats on the courts of appeals, each of which has jurisdiction over cases from a number of states. On most circuit courts of appeals, however, it is traditional that each state have a certain representation on the court at all times.

Once the nomination is made, it is sent from the White House to the Senate, where it is referred to the Senate Judiciary Committee. Hearings are held on virtually every nomination, but they are rarely more than perfunctory proceedings of brief length. The Senate committee then routinely recommends that the Senate confirm the nominees, which usually occurs by voice vote and without debate.

Senatorial Courtesy

Prior to confirmation, a senator can object to a nominee for specific reasons or using the stock, but rare, objection that the nominee is "personally obnoxious" to him. In this case, the other senators usually join in blocking confirmation out of courtesy to their colleague.

This practice of "senatorial courtesy" began as early as 1789 when the Senate refused to confirm Benjamin Fishbourn, nominated naval officer for the port of Savannah, Ga., by George Washington. More recently, in 1976, the Senate Judiciary Committee tabled, and thereby killed, President Ford's nomination of William B. Poff to a federal judgeship in Virginia, a selection objected to by Sen. William Lloyd Scott, R-Va.

Recess Appointments

Aside from the regular appointment route outlined above, a president can make a "recess" appointment to the Supreme Court or any other federal court vacancy. The Constitution states that "The President shall have the power to fill up all vacancies that may happen during the recess of the Senate, by granting commissions which shall expire at the end of their next session."

The president can fill a vacant post while Congress is not in session and the new judge can take his seat without confirmation. When Congress reconvenes, the president has 40 days within which to submit the recess appointee's name for confirmation. If he does not do so, the judge's pay is terminated. If the name is submitted, but Congress fails to confirm or reject the nomination during the session, the appointment is good until Congress adjourns.

Chief Justice Earl Warren and Justices William J. Brennan Jr. and Potter Stewart were the last three men to accept recess appointments to the Supreme Court.

Rejection of Nominees

Starting with George Washington, 15 presidents have seen 26 of their nominees for the Supreme Court fail to win Senate confirmation — among a total of 139 appointments. One nominee, Edward King, failed to be confirmed despite two attempts in 1844, for a total of 27 unsuccessful nominations. In contrast, only eight Cabinet nominees have been rejected by the Senate. The last time a Cabinet nomination was rejected was in 1959, when Senate Democrats refused to approve President Eisenhower's selection of Lewis L. Strauss as secretary of commerce.

Although Congress also has authority to remove federal judges by impeachment, only one such attempt with respect to a Supreme Court justice has moved past the preliminary stage, and that attempt failed. In 1804 the House impeached Justice Samuel Chase, a staunch Federalist who had rankled Republicans with his partisan political statements and his vigorous prosecution of the Sedition Act, which had finally been repealed in 1802. But Chase was not convicted by the Senate even though his opponents obtained a majority on three of the eight articles of impeachment. (A total of 23 senators — two-thirds of the Senate — was necessary for conviction. The greatest number of votes for conviction on any of the articles was 19.) After the trial, President Jefferson, a strong foe of the Federalist-dominated court, criticized impeachment as "a bungling way of removing judges" and "a farce which will not be tried again" in a letter of Sept. 6, 1819, cited in Warren's book *The Supreme Court in United States History.*

Senate rejection of court nominations was common in the 19th century, when political ideology often colored the confirmation process. But from 1900 to 1968 the Senate refused a seat on the Supreme Court to only one man, John J. Parker in 1930. Then, in a 19-month period from late 1968 to early 1970, the Senate refused to approve four Supreme Court nominees — Abe Fortas and Homer Thornberry, nominated by President Johnson, and Clement F. Haynsworth Jr. and G. Harrold Carswell, nominated by President Nixon. (Fortas, already an associate justice, had been nominated for chief justice. Thornberry was to take his place as an associate justice. Both nominations were withdrawn when Senate supporters of the nominees were unable to break a Republican-Southern Democratic filibuster on the Fortas nomination.)

President Hoover thought Parker would be a noncontroversial nominee. He was a federal judge and a Republican from North Carolina. Hoover later wrote in his memoirs that "No member of the Court at that time was from the southern states, and the regional distribution of justices had always been regarded as of some importance." But Hoover misjudged the temper of the times. Social and economic issues were more important than geography. A bipartisan group in Congress charged that Parker had made anti-Negro statements as a political candidate and an anti-Negro ruling from the bench. His nomination was rejected, 39 to 41.

The Senate's refusal to take up the Fortas and Thornberry nominations resulted largely from Fortas' affirmative votes in some of the most controversial decisions of the Warren court and from the desire of Senate Republicans to have a Republican president name the new chief justice. The GOP strategy paid off when Republican presidential candidate Richard M. Nixon won the 1968 election. But after Nixon's nominee for Chief Justice, Warren E. Burger, had been confirmed, Senate Democrats retaliated for the Fortas affair by successfully opposing confirmation of the president's next two court nominees — Haynsworth and Carswell. Critics of the nominations based their opposition primarily on allegations that Haynsworth had failed to observe high standards of professional ethics while serving as an appellate judge, and that Carswell was not qualified for such a high judicial post. Republicans contended, however, that the avowedly conservative views of both men were responsible for their rejection.

Despite the low incidence of rejection for most of the 20th century, at least four other court nominations faced stiff opposition — those of Louis D. Brandeis in 1916, Harlan F. Stone in 1925, Charles Evans Hughes in 1930, and Thurgood Marshall, the only black ever named to the court. The Senate Judiciary Committee, under the chairmanship of Sen. James O. Eastland, D-Miss., held up Mar-

Federal Judicial System

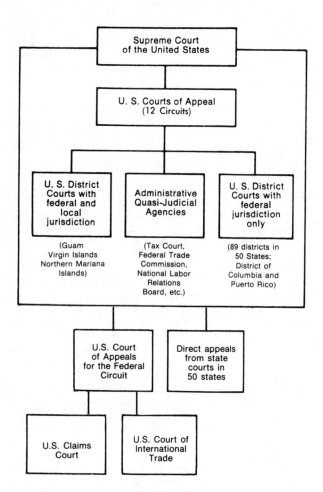

Supreme Court of the United States

U. S. Courts of Appeal (12 Circuits)

U. S. District Courts with federal and local jurisdiction

Administrative Quasi-Judicial Agencies

U. S. District Courts with federal jurisdiction only

(Guam Virgin Islands Northern Mariana Islands)

(Tax Court, Federal Trade Commission, National Labor Relations Board, etc.)

(89 districts in 50 States; District of Columbia and Puerto Rico)

U.S. Court of Appeals for the Federal Circuit

Direct appeals from state courts in 50 states

U.S. Claims Court

U.S. Court of International Trade

State Judicial System

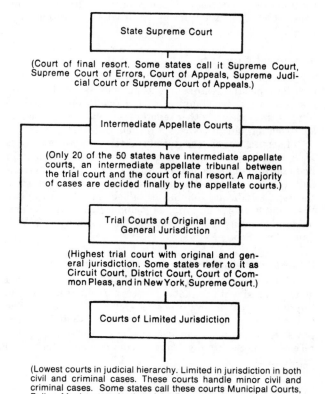

State Supreme Court

(Court of final resort. Some states call it Supreme Court, Supreme Court of Errors, Court of Appeals, Supreme Judicial Court or Supreme Court of Appeals.)

Intermediate Appellate Courts

(Only 20 of the 50 states have intermediate appellate courts, an intermediate appellate tribunal between the trial court and the court of final resort. A majority of cases are decided finally by the appellate courts.)

Trial Courts of Original and General Jurisdiction

(Highest trial court with original and general jurisdiction. Some states refer to it as Circuit Court, District Court, Court of Common Pleas, and in New York, Supreme Court.)

Courts of Limited Jurisdiction

(Lowest courts in judicial hierarchy. Limited in jurisdiction in both civil and criminal cases. These courts handle minor civil and criminal cases. Some states call these courts Municipal Courts, Police, Magistrates, Justice of the Peace, Family, Probate, Small Claims, Traffic, Juvenile Courts, and other titles.)

shall's confirmation as a judge of the Second Circuit Court of Appeals for a year before approving it. But in 1965 the same committee approved Marshall's nomination as solicitor general in less than a month, and in 1967 Marshall's nomination to the Supreme Court was confirmed by a comfortable 69-11 vote.

Action on the Brandeis nomination a half-century earlier was delayed for months by the same committee while it pondered the nominee's "radical views." While opposition to the nomination focused on Brandeis' liberal economic, political and social posture, there is evidence that much of it was motivated by anti-Semitic prejudice.

The nomination of Hughes as chief justice was made in 1930 when the country was entering the Great Depression and the nominee's views were attacked as too conservative.

Stone, at the time of his nomination, was U.S. attorney general and was in the midst of prosecuting Burton K. Wheeler, a recently elected Democratic senator from Montana. Wheeler was accused, but later acquitted of charges of participating in an oil-land fraud.

Wheeler's home state Democratic colleague, Sen. Thomas J. Walsh, used the committee hearings on the Stone nomination to criticize the Justice Department's handling of the Wheeler case.

To these four might be added the name of Hugo L. Black, who encountered difficulties after his confirmation when it was learned that he had once been a member of the Ku Klux Klan.

Black repudiated his Klan involvement in a dramatic radio broadcast and criticism waned.

Convicted on Three Articles:

Senate Finds Claiborne Guilty, Strips Him of Federal Judgeship

The Senate Oct. 9, 1986, removed imprisoned U.S. District Judge Harry E. Claiborne from office after convicting him of "high crimes and misdemeanors" related to his 1984 conviction for tax fraud.

An overwhelming majority of senators voted to convict Claiborne on three articles of impeachment, but he was acquitted on a fourth.

Last-minute court appeals Oct. 8-9 to block the final Senate vote were unsuccessful. A federal district judge and an appeals court panel in Washington, D.C., said they had no authority to tell the Senate how to conduct an impeachment trial. And two hours before the final vote, Chief Justice William H. Rehnquist denied Claiborne's request for a stay.

The House July 22 voted the four articles of impeachment against the 69-year-old Claiborne — all stemming from his conviction for filing false income tax returns. The first two articles alleged that Claiborne willfully underreported his income by $18,741 in 1979 and by $87,912 in 1980. The third alleged that he should be removed from office because of the 1984 conviction, and the fourth asserted that he betrayed the trust of the people and brought disrepute on the federal judiciary. *(1986 CQ Weekly Report p. 2383; text of impeachment articles p. 1498)*

Dramatic Roll Call

The judge, who has maintained his innocence since his 1983 indictment, listened intently as the roll was called, whispering once or twice with his two lawyers, Oscar B. Goodman of Las Vegas, Nev., and former Sen. Howard W. Cannon, D-Nev. (1959-83), who were keeping tallies.

Instead of answering "aye" or "no," the traditional response during a vote, the senators were instructed to stand and say "guilty," "not guilty," or "present."

In a gesture that underscored the solemnity and importance of the occasion, even John C. Stennis, D-Miss., who lost a leg to cancer two years ago, pulled himself to a standing position each time his name was called.

On Article I, the Senate found Claiborne guilty 87-10, with Ted Stevens, R-Alaska, voting present. This was 21 more than the two-thirds required to convict. *(Vote 335, 1986 Weekly Report p. 2568)*

On Article II, 90 voted guilty and seven voted not guilty, with Stevens voting present. *(Vote 336, p. 2568)*

On Article III, the vote was 46 guilty, 17 not guilty, with 35 voting present. Claiborne was acquitted on this article. *(Vote 338, p. 2568)*

On Article IV, there were 89 guilty votes and eight not-guilty votes, with Stevens again voting present. *(Vote 338, p. 2568)*

Claiborne was automatically removed from office as soon as he was convicted on the first article.

Shortly after the final vote was cast, the former judge was hustled out of the chamber by the U.S. marshals.

"A part of my soul died here today . . ."
—Harry E. Claiborne

Claiborne did not speak to reporters, but he did give a handwritten note to his longtime friend, Hank Greenspun, publisher of the Las Vegas *Sun*. The note, which was printed in the *Sun*, said: "A part of my soul died here today. Not because of defeat but because everything that I believed in was assaulted beyond repair in that the most responsible body in the world . . . has violated their constitutional obligation and duty by refusing to grant me the trial in the Senate that the Constitution dictates, but instead decided to circumvent their responsiblities by a 'rush to judgment' in order to get to their homes and campaign or otherwise take advantage of their recess."

Goodman plans to return to court to challenge the impeachment.

Several senators said after the proceedings they had voted against conviction on Article III because it would set a bad precedent. Sam Nunn, D-Ga., said senators worried that removing Claiborne simply because he had been convicted could be interpreted to mean that conviction is the equivalent of impeachment and an acquittal would mean a person could not be impeached.

The Senate's decision could affect another case that may come before Congress in 1987. Florida federal Judge Alcee L. Hastings was acquitted in 1983 of bribery charges, but the 11th U.S. Circuit Court of Appeals has recommended that he be removed from office. *(1986 Weekly Report p. 2280)*

Claiborne became the first official to be removed from office in 50 years and the fifth in the history of the nation. The last was Judge Halsted Ritter of Florida.

Full Trial Sought

For the first time in its history, the Senate used a special 12-member committee to gather evidence for the trial. The special committee, chaired by Sen. Charles McC. Mathias Jr., R-Md., took testimony for seven days, nearly two of them devoted to hearing from Claiborne. The members produced a voluminous report for the Senate, and the thick bound volumes were on top of each senator's desk during the proceedings.

In a critical vote Oct. 8, the Senate decided 61-32 to rely on the committee's report and not to question any witnesses directly. *(Vote 334, 1986 Weekly Report p. 2568)*

Goodman contended that this was a fatal mistake. He charged that the committee procedure violated Claiborne's constitutional rights and asserted that the judge was entitled to have the entire Senate hear the evidence against him.

After the conviction, Goodman said, "Harry Claiborne is no longer the fight. The fight is whether the Constitution is worth the paper it's written on." The Constitution, he said, "is a fragile document. Today it was bruised if not broken."

Goodman criticized senators — whom he declined to name — for not being informed about Claiborne's case. He said it appeared to him that many members had not touched the committee transcripts.

David Pryor, D-Ark., who voted to acquit Claiborne on all the articles, told reporters later that he believed Claiborne got a fair trial. However, Pryor, who served on the special committee, said senators had little time to master the facts and issues in the case.

"I truly feel time was running against Judge Claiborne," he said, but then added, "Under the circumstances, they gave him the best trial they knew how."

The Senate's decision to use the special committee was dictated in large part by the press of other business and the lateness of the session. The Republican and Democratic leadership concluded there was not enough time for the full Senate to hear all the testimony and felt they could not postpone the trial to a lame-duck session or until the next Congress.

Under the Constitution, Claiborne could be removed from office only through impeachment. While in jail, he continued to receive his $78,700 annual salary. That fact, coupled with the fact that a convicted felon was still on the bench, helped create a sense of urgency.

During the Oct. 7 debate on whether to hold a full trial, Rep. William J. Hughes, D-N.J., contended that the Senate had the right to try Claiborne the way it wanted to. He said delegating to the committee was "wise, prudent and constitutional."

"The only conduct that is relevant in these proceedings," Hughes concluded, "is the defendant's conduct."

The Senate deliberated in closed session for nearly three hours Oct. 8 on Goodman's motion for a full trial.

When the deliberations concluded, Majority Leader Robert Dole, R-Kan., told colleagues the Senate had to decide whether it wanted to get on with the trial and then he offered a motion barring any other witnesses.

After the 61-32 vote on Dole's motion, several senators who had voted against it expressed unhappiness.

"We weren't satisfied with just having a bunch of books handed to us," said J. James Exon, D-Neb.

Carl Levin, D-Mich., and Daniel J. Evans, R-Wash., said the chance to see and question witnesses was particularly important for Articles I and II, which specifically refer to Claiborne's state of mind.

Evans voted to acquit Claiborne on all the articles; Levin voted for acquittal on Articles I and II.

But Dale Bumpers, D-Ark., said the committee had compiled a good record. "When you look at what the witnesses said," Bumpers added, "it doesn't matter to me whether they were frowning or smiling."

Goodman's Motions

The request for a full Senate trial was only one of several motions presented by Goodman when the proceedings began Oct. 7.

After the arguments, the Senate went into closed session for several hours. (By precedent, Senate impeachment deliberations are private.)

Goodman asked the Senate to postpone the trial until procedural claims Claiborne had filed in the 9th U.S. Circuit Court of Appeals were decided. The Senate rejected that motion by voice vote.

He also asked the Senate to adopt a "guilty beyond a reasonable doubt" standard of proof for conviction.

Vice President George Bush, who was presiding, ruled that each senator could decide for himself what the standard should be.

Orrin G. Hatch, R-Utah, asked for a vote on Claiborne's motion; it failed 17-75. *(Vote 333, 1986 Weekly Report p. 2568)*

Goodman contended the "beyond a reasonable doubt" standard was appropriate for an impeachment trial, and he was convinced his client would have been acquitted had it been used.

He and Claiborne maintain that the judge did not intentionally or willfully under-report his taxes. They blame his tax preparers.

When Goodman and the House managers had completed their arguments Oct. 7, Claiborne made a dra-

matic address to the Senate. He said he wanted to speak to the members "primarily, I think, to let you see me."

Referring to the preceding arguments, Claiborne said, "I kind of feel like a piece of meat that is thrown out to a couple of dogs, jerked back and forth for possession ... between the House managers and my lawyers."

Claiborne again said he was innocent of wrongdoing. "I am not fighting for a judgeship. That may be forever gone," he said. "I am not fighting for my freedom because I have given up a large part of that.... What is involved is a sense of honesty and decency and what is involved is the independence of the American judiciary."

Vendetta Charges

Claiborne has contended since his indictment in 1983 that he was the victim of a vendetta by federal officials who wanted to force him off the bench. And some senators have expressed concern about the conduct of federal officials.

Pryor said he voted to acquit Claiborne "because of the long and abusive arm of the federal government."

Citing the FBI and the Internal Revenue Service, Pryor asserted that "without their involvement, without their targeting, without their harassment, I have great doubt that he would have been convicted in the first place."

Pryor said he would introduce a resolution calling for an investigation next year of FBI strike force activities.

Claiborne's trial was a departure from the usual order of Senate business in a number of ways. The "well," or front of the chamber, was set up to resemble a courtroom. On one side of the podium was a table for Claiborne and his lawyers. On the other side was a table for the nine House managers, or prosecutors, and their special counsel, Nicholas D. Chabraja.

Between the tables was a speaker's stand, where Goodman and the House managers made their arguments.

Normally there are only a few senators on the floor when legislation is pending, and they often visit with one another. The atmosphere is informal.

During the impeachment trial, however, there were between 40 and 50 senators on the floor and even more during the final deliberations.

The senators were unusually attentive and several took notes. "Everybody takes this assignment seriously," said Donald W. Riegle Jr., D-Mich. "I think we all feel an obligation to make an independent judgment." ∎

Reagan's Arguments Rebuffed by High Court

It will take more than the appointment of conservative Judge Antonin Scalia to win the Supreme Court over to President Reagan's point of view.

That much is clear after a 1985-86 term in which a fragmented but tenacious majority of the court consistently rebuffed the administration on virtually every social policy argument it raised.

Coupled with a similar record in the 1984-85 term, the court's chilly reception for Reagan's initiatives demonstrates that the 1983-84 term, in which the court seemed to turn sharply to the right, was an aberration, not the beginning of a new conservative era at the court. *(1984 CQ Almanac p. 3-A)*

Indeed, during the term that began Oct. 7, 1985, and ended July 7, 1986, the court emphatically reaffirmed two "liberal" tenets that the White House, with equal consistency, rejects.

First, the court declared — in decisions about jury selection, voting rights and affirmative action — that the nation must continue to work actively toward the goal of equality for all of its citizens.

Reagan espouses a "colorblind" society, but he argues that sufficient progress has been made toward that goal to permit an end to some of the more aggressive civil rights measures, such as affirmative action.

Second, the court continued to claim a major role for the federal courts in preserving and protecting individual rights.

Not only did the justices reaffirm a woman's right to have an abortion, but they also refused to curtail access to the courts or curb judges' power to order the losing side in a civil rights case to pay the legal fees of the winners.

This, too, ran directly counter to the Reagan administration's argument that judges should do less and elected officials more.

"This term witnessed the most significant defeats for the policy objectives of a chief executive in half a century," said Bruce Fein, an adjunct scholar at the American Enterprise Institute who has written extensively on the contemporary court.

"Not since the Supreme Court scuttled President Franklin D. Roosevelt's efforts to fashion a domestic New Deal program in a flurry of 1935 rulings has a president's policy agenda fared so poorly before the high court," he added.

Swapping One Vote for Another

The only two justices who consistently supported the administration's position were Chief Justice Warren E. Burger, who retired in September 1986, and Justice William H. Rehnquist, who was selected as his successor. Scalia, a conservative member of the U.S. Court of Appeals for the District of Columbia, was named to fill the seat Rehnquist vacated. *(See story, p. 72)*

Because Scalia's appointment simply replaced one conservative vote — Burger — with another, it was unlikely to have any immediate impact on the court's responsiveness to Reagan's social agenda.

What may be more significant for the new term is the movement of Reagan's first Supreme Court appointee, Justice Sandra Day O'Connor, away from the consistently conservative stands of Burger and Rehnquist, which she had generally supported in the past, toward a more centrist position on the court. That shift, which began in 1985, became more pronounced during the 1985-86 term. *(Box, this story)*

Reagan's Crusade

Despite major disappointments in the

Major Rulings of 1985-86 Court Term

Abortion. Reaffirmed a woman's right to have an abortion, by 5-4, compared with the original 7-2 ruling in 1973 *Roe v. Wade* decision.

Affirmative Action. Ruled that neither the Constitution nor Title VII of the 1964 Civil Rights Act prohibits the use of affirmative action plans to remedy discrimination in employment, even when those plans benefit blacks who were not personally victims of bias.

'Baby Doe' Rules. Struck down Reagan administration regulations designed to force hospitals to provide aggressive medical treatment to newborns with severe birth defects, regardless of parental wishes.

Capital Punishment. Held that opponents of the death penalty may be excluded from trial juries in capital cases, even if that increases the likelihood of conviction.

Gerrymandering. Decreed for the first time that partisan political gerrymanders are subject to constitutional challenge. But results of a single election are not enough to prove unconstitutional discrimination.

Gramm-Rudman. Struck down the key provision of the 1985 Gramm-Rudman-Hollings law, which was designed to balance the federal budget within five years.

Jury Selection. Ruled that prosecutors may not use peremptory challenges to keep blacks off juries, and held that anyone indicted by a grand jury selected in a racially discriminatory fashion was entitled to a new trial.

Libel Law. Made it easier for the press to win pretrial dismissal of libel suits involving public figures, and ruled that private individuals must prove that a challenged story was false before they can collect libel damages.

Sexual Harassment. Ruled that sexual harassment in the work place is sex discrimination prohibited by Title VII of the 1964 Civil Rights Act.

Sexual Privacy. Declared that the Constitution's implied right of privacy does not protect adult, consenting homosexuals from prosecution for sodomy, even when the conduct occurs in their own homes.

Voting Rights. Ruled that the occasional election of a black candidate from a particular election district does not immunize that district from challenges under the Voting Rights Act as amended in 1982.

1984-85 term, especially in its drive to lower the wall between church and state, the administration in summer 1985 intensified its campaign to swing the court to a more conservative stance. *(1985 Almanac p. 3-A)*

Attorney General Edwin Meese III criticized the court for opinions that were "on the whole, more policy choices than articulations of constitutional principle." He urged the court to abandon this "jurisprudence of idiosyncrasy" and adopt a jurisprudence of original intent, relying upon the views of the men who wrote the Constitution as the standard for interpretation. *(1985 Weekly Report p. 1463)*

As part of the administration's stepped-up crusade, Solicitor General Charles Fried filed briefs arguing that the court should overturn the 1973 *Roe v. Wade* ruling legalizing abortion and that it should proclaim most affirmative action plans unconstitutional. In the past, the administration had stopped short of asking the court to reverse itself on these issues.

The new, harder line did not play well at the court. First the justices denied Fried's request that he be permitted to make his arguments in person. Then it rejected the arguments.

As in previous terms, many of the administration's most controversial positions were outlined in advisory *amicus curiae* ("friend-of-the-court") briefs in cases in which the government was not directly involved.

The Reagan administration has filed a record number of these briefs. Almost half the briefs filed by the solicitor general this term fell in that category. But Fried said in March 1986 that "the really important part of the story is whether we got it right" — whether the court agreed with the points made in the government's briefs. *(1986 Weekly Report p. 616)*

Evaluating that record at the end of the term, Fried said he felt "pretty good" about the court's response.

Of the 39 *amicus* briefs filed in cases resolved on the merits by the court, only nine were clear losses.

Twenty-six were victories. In four cases, the outcome was in line with what the administration sought, but the court did not adopt the policy stance Fried had suggested.

Although Fried objects strenuously to any characterization of certain *amicus* cases as more important than others, it is difficult to overlook the fact that the administration's losses included major rulings on abortion, affirmative action, voting rights, attorneys' fees and racial bias in jury selection.

Fried lists as significant victories decisions upholding the disciplinary authority of school officials, curtailing inmate suits against prison officials, refusing to expand existing protection for suspects' rights, and recognizing First Amendment concerns in cable television franchise disputes.

A Divided Court

There was far more discord among the justices in the 1985-86 term than in the last several years. Two out of three cases in the 1983-84 and 1984-85 terms were decided with little or no dissent. But in the 1985-86 term, the level of agreement within the court dropped precipitously. Almost half of the 158 decisions came by margins of 6-3 and 5-4. The number of cases closely dividing the court jumped from 48 last term to 72 in 1985-86.

Justice Lewis F. Powell Jr., a centrist, once again played a critical role on a number of split decisions, voting with the majority on 28 of the 36 cases decided by 5-4 votes.

Among the cases in which he cast the decisive vote were those involving abortion, affirmative action and the Reagan administration's "Baby Doe" regulations, which required aggressive treatment of all newborns with birth defects, regardless of parental wishes. With Powell casting the fifth vote, the court invalidated those regulations, 5-3. Rehnquist did not take part in that decision.

Powell dissents less than any of his colleagues, but in the 1985-86 term, he dissented in almost twice as many cases as last term — 15 vs. eight.

While O'Connor's dissent rate dropped almost as low as his, that was offset by a dramatic increase in dissents by Justice Harry A. Blackmun, from 19 in the 1984-85 term to 41 in the 1985-86 term.

Fallout to Come

Some of the court's decisions in the 1986-87 term are certain to have major political reverberations.

Congress, for example, will be scrambling for months to deal with the July 7 decision striking down the key provisions of the Gramm-Rudman-Hollings budget-balancing law. *(1986 Weekly Report, p. 1559)*

And in a June 30 decision, *Davis v. Bandemer,* the justices opened the doors of federal courthouses around the country to suits challenging political gerrymanders — the rigging of electoral district lines to benefit one party. *(1986 Weekly Report p. 1523)*

First Amendment Issues

In contrast to 1985 when the administration lost arguments over silent prayer and aid to parochial schools, the court issued no major church-state decisions.

The cases it did resolve in this area involved narrower questions — whether a rabbi in the Air Force could wear his yarmulke in violation of uniform regulations (no), whether a blind ministry student could receive state vocational rehabilitation aid (yes), and whether an Indian family could claim a religious exemption from a requirement that they list their child's Social Security number on a food stamp application (no).

Other First Amendment rights, notably those of free press and free speech, were at stake in some important rulings in the 1985-86 term.

The news media won two major libel decisions. The court made it easier to win dismissal of such charges before trial, and more difficult for private figures to recover damages. *(1986 Weekly Report pp. 1515, 934)*

In addition, the justices reaffirmed the right of press and public to attend pretrial hearings in criminal cases. *(1986 Weekly Report p. 1526)*

On the last day of the term, the court upheld, 7-2, the power of school officials to discipline students for using vulgar language, and endorsed, 6-3, the use of public nuisance statutes to close an "adult" bookstore where prostitution and other lewd activities occurred.

Earlier in the term, the court had approved a city's use of its zoning power to keep "adult" theaters and bookstores out of residential neighborhoods. *(1986 Weekly Report p. 512)*

And in a different kind of free-speech case, the justices ruled that states could not require corporations to enclose messages with which they disagreed in bills to their customers. However, the court allowed governments to ban advertising for certain legal but "harmful" products and services — in this case, casino gambling in Puerto Rico. *(1986 Weekly Report pp. 512, 1526)*

Individual Rights

The court's decisions endorsing the continued use of affirmative action were not its last words on that issue. *(1986 Weekly Report pp. 1181, 1525)*

On July 7, the justices accepted two more affirmative action cases for review in the term that began Oct. 6.

One of them, *Johnson v. Transportation Agency, Santa Clara County, Calif.*, is the first test of alleged "reverse discrimination" based on sex, rather than race.

The other, *United States v. Paradise*, involves the court-ordered use of racial quotas for promotions.

On questions of personal privacy, the court struck down a Pennsylvania law regulating abortion but upheld a Georgia law making sodomy a crime. *(1986 Weekly Report pp. 1334, 1527)*

The justices rejected the administration's "Baby Doe" regulations, but accepted its view that the federal ban on discrimination against the handicapped did not apply to commercial airlines, even though they benefit from the federally funded air traffic control system. *(1986 Weekly Report pp. 1334, 1515)*

The court for the first time defined sexual harassment as unlawful sex discrimination, and the justices made it easier for blacks to win voting rights challenges against multi-member electoral districts and other practices that dilute their political influence. *(1986 Weekly Report pp. 1405, 1524)*

Crime and Punishment

A decade after reinstating capital punishment in the United States, the court was still facing a variety of questions about the death penalty.

In the most significant of its eight capital punishment cases this term, the court ruled 6-3 that opponents of the death penalty may be excluded from juries in capital cases, even if that increases the likelihood that the jury will convict the defendant. Virtually all of the 1,714 people on death row in May 1986 were convicted by such juries; the ruling was expected to expedite the pace of executions. *(1986 Weekly Report p. 1054)*

But on July 7, the court accepted for review in the 1986-87 term what may be the last major challenge to use of the death penalty. In *McCleskey v. Kemp*, a black man sentenced to die for killing a white police officer argues that someone who kills a white person is far more likely to receive the death penalty than someone who kills a black person.

Death row inmates won three of this term's capital cases. Among their victories were rulings that it is unconstitutional to execute someone who has lost the mental ability to understand what is happening and why, and that a defendant in a capital case, whose victim was of a different race, has a right to have prospective jurors asked about their racial biases. *(1986 Weekly Report pp. 972, 1516)*

In other decisions, the court made clear that racial bias has no place in the nation's courtrooms, holding that blacks may not be excluded from juries and guaranteeing a new trial for anyone indicted by a grand jury from which blacks had been shut out. *(1986 Weekly Report pp. 127, 972)* ∎

Rehnquist, Scalia Win Senate Confirmation

After five days of debate, the Senate Sept. 17, 1986, voted to confirm William Hubbs Rehnquist as the 16th chief justice of the United States and Antonin Scalia as an associate justice of the Supreme Court.

The vote to confirm Rehnquist was 65-33. Republicans Charles McC. Mathias Jr., R-Md., and Lowell P. Weicker Jr., R-Conn., joined 31 Democrats in opposing Rehnquist's elevation to chief justice. *(Vote 266, 1986 CQ Weekly Report p. 2240)*

Those who opposed Rehnquist's confirmation did so because of concern about his 15-year record on the high court, his views on minority and individual rights, and his candor in testifying to the Judiciary Committee. *(Box, this story)*

He had more votes cast against him than any other successful Supreme Court nominee in the twentieth century. Rehnquist also tied for the second-highest number of "nays" — the 26 cast against him when he was confirmed in December 1971.

In 1930, the Senate confirmed Charles Evans Hughes by 52-26. Hughes, who like Rehnquist previously had served as an associate justice, went on to become one of the nation's most respected chief justices. The Senate has refused to confirm a high court nominee five times since 1900.

Scalia, 50, since 1982 a judge on the U.S. Court of Appeals for the District of Columbia, was confirmed 98-0. He was the second justice to be put on the court by President Reagan, who appointed Sandra Day O'Connor in 1981. *(Vote 265, 1986 Weekly Report, p. 2240; 1981 CQ Almanac p. 409)*

In sharp contrast to the hours of floor debate over Rehnquist's nomination, there were only a few moments of speeches about the equally conservative Scalia before he was confirmed. Scalia became the 103rd person to serve on the Supreme Court and the first justice of Italian-American descent.

By coincidence, Rehnquist's confirmation came on the 79th birthday of the man he succeeded as chief justice, Warren Earl Burger. At White House ceremonies Sept. 26, Burger administered the oath of office to Scalia and Rehnquist, who celebrated his 62nd birthday on Oct. 1.

The Cloture Showdown

Hours before the confirmation roll call, the Senate voted 68-31 to invoke cloture and limit debate on the Rehnquist nomination. A minimum of 60 votes was needed. *(Vote 265, 1986 Weekly Report p. 2240)*

On that key vote, 16 Democrats joined 52 Republicans to approve the cloture petition filed by Senate Majority Leader Robert Dole, R-Kan. The only absentee was Jake Garn, R-Utah, recuperating from surgery to donate a kidney to his daughter.

Dole filed the cloture petition Sept. 15 after negotiations with those who opposed the Rehnquist nomination failed to produce an agreement on a time for a final vote.

The informal coalition of civil rights and civil liberties groups that had worked to block confirmation of Rehnquist knew that their effort was doomed when Edward M. Kennedy, D-Mass., a leading Rehnquist opponent, emerged dejected from an after-lunch caucus of Democratic senators. At that session, he had tried unsuccessfully to persuade Minority Leader

Robert C. Byrd, D-W.Va., to make the issue a partisan test. (Byrd later voted against confirming Rehnquist.)

Weicker announced his opposition Sept. 16, criticizing Rehnquist for "exercises in sophistry," and for an "unrelieved predisposition toward achieving a specific philosophical end while leaving reality unexplained or misspoken."

Mathias had voted for the Rehnquist nomination when the Judiciary Committee approved it 13-5 on Aug. 14. But he said Sept. 17 that he was voting against confirmation because of new evidence that had emerged regarding Rehnquist's failure to recuse himself from participating in the court's 1972 consideration of a challenge to the Army's domestic surveillance program. In that case, *Laird v. Tatum,* Rehnquist cast the deciding vote to dismiss the challenge, even though he had taken part as an assistant attorney general in discussions involving the program.

Senate Hearings

Rehnquist easily survived 13 hours of exhaustive cross-examination by the Senate Judiciary Committee July 29-Aug. 1. A trio of Democrats, Joseph R. Biden Jr., Del., Edward M.

Chief Justice William H. Rehnquist, left, and his replacement as an associate justice of the Supreme Court, Antonin Scalia, were sworn in Sept. 26, 1986.

Bias Charges Aired at Rehnquist Hearings

During Senate hearings on his nomination as chief justice, William H. Rehnquist defended himself against allegations that he had harassed voters, knowingly accepted anti-semitic restrictions on his property, lacked sympathy to civil rights and was in uncertain health.

The voter harassment charges first surfaced in 1971 at the end of Rehnquist's confirmation hearings as associate justice. He was asked at that time to respond in writing to allegations that he had intimidated or challenged Phoenix voters. In response, he wrote James O. Eastland, D-Miss. (1943-78), then Judiciary chairman, that "in none of these years [1958-68] did I personally engage in challenging the qualifications of any voters."

Rehnquist repeated his assertions in July and August 1986 when Democratic senators Edward M. Kennedy, Mass., and Howard M. Metzenbaum, Ohio, questioned him about new allegations made by 10 persons who said they witnessed harassment. Rehnquist repeatedly denied the charges and told Kennedy the witnesses were wrong. "I think they're mistaken. I just can't offer any other explanation," he said.

On Aug. 1, the committee heard from five witness who seemed to contradict Rehnquist's testimony and one who backed it up. One of the five, James J. Brosnahan, an assistant U.S. attorney in Phoenix in 1962, said he was with FBI agents who were called to one polling station after voters complained they had been intimidated.

Brosnahan said Rehnquist was there and some voters accused him of challenging their right to vote. Brosnahan told the committee Rehnquist did not deny being a vote "challenger." However, Brosnahan added, he did not actually see Rehnquist challenge anyone's credentials.

Later William Turner said he was with Rehnquist on Election Day in 1962 and that "At no time in our presence did Bill Rehnquist assume the role of challenger."

Charges of Racial Bias

Democrats questioned Rehnquist on his civil rights views, particularly those he held as a young man working as a law clerk for then-justice Robert H. Jackson.

Joseph R. Biden Jr., Del., grilled him about a memo he had written to Jackson when the Supreme Court was first considering the landmark 1954 *Brown v. Board of Education* decision, which held that official segregation of schools was unconstitutional.

In the memo, Rehnquist argued that it was permissible to have separate but equal facilities for blacks and whites. That doctrine had been upheld in an 1890 case, *Plessy v. Ferguson*.

Rehnquist said in 1971 that the memo represented Justice Jackson's views, not his own, but Metzenbaum challenged that and Biden demanded to know how Rehnquist felt about both the *Plessy* decision and what conclusion he came to when the *Brown* case was being decided.

Rehnquist said he believed the *Plessy* decision was wrong and that "it was not a good interpretation of the equal protection clause to say that when you segregate people by race there's no denial of equal protection." He told Biden he had never completely decided what the court should do on *Brown*. "I had ideas on both sides. I don't think I truly decided in my own mind," he said.

When Biden pressed him, Rehnquist said, "Senator, I don't think I reached a conclusion. Law clerks don't have to vote." "No," Biden retorted, "but they surely think."

When Paul Laxalt, R-Nev., told Rehnquist there was concern among women and blacks about his civil rights views, Rehnquist conceded that some of his opinions resulted in "less favorable rulings for women and blacks than would a broader reading of the equal protection [clause of the Constitution]." But Rehnquist insisted he treats all parties equally: "It is the same with respect to corporations," he said. "I give the best interpretation I know how."

"Are women going to be prejudiced by your being chief justice?" Laxalt then asked. "I don't believe so, Senator," Rehnquist replied.

Restrictive Covenants

Patrick J. Leahy, D-Vt., asked Rehnquist July 30 about a property deed to a Vermont home that contained the covenant barring sales to Jews. Rehnquist said he had not known of the covenant until the FBI uncovered it in a routine screening investigation. He said he could not recall reading the deed.

Rehnquist added that the language was meaningless because it could not be enforced in a court, but he added that he considered the language "obnoxious." At first Rehnquist said he saw no point in having the clause removed, but after Leahy raised the issue of appearances, Rehnquist said he would take steps to remove it.

A day later, Kennedy told Rehnquist that records showed a home he had owned in Phoenix included a covenant barring sales to non-whites. Rehnquist, who no longer owns that property, said he did not know of that restrictive language either.

Orrin G. Hatch, R-Utah, criticized the Democrats for "blowing this out of proportion," adding it was "ridiculous to make a big brouhaha" over the unenforceable covenants.

The Health Issue

Senators avoided all but the most general questions about Rehnquist's health. However, the evening of July 31, Chairman Strom Thurmond, R-S.C., announced that the committee had appointed an independent physician to review Rehnquist's medical records and interview the justice's doctors, if necessary. It was not clear whether the independent doctor's findings would be made public.

Concern about Rehnquist's health stemmed from chronic, low-back problems that required hospitalization in January 1982 because of an adverse reaction to a drug prescribed for pain.

In response to questions from Howell Heflin, D-Ala., Rehnquist said he "certainly would not have accepted the nomination" as chief justice if he did not believe he was in good health.

Kennedy, Mass., and Howard M. Metzenbaum, Ohio, grilled Rehnquist about his views on civil rights; allegations that he harassed Phoenix, Ariz., voters in the 1960s; and the fact that two of his homes included restrictive covenants, or property agreements, barring sales to non-whites and people of "the Hebrew race."

Rehnquist steadfastly denied that he was biased against minorities or that he had engaged in voter intimidation while he was a lawyer in Phoenix. He said he had not known his deeds contained restrictive covenants, and noted they were unenforceable.

But on Aug. 1, five other witnesses contradicted his assertions that he had not harassed voters. And at the end of the day it was clear the mens' testimony had reinforced Democrats' concerns over the nomination.

Throughout his many hours in the witness chair July 30-31, Rehnquist seemed unflappable, thoughtful, easygoing and, on occasion, firm in his refusal to answer questions he deemed inappropriate for a sitting justice.

When asked to explain some of his court opinions, Rehnquist said he believed he was being "called to account" for a judicial act and he declined to answer.

After Rehnquist was excused by the committee, Democrats tangled with Justice Department officials who refused to turn over memos Rehnquist wrote while he was a top department official during the administration of President Richard Nixon.

Rehnquist said he had no objection to releasing the memos, but department officials claimed executive privilege and refused to provide the documents, which deal with civil rights, civil liberties, wiretapping and surveillance of radical groups.

Rehnquist was nominated June 17 by President Reagan, after Burger announced he was retiring. Unlike most judicial nominees, Rehnquist was a known quantity to the Judiciary Committee. Senators had the nominee's 1971 confirmation hearings to study and 15 years of opinions Rehnquist had written — many in dissent — as an associate justice.

Rehnquist has been considered the court's leading conservative. His opinions reflect a literal approach to individual rights. For example, he finds no specific right of privacy in the Constitution and he has consistently dissented from the court's rulings protecting a women's privacy-based right to have an abortion.

In announcing his his opposition to Rehnquist July 29, Kennedy asserted that the nominee "is too extreme on race, too extreme on women's rights, too extreme on freedom of speech, too extreme on separation of church and state to be chief justice."

Responding to the criticisms, Rehnquist made these points during the hearings:

● He said he did not believe a chief justice, by himself, could sway the tenor of a court. Rehnquist said that no chief justice "could pull the wool over [colleagues'] eyes and make them think that green is blue." He said a chief justice can exert influence by trying to make the court work smoothly. "The chief does have a leadership role, but I don't think it has much to do with the philosophical bent of the court."

● Rehnquist said he believed it was important for the court to speak clearly with one voice whenever possible. When there are several opinions, he said, "it tends to muddy the message." He added that he would try to restrain himself from writing a separate opinion simply because he had not liked the way a colleague phrased the decision.

● He said he believed he should be judged on whether he had "fairly construed the Constitution in my 15 years on the court."

Scalia Avoids Controversy

Although Scalia had a shorter judicial record than Rehnquist, senators nonetheless had a body of appeals court decisions and public speeches from which to assess his views on basic issues, particularly his belief in a restrictive role of the courts.

Scalia, whose nine children all attended the hearing, is known for his sense of humor and affable personality. He displayed flashes of wit during his day-long questioning by senators, and his appearance had none of the confrontational tone that characterized much of the Rehnquist hearing.

On several subjects, Scalia declined to answer questions, saying they involved issues before his court

or that he would surely confront them once on the high court. This included subjects such as abortion and the Freedom of Information Act.

For example, Kennedy asked Scalia if he would vote to overrule the landmark *Roe v. Wade* decision, which made abortion legal. "It is not proper for me to answer," Scalia said, adding he would be "in a very bad position to adjudicate the case without being accused of having a less than impartial view."

When Kennedy pressed him, Scalia said: "I assure you I have no agenda with a list of things I want to do. My only agenda is to be a good judge and decide the cases that are brought before me according to the law as I can best figure it out."

Later, in response to abortion questions, Scalia said he would remove himself from a case if he believed he could not make "an impartial judgment of the Constitution." He added that he did not believe "reasonable people think the moral views [of

---

> *The nominee "is too extreme on race, too extreme on women's rights, too extreme on freedom of speech, too extreme on separation of church and state to be chief justice."*
>
> —Sen. Edward M. Kennedy, D-Mass.

---

judges] so automatically becloud their judgments that they must disqualify themselves."

The nominee's reluctance to give specific answers irritated some senators, particularly Democrats Howell Heflin, Ala., and Dennis DeConcini, Ariz., who said Scalia was being more cautious than necessary.

And at one point, Biden, somewhat frustrated, said, "Let yourself go. It's pretty boring so far."

Scalia also addressed these issues:

● On the Constitution: "I cannot say I have a fully formed omnibus view of the Constitution.... The Constitution is obviously not meant to be evolvable so easily.... It is intended as insulation against the current trend."

● Scalia said he supported the 1966 *Miranda v. Arizona* ruling, which requires police to warn arrested suspects of their rights to remain silent and to have a lawyer present at any interrogation. "I think — as far as I know, everybody thinks — it's a good idea to warn a suspect of his rights."

● On affirmative action, Scalia said,

In contrast to Rehnquist, Judge Scalia had an easy time with the Senate Judiciary Committee. At one point, Sen. Joseph R. Biden Jr., D-Del., above, joked: "It's pretty boring so far."

"When you favor one person because of his race, you're automatically disfavoring another because of his race." Later he went on to say, "There should be no doubt about my commitment to a society without discrimination."

● On the death penalty, Scalia said he had not thought about how much due process should be available to a prisoner on death row appealing his sentence. He said he was certain such decisions were "a hard call," adding, "I don't look forward to that as the most enjoyable part of the job."

● Concerning the importance of committee reports in understanding legislation, Scalia said, "Congress does not act in committee reports. Congress can only act by passing a law."

At one point in an exchange with DeConcini about the role of Congress in lawmaking, Scalia said, "You write it. I'll enforce it."

For and Against

When Scalia finished testifying, nearly three dozen witnesses presented testimony. Prominent lawyers and academics as well as conservative groups such as Concerned Women for America and United Families of America lavished praise on his nomination, while several civil rights groups were highly critical.

Among the strong Scalia supporters were Carla Hills, former secretary of housing and urban development under President Gerald R. Ford; Erwin Griswold, a former solicitor general of the United States; Lloyd Cutler, a well-known Washington, D.C., lawyer who served in President Jimmy Carter's White House; Gerhard Casper, dean of the University of Chicago law school; and Paul Verkuil, dean of the College of William & Mary in Williamsburg, Va.

All praised Scalia's skills and said he would make an excellent addition to the Supreme Court. In response to questions about Scalia's conservative views, Verkuil said he did not believe Scalia was an extremist. "Judge Scalia practices judicial restraint," he said.

But a different picture was painted by Audrey Feinberg, a lawyer who helps monitor the Supreme Court for the Nation Institute, a New York civil rights research foundation.

Feinberg asserted that Scalia's opinions show "a record that is far removed from mainstream judicial thought. During his few years on the bench, Judge Scalia's rulings have repeatedly espoused extreme views far to the right of even traditional legal thought." ∎

Reagan Woos Conservatives With New Court

Time was running out when President Reagan finally got his chance to reshape the Supreme Court into the conservative bench he wishes to bequeath to the nation when he leaves the White House.

Despite predictions dating back to Reagan's first year of office that the advanced age of several sitting justices virtually assured him several Supreme Court appointments, it was not until six years into his presidency that Reagan got the opportunity to place his second justice on the bench, thereby giving the court's conservative wing what could be a decisive force in split decisions.

On balance, the administration's effort to advance its conservative social agenda in the Supreme Court that was presided over by Chief Justice Warren E. Burger until his retirement in September 1986 has been far from a sterling success. In the past two years, the court has rebuffed the Reagan administration's call for change on several key social issues, including school prayer, affirmative action and abortion.

The role of Sandra Day O'Connor, Reagan's first appointment to the high court, during this period illustrates the riskiness of predicting a justice's voting pattern once the justice is elevated to the high court. Tapped by Reagan in 1981, O'Connor brought to the court's conservative wing an articulate conservative voice that was in harmony with the administration's ideology, but her addition alone was not enough to put the court's conservatives in control. Moreover, in recent years O'Connor has turned in an increasingly independent voting record, siding on occasion with the liberal wing of the court that handed the administration defeats on such high-profile issues as prayer in school and affirmative action.

With Burger's announcement in June 1986 that he would retire, Reagan was given a crucial opportunity to further rearrange the court's membership. This opportunity was a dual one because Reagan could both designate a new chief justice, thus securing the special powers of that office in chosen hands, as well as bring a brand new vote onto the court.

For chief justice, Reagan selected William H. Rehnquist, a staunch conservative who was appointed almost 15 years ago by President Nixon. After a noisy but probably foredoomed effort by Senate Democrats to discredit Rehnquist's commitment to civil rights, he was confirmed as expected by the Republican-controlled Senate Sept. 17. As the court's newest justice, Reagan chose Antonin Scalia, a conservative federal appeals court judge with a reputation for an awesome legal intellect and a talent for consensus-building. Scalia's nomination sailed through Senate confirmation Sept. 17.

On the opening of the new court's first term, which began Oct. 6, the question of how Rehnquist's elevation and Scalia's arrival will affect the court's collective view of the Constitution loomed at least as large in the minds of observers as the big lineup of cases on its docket, which includes challenges to Reagan's use of the pocket veto, to state laws requiring "closed" primary elections and to affirmative action plans.

Because of the strong similarity in the views of Rehnquist, Burger and Scalia, a sudden shift in the court's stance on key issues appeared unlikely. But personal chemistry among the justices would be a significant factor, especially on a court that in recent years has been closely divided in many of its opinions.

In the Rehnquist court, as in the Burger court, much will depend on the art of persuasion among the justices, as the court's conservative and liberal wings try to woo crucial swing votes on key issues, notably those of Justices Byron R. White, Lewis F. Powell Jr. and O'Connor. In the past, Rehnquist has not been notably successful in winning support for his position, dissenting alone more than other justices.

Scalia, on the other hand, already has the reputation for being an artful persuader, which suggests that he will be an asset to the court's conservative wing from the outset. Both men are considered personable and get along well with their colleagues.

Thus, while conservative domination of the high court is by no means assured, it is, perhaps, within grasp for the first time in half a century. If Rehnquist and Scalia become an effec-

Chief Justice William H. Rehnquist, center. From the left: Justices Sandra Day O'Connor, Lewis F. Powell Jr., Thurgood Marshall, William J. Brennan Jr., Rehnquist, Byron R. White, Harry A. Blackmun, John Paul Stevens and Antonin Scalia.

tive team, they could build a conservative coalition that could dominate the court, speculates University of Virginia law Professor A. E. Dick Howard, a close observer of the court. At the very least, the pressure of debate is likely to rise on the Rehnquist court. "The tempo of the debate will pick up this term," Howard predicted, "intensifying the pressure on [the] justices in the middle to choose sides."

Rehnquist: Tough Opinions

In selecting a chief justice to lead his conservative campaign inside the conference room of the Supreme Court, Reagan chose a known quantity in Rehnquist. In almost 15 years on the court, he voiced his views on hundreds of issues. Most of the time they coincided with Reagan's own belief in a limited judicial role and a literal approach to the Constitution.

Federal judges, Reagan argues, should not be policy makers. That is the job of elected officials in the executive and legislative branches. Judges should simply tell these lawmakers when they overstep their proper roles. Reagan views the Constitution as the source of government's power — and of limits on those powers. Because he asserts a belief in limited government, he tends to read the Constitution's restrictive provisions literally — and wants judges he appoints to do the same.

In his opinions, Rehnquist, who turned 62 Oct. 1, 1986, has consistently argued for a posture of judicial restraint. He argues that the Supreme Court should be the brakes, not the accelerator on the engine of government. The courts are simply there to halt trends that violate the Constitution.

A native of Wisconsin with degrees from Stanford and Harvard universities, Rehnquist became the youngest justice on the court when he was picked by Nixon in 1971. Previously, Rehnquist had served for two-and-a-half years as assistant attorney general in charge of the office of legal counsel under Attorney General John N. Mitchell.

On the court, Rehnquist quickly staked out his position as its most extreme justice. He has, notes John P. Frank, another close observer of the court who writes frequently on the subject, "an amazingly integrated view of the universe to which all issues relate." In one of Rehnquist's first decisions, he criticized the majority's view that there were certain "fundamental

personal rights" protected — even if not mentioned — by the Constitution. That position is the basis of his consistent objection to rulings denying states the power to ban or regulate abortions.

Protesting the court's 1972 decision in *Weber v. Aetna Casualty & Surety Co.* (1972), to strike down existing capital punishment laws on a variety of constitutional grounds, Rehnquist emphasized his belief that over the long run, it is more important for the court to defer to the other branches of the government than to vindicate the rights of particular individuals. It is a mistake for judges to strike down a law in order to protect the rights of an individual, he wrote, because the result "is . . . to impose upon the nation the judicial fiat of a majority of a court of judges whose connection with the popular will is remote at best."

In the years that followed, Rehnquist has consistently sounded these themes, often in dissent. He has dissented by himself 47 times — more than any other sitting justice. Eleven of those lone dissents have been in criminal cases, 12 in cases applying the equal protection guarantee to laws challenged as discriminating against aliens, women or illegitimate children, and 10 in First Amendment cases (*Furman v. Georgia*, 1972).

Rehnquist alone among his colleagues is completely at ease with the Reagan administration's argument that the original intent of the men who wrote the Constitution and the Bill of Rights is the proper standard for applying that document.

When the court in 1985 struck down a law instituting the observation of a moment of silence in public schools as an abridgment of the First Amendment guarantee of separation of church and state, he dissented.

"It is impossible to build sound constitutional doctrine upon a mistaken understanding of constitutional history," he argued, criticizing as a "misleading metaphor" Thomas Jefferson's often-quoted statement that the First Amendment built "a wall of separation between church and State" (*Wallace v. Jaffree*).

Arguing for the moment of silence and against complete separation, Rehnquist contended that the majority held an erroneous view of the Establishment Clause. That clause, he said, was intended simply to prevent Congress from establishing a national religion, citing as his authority James

Madison's remarks on the House floor in 1789, when Congress was considering whether to approve the First Amendment. "Congress should not establish a religion and enforce the legal observation of it by law, nor compel men to worship God in any manner contrary to their conscience," Madison said.

In comparison with Burger, Rehnquist's views on legal issues are similar. The two agreed on at least three out of four cases every term, and in recent terms almost nine of 10 cases.

In style, however, Rehnquist and Burger are very different personalities, and that difference is expected to result in an immediate change in the atmosphere of the court. Burger is a rather formal man, while Rehnquist is informal in his dress, his manner and his general approach. In a characteristic contrast, Burger adamantly opposed televising public sessions of the court, while Rehnquist has said he would be open to the idea. Burger had many difficulties in his relationships on the court. Bruce Fein, an adjunct scholar at the American Enterprise Institute of Public Policy Research (AEI), described Burger as a "porcupine" at a July 1986 AEI seminar. Rehnquist, however, is universally liked by his colleagues.

"The court will surely be a more congenial place," under Rehnquist, comments Howard. "On balance, it will be a friendlier place, more like the days of Earl Warren [chief justice 1953-69], and that may take some edge off the ideological passions" that Rehnquist's promotion is certain to generate.

Rehnquist probably will view the administrative aspects of his new job as less absorbing than did Burger, who devoted a great deal of time and energy to issues of judicial efficiency and reform, arguing frequently that the court was overworked and needed relief.

Although Rehnquist has generally supported the idea that Congress might create a new judicial panel to assist the Supreme Court with some of its work, he does not share the view that it is overworked. His own regular office hours are from 9 a.m. to 3 p.m.

Scalia: Independent Voice

Even before his selection in June, attention began focusing on Scalia as a prime candidate for a Reagan nomination to the Supreme Court.

In March 1985, *The American*

Lawyer profiled him as a "live wire" newcomer on the U.S. Circuit Court of Appeals for the District of Columbia, one of the busiest and for years most liberal appeals courts in the country. Burger was a member of that court when he was named chief justice.

Scalia, 50, is the first Supreme Court justice of Italian-American ancestry. He was born in Trenton, N.J., grew up in Queens, N.Y., and is a Roman Catholic with nine children. A graduate of Georgetown University and Harvard Law School, he has practiced law in Cleveland, taught at the University of Virginia and University of Chicago law schools, and held several legal posts within the Nixon and Ford administrations, including that of head of the office of legal counsel from 1974-76, the job Rehnquist held from 1969-71.

In his writings on and off the bench, Scalia seems as congenial to the views of the Reagan administration as Rehnquist does. A key issue on which Scalia's personal views are in harmony with those of the Reagan administration is affirmative action, the notion that racial preferences may be used to temporarily favor members of a group that has previously suffered discrimination. Scalia and Reagan both view this as impermissible "reverse discrimination."

In other areas that are prominent on the Reagan social agenda, Scalia's religion and family background seem to justify the assumption that he opposes abortion and favors school prayer, though he has never made public his views on these issues.

Like Rehnquist, Scalia closely scrutinizes claims of constitutional rights and generally declines to expand their scope. When an activist group challenged administration regulations barring sleeping in Lafayette Park across from the White House, (*Clark v. Community for Creative Non-Violence*, 1984) arguing that sleeping should be protected as part of their First Amendment freedom of expression, Scalia flatly rejected the idea that "sleeping is or ever can be speech for First Amendment purposes."

Also like Rehnquist, Scalia argues for judicial restraint, contending that it is not the job of judges to create new rights or to expand existing ones. At the same time, however, Scalia has agreed with critics of judicial restraint that its advocates sometimes are more interested in results than in the principle.

There may come a moment of truth, he has noted, when conservative critics of the courts have to decide "whether they really believe ... that the courts are doing too much, or whether they are actually nursing only the less principled grievance that the courts have not been doing what they want."

Scalia, like Reagan, takes a strict view of the separation of powers, opposing experiments like the legislative veto that threaten the traditional separation of powers. He was, for example, one of the three judges voting in February 1986 to strike down a key provision of the Gramm-Rudman-Hollings Deficit Reduction Act as unconstitutional, a ruling upheld in July by the Supreme Court (*Bowsher v. Synar*, 1986).

Scalia's advocacy of free-market principles gives him the distinction of being the first modern economic conservative to sit on the Supreme Court. He believes that "the free market ... has historically been the cradle of broad political freedom, and in modern times the demise of economic freedom has been the grave of political freedom as well."

However he votes, Scalia — a man of considerable personal charm and energy — is unlikely to vote alone. In four years on the appeals court, he demonstrated his ability to build a consensus, quite an achievement on a court well-known for antagonistic relationships among its members.

Reagan's Court Campaign

Reagan's hope for a conservative court is integral to his plan to lighten the hand of government in the lives of American citizens.

"It is no coincidence," he said in his first inaugural address, "that our present troubles parallel and are proportionate [to] the intervention and intrusion in our lives that have resulted from unnecessary and excessive growth of government."

From the beginning, the Reagan administration has argued that the Supreme Court should reconsider — and redirect — national policy on issues ranging from antitrust and abortion to questions of criminal law and the relationship between church and state.

These arguments had a common theme: they urged the court to relax the grip of government on individual decisions — those of businessmen, educators, employers and administrators. Only a few of these arguments have met a warm reception at the court, however, giving Rehnquist ample opportunity to dissent. Even some instances in which the administration appeared to prevail during Reagan's first term were subsequently turned into defeats when later cases were decided the other way during his second term.

Issues on which the the administration prevailed include its arguments in favor of permitting more public use of religious symbols, curtailing certain affirmative action plans and approving some exceptions to a controversial rule barring the use of illegally obtained evidence in criminal trials (*Lynch v. Donnelly*, 1984; *Firefighters Local Union #1784 v. Stotts*, 1984; *United States v. Leon*, 1984; *New York v. Quarles*, 1984).

Issues in which the court rebuffed the administration include its arguments in favor of granting tax-exempt status to private schools that discriminate against black students, of giving states more leeway to regulate abortions and of permitting regulatory agencies to rescind health and safety regulations (*Bob Jones University v. U.S.*, 1983; *Akron v. Akron Center for Reproductive Health*, 1983; *Motor Vehicle Manufacturers Association v. State Farm Mutual Automobile Insurance Co.*, 1983).

Two administration defeats — on abortion and school prayer — came in high-profile cases in which it pressed the court most aggressively. Such arguments seem to have had a particularly adverse effect on the key justices in the court's center. Both Powell and O'Connor voted against the administration on a 1985 school prayer case (*Thornburgh v. American College of Obstetricians and Gynecologists*, 1986; *Wallace v. Jaffree*, 1985).

Debate over Original Intent

During the summer of 1985, in an unusually heated clash between the court and the executive branch the administration went public with its challenge to the court's reading of the Constitution. Attorney General Edwin Meese III delivered two scathing attacks, characterizing the court's decisions as "a jurisprudence of idiosyncracy" and urging its return to a more principled "jurisprudence of original intention."

"The original meaning of constitutional provisions and statutes" is "the only reliable guide for judgment," Meese declared. "Those who framed the Constitution chose their words carefully; they debated at great length the most minute points. The language they chose meant something. It is incumbent upon the court to determine what that meaning was."

A few months later, Justice William J. Brennan Jr. — the most senior and most liberal justice — responded. "We current Justices read the Constitution in the only way we can: as 20th-century Americans," he said. "The genius of the Constitution rests not in any static meaning it might have had in a world that is dead and gone, but in the adaptability of its great principles to cope with current problems and current needs. What the constitutional fundamentals meant to the wisdom of other times cannot be their measure to the vision of our time."

If there were any doubt that the Reagan social agenda faced dim prospects in the Burger court, that uncertainty probably was dispelled last term, when the court handed down some stinging rebuffs to the administration.

On issues ranging from abortion to voting rights, the court underscored its continuing commitment to two liberal tenets that are anathema to the current occupants of the White House.

First, the court made clear that the government must continue to work actively to realize the goal of equality for all of its citizens. The administration has repeatedly declared that the nation has made enough progress toward a colorblind society and can abandon such remedial strategies as busing, racial quotas and hiring goals. In cases involving affirmative action, voting rights and jury selection, the court flatly refused to adopt that view (*Wygant v. Jackson Board of Education*, 1986; *Thornburgh v. Gingles*, 1986; *Batson v. Kentucky*, 1986).

Second, the court upheld a continuing major role for federal courts in protecting and preserving individual rights. This was dramatically illustrated in decisions striking down federal regulations requiring hospitals to aggressively treat severely handicapped newborns, even over parental objections, and, in another case, reaffirming its view that government has little or no business interfering in a woman's right to have an abortion (*Brown v. American Hospital Association; Thornburgh v. American College of Obstetricians and Gynecologists*).

"There is "a certain private sphere of individual liberty" that should "be kept largely beyond the reach of government," the court declared. The administration had urged the court to uphold the so-called "Baby Doe" regulations involving handicapped infants, and reverse itself to permit states free rein to regulate or ban abortions. Justices Rehnquist and O'Connor took the government's side in both cases.

First Tests

In its busy first term, the Rehnquist court will address constitutional and statutory issues ranging from affirmative action to freedom of speech, from church and state to separation of powers. Speculating on the character of the new court, Howard of the University of Virginia said he expects a "sharpening of ideological divisions." He sees the court as becoming more divided into liberal and conservative camps with an end to the splintering and fragmentation that characterized the Burger court's response to many difficult issues it confronted.

Bruce Fein of AEI agreed. During the Burger era the court was "philosophically at sea," he said, but now the court will have at least two conservative members who will work to build a "philosophically consistent theme of jurisprudence."

One of the most significant in-house powers Rehnquist will assume as chief justice is the power to assign the task of writing the court's opinion in a case. Having heard each justice state his or her views in conference, the chief justice can influence the shape of the precedent by selecting who will write the opinion, knowing already whether that justice views the ruling as narrow or expansive. However, the chief justice retains the power of assignment only if he is part of the majority. It is illustrative of the ideological divisions Howard foresees that on this court that power — when Rehnquist is in dissent — will pass to veteran justice Brennan, to the court's most systematic and outspoken liberal.

Scalia-Rehnquist a Team?

If Rehnquist and Scalia become an effective team, Reagan's campaign for a conservative court will finally move from the courtroom to the conference room, where the justices argue the merits of cases and state their opinions. But the conservative campaign will succeed only if his appointees agree with each other — and can persuade at least some of the more moderate members of the court to go along.

There are certain traditions that could facilitate the development of this team — and would certainly enhance its effectiveness. As chief justice, Rehnquist speaks first on each case in conference. As the most junior justice, Scalia votes first on each case. By thus bracketing the court's discussion, these two justices could have an impact far beyond their own two votes.

Frank described as "vast" the power that a chief justice can wield as a result of setting the agenda and opening the discussion in conference. "Frequently the person who sets the agenda controls the meeting," Frank said. "The chief will be able to focus on the questions he wants to talk about; anyone who wants to talk about something else will have to disrupt that pattern."

Rehnquist and Scalia are the court's most committed conservatives. Brennan and Thurgood Marshall are equally consistent liberals. The balance of power on close questions is held by the remaining justices: O'Connor, White and Powell, who tend to — but don't always — take the conservative view of matters, and Harry A. Blackmun and John Paul Stevens, who tend to take the liberal view.

Howard predicts that the tempo of the debate will pick up, increasing the pressure on the justices in the middle to choose sides. "The argument on the conservative side will be more carefully worked out," he said, referring to Scalia's powerful legal intellect. "That will have a polarizing effect, attracting or repelling these other justices."

O'Connor's Next Move

The impact of that polarizing effect on O'Connor is significant and unpredictable. Rehnquist's promotion and Scalia's arrival come just as O'Connor seems to be shifting away from her steady alliance with Rehnquist toward a more centrist role on the court.

After four years of consistently voting with Burger and Rehnquist, O'Connor in 1986 made clear that she did not always agree with them. Such independence had been foreshadowed in June 1985, in *Wallace v. Jaffree*, when she, with Powell, refused to go along with the administration's approval of the public school moment of silence law.

The intensification of conservative arguments could drive O'Connor into a more frequent alliance with the liberals, Howard speculates, particularly on questions of religious freedom and sex discrimination, another issue on which she has consistently taken a more liberal stance than Rehnquist.

Although both have dissented from the court's recent rulings striking down state and local efforts to regulate abortion, O'Connor's stance on that issue differs from Rehnquist's. He is ready to overturn *Roe v. Wade* — the landmark 1973 decision that legalized abortion — and return control over this matter to the states, as the administration has urged. But O'Connor does not go so far, advocating instead that states be given more leeway to regulate abortion as long as they do not "unduly burden" a woman's choice to terminate a pregnancy (*Thornburgh v. American College of Obstetricians and Gynecologists*).

O'Connor went out of her way in May, when the court held a particular affirmative action plan unconstitutional, to point out that the majority agreed that some such plans were in-deed permissible to remedy job bias. And she split with Rehnquist to join the majority in two libel rulings, each of which were hailed as major victories for the press. (*Wygant v. Jackson Board of Education; Liberty Lobby v. Anderson; Hepps v. Philadelphia Newspapers Inc.*).

Powell to Swing Conservative?

O'Connor's move toward the center has aligned her with Powell, who throughout nearly 15 years on the court, has maintained just enough independence from a conservative label to wield considerable power when the court is divided closely on an issue.

No better example of his pivotal vote can be found than the court's much discussed sodomy ruling in June 1986. By a 5-4 vote — with Powell and O'Connor in the majority — the court upheld a state law criminalizing sodomy (*Bowers v. Hardwick*).

Soon after the ruling, *The Washington Post* reported that Powell had been the key vote — that he had first voted to strike the law down and then had changed his vote to uphold it. Powell acknowledged that this was the case, emphasizing that the man bringing the case had not in fact been prosecuted. Powell made clear in his concurring opinion that he would not vote to uphold such laws if they were used to justify severe punishment for such activity.

If Scalia can use his considerable talents of intellectual and personal persuasion to swing Powell and O'Connor firmly into the conservative wing of the court, only one more vote would be needed to secure conservative dominance in decision-making on a variety of issues.

Observers think such a swing could happen, particularly if Rehnquist and Scalia forge a good working relationship.

Fein said he thinks they will work "splendidly together," noting that both are congenial, unpretentious men who enjoy good rapport with their colleagues.

"It could be quite a team," said Howard, "with one assigning the opinions, and the other employing as powerful a mind as the court will have. ∎

Biographies of Supreme Court Justices

The following are biographical sketches of each of the justices who currently serve on the Supreme Court.

William Hubbs Rehnquist

Reagan's appointment of William H. Rehnquist as chief justice clearly indicated that the president was hoping to shift the court to the right. Since his early years as an associate justice in the 1970s Rehnquist has been the court's most conservative justice. An ardent advocate of judicial restraint, he feels that the court should simply call a halt to unconstitutional policies — and stop at that. Innovation in public policy, he believes, is the prerogative of elected officials, not appointed judges.

Rehnquist, the fourth associate justice to become chief, is the only justice completely comfortable with the argument that the original intent of the framers of the Constitution and the Bill of Rights is the proper standard

for interpreting those documents today. He also takes a literal approach to individual rights. These beliefs have led him to dissent from the court's rulings protecting a woman's privacy-based right to abortion, to argue that there is no constitutional barrier to school prayer, and to side with police and prosecutors on questions of criminal law.

Born in Milwaukee, Wis., Oct. 1, 1924, Rehnquist went west to college. At Stanford University, where he received both his undergraduate and law degrees, classmates recalled him as a brilliant student whose already well-entrenched conservative views set him apart from his more liberal classmates.

After graduating from law school in 1952, Rehnquist traveled east to Washington, D.C., to serve as a law clerk to Supreme Court Justice Robert H. Jackson. There in 1952, he wrote a memorandum that later would come back to haunt him during his Senate confirmation hearings. In the memorandum, Rehnquist favored separate but equal schools for blacks and whites. Asked about those views by the Senate Judiciary Committee in 1971, Rehnquist repudiated them, declaring that they were Justice Jackson's not his own.

Following his clerkship, Rehnquist decided to begin law practice in the Southwest. In 1953, Rehnquist moved to Phoenix, Ariz., and immediately became immersed in state Republican politics. From his earliest days in the state, he was associated with the party's most conservative wing. A 1957 speech denouncing the liberality of the Warren court typified his views at the time.

During the 1964 presidential campaign, Rehnquist campaigned ardently for Barry Goldwater. It was during the campaign that Rehnquist met and worked with Richard G. Kleindienst, who later as President Nixon's deputy attorney general, would appoint Rehnquist to head the

Justice Department's Office of Legal Counsel as an assistant attorney general.

Rehnquist quickly became one of the administration's chief spokesmen on Capitol Hill, commenting on issues ranging from wiretapping to the rights of the accused. It was Rehnquist's job to review the legality of all presidential executive orders and other constitutional law questions in the executive branch. He frequently testified before congressional committees in support of the administration's policies — most of which matched his own conservative philosophy. So tightly reasoned and articulate was his testimony backing government surveillance of American citizens and tighter curbs of obscene materials, that even some liberal members of Congress applauded his ability.

In 1971, the once-obscure Phoenix lawyer was nominated by President Nixon to the Supreme Court.

Rehnquist has been married since 1953 to Natalie Cornell. They have two daughters and a son.

Born Oct. 1, 1924, Milwaukee, Wis.; Stanford University B.A. (1948); Phi Beta Kappa; LL.B (1952); Harvard University M.A. (1949); law clerk to Justice Robert H. Jackson, U.S. Supreme Court 1952-53; married 1953; two daughters, one son; practiced law 1953-69; assistant U.S. attorney general, Office of Legal Counsel 1969-71; nominated as associate justice, U.S. Supreme Court, by President Nixon Oct. 21, 1971; confirmed Dec. 10, 1971; nominated as chief justice of the United States, by President Reagan June 17, 1986; confirmed Sept. 17, 1986.

William Joseph Brennan Jr.

As a member of the activist Warren court, William J. Brennan Jr. became known as an articulate judicial scholar, who framed some of the court's key decisions. On the more conservative Burger court, however, Brennan has been

largely confined to writing dissents. But while he has been relegated to a minority voice on the court, Brennan has continued to rise in the esteem of legal scholars, some of whom characterize him as the court's most eminent jurist.

Brennan was born April 25, 1906, in Newark, N.J., the second of eight children of Irish parents who immigrated to the United States in 1890. Brennan displayed impressive academic abilities early in his life. He was an outstanding student in high school, an honors student at the University of Pennsylvania's Wharton School of Finance and graduated in the top 10 percent of his Harvard Law School class in 1931.

Following law school, Brennan returned to Newark, where he joined the law firm of Pitney, Hardin and Skinner. After several years of general practice and the passage of the Wagner Labor Relations Act in 1937, he began to specialize in labor law. With the outbreak of World War II, Brennan entered the Army, serving as a manpower trouble-shooter on the staff of Under Secretary of War Robert B. Patterson.

At the conclusion of the war, Brennan returned to his old law firm. But as his practice swelled, Brennan, a dedicated family man, began to resent the demands which it placed on his time. "My practice was bidding to kill me," he once recalled.

A desire to temper the pace of his work was one of the reasons which prompted Brennan to accept an appointment to the newly-created New Jersey Superior Court. Brennan had been a leader in the movement to establish the court as part of a larger program of judicial reform. Thus it was not surprising when Republican Governor Alfred E. Driscoll named Brennan, a registered, but inactive Democrat, to the Superior Court bench in 1949.

During his tenure on the Superior Court, Brennan's use of pretrial procedures to speed up the disposition of cases brought him to the attention of New Jersey Supreme Court Justice Arthur T. Vanderbilt. It was reportedly at Vanderbilt's suggestion that Brennan was moved first in 1950 to the appellate division of the Superior Court and then in 1952 to the state Supreme Court. Late in 1956, President Eisenhower gave Brennan a recess appointment to the United States Supreme Court, sending his nomination to Congress early in 1957 when the new Congress convened.

Brennan is a football fan and a walker. Aside from these diversions, he is committed to his family and the law. Brennan was married in 1928 to Marjorie Leonard and has three children. After his wife's death in 1982, he married Mary Fowler in March 1983.

Born April 25, 1906, in Newark, N.J.; University of Pennsylvania B.S. (1928); Harvard Law School LL.B (1931); married 1928; two sons, one daughter; practiced law Newark 1931-49; N.J. Superior Court judge 1949; appellate division 1951-52; associate justice N.J. Supreme Court 1952-56; received recess appointment as associate justice, U.S. Supreme Court, from President Eisenhower Oct. 16, 1956; nominated as associate justice by President Eisenhower Jan. 14, 1957; confirmed March 19, 1957.

Byron Raymond White

Byron R. White is noted for his quick and precise legal mind, and his peppery and incisive questioning during oral argument.

White was born June 8, 1917, in Fort Collins, Colo., but grew up in Wellington, a small town in a sugar beet growing area of the state. Ranking first in his high school class, White won a scholarship to the University of Colorado, which he entered in 1934.

At the university White earned his reputation as an outstanding scholar-athlete. He was first in his class, a member of Phi Beta Kappa and the winner of three varsity letters in football, four in basketball and three in baseball. By the end of his college career in 1938 he had been dubbed "Whizzer" White for his outstanding performance as a football player, a performance which earned him not only a national reputation but also a one-year contract with the Pittsburgh Pirates (now the Steelers). White had already accepted a coveted Rhodes Scholarship for study at Ox-

ford, but decided to postpone his year in England.

Despite his success as a pro football player, at the end of the football season, White sailed for England to attend Oxford. When the European war broke out in September 1939, White returned to the United States and entered Yale Law School. But during 1940 and 1941, he alternated law study with playing football for the Detroit Lions.

After the United States entered the war, White served in the Navy in the South Pacific. There he renewed an old acquaintance with John F. Kennedy, whom he had met in England and who later would nominate White to the Supreme Court. After the war, White returned to Yale, earning his law degree *magna cum laude* in 1946. Following graduation, White served as law clerk to U.S. Chief Justice Fred M. Vinson. In 1947, he returned to his native Colorado, where for the next 14 years he practiced law with the Denver firm of Lewis, Grant and Davis.

White renewed his contact with Kennedy during the 1960 presidential campaign, leading the nationwide volunteer group, Citizens for Kennedy. After the election, Kennedy named White to the post of deputy attorney general, a position he held until his Supreme Court appointment in 1962.

White has been married since 1946 to Marion Stearns. They have one son and one daughter.

Born June 8, 1917, in Fort Collins, Colo.; University of Colorado B.A. (1938); Phi Beta Kappa; Rhodes scholar, Oxford University; Yale Law School LL.B *magna cum laude* (1946); married 1946; one son, one daughter; law clerk to Chief Justice Fred M. Vinson, U.S. Supreme Court 1946-47; practiced law, Denver, 1947-60; U.S. deputy attorney general 1961-62; nominated as associate justice, U.S. Supreme Court, by President Kennedy March 30, 1962; confirmed April 11, 1962.

Thurgood Marshall

Unlike some jurists who undergo striking philosophical changes once elevated to the Supreme Court, Thurgood Marshall has deviated little from his earlier convictions. For more than a quarter of a century, Marshall exemplified, through his work with the National Association for the Advancement of Colored People (NAACP), that part of the civil rights movement which sought change through legal processes. Once on the court, Marshall has continued to champion the rights of minorities. And as a member of the court's minority liberal wing, Marshall has persisted in his defense of individual rights.

Marshall was born July 2, 1908, in Baltimore, Md., the son of a primary school teacher and a club steward. In 1926, he left Baltimore to attend all-black Lincoln University in Chester, Pa., where he developed a reputation as an outstanding debater. After graduating *cum laude* in 1930, Marshall decided to study law, and in 1931 he entered Howard University in Washington, D.C.

During his law school years, Marshall began to develop an interest in civil rights. After graduating first in his law school class in 1933, Marshall commenced a long and historic involvement with the NAACP.

In 1940 Marshall became the head of the newly formed NAACP Legal Defense and Educational Fund, a position he held for more than 20 years.

Over the next two and one-half decades, Marshall coordinated the fund's attack on segregation in voting, housing, public accommodations and education. But the culmination of his career as a civil rights attorney came in 1954 as chief counsel in a series of cases grouped under the title *Brown v. Board of Education.* In that historic case, which Marshall argued before the court, civil rights advocates convinced the court to declare that segregation in public schools was unconstitutional.

In 1961, Marshall was appointed by President Kennedy to the U.S. Court of Appeals for the 2nd Circuit, but because of heated opposition from Southern Democratic senators, he was not confirmed until a year later.

Four years after he was named to the circuit court, Marshall was chosen by President Johnson to be the nation's first black solicitor

general. During his years as the government's chief advocate before the Supreme Court, Marshall scored impressive victories in the areas of civil and constitutional rights. He won Supreme Court approval of the 1965 Voting Rights Act, voluntarily informed the court that the government had used electronic eavesdropping devices in two cases, and joined in a suit that successfully overturned a California constitutional amendment that prohibited open housing legislation.

On June 13, 1967, Marshall became the first black appointed to be a justice of the Supreme Court, chosen by President Johnson.

Marshall was married in 1955 to Cecelia A. Suyat. He has two sons by his first wife who died in 1955.

Born July 2, 1908, in Baltimore, Md.; Lincoln University B.A. (1930); Howard University LL.B (1933); practiced law 1933-37; assistant special counsel NAACP 1936-38; special counsel 1938-50; married 1955; two sons; director-counsel, NAACP Legal Defense and Educational Fund 1940-61; judge, U.S. Court of Appeals for the 2nd Circuit 1961-65; U.S. Solicitor General 1965-67; nominated as associate justice, U.S. Supreme Court, by President Johnson June 13, 1967; confirmed Aug. 30, 1967.

Harry Andrew Blackmun

During his first years on the court Harry A. Blackmun was frequently described as one of the "Minnesota Twins" along with the court's other Minnesota native, Chief Justice Warren E. Burger. Blackmun and Burger are lifelong friends who initially voted together on important court decisions.

However, Blackmun, who originally impressed observers as a modest, even meek, addition to the court's conservative bloc, has authored some of the court's most controversial decisions, among them its 1973 ruling upholding a

woman's right to an abortion. And he has broken frequently enough with his conservative colleagues to earn a reputation as an independent, if still fundamentally conservative, justice.

Blackmun was born in Nashville, Ill., on November 12, 1908, but spent most of his early years in Minneapolis-St. Paul, where his father was an official of the Twin Cities Savings and Loan Co. It was in grade school that Blackmun began his lifelong friendship with Burger.

"A whiz at math," according to his mother, Blackmun went East after high school to attend Harvard College on a scholarship. At Harvard, Blackmun majored in mathematics and toyed briefly with the idea of becoming a physician.

But Blackmun chose the law instead. After graduating from Harvard in 1929, Phi Beta Kappa, Blackmun entered Harvard Law School, from which he graduated in 1932. During his law school years, Blackmun supported himself with a variety of odd jobs, including tutoring in math and driving the launch for the college crew team.

Following law school, Blackmun returned to St. Paul, where he served for a year-and-a-half as a law clerk to United States Circuit Court Judge John B. Sanborn, whom Blackmun succeeded 20 years later. He left the clerkship at the end of 1933 and joined the Minneapolis law firm of Dorsey, Colman, Barker, Scott and Barber. At the same time he taught for a year at William Mitchell College of Law in St. Paul, Chief Justice Burger's alma mater. In addition to his practice he also taught for two years during the 1940s at the University of Minnesota Law School.

In 1950 he accepted a post as "house counsel" for the world-famous Mayo Clinic in Rochester, Minn.

Among his colleagues at the clinic, Blackmun quickly developed a reputation as a serious man, totally engrossed in his profession.

The reputation followed him to the bench of the U.S. Court of Appeals for the 8th Circuit, to which Blackmun was appointed by Eisenhower in 1959. As a judge, he was known for his scholarly and thorough opinions.

Blackmun's total devotion to the law leaves little time for outside activities. He is an avid reader, delving primarily into judicial tomes. Over the years, he has also been active in Methodist church affairs. Before a knee gave out, Blackmun was a proficient squash and tennis player. It was on the tennis court that Blackmun met his future wife, Dorothy E. Clark. They were married in 1941 and have three daughters.

Born Nov. 12, 1908 in Nashville, Ill.; Harvard College B.A. (1929); Phi Beta Kappa; Harvard Law School LL.B. (1932); clerk, John Sanborn, U.S. Court of Appeals for the 8th Circuit, St. Paul 1932-33; practiced law, Minneapolis, 1934-50; married 1941; three daughters; resident counsel, Mayo Clinic, Rochester, Minn. 1950-59; judge, U.S. Court of Appeals for the 8th Circuit 1959-70; nominated as associate justice U.S. Supreme Court, by President Nixon April 14, 1970; confirmed May 12, 1970.

Lewis Franklin Powell Jr.

At the time of his nomination to the Supreme Court in 1971, former American Bar Association President Lewis F. Powell Jr. was hailed for his professional excellence and for the moderation of his political views. Those views had been fashioned by a lifetime of private law practice in Richmond, Virginia, years of active participation in the American Bar Association, and deep involvement in the sensitive question of desegregating Virginia's public schools.

Following his appointment to the Supreme Court, Powell continued to build a reputation as a moderate. And, according to observers, Powell quickly rose to a position of influence among the other eight justices disproportionate to his low seniority on the court.

Powell was born September 19, 1907, in Suffolk, Va., but he spent most of his life in Richmond. He attended

college and law school at Washington and Lee University in Lexington, Va., earning his B.S. in 1929 and law degree in 1931. From Lexington, Powell journeyed north to Cambridge, Mass., where he attended Harvard Law School, earning a master's degree in 1932.

Following his year at Harvard, Powell returned to Virginia, where he joined one of the state's oldest and most prestigious law firms, later called Hunton, Williams, Gay, Powell and Gibson. Powell rose to become a senior partner, continuing his association with the firm until his nomination to the Supreme Court.

Over the years, Powell's practice made him no stranger to blue chip board rooms. Among the companies Hunton, Williams represented during Powell's years with the firm were the Baltimore & Ohio Railroad Co., the Prudential Insurance Co. and the Virginia Electric and Power Co. Powell himself did no work for these corporations.

Powell's reputation as a moderate stemmed from his work as president from 1952-61 of the Richmond school board, and later as a member of the state board of education. According to civil rights advocates in Richmond, Powell, in the face of intense pressure to "massively" resist desegregation, consistently advocated keeping the city schools open.

A one-year stint, from 1964-65, as the president of the American Bar Association (ABA) provided Powell with a national platform from which to express his views on a range of subjects. The exposure enhanced his reputation as a moderate. On the liberal side, Powell spoke out against inadequate legal services for the poor and worked to create the legal services program of the Office of Economic Opportunity. A more conservative tone characterized his pronouncements against "excessive tolerance" by parents and his stern denunciations of civil disobedience and other forms of civil demonstrations. And, as a member in 1966 of President Johnson's Crime Commission, Powell participated in a minority statement criticizing Supreme Court rulings upholding the right of criminal suspects to remain silent. Powell was the only Democrat among President Nixon's Supreme Court appointees.

A first-rate tennis player, Powell is also an avid sports fan. Powell has been married since 1936 to Josephine Rucker. They have three daughters and a son.

Born Sept. 19, 1907, Suffolk, Va.; Washington and Lee University B.S. (1929); Phi Beta Kappa; LL.B (1931); Harvard Law School LL.M (1932); practiced law in Richmond, 1932-71; married 1936; three daughters, one son; president, American Bar Association 1964-65; president, American College of Trial Lawyers 1968-69; nominated associate justice, U.S. Supreme Court, by President Nixon Oct. 21, 1971; confirmed Dec. 6, 1971.

John Paul Stevens

When President Ford nominated federal appeals court Judge John Paul Stevens to the Supreme Court seat vacated by veteran liberal William O. Douglas in 1975, court-watchers and other observers struggled to pin an ideological label on the new nominee. The consensus which

emerged was that Stevens was neither a doctrinaire liberal nor conservative, but a judicial "centrist," whose well-crafted, scholarly opinions made him a "judge's judge." His subsequent opinions bear out this description.

A soft-spoken, mild-mannered man who occasionally sports a bow tie under his judicial robes, Stevens had a long record of excellence in scholarship. A member of a prominent Chicago family, Stevens graduated Phi Beta Kappa from the University of Chicago in 1941. After a wartime stint in the Navy, during which he earned the Bronze Star, he returned to Chicago to enter Northwestern University Law School, from which he graduated *magna cum laude* in 1947. From there, Stevens left for Washington, where he served as a law clerk to Supreme Court Justice Wiley Rutledge. He returned to Chicago to join the prominent law firm of Poppenhusen, Johnston, Thompson and Raymond, which specialized in antitrust law. Stevens developed a reputation as a pre-eminent antitrust lawyer, and after three years with Poppenhusen, he left in 1952 to form his own firm, Rothschild, Stevens, Barry and Myers. He remained there, engaging in private practice and teaching part-time at Northwestern and the University of Chicago law schools, until his appointment by President Nixon in 1970 to the U.S. Court of Appeals for the 7th Circuit.

Stevens developed a reputation as a political moderate during his undergraduate days at the University of Chicago, then an overwhelmingly liberal campus. But although he is a registered Republican, he has never been active in partisan politics. Nevertheless, Stevens did serve as Republican counsel in 1951 to the House Judiciary Committee's Subcommittee on the Study of Monopoly Power. He also served from 1953 to 1955, during the Eisenhower administration, as a member of the Attorney General's National Committee to Study the Antitrust Laws.

An enthusiastic pilot, Stevens flies his own small plane. According to friends, he is also a creditable bridge player and golfer. Stevens underwent open heart surgery several years ago, from which he is said to have recovered fully. However, the operation did force him to give up the game of squash. In 1942, Stevens married Elizabeth Jane Sheeren. They have four children. They were divorced in 1979. Stevens subsequently married Maryan Mulholland Simon, a longtime neighbor in Chicago.

Born April 20, 1920, Chicago, Ill.; University of Chicago B.A. (1941); Phi Beta Kappa; Northwestern University School of Law J.D. (1947); *magna cum laude;* married 1942; three daughters, one son; divorced 1979; married Maryan Mulholland Simon 1980; law clerk to Justice Wiley Rutledge, U.S. Supreme Court 1947-48; practiced law Chicago, 1949-70; judge, U.S. Court of Appeals for the 7th Circuit 1970-75; nominated as associate justice, U.S. Supreme Court, by President Ford Nov. 28, 1975; confirmed Dec. 17, 1975.

Sandra Day O'Connor

Pioneering came naturally to Sandra Day O'Connor. Her grandfather left Kansas in 1880 to take up ranching in the desert land that would eventually become the state of Arizona. O'Connor, born in El Paso where her mother's parents lived, was raised on the Lazy B Ranch, the 162,000-acre spread that her grandfather had founded in southeastern Arizona near Duncan. She spent her school years in El Paso, living with her grandmother and attending the schools there. She graduated from high school at age 16 and then entered Stanford University.

Six years later, in 1952, Sandra Day had won degrees, with great distinction, both from the university, in economics, and from Stanford Law School. There she met John J.

O'Connor III, her future husband, and was also a classmate of William H. Rehnquist, a future colleague on the Supreme Court. During her law school years, Sandra Day was an editor of the Stanford Law Review and a member of Order of the Coif, both reflecting her academic leadership.

But despite her outstanding law school record, she found it difficult to locate a job as an attorney in 1952 when relatively few women were practicing law. She applied, among others, to the firm in which William French Smith — attorney general in the Reagan administration — was a partner, only to be offered a job as a secretary.

After a short stint as deputy county attorney for San Mateo County (Calif.) while her new husband completed law school at Stanford, the O'Connors moved with the U.S. Army to Frankfurt, Germany. There Sandra O'Connor worked as a civilian attorney for the Army, while John O'Connor served his tour of duty.

In 1957, they returned to Phoenix to live. In the next eight years, their three sons were born and O'Connor's life was a mix of mothering, homemaking, volunteer work and some "miscellaneous legal tasks" on the side.

In 1965, O'Connor resumed her legal career full time, taking a job as an assistant attorney general for Arizona.

After four years in that post, she was appointed to fill a vacancy in the state Senate, where she served on the judiciary committee. In 1970, she was elected to the Senate, and two years later was chosen its majority leader; the first woman in the nation to hold such a post.

O'Connor was active in Republican Party politics and was co-chairman of the Arizona Committee to Re-Elect the President in 1972.

In 1974, she was elected to the Superior Court for Maricopa County where she served for five years. Then in 1979, Gov. Bruce Babbitt — acting, some said, to remove a potential rival for the governorship — appointed O'Connor to the Arizona Court of Appeals. It was from that seat that President Reagan chose her as his first nominee to the Supreme Court, describing her as "a person for all seasons."

She was confirmed unanimously Sept. 21, 1981, by the Senate as the first woman associate justice of the U.S. Supreme Court.

Born March 26, 1930 in El Paso, Texas; Stanford University, B.A. (1950); *magna cum laude*; Stanford University Law School, LL.B. (1952); with high honors; deputy county attorney, San Mateo, Calif., 1952-53; assistant attorney general, Arizona, 1965-69; Arizona state senator, 1969-1975, Senate majority leader, 1972-75; judge, Maricopa County Superior Court, 1974-79; judge, Arizona Court of Appeals, 1979-81; married John J. O'Connor III, Dec. 20, 1952; three sons; nominated associate justice U.S. Supreme Court, by President Ronald Reagan Aug. 19, 1981, to replace Potter Stewart, who retired; confirmed by the U.S. Senate Sept. 21, 1981, by a vote of 99-0.

Antonin Scalia

When Warren Burger resigned and President Reagan named William Rehnquist to be the new chief justice, it was not surprising that he would appoint Antonin Scalia to the Supreme Court. On issues dear to Reagan, it was clear

that Scalia met the president's tests for conservatism. Scalia, whom Reagan named to the U.S. Court of Appeals for the District of Columbia in 1982, became the first justice of Italian ancestry. A Roman Catholic, he has nine children and opposes abortion. He has also expressed opposition to "affirmative action" preferences for minorities.

The president is a strong advocate of deregulation, a subject of considerable interest to Scalia, a specialist in administrative law. Scalia was from 1977-82 editor of the magazine *Regulation*, published by the American Enterprise Institute for Public Policy Research.

Born in Trenton, N.J., on March 11, 1936, Scalia grew up in Queens, N.Y. He graduated from Georgetown University in 1957 and from Harvard Law School in 1960.

He worked for six years at the firm of Jones, Day in Cleveland and then taught contract, commercial and comparative law at the University of Virginia Law School.

Scalia served as general counsel of the White House

Office of Telecommunications Policy in 1971-72. He then headed the Administrative Conference of the United States, a group that advises the government on questions of administrative law and procedure. From 1974 through the Ford administration he headed the Justice Department's Office of Legal Counsel, a post Rehnquist held three years earlier. Scalia then returned to academia, to teach at the University of Chicago Law School.

Scalia has shown himself a hard worker, an aggressive interrogator and an articulate advocate. He has been impatient with what he sees as regulatory or judicial overreaching. In 1983, he dissented from an appeals court ruling requiring the Food and Drug Administration to consider whether drugs used for lethal injections met FDA standards as safe and effective. The Supreme Court agreed, reversing the appeals court in 1985.

Scalia was thought to be the principal author of an unsigned decision in 1986 that declared key portions of the Gramm-Rudman-Hollings budget-balancing act unconstitutional. The Supreme Court upheld the decision later in the year.

Born March 11, 1936, Trenton, N.J.; Georgetown University A.B. (1957); Harvard University, LL.B. (1960); practiced law in Cleveland, 1960-67; married to Maureen McCarthy; nine children; taught at the University of Virginia, 1967-71; general counsel, White House Office of Telecommunications Policy 1971-72; chairman Administrative Conference of the United States 1972-74; head Office of Legal Counsel 1974-77; taught at the University of Chicago Law School 1977-82; judge, U.S. Court of Appeals, District of Columbia; nominated as associate justice, U.S. Supreme Court June 17, 1986; confirmed Sept. 17, 1986.

Reference Guide to the Supreme Court

Biographical Directory of the Federal Judiciary — Biographical data on judges of the Supreme Court, Court of Appeals, District Courts, Court of Claims; statistical data on religious and political persuasions. Detroit, Michigan, Gale Research Corp., 1983.

Black's Law Dictionary edited by Henry C. Black — Definitions of terms and phrases of American and English jurisprudence. St. Paul, Minnesota, West Publishing Co., 1979.

Congressional Quarterly's Guide to the U.S. Supreme Court — A 1,000-page volume documenting the development and working of the court. Includes summaries of major decisions and biographies of all justices. Washington, D.C., Congressional Quarterly Inc., 1979.

The Constitution of the United States of America: Analysis and Interpretation — Discussion of each phrase of the Constitution and annotations of cases decided by the Supreme Court. Washington, D.C., Government Printing Office, 1979.

Court and Constitution in the Twentieth Century by William F. Swindler — Two-volume history of the court from 1889 through 1968. Indianapolis, Bobbs-Merrill, 1969.

Justices and Presidents: A Political History of Appointments to the Supreme Court by Henry J. Abraham — History of appointments to the Supreme Court from George Washington through Lyndon Johnson. New York, Oxford University Press, 1974.

The Justices of the United States Supreme Court: Their Lives and Major Opinions, edited by Leon Friedman and Fred Israel — Five volumes on the lives and major opinions of the Supreme Court justices from 1789 through 1971. New York, R.R. Bowker.

Landmark Briefs and Arguments of the Supreme Court of the United States: Constitutional Law, edited by Philip B. Kurland and Gerhard Casper — Includes briefs, transcripts of oral arguments and decisions of the Supreme Court on major constitutional law cases from 1793 through 1973. Washington, D.C., University Publications of America Inc., 1975.

Lawyer's Edition of the United States Supreme Court — Weekly report of court opinions, summary of arguments, digest of court decisions; bound volumes issued annually. Rochester, N.Y., Lawyer's Cooperative Publishing Co.

Significant Decisions of the Supreme Court by Bruce E. Fein — Annual review of all major opinions and analyses since 1969. Washington, D.C., American Enterprise Institute for Public Policy Research.

The Supreme Court by Lawrence Baum — Analysis of the Supreme Court's policy-making role. Washington, D.C., CQ Press, 1985.

The Supreme Court in United States History by Charles Warren — Two volume history covers the period 1789 through 1918. Boston, Little, Brown and Co., 1922.

A Different Justice by Elder Witt — Examination of President Reagan's influence on the Supreme Court. Washington, D.C., Congressional Quarterly Inc., 1985.

Supreme Court Practice by Robert L. Stern and Eugene Gressman. Washington, D.C., Bureau of National Affairs, 1978.

Supreme Court Reporter — Bimonthly coverage of Supreme Court decisions and proceedings; bound cumulative reports issued annually. St. Paul, Minnesota, West Publishing Co.

The United States Law Week — Digest and analysis of current developments, opinions and rulings of the Supreme Court. Washington, D.C., Bureau of National Affairs.

The United States Reports — Official record of Supreme Court decisions and proceedings; issued daily in "slip opinions"; cumulative volumes issued annually. Washington, D.C., Government Printing Office.

LOBBIES

The Washington Lobby: A Continuing Effort To Influence Government Policy

Of all the pressures on Congress, none has received such widespread publicity and yet is so dimly understood as the role of Washington-based lobbyists and the groups they represent. The popular image of a rotund agent for special interests buying up members' votes is a vast over-simplification. The role of today's lobbyist is far more subtle, his or her techniques more refined.

Lobbyists and lobby groups have played an increasingly active part in the modern legislative process. The corps of Washington lobbyists has grown steadily since the New Deal, but especially since the early 1970s. The growth in the number of lobbyists has paralleled the growth in federal spending and the expansion of federal authority into new areas. The federal government has become a tremendous force in the life of the nation, and the number of fields in which changes in federal policy may spell success or failure for special interest groups has been greatly enlarged.

With the drive to reduce federal spending that gained impetus during the Reagan administration, the competition for the dwindling supply of federal dollars has become more intense. Lobbyists have to compete with one another to safeguard traditional spending in their area of interest or to gain some portion of the smaller federal pool of. funds. Thus commercial and industrial interests, labor unions, ethnic and racial groups, professional organizations, citizen groups and representatives of foreign interests — all from time to time and some continuously — have sought by one method or another to exert pressure on Congress to attain their legislative goals.

The pressure usually has selfish aims — to assert rights or to win a special privilege or financial benefit for the group exerting it. But in other cases the objective may be disinterested — to achieve an ideological goal or to further a group's particular conception of the national interest.

Lobbying: Pros and Cons

It is widely recognized that pressure groups, whether operating through general campaigns designed to sway public opinion or through direct contacts with members of Congress, perform some important and indispensable functions. Such functions include helping to inform both Congress and the public about problems and issues, stimulating public debate, opening a path to Congress for the wronged and needy, and making known to Congress the practical aspects of proposed legislation — whom it would help, whom it would hurt, who is for it and who against it. The spinoff from this process is considerable technical information produced by research on legislative proposals.

Against benefits to the public that result from pressure activities, critics point to certain serious liabilities. The most important is that in pursuing their own objectives, the pressure groups are apt to lead Congress into decisions that benefit the pressure group but do not necessarily serve other parts of the public or the national interest. A group's power to influence legislation often is based less on its arguments than on the size of its membership, the amount of financial and manpower resources it can commit to a legislative pressure campaign and the astuteness of its representatives.

Origins of Lobbying

Representatives of special interests haunted the environs of the First Continental Congress, but the word "lobby" was not recorded until 1808 when it appeared in the annals of the 10th Congress. By 1829 the term "lobby-agents" was applied to favor-seekers at the state capitol in Albany, N.Y. By 1832 it had been shortened to "lobbyist" and was in wide use at the U.S. Capitol.

Although the term had not yet been coined, the right to "lobby" was made implicit by the First Amendment to the Constitution, which provided that "Congress shall make no law ... abridging the freedom of speech or of the press; or the right of the people peaceably to assemble and to petition the Government for redress of grievances." Among the Founding Fathers, only James Madison expressed concern over the dangers posed by pressure groups. In *The Federalist* (No. 10), Madison warned against the self-serving activities of the "factions." "Among the numerous advantages promised by a well-constructed union," he wrote, "none deserves to be more accurately developed than its tendency to break and control the violence of faction.... By a faction, I understand a number of citizens, whether amounting to a majority or minority of the whole, who are united and actuated by some common impulse of passion, or of interest, adverse to the rights of other citizens, or to the permanent and aggregate interests of the community." A strong federal government, Madison concluded, was the only effective counterbalance to the influence of such "factions."

Sources of Pressure

Traditionally, pressure groups in the United States have been composed of similar economic or social interests. Classic examples of such traditional lobbies are those representing farmers, business executives and labor union members. Each of these groups has specific interests that usually draw the support of a large majority of its members.

As the federal government broadened its activities, a new type of pressure group developed — the coalition of diverse economic and social interests brought together by concern for a certain issue. Most major legislation is backed by alliances of interest groups on one side and opposed by alliances on the other. Such lobby coalitions, while having the advantages of bigger memberships and more financial resources for lobbying, may be difficult to control because of the differences of opinion that are likely to arise within any coalition. Despite these inner tensions, lobby coalitions nonetheless have been instrumental in obtaining passage of much major legislation, such as the civil rights and Alaska lands bills.

A notable effort that did not succeed was the coalition for ratification of the Equal Rights Amendment (ERA), which failed to win ratification by the deadline of June 30, 1982. Only 35 states approved it, three short of the necessary 38. Also traditional secular and religious advocates for the underprivileged that have formed a coalition for the poor — such as the National Conference of Catholic Bishops, the National Low Income Housing Coalition and the Food Research and Action Center — have been challenged by the budget cutbacks of the conservative administration of Ronald Reagan.

Executive Branch. Equally prominent among forces exerting pressures on Congress is the executive branch. Executive lobbying activities have been described as the most pervasive, influential and costly of any of the pressures converging on Capitol Hill.

Although every president since George Washington has sought to influence the content of legislation, it was not until the administration of Dwight D. Eisenhower that a formal congressional liaison office in the White House was created. In addition, each executive department has a congressional liaison office charged with selling the department's legislative program to Congress.

While senators and representatives sometimes criticize what they regard as excessive executive pressures, they tend on the other hand to complain of lack of leadership when executive influence is missing. The inter-branch pressure process also works in reverse. Members of Congress exert pressure on executive agencies, if only through inquiries that demonstrate an interest on the part of the body that must pass agency appropriations.

Foreign Interests. Since World War II, lobbying by foreign interests and by American groups with foreign members or interests has become an increasingly important factor in Washington legislative and executive decision making. Foreign-oriented lobbying is based on international politics, world trade and many American domestic issues, for any action by the U.S. government may have foreign or global implications.

Approximately 800 active registered agents representing the interests of foreign principals (governments, political parties, corporations and individuals) were listed with the Justice Department under the Foreign Agents Registration Act in mid-1985, despite Congress' narrowing of the act's coverage in 1966. Counting partners and associates who may participate in representing overseas clients, the number of individuals listed as being in the service of foreign "principals" swelled to over 7,000.

Public Interest Lobbies. Finally there is a collection of groups with no single special interest to promote or

protect. These self-styled citizens' or public interest lobbies are concerned with a vast array of issues, and usually have large numbers of individual members. Two of the oldest public interest lobbies are the League of Women Voters and Americans for Democratic Action. Their activities set the pattern for the public interest groups that followed in this relatively new lobbying development.

Two groups, Common Cause and Public Citizen, have attracted wide attention over the last decade and have come almost to characterize liberal public interest lobbies. Developed by Ralph Nader, Public Citizen groups pursue a broad agenda of substantive economic, consumer, environmental, legal and social policy issues. Common Cause has focused on issues of political structure and procedure.

Conservative public interest groups have gained in prominence in recent years as well. Evangelical lobby groups, including the Moral Majority and Christian Voice, have joined other more traditional conservative groups, including the Conservative Caucus, in legislative fights against abortion, homosexual rights, and the Equal Rights Amendment, and in favor of budget-balancing, an anticommunist foreign policy and heavier defense spending. This loose coalition of conservative groups has come to be called The New Right.

Pressure Methods

A Washington lobby group is out to get results. It pursues them wherever they are likely to be found in the governmental process. Many organizations, directed by professionals in the art of government, focus major efforts at key points where decisions are made and policy interpreted into action. If a group loses a round in Congress, it may continue the fight in the agency charged with implementation of the legislation or in the courts. A year or two later, it may resume the struggle in Congress. This process can continue indefinitely.

Whether they focus on Congress or the executive branch, lobbyists use the methods they deem appropriate for the circumstances within the limits of their resources, group policies and ethical outlook.

Bribery

Bribery of members of Congress was a well-documented occurrence in the 19th and early 20th centuries.

When Congress in the 1830s became embroiled in President Andrew Jackson's battle with the Bank of the United States, it was disclosed that Daniel Webster, then a senator from Massachusetts, enjoyed a retainer from the bank. On Dec. 21, 1833, Webster complained to bank President Nicholas Biddle: "My retainer has not been renewed or refreshed as usual. If it is wished that my relation to the Bank should be continued, it may be well to send me the usual retainers."

Col. Martin M. Mulhall, a lobbyist for the National Association of Manufacturers (NAM), stated publicly in 1913 that he had bribed members of Congress for legislative favors, had paid the chief House page $50 a month for inside information from the cloakrooms, and had influenced House leaders to place members friendly to the NAM on House committees and subcommittees. In a subsequent congressional probe, six members were exonerated but one was censured and resigned.

After World War II, direct vote-buying by lobbyists

Ex-Members as Lobbyists

Among the most influential and active lobbyists in Washington are former members of Congress, who, after leaving office, are hired as lobbyists for private organizations.

In some cases, former members become permanently associated with a single organization whose views they share. On the other hand, some former members work for many different organizations as lobbyists, frequently changing or adding employers from year to year.

Because of their service in Congress, former members of the House or Senate enjoy several advantages in lobbying activities. They have an excellent knowledge of the legislative process and frequently a good "feel" for the operations of the House or Senate, which help them decide precisely when and what kind of pressure to exert on behalf of their clients. They often enjoy easy access to congressional staff members and members who are friends and former colleagues. This enables them to see and speak with key legislative personnel, perhaps the chairman of a committee or subcommittee, at the proper time. The ordinary lobbyist might spend weeks trying to obtain an appointment. Former members also frequently have an expert knowledge of the subject matter of legislation through having dealt with it while in Congress.

The privileges of being admitted to the floor and adjacent halls of the House and Senate, which is granted in each chamber to former members of that chamber, is used relatively little by former members directly for lobbying purposes, although it is useful for maintaining contacts and acquaintances. In the House, use of the floor by former members for lobbying purposes has been circumscribed by House Rule 32 and a chair ruling in 1945 by Speaker Sam Rayburn, D-Texas. Under the "Rayburn rule," a former member is forbidden the privilege of the floor at any time the House is debating or voting on legislation in which he is interested, either personally or as an employee of some other person or organization.

No similar formal rule exists in the Senate. But as a matter of custom it is considered improper for a former senator, or any other non-member granted the privilege of the floor, to use that privilege to lobby for legislation.

was replaced, for the most part, by more sophisticated techniques. Indirect, grass-roots pressures and political support became more powerful tools of persuasion. But bribery did not disappear altogether and the Abscam scandal that surfaced in 1980 demonstrated its persistence. The government undercover investigation of political corruption — known as "Abscam" — in which agents of the Federal Bureau of Investigation, posing as businessmen or wealthy Arabs, attempted to bribe members of Congress and other elected officials to help Arabs obtain U.S. residency, get federal grants and arrange real estate deals, resulted in the convictions of seven members of Congress — six representatives and one senator. The charges ranged from bribery to conspiracy.

Campaign Support

Campaign contributions to members of Congress serve two important functions for lobbying organizations. Political support may not only induce a congressman to back the pressure group's legislative interests in Congress but also helps assure that members friendly to the group's goals will remain in office.

While corporations have been barred since 1907, and labor unions since 1943, from making direct contributions to campaigns for federal office, contributors have found numerous ways to get around the restrictions. Although unions are prohibited from using dues money to assist political candidates in federal elections, it is legal for them to set up separate political arms, such as the AFL-CIO's Committee on Political Education (COPE), which collect voluntary contributions from union members and their families and use the funds for political expenditures calculated to benefit senators and representatives friendly to labor. It is also legal for unions to endorse political candidates.

Similarly, while corporations are prohibited from making direct campaign contributions, they can set up corporate political action committees (PACs) to seek contributions from stockholders and executive and administrative personnel and their families. Corporate PACs have proliferated in recent years and their influences rival, if not surpass, those of labor.

Twice a year union and corporate political action committees may seek anonymous contributions by mail from all employees, not just those to which they are initially restricted.

The same general resources for political support and opposition are available to members of citizens' groups and, indeed, to a wide range of organizations seeking to exert political pressure on members of Congress.

In approaching the typical member, a pressure group has no need to tell the member outright that future political support or opposition, and perhaps future political expenditures and the voluntary campaign efforts of its members, depend on how the member votes on a particular bill or whether, over a long period, the member acts favorably toward the group. The member understands this without being told. He or she knows that when the vital interests of some group are at stake in legislation, a vote supporting those interests would normally win the group's friendship and future support, and a vote against them would mean the group's enmity and future opposition.

Lobbyists themselves frequently deny that this is the intention of their campaign support. But lobbyists do admit that political support gives them access — that they otherwise might not have — to the legislator to present their case.

Grass-Roots Pressures

Except on obscure or highly specialized legislation, most lobby campaigns now are accompanied by massive propaganda or "educational" drives in which pressure groups seek to mobilize public opinion to support their aims. In most cases, citizens are urged to respond by contacting members of Congress in support of or opposition to a particular bill.

The most outstanding example of a successful grass-roots lobbying group is the National Rifle Association (NRA). Despite polls showing a majority of Americans favoring some strengthening of gun controls, and despite periodic waves of revulsion brought on by the shooting of public figures, efforts aimed at stricter gun control legislation have been consistently subdued by the NRA, and other similar groups.

NRA has all the advantages of a successful grass-roots lobby organization going for it: a large, well-organized, passionately concerned constituency, concentrated on a single issue.

"In politics you learn to identify the issues of the highest intensity," said Rep. Dan Glickman, a Democrat from Kansas. "This issue [gun control] is of the highest intensity. Those people who care about guns, care very strongly, almost to the exclusion of other issues."

Even in the aftermath of the assassinations of President John F. Kennedy, the Rev. Martin Luther King Jr. and Sen. Robert F. Kennedy, D-N.Y. (1965-68), the gun lobby, through an outpouring of mail opposing tighter gun controls, was able to bottle up proposals for tough controls. All that was passed in 1968 was watered-down legislation not vigorously opposed by the NRA. And it was widely perceived that the only real legislative impact of the shootings of John Lennon in December 1980 and President Reagan in March 1981 would be to diminish NRA's chances of rolling back the 1968 law.

Disadvantages. Despite the frequent success of grass-roots lobbying, such an approach has several inherent limitations that make its use questionable unless it is carefully and cleverly managed. If a member's mail on an issue appears artificially generated, by a professional public relations firm for instance, the member may feel that the response is not representative of the member's constituency. Such pressure mail is easily recognized because the letters all arrive at about the same time, are mimeographed or printed, or are identically or similarly worded.

G. Colburn Aker, a Washington lobbyist, said: "Anybody who believes you can use advertising or public relations techniques to create a groundswell that doesn't have a good basis to begin with is misconceiving the power of those techniques."

But others say a sense of insecurity has pervaded Congress recently, especially among the large number of relative newcomers. Skittish members are more eager to avoid controversy. Norman J. Ornstein, a politics professor associated with the American Enterprise Institute, agreed that the dramatic turnovers in the past few elections have taught many politicians to practice "damage limitation" — never taking a chance of making someone angry.

But Ornstein said that as lawmakers gather experience they likely will learn when it is safe to trust their own judgment.

Direct Lobbying

Much lobbying still is conducted on a face-to-face basis. In a study of pressures on the Senate, Donald R. Matthews, a political scientist, observed that the vast majority of such lobbying was directed at members "who are already convinced." He added: "The services a lobby can provide a friendly senator are substantial. Few senators could survive without them. First, they can perform much of the research and speech-writing chores of the senator's office. This service is especially attractive to the more publicity-oriented senators. Members of the party that does not control the White House also find this service especially valuable, since they cannot draw upon the research services of the departments as much as can the

other members. But most senators find this service at first a convenience and soon a necessity."

Once established, Matthews has said, "Senator-lobbyist friendships also tend to reinforce the senator's commitment to a particular group and line of policy.... Relatively few senators are actually changed by lobbyists from a hostile or neutral position to a friendly one. Perhaps a few on every major issue are converted and this handful of votes may carry the day. But quantitatively, the conversion effect is relatively small."

Ensuring continued access to members of Congress requires considerable tact on the part of the lobbyist. Lobbyists must be particularly wary of overstaying their welcome and appearing overly aggressive. Rep. Emanuel Celler, D-N.Y. (1923-73), wrote: "The man who keeps his appointment, presents his problem or proposal and lets the congressman get on with his other work comes to be liked and respected. His message has an excellent chance of being effective. The man who feels that it somehow adds to his usefulness and prestige to be seen constantly 'in the company of one legislator or another, or who seeks to ingratiate himself with congressional staffs, gets under foot and becomes a nuisance. He does his principal and cause no good."

Above all, the lobbyist must be certain that the information he gives the member is accurate and complete. In their book, *Interest Groups, Lobbying and Policymaking*, Norman J. Ornstein and Shirley Elder quoted a member of Congress: "It doesn't take very long to figure which lobbyists are straightforward, and which ones are trying to snow you. The good ones will give you the weak points as well as the strong points of their case. If anyone ever gives me false or misleading information, that's it — I'll never see him again."

Strategic Contacts. In fights over a specific bill, most direct approaches by lobbyists are likely to center on a few strategic members instead of a large part of the membership of the House or Senate. Generally the key members sit on the committees that have jurisdiction over the legislation in question. As one former member of the House said in 1970, "The committee system is still the crux of the legislative process and is still the basis for congressional action. Laws are not really made here on the floor of the House or on the floor of the other body. They are only revised here. Ninety percent of all legislation that has been passed was passed in the form reported by the committee to the floor."

The committee's power to prevent legislation or to determine its nature narrows down the number of targets for the great majority of specialized interests. Their Washington representatives become experts not only in their field but also on the House and Senate committees that deal with that specialty. This focus in some cases narrows still further to certain subcommittees.

Pressure groups pay their Washington staffs to keep them abreast of developments in government that could affect their constituents. These agents make it their business to watch the work of committees in which they have an interest, to establish and maintain working relationships with key members and staff members and to stay informed on potential and actual legislative developments.

Testimony at Hearings

Another useful technique for lobbyists is testimony at congressional hearings. The hearing provides the lobbyist with a propaganda forum that has few parallels in Washington. It also provides access to key members whom the lobbyist may not have been able to contact in any other way. On important legislation, lobbyists normally rehearse their statements before the hearing, seek to ensure a large turnout from their constituency on the hearing day, and may even hand friendly committee members leading questions for the group's witness to answer.

The degree of propaganda success for the hearing, however, is likely to depend on how well the committee's controlling factions are disposed to the group's position. In his book, *House Out of Order,* Rep. Richard Bolling, D-Mo. (1949-1983), says that within congressional committees "proponents and opponents of legislation jockey for position — each complementing the activities of their alter egos in lobbies outside." He points out: "Adverse witnesses can be kept to a minimum, for example, or they can be sandwiched among friendly witnesses in scheduled appearances so that their testimony does not receive as much attention from the press as it deserves. Scant attention will be given, for example, to a knowledgeable opponent of the federal fallout shelter program if he is scheduled to testify on such legislation on the same day as are Dr. Edward Teller, an assistant secretary of Defense and a three-star general. The opponent is neatly boxed in."

Regulation of Lobbying

In the 19th and 20th centuries, abundant evidence accumulated that venal, selfish or misguided methods used by pressure groups could often result in legislation designed to enrich the pressure group at the expense of the public or to impose the group's own standards on the nation.

The first regulation of lobbyists occurred in 1876 when the House passed a resolution requiring lobbyists to register during the 44th Congress with the clerk of the House. Since the advent of the 62nd Congress in 1911, federal legislation to regulate lobbyists and lobbying activities has continued to be proposed in practically every Congress. Yet only one comprehensive lobbying regulation law and only a handful of more specialized measures have been enacted.

The principal method of regulating lobbying has been

disclosure rather than control. In four laws, lobbyists have been required to identify themselves, whom they represent and their legislative interests. In one law, lobbyists also have been required to report how much they and their employers spend on lobbying. But definitions have been unclear, and enforcement has been minimal. As a result, the few existing disclosure laws have produced only limited information, and its effects have been questionable.

One reason for the relative lack of restrictions on lobbies has been the difficulty of imposing meaningful restrictions without infringing on the constitutional rights of free speech, press, assembly and petition. Other reasons include a fear that restrictions would hamper legitimate lobbies without reaching more serious lobby abuses; the consolidated and highly effective opposition of lobbies to restrictions; and the desire of some members to keep open avenues to a possible lobbying career they may wish to pursue later.

The two major lobbying laws that Congress has succeeded in enacting have dealt with lobbyists in general who meet certain definitions of lobbying. The Foreign Agents Registration Act was first enacted in 1938 amid reports of fascist and Nazi propaganda circulating in the United States in the period before World War II. It has been amended frequently since then, and its history is as much a part of this country's struggle with internal security as it is a part of efforts to regulate lobbying.

The one existing omnibus lobbying law, the Federal Regulation of Lobbying Act, was enacted in 1946 as part of the Legislative Reorganization Act. It requires paid lobbyists to register with the House and the Senate and to file quarterly reports with the House. However, large loopholes in the law exempt many interests from registering. The 1954 U.S. Supreme Court decision in *United States v. Harriss* further limited the scope of the law.

Since then congressional committees have investigated the situation and proposed replacements for the 1946 act. Both the House and Senate passed versions of a new bill in 1976 but conferees were not able to resolve differences between the two versions before Congress adjourned. Although various versions of a lobby disclosure bill have been introduced each year since then, including one passed by the House in 1978, no bill has been enacted.

Lobbyists See Challenge in New Tax Law

"We desperately need a tax sabbath — a rest," said Kenneth C. O. Hagerty, vice president for government operations of the American Electronics Association.

It was a surprising statement, considering the source, because the members of Hagerty's organization were among those who considered themselves big losers under the tax-overhaul bill (HR 3838) that finally passed Congress, Sept. 27, 1986, after two years of work. They considered elimination of the special low tax rate on capital gains a threat to continued innovation and prosperity in the high-tech industries. *(Tax bill, p. 45; CQ 1986 Weekly Report, provisions, p. 2350)*

Hagerty's views were not unusual, however, either in Congress or in the lobbying community.

Most of those who wanted to see the tax law changed again, and quickly, simply did not figure their chances were very good.

But they were not really resting. They were thinking and planning how to take advantage of the right moment, when it came.

The numbers of those who were calculating how to change the law before the ink of a presidential signature was even applied, let alone dried, were large and their objectives were diverse. Their aims went far beyond traditional business concerns to include items that have been the subject of almost no congressional or public discussion, such as whether the new law treats the blind or renters unfairly.

In addition, business lobbyists, in particular, were beginning to talk among themselves about the need to devise whole new approaches to what the tax law should be. That would obviously be a more time-consuming task than merely marshaling the arguments for restoring an old tax break that was taken away.

Letting the Law Sink In

On the other side, opposing changes in the near future, were those who really wanted some time to rest, and perhaps more important, time for Congress and the nation to find out

whether the results of this major rewrite of the tax law were good or bad.

Rep. Dan Rostenkowski, D-Ill., chairman of the Ways and Means Committee, opened the House debate on the tax bill with some comments on that point.

"If I have one philosophic quest as chairman," he said, "it's to check the annual sport of tightening and loosening the federal tax code. I don't want to come back next year and open another round of rearranging tax preferences."

Even members of Congress who did not like HR 3838 at all agreed that it would be hard to change any time soon.

Sen. John C. Danforth, R-Mo., who was the leading spokesman for the opposition in the Senate, said,

---

Everyone agreed that the deficit would keep the pressure on 1987 for a tax increase. Even if new revenues came from excise taxes on gasoline, alcohol and tobacco, that could reopen the whole tax code.

"There's going to be great resistance to reopening the tax law during the balance of the Reagan administration. The president likes the bill and he'll be very reluctant to see any change in the rates. And if we don't move off the rates, I don't see where the money will come from to restore" major tax breaks that have been repealed or curtailed.

The views of the president figured into everyone's thinking about the prospects for future changes in the tax law.

Rep. Bill Archer, R-Texas, who was the leader of the opposition in the House, was among those who thought the tax bill would reduce revenue collections over five years, though it was not supposed to, thus increasing the already huge budget deficit, and forc-

ing President Reagan to agree either to a smaller defense spending buildup or to some tax increases.

"The White House is going to have to choose," Archer said.

What's more, there was a story going around in well-connected circles in Washington that several members of Reagan's Cabinet were so deeply concerned about the deficit — they were said to include Secretaries James A. Baker III of Treasury, Malcolm Baldrige of Commerce and William E. Brock of Labor — that they were working together to change Reagan's mind about tax increases, since the tax overhaul bill was successfully out of the way.

Heat From the Deficit

Whether the Cabinet group existed precisely as the story had it, and whether it or anyone else would succeed in altering Reagan's resistance to increased taxes, everyone agreed that the deficit would create continuing pressure in 1987 for new revenues.

Even if the increases were limited to items such as excise taxes on gasoline, alcohol and tobacco, that could reopen the whole tax code.

So could another deficit-reducing idea that was just beginning to be heard on Capitol Hill: postponing the full tax cut scheduled for 1988 for at least a year.

That would cut the fiscal 1988 deficit by more than $20 billion. The deficit would be cut by more than $30 billion if the scheduled 1988 increases in the personal exemption and standard deduction were postponed as well.

Under such a plan, the public would still get the benefits of the first phase of the tax reduction, which goes into effect for 1987.

Two other factors figured into the thinking of those who had hopes for changing the new tax law that went onto the statute books in October 1986.

The first was the universally agreed need to correct the inevitable errors in HR 3838 — to make what are generally called technical corrections in the law. Both lobbyists and members of Congress quoted a gag gener-

"There's going to be great resistance to reopening the tax law during the balance of the Reagan administration. The president likes the bill and he'll be very reluctant to see any change in the rates."

—Sen. John C. Danforth, R-Mo.

ally attributed to Sen. Russell B. Long of Louisiana, who retired in 1986 as the ranking Democrat on the Senate Finance Committee.

Long reportedly once said that "a technical correction is whatever 51 senators agree it is."

The other reason why some believed the tax law would be reopened in 1987, despite widespread reluctance, was the possibility that the economy was slipping into a downturn.

If so, there would be pressure to make tax changes aimed at stimulating the economy. Chief among these would be restoration of tax incentives for business investment in new machinery and equipment and a loosening of new restrictions on consumer interest deductions.

Such changes could have been made even if it was really much too soon for anyone to demonstrate that the new law had actually caused the recession, or made it worse.

Pressure Points

It was too soon to begin predicting which sections of HR 3838 might be the first to be amended.

Which parts of the law are most vulnerable are not always clear in advance. For example, there was a provision of the 1984 Deficit Reduction Act (PL 98-369) that required persons who use the same automobile for both business and personal travel to keep detailed daily records of their trips. The provision did not attract very much attention as it went through Congress, but once it was on the books it aroused so many complaints that it was repealed in just four months.

(1985 CQ Almanac p. 478)

What follows is nonetheless a list of some of the main items cited as prime candidates for change, if Congress were to reopen the tax law:

● **Passive Loss Provisions.** These sections of HR 3838 were aimed at putting a stop to investments in tax shelters, especially in real estate, whose sole purpose is the creation of paper losses that investors can use to reduce their taxable income.

Among those who thought the bill went beyond that objective and would harm people actually in the real estate business, and not just tax-motivated, was Sen. Lloyd Bentsen, D-Texas. He tried to soften this provision in the Finance Committee but lost by one vote. Bentsen also thought the bill's retroactive reach was unfair.

● **The Elderly and Blind.** The bill would take away the extra personal exemption that blind or elderly persons were getting, substituting an increase in the standard deduction. Archer, among others, noted that such a change did not compensate those who itemize their deductions for the loss of the extra exemption. He assigned a high priority to changing this.

● **Interest Deductions for Renters.** Congress got itself into some complications because it decided to preserve interest deductions on home mortgages but disallow them on other consumer purchases.

To deal with the obvious loophole they had created — homeowners with some equity could merely refinance their house and use the proceeds to buy a car, for example — legislators put restrictions on the amount of such refinancings. But they put no limits on

how much anyone could borrow against a first or second residence if the proceeds of the loan were used for educational or medical purposes.

Members reported that they were hearing from constituents who protested that it was unfair to give these interest deductions to homeowners but not renters.

● **Individual Retirement Accounts.** Surprisingly, since limits on tax-free contributions to these retirement savings plans produced by far the largest volume of mail Congress got on any aspect of the tax bill, there was little continuing protest. Thus it was not clear if loosening the restrictions on IRAs would be one of the main targets for early amendment. Major additions to the tax-free contributions that were still permitted under the bill would cost considerable revenue.

● **Charitable Contributions.** Robert Smucker, vice president for government relations of Independent Sector, a coalition of charitable, educational and other tax-exempt organizations, said he and others "plan to make a major effort in the next Congress to restore the deduction" for charitable contributions for persons who do not itemize other deductions.

He noted that 265 House members — more than a majority — sponsored legislation to create that deduction and that an effort to keep its repeal out of the Senate version of the 1986 tax bill failed by only four votes.

Despite this arithmetic, he conceded that "it's going to be tough to get any major changes in the tax bill in the next several years." But then he added, "There's nothing as certain as

"If I have one philosophic quest as chairman, it's to check the annual sport of tightening and loosening the federal tax code. I don't want to come back next year and open another round of rearranging tax preferences."

—Rep. Dan Rostenkowski, D-Ill.

change in Washington."

● **Investment Tax Credit, Rapid Depreciation and Capital Gains.** Restoration of at least part of what was taken away from these incentives for capital investment was the main objective for many businesses, though all recognized that the big tax losses involved were a problem.

Hagerty of the electronics association said, "It is going to take us a while to document the case" for restoration of a preferential capital gains rate, although he expected the impact to be "huge."

He added that his organization had not yet developed a consensus on its "single immediate highest priority" in the tax area, partly because the credit for business research and development outlays had been extended only through 1988. He noted that they would have to fight that battle again then.

Other business lobbyists spoke of similar uncertainties about their priorities without being willing to be quoted by name.

Some were also still thinking out the exact new provisions they ought to propose, even though they knew what their basic economic objectives were.

Charls E. Walker, head of the lobbying firm that bears his name, said he expected that "Congress will be looking at investment incentives if the economy drops off sharply next year." But he added that he did not care greatly whether they restored the investment tax credit, as such, or gave businesses the same degree of tax incentives for new investment with heavy first year depreciation writeoffs.

His concern, he said, was simply that U.S. businesses be able to recover their capital investments at a pace competitive with the rest of the world.

Walker conceded that the ITC had acquired "a bad image" since 1962, when it was first enacted. It had been taken off the statute books and then restored three times since.

Ernest S. Christian, a lawyer with the Washington lobbying firm of Patton, Boggs & Blow also thought "it's going to be hard to get Congress to put back what they just took away. But maybe there are other ways to ameliorate the effects. We haven't reached the limits of human intelligence on this tax bill. I expect that over the next three to six months, you're going to see a number of new ideas."

A somewhat different approach was suggested by Mark Bloomfield, president of the American Council for Capital Formation.

"We don't know what members of Congress want to do next, if anything," he said. "That 'Gone fishin' sign Rostenkowski has on the door is real. I never think of what issues are important and try to sell them. I try to find out what members of Congress are interested in and work with them." ▪

Senate Votes to Restrict PAC Contributions

After months of fits and starts, the Senate the week of Aug. 11, 1986, came to the brink of passing sweeping campaign finance reforms designed to loosen the binds of special interest groups on congressional office seekers.

But in the partisan drive to gain the higher ground on the sensitive election-year issue, Republicans and Democrats played a high-stakes game of "political chicken" and eventually dodged a final decision.

Senators went on record twice in favor of strict new controls on campaign fund-raising, but in the end failed to pass legislation to that effect.

On a 69-30 vote, the Senate approved a measure by David L. Boren, D-Okla., to limit the amount of money that political action committees (PACs) can give congressional candidates.

Then, on a 58-42 roll call, the Senate approved a GOP countermeasure by Rudy Boschwitz, Minn., to stifle PAC contributions to political parties and force party operations to disclose all hidden sources of their funds. *(1986 CQ Weekly Report, p. 1912)*

Both amendments were attached to an unrelated bill (S 655) that had been stripped of its other provisions in 1985. The two sides earlier had agreed to delay further action on the bill as amended until after Congress returned from its August recess.

A last-minute effort to bring S 655 to a final vote immediately — thus sending the PAC-limiting measure to the House — was stymied by partisan maneuvering and tactical infighting.

Majority Leader Robert Dole, R-Kan., a vocal opponent of the bill, appeared willing to allow a final vote after both amendments were approved. Boren, despite the reluctance of some Democrats, was ready to take up the offer.

But Boschwitz, who had devised his amendment partly to embarrass Democrats whose national party apparatus relies most heavily on PAC donations, ultimately nixed the idea of passing the bill as a political gambit.

- "People are playing chicken with each other," Boschwitz said. "This is a political exercise, by and large, and it should be seen for what it is."

The Boren and Boschwitz amendments were the only votes allowed on S 655 under a complicated agreement guaranteeing action before the Senate's scheduled Aug. 15 recess on two other issues, South Africa sanctions and U.S. aid to the Nicaraguan "contras." *(1986 Weekly Report, p. 1878)*

Ironically, Republicans who opposed Boren's amendment said pressure on both sides of the aisle to force action on the two foreign policy issues would have given Boren leverage to insert a final vote on S 655 in the agreement.

But Boren, who had been angling for Senate action on his PAC-limita-

"People are playing chicken with each other.... This is a political exercise, by and large, and it should be seen for what it is."
—Sen. Rudy Boschwitz, R-Minn.

tion measure since January, seemed content with the recorded vote in favor of his proposal. "This is not a vote they could cast without it coming back to haunt them," Boren said afterward. "This cause has a momentum now. It's not going to be stopped."

Prime PAC Opponent

Boren has been the primary instigator in the Senate to limit PAC contributions to congressional campaigns. Though he has attracted bipartisan support — including Barry Goldwater, R-Ariz., and John C. Stennis, D-Miss. — for the most part he has conducted a lonely crusade to force Senate action. *(Boren, box, next page)*

He introduced a bill (S 1806) in October 1985 and forced temporary

Senate action on the measure when he offered it as an amendment to S 655 in December. *(1985 CQ Almanac p. 33)*

But the anticipated showdown in 1985 dissipated after both sides said they were uncertain how the votes were lining up. Dole promised Boren future action on his bill, including hearings in the Senate Rules Committee and a subsequent floor vote, and Republicans and Democrats then joined in an overwhelming 7-84 vote against killing the Boren bill.

Boren's Key Provisions

The crux of Boren's attack on PACs is creation of a limit on how much each Senate and House candidate may accept from all PACs, and the setting of new limits on how much each can receive from one PAC, in any two-year election "cycle."

The cap on receipts from PACs overall would be $100,000 for House candidates and between $175,000 and $750,000 for Senate candidates, depending on the populations in their states. The limits would be increased to allow for contested primaries and runoff elections.

The Boren measure also would reduce from $5,000 to $3,000 the cap on what a PAC can give to one candidate per election. It would at the same time increase the limit on what an individual contributor can give a candidate from $1,000 to $1,500 per election.

In addition, Boren would close an existing loophole in campaign finance law that allows a PAC to exceed cur-

Sen. Boren Refuses PAC Contributions . . .

David L. Boren, D-Okla., the driving force behind the Senate vote to limit political action committee contributions, makes a virtue of not accepting PAC money himself. But that doesn't mean he won't take a campaign donation from a special interest.

A detailed Congressional Quarterly study of Boren's 1983-84 campaign finances shows that at least 25 percent of the $983,553 he raised came from donors who were executives or employees of companies in two industries: energy, and banking and finance. They contributed at least $246,950, according to records on file with the Federal Election Commission.

Boren, a member of the tax-writing Finance Committee, received close to $10,000 from presidents and chief executive officers of some of the nation's largest corporations, and at least $25,000 from Washington, D.C., lawyers and lobbyists.

Other attorneys, mainly in Oklahoma, Texas and Louisiana, contributed $48,200. And nearly 7 percent of his total receipts came from contributors who listed themselves simply as "homemaker," although some were apparent relatives of wealthy executives who also contributed to Boren's last re-election campaign.

There is nothing unusual in members accepting donations from individuals who may represent specific economic interests over which the member has legislative purview. What makes Boren different is his unrelenting stand against existing campaign finance laws and his refusal to take PAC money. His anti-PAC amendment passed the Senate Aug. 12, 1986.

The senator, who says he is not opposed to PACs per se and might someday accept money from them if necessary, is concerned about their growing impact on politics.

"They're taking on an undue amount of influence by providing too great a proportion of the campaign financing," he said in an interview. "What we've seen is the percentage of contributions coming from small [contributors] declining rapidly over the past 10 years."

To finance his campaigns, Boren relies on money from individual contributors — much of it in large sums. And he takes pride in noting that most of them come from Oklahoma. He agreed that banning PAC money would not end the special interest nature of many campaign contributions but declared that there is a major difference between an individual donation and a PAC gift.

"An individual can contribute based upon the individual's assessment of the candidate's total [record]," he said. "But a PAC can't do that. A PAC has to say, 'Well, how did he vote on real estate, banking issues, this union's issue, or something else?'"

Of the $983,553 he raised in 1983-84, he reported that $264,333 came from contributors who gave amounts totaling less than $200. CQ's study focused on the remaining, larger contributions, and, where possible, identified them as coming from employees or executives of certain industries. Those not easily identified were not included in the study.

The results showed that a majority of his contributors live in Oklahoma, but sizable numbers also come from Texas, Louisiana and Washington, D.C.

At least $122,000 — about 12 percent of his total — came from executives and employees of companies specializing in energy, a staple of the Oklahoma economy. The largest amount, $84,650, came from con-

tributors involved in oil and gas. These ranged from small-time independent oil producers to better-known corporate oil men such as Rawleigh Warner Jr., chairman and chief executive officer of Mobil Corporation.

Boren has an excellent legislative record as far as oil producers are concerned. He is one of only four senators — and the only Democrat — to get a 100 percent rating from the Independent Petroleum Association of America for his votes in Congress through the end of 1984.

Boren also got $21,250 from donors involved in drilling and exploration; $8,250 from those providing supplies, such as pipelines, to energy companies; and $7,850 from miscellaneous energy-related interests.

A slightly larger portion of Boren's contributions, 13 percent, came from the finance industry. Some $124,950 of his total receipts came from donors involved in investment, banking, accounting and insurance. That does not include $38,650 from persons listed as self-employed who described their occupation as "investments."

A swing vote on the Finance Committee, Boren is ranking Democrat on the Estate and Gift Taxation Subcommittee, and a member of the Health and International Trade subcommittees.

He received at least $58,850 from contributors employed in banking, $43,650 from investment executives and $18,100 from insurance executives. Some $4,350 came from accountants and others in the accounting business.

Some of these contributions came from Oklahoma bankers, but others represented larger interests. Executives of one firm — Lomas and Nettleton, the Dallas-based financial company — gave $5,500, while executives of the New York-based brokerage firm of Goldman, Sachs & Co. contributed at least $5,000.

Other large contributors included a number of prominent Washington lawyers, including tax and energy specialists, and some well-known "super lobbyists," such as Robert S. Strauss and J. D. Williams.

. . . But Still Accepts Special Interest Money

Among the corporations for whom Strauss' Dallas-based law firm — Akin, Gump, Strauss, Hauer & Feld — lobbied in Washington in 1984 were the Gulf, Mobil and Texaco oil companies and two investment firms, the Bache Group and Goldman, Sachs. Among the clients represented by Williams' law firm, Williams & Jensen, were the Domestic Petroleum Council, E. F. Hutton and Cigna, the insurance company.

The large category of contributors, all women, listed simply as "homemaker," included a number of people who appeared to be relatives of other Boren donors. Among them were Beatrice Carr Pickens, who gave $1,000 and listed the same address as T. Boone Pickens Jr., the charismatic president of Mesa Petroleum, and Mrs. J. D. Williams, who made contributions throughout the election cycle along with Williams, the Washington lobbyist.

Other major groups of Boren contributors include those involved in engineering and construction, who gave at least $21,800; agriculture, $20,500; real estate and land development, $16,050; health, $13,100; and automobiles and transportation, $12,500.

. . .By Any Other Name

Some people who follow campaign finance see little significant distinction between a PAC contribution and a large donation from an individual. even the vehemently anti-PAC organization Common Cause, the self-styled citizens' lobby, which supported Boren's amendment, views large donations as special interest money.

"We've never thought that the only special interest money is PAC money," says Randy Huwa, Common Cause vice president for communications, noting however that the difference between individual donations and PAC contributions is that PAC's generally have a lobbying agenda, which is not always the case with an individual.

"That's why our long-term goal has been a system of public financing or some other mechanism for encouraging small contributions," Huwa

Selected Boren Contributors

Washington, D.C., Lawyers Giving $500 or More

Attorney	Firm	Legal Specialty [1]	Contribution
Harry E. Barsh	Camp, Carmouche	Energy	$1,000
Carl E. Bates	Camp, Carmouche	Tax	1,000
David Busby	Busby, Rehm & Leonard	Trade	500
Thomas A. Davis	Davis & McLeod [2]	Tax	1,500
W. Peyton George	Miles & Stockbridge	General	1,000
Robert E. Glennon	Williams & Jensen	Tax	500
William B. Harmon	Davis & Harmon	Insurance, Tax	1,000
Gail Harrison	Wexler, Reynolds	Government Relations	666
J. Steven Hart	Williams & Jensen	Lobbying	950
Joel Jankowsky	Akin, Gump	Legislative	1,000
Robert E. Jensen	Williams & Jensen	General	1,100
Richard A. Kline	Kline, Rommer	Patents	1,000
Jim Lake	Heron, Burchette	Government Relations	1,000
Jim C. Langdon	Akin, Gump	Energy	1,000
John Montgomery	Barrett, Montgomery	Washington Representative	1,000
Carl A. Nordberg	Groom & Nordberg	Tax	1,000
John Rainbolt	Miles & Stockbridge [2]	Commodities	1,000
Jonathan C. Rose	Jones, Day	(unavailable)	500
Cornelius Shields	Pepper, Hamilton [2]	Tax	1,000
Robert S. Strauss	Akin, Gump	General	1,000
Dennis Whittlesey	Keck, Mahin	Tax, Indians, Environment	1,000
J. D. Williams	Williams & Jensen	Lobbying	2,000

Industry Leaders

Contributor	Title	Company	Amount
A. Dan Davis	President/CEO	Winn-Dixie	1,000
Robert D. Davis	Chairman	Winn-Dixie	1,000
Robert D. Kirkpatrick	Chairman/CEO	Cigna	500
Robert W. Lundeen	Chairman	Dow Chemical	1,000
Dean A. McGee	Chairman	Kerr-McGee	500
Lee. L. Morgan	Chairman	Caterpillar Tractor	500
T. Boone Pickens Jr.	President	Mesa Petroleum	1,500
Rawleigh Warner Jr.	Chairman/CEO	Mobil	800

[1] *According to law firm*   [2] *No longer with firm*

SOURCE: Federal Election Commission reports

said.

Richard P. Conlon, executive director of the Democratic Study Group, the House Democrats' research arm, sees little difference between PAC money and big contributions.

"The PAC wants to further its legislative agenda," Conlon says. "The same can be said for big contributions. Certainly, big contributions are 90 percent or more contributions from people with an interest in legislation. They are peo-

ple who [want] access the same as a PAC."

But Larry J. Sabato, a PAC expert at the University of Virginia, does find one difference between PAC money and large contributions. "Special interests may come in many forms," he says. "The difference being that PAC money, since it's pooled . . . is easily identified by interest. Individual gifts are much more difficult to trace and, therefore, the special influence can be far more insidious than PAC money."

rent limits by "bundling" further donations from individuals and passing those on to candidates in the PAC's name.

Besides limiting PAC contributions to candidates, Boren's bill attacks the practice of using PAC money to campaign against one candidate without the money being covered by an opponent's campaign spending limits.

Boren would require that such advertising announce that it is not subject to campaign contribution limits. It would also require broadcasters to give equal time to the subjects of "negative" ads.

Tenfold Increase

Boren and other supporters of PAC limits repeatedly invoked statistics that show PAC spending on congressional campaigns has risen nearly tenfold in the past decade. In 1974, 608 PACs gave candidates for Congress a total of $12.5 million. In the 1984 campaigns, House and Senate candidates received $104 million from 4,000 registered PACs.

The rise in the number of PACs and their influence in political campaigns has put lawmakers on the defensive against a public perception that special-interest groups have undue influence on politicians.

"We have formalized and legalized political corruption," said Sen. William Proxmire, D-Wis.

Senate Minority Leader Robert C. Byrd, D-W.Va., complained bitterly that legislators have become obsessed with raising money for their re-election campaigns. "It's going to kill this institution," he said.

But opponents of the proposed limits insisted that Boren's bill would do little to contain the flow of PAC money into campaigns, because PACs would merely funnel their funds into more negative advertising and other forms of "independent" expenditures.

"The Boren plan will only worsen the problems that he seeks to resolve," Boschwitz said, adding that PACs were formed in the post-Watergate era of the mid-1970s as a result of campaign reforms that sought to control the influence of wealthy individuals.

GOP Counterpoint

Boschwitz became the point man for Republican opposition to the Boren plan when Dole appointed him to head a special GOP task force to come up with an alternative.

Boschwitz came back with a countermeasure to prohibit PAC contributions to national political parties, which include the partisan campaign committees run by leaders of the House and Senate.

Boschwitz' amendment also would require political parties to disclose the so-called "soft money" they accept from corporations, unions and other donors that currently goes unreported.

Soft money is used for general "party-building" purposes, such as paying for campaign headquarters or bolstering the coffers of state party organizations, rather than for a particular candidate's campaign. The practice allows wealthy donors to exceed limits on individual contributions and allows party organizations to provide indirect support for candidates with money that would be illegal if given directly to a candidate.

Boschwitz' amendment was assailed as a blatantly partisan attempt to embarrass Democrats, who traditionally rely more heavily on PAC contributions to party organizations than do Republicans, who get most of their donations from individuals.

In the 1984 congressional elections, national Democratic Party organizations, such as the Democratic Senatorial Campaign Committee (DSCC) and the Democratic Congressional Campaign Committee (DCCC), received $6.5 million in contributions from PACs, compared with $58.3 million from individuals, according to the Federal Election Commission.

On the other hand, Republican organizations, including the National Republican Senatorial Committee and the National Republican Congressional Committee, received only $1.7 million from PACs, compared with $262 million from individual contributors.

Sen. George J. Mitchell of Maine, chairman of the DSCC, called the Boschwitz amendment a "plainly, openly, cynically partisan" attempt to give Republicans an even bigger edge in campaign fund-raising.

"If those figures were reversed, there would be no attempt to offer this amendment," Mitchell said.

Boschwitz acknowledged that his amendment was crafted with a political strategy in mind. The amendment and the rules governing the two votes were designed to give Republicans a way to vote successively for the Boren amendment and the Boschwitz alternative, working on the assumption that the Democratic-controlled House would probably not want to act on a bill that contained both measures.

"Most senators voted for it know-ing it would not solve the problem," said Pete V. Domenici, R-N.M.

"They also voted for it hoping against hope that it wouldn't pass. There are not 51 senators that would vote for that Boren amendment if they thought it would become law," he said.

Bill's Future Uncertain

While the vote on the Boren amendment drew broad bipartisan support, the tally on Boschwitz' proposal proceeded almost strictly along party lines, until the outcome in the Republicans' favor was assured and a handful of Democrats joined with Boschwitz.

Once the votes were taken, the plan was to let the issue drop until September.

But according to one Republican aide, Dole, Boschwitz, Phil Gramm, R-Texas, and John Heinz, R-Pa., huddled in the GOP cloakroom and decided to press for final passage on the assumption that Boren and the Senate Democrats would take the Boschwitz amendment to get Boren's.

Standing in their way, however, were several senators on both sides of the aisle who wanted to offer amendments of their own. Because the bill was still tied up in the unanimous consent agreement governing debate on South Africa and Nicaragua, an individual senator could block a final vote on S 655.

Jesse Helms, R-N.C., and Gordon J. Humphrey, R-N.H., wanted to include a measure to prevent unions from using member dues for political contributions. Lloyd Bentsen, D-Texas, had an amendment to prohibit foreign-controlled PACs from contributing to any political campaign.

In the end, however, it was Boschwitz who halted further action on S 655, although an aide said he was also objecting to final passage on behalf of an unnamed Democrat, as well.

Throughout the debate Boschwitz described the issue as too politically charged for Congress to be able to deal with objectively. He called for a bipartisan commission to come back in a year with recommendations for campaign finance reform; a bill (S 528) to that effect was passed by the Senate Governmental Affairs Committee Aug. 12.

"Don't get me wrong. I'm not opposed to PAC reform," Boschwitz said. "The motivation for going to final passage is political. If we're going to do it, we're going to do it right." ∎

Former Reagan Aide Target of Lobby Probe

A special prosecutor was named in May 1986 to probe allegations that Michael K. Deaver violated conflict-of-interest laws by lobbying White House officials after he resigned as President Reagan's deputy chief of staff in May 1985. Whitney North Seymour Jr. was appointed after the Justice Department determined that an independent counsel for Deaver's case was warranted under the Ethics in Government Act.

Deaver left the administration to run a public relations firm that represented Canada, South Korea, Mexico, Saudi Arabia and Caribbean sugar producers, among others. Deaver's activities were controversial because, in addition to his professional connection to the administration, he was a long-time personal friend of President and Nancy Reagan. Upon leaving his post, Deaver kept his White House pass and continued to receive a copy of Reagan's daily schedule. He also played tennis on the White House courts.

The Deaver case spurred the consideration of new conflict-of-interest legislation in the 99th Congress (1985-87), focusing particular attention on government officials — and members of Congress — who go to work for foreign governments. However, the outlook for final passage of a bill was poor as Congress rushed to adjourn before the November 1986 elections.

GAO Report

Earlier in the year, on May 12, the General Accounting Office reported that Deaver appeared to have violated conflict-of-interest laws by representing Canada on acid rain shortly after determining administration policy on the issue as a White House official. Contending that it was being damaged by acid rain caused by American factories and power plants, Canada was seeking U.S. government action to control air pollution. After a five-month investigation that involved interviews with about 10 White House officials, the GAO concluded that Deaver could have violated four sections of the ethics law governing postemployment conflict of interest:

● A lifetime ban for any executive branch employee on lobbying a "particular matter involving a specific party" if the official "participated personally and substantially" in the issue while in office.

The GAO said Deaver participated in 15 White House discussions on acid rain in preparation for the March 1985 summit meeting between President Reagan and Canadian Prime Minister Brian Mulroney and became a supporter of the decision to appoint a special envoy for acid rain. Deaver discussed with national security adviser Robert C. McFarlane two potential nominees for the job, former interior secretary William P. Clark and former transportation secretary Drew Lewis, who eventually got the volunteer position.

Michael K. Deaver entering the Capitol to testify before a House subcommittee in May 1986.

● A two-year lobbying prohibition for federal officials on specific matters that fell under the official's responsibility in the last year of federal service.

The GAO said Deaver's attorney reported that Deaver shared "overall responsibility" for the U.S.-Canadian summit, but that other White House officials had specific responsibility for the acid rain issue. "Given the apparently broad scope of Mr. Deaver's White House duties," the GAO reported, "it may be that the issue of whether the United States should agree to appoint a special envoy for acid rain was a matter that was 'actually pending' under his official responsibility within the year prior to his resignation."

● A two-year ban for a specific group of top-level civilian and military officials against representing, counseling, assisting or advising on an issue in which the official "participated personally and substantially."

Five months after he left the White House, Deaver accompanied Canadian officials to the River Club in New York City, where he met with Lewis, the GAO said. Lewis told GAO that the group discussed the content and timing of a special envoy report, with the Canadians pressing the administration for a funding commitment to control acid rain. Deaver did not discuss the content of the report, but merely the timing of its release. But GAO said Deaver's very presence at that meeting appeared to constitute lobbying an officer of the United States.

● A one-year ban on senior government officials lobbying their former agency or department.

The question was whether the special envoy was a State Department official or a White House official. Deaver maintained that Lewis was attached to the State Department, where Deaver was free to make contacts. But GAO concluded that Lewis worked mainly out of the White House and reported directly to the president.

The role of employer, according to the GAO, appeared to have been served by the White House Office and the Office of Policy Development. The Office of Government Ethics ruled in 1983 that these two offices together are considered a separate "agency" in the Executive Office of the President. Deaver, as a former member of the White House Office, was barred from contacts with anyone in that office or in the Office of Policy Development. If Lewis was part of the latter office, Deaver violated the law by seeing him in New York City, the GAO said.

On Jan. 8, 1986, the special envoys of Canada and the United States issued a joint report containing a recommendation that the U.S. government implement a five-year, $5 billion demonstration program to control acid rain. On March 19, Reagan reversed a longstanding policy and agreed to this recommendation.

GAO deputy counsel James F. Hinchman said there was "enough basis" for believing that the post-employment laws were violated to justify referring the case to the Justice Department. The department was already conducting a preliminary investigation into Deaver's lobbying activities. An FBI probe was triggered April 24 by a letter from five Democratic members of the Senate Judiciary Committee, who asked Attorney General Edwin Meese III to determine if sufficient grounds existed to ask a special federal court to appoint an independent counsel to look into Deaver's

activities. Deaver himself joined the call for a special prosecutor, saying in an April 28 letter to Meese that it was the only way to clear his name.

Deaver Testimony

Reacting to the mounting publicity against him, Deaver defended his occupation and his reputed influence with the Reagans in private testimony May 16, 1986, before the House Energy and Commerce Subcommittee on Oversight and Investigations. The subcommittee, headed by John D. Dingell, D-Mich., questioned Deaver's work for the Canadian government on acid rain, as well as other lobbying efforts on behalf of foreign trading partners of the United States.

Deaver told the subcommittee he has stayed "within the law at all times" and "faithfully adhered" to the Foreign Agents Registration Act. Deaver said he has been attacked "virtually without restraint or qualification" by critics who believed it was improper for a former presidential adviser to represent a foreign government before the U.S. government. But Congress "never has even suggested the impropriety of, much less prohibited by legislation, what these critics now assert," Deaver said. "I submit that if there is a dispute over what the nation's policy with respect to this issue should be, then such criticism should be directed to Congress, not to individual citizens."

Subcommittee Staff Report

The subcommittee Aug. 12 unanimously adopted a scathing report alleging Deaver could have committed "perjury" and "obstruction of justice." The subcommittee voted 17-0 to turn evidence of Deaver's possible criminal violations over to the special prosecutor.

The report, prepared by the majority and minority staff members, said Deaver "knowingly and willfully" made false statements when he testified before the subcommittee. The report alleged Deaver failed to tell members about a conversation in 1985 with a national security adviser on getting tax breaks for Puerto Rico, did not tell them about contacts with two U.S. ambassadors on behalf of clients and misrepresented his dealings with the administration's budget director on behalf of a defense contractor. The report concluded that Deaver "may have violated federal statutes relating to perjury, false statements and obstruction of a congressional investigation."

The subcommittee's action effectively requested that the independent counsel decide if Deaver committed the federal offense of perjury in his sworn testimony before the panel. Dingell stressed that Seymour would have to judge whether prosecution on that charge was warranted. Resolution of the Deaver case was still pending as of October 1986. ∎

Evangelicals Become Electoral Force

After making a strong early showing in the campaigning that led up to Michigan's Aug. 5, 1986, Republican primary, television evangelist Marion G. "Pat" Robertson expressed jubilation about the early success of his exploratory 1988 presidential campaign. "The Christians have won!" he had written to some 50,000 supporters in June. The comment seemed to sum up both the emerging political strength of Robertson and others on the "Christian Right," as well as, in the eyes of some people, the potentially dangerous impact of a powerful religious movement on American political life.

Whatever the outcome of Robertson's campaign, his fellow political conservatives among the nation's estimated 35 million "evangelical" Christians are becoming a major force in politics and social issue lobbying. These theologically conservative evangelical Protestants, who stress the authority of the Bible and the need for a personal relationship with Jesus Christ, are opposed to what they see as the moral decay of American society, as exemplified by legal abortions, the banning of prayer in public schools and the toleration of pornography. In the past decade they have moved away from their traditional distrust of politics, and they are showing a growing allegiance to the Republican Party. Along with other demographic groups who are moving to the Republicans, evangelicals may be contributing to a realignment process that could make the GOP the nation's majority party. Their new political activism, symbolized by such organizations as Robertson's Freedom Council and the Liberty Federation (formerly, the Moral Majority) of Rev. Jerry Falwell, is reshaping the Republican Party at the grass roots.

The Christian Right will be, in the words of University of Virginia sociologist Jeffery Hadden, "one of the most important social movements in this country for the remainder of the century." But the movement is also stirring up a backlash among people who worry that zealots will use the power of government to force their religious views on others.

"There is an antipathy to the involvement of clergy in politics — especially if clergy tell people how to vote," Robertson told a group of Washington reporters Aug. 12. "I think it's wrong to stand up and say you're God's candidate."

Boon for GOP

While evangelicals are found in all walks of life, they traditionally have shared some common characteristics. Evangelicals are found much more frequently in the South, especially in rural areas. They are predominantly white and mostly women. Their incomes have tended to be below those of members of mainline Protestant denominations, as has their degree of education. In recent years, however, the evangelical population has changed somewhat, particularly through the development of "super churches," with many thousands of members, in fast-growing cities of the Sun Belt. Those churches have drawn many upwardly mobile, better-educated people originally from other areas.

Those traditional characteristics had political consequences. Evangelicals' relatively low social standing made them less likely to be involved in politics. While they held conservative views on some social issues, such as school prayer and abortion, their eco-

Televangelist Pat Robertson

nomic condition often led to relatively liberal stands on issues such as government aid to the poor. Concentrated as they were in the South, they tended to be Democrats out of the historic loyalty of their region. But analysts generally argued that their religion did not constitute a major factor in determining their political viewpoints.

In recent decades, however, evangelical political attitudes have changed. Most importantly, evangelicals are leaving their traditional Democratic home and becoming Republicans in great numbers. The Republican trend in evangelical voting for president, evident since about 1960, had become a mass movement by 1984. The exceptions to this trend were in 1976 and 1980, when Jimmy Carter — who stressed his "born-again" experience and southern roots — captured the votes of many evangelicals in the South. According to television network exit polls and surveys by the University of Michigan's Center for Political Studies, at least 80 percent of white evangelicals backed President Reagan's re-election.

A 1984 survey of Southern Baptist ministers found that 66 percent identified with the Republican Party, while only 26 percent considered themselves Democrats. As recently as 1980, Democrats had outnumbered Republicans, 41-29 percent. According to political scientist Corwin Smidt, the shift has been strongest among young evangelicals. "Young Southern whites in particular are showing a very strong movement to the Republican Party," he said.

Evangelicals also are going to the polls in greater numbers, after many years of voting at lower rates than non-evangelicals. Indeed, in 1980 — when Reagan, Carter and independent presidential candidate John B. Anderson all had ties to the evangelical movement — evangelicals voted at a higher rate (77 percent) than non-evangelicals (72 percent). Evangelical turnout fell back in 1984, to 70 percent, but remained at a level just below that of the rest of the population (76 percent). Christian Right groups have laid great emphasis on improving voter registration and turnout among evangelicals. The groups' efforts appear to have paid off in the election of at least seven Republican House candidates in 1984, according to election analyst Albert J. Menendez of Americans United for Separation of Church and State. In those seven districts, located in Texas, North Carolina and Georgia, substantial evangelical populations and increased voter-turnout rates appear to have played a role in GOP victories. Stepped-up evangelical voting also apparently helped North Carolina Republican Sen. Jesse Helms win a tough 1984 re-election contest.

The Republican Party's stand on social issues has been the key reason for the shift. The party favors abortion curbs, school prayer and other positions backed by most evangelicals. Moreover, Republicans have worked hard to woo them, appointing evangelical liaisons at the Republican National Committee and other party organizations. In contrast, many evangelicals see the Democratic Party as abandoning them in pursuit of homosexual and feminist support. "One party has chosen to appeal to them [evangelicals], and one party has cultivated other constituencies," said Robert P. Dugan Jr., director of public affairs for the National Association of Evangelicals (NAE).

Voter Drives

The mass movement of evangelicals to the GOP has been accompanied by the emergence of a smaller cadre of activist evangelicals who are highly involved in politics. The best-known representatives of this activist core are several national organizations, including Falwell's Liberty Federation and Robertson's Freedom Council. The Liberty Federation has a mailing list of about six million households, although many fewer people are active in the organization; the Freedom Council says it has about 500,000 members. Among other national groups is Christian Voice, a 350,000-member lobbying and political organization that distributes a "Biblical Scoreboard" on the voting records of members of Congress. The American Coalition for Traditional Values (ACTV) claims to represent the leaders of "110,000 Bible-believing churches" in a battle against "secular humanism," the philosophy that man, not God, is at the center of life.

These and similar organizations are putting their main efforts into increasing political participation among evangelicals. According to Gary Jarmin, consultant to Christian Voice, the aim of that group is to spread "campaign technology as applied to the church." The organizations are trying to create networks of activists on the state and local level, in order to mobilize evangelical voters and provide grass-roots support for lobbying campaigns in Congress. While avoiding specific endorsements of candidates, the groups hope to aid candidates of the Right. "If you go fishing in a conservative pond, you're going to catch conservative fish," said Falwell administrative assistant Mark DeMoss.

The legislative agenda of these organizations focuses on social issues. ACTV's 10-point program, for example, lists constitutional amendments banning abortion and allowing voluntary prayer in the public schools as top priorities. The organization also calls for opposition to "gay rights" legislation, pornography and the Equal Rights Amendment. The Christian Right groups emphasize some foreign policy and economic issues as well. Christian Voice's 1986 scoreboard listed support for the Strategic Defense Initiative, aid to anti-communist guerrillas in Angola and Nicaragua and a balanced-budget constitutional amendment as representing the "biblical" position.

Despite their high profile, however, these organizations represent only a relatively small sector of the evangelical community. A Robertson presidential campaign could not count on the support of evangelicals as a bloc; an April poll of church leaders by NAE found that Robertson ran well behind New York Rep. Jack F. Kemp and Colorado Sen. William L. Armstrong as the preferred Republican presidential candidate. "The organizations on the Christian Right are separate from the larger movement of evangelicals," said Furman University political scientist James L. Guth. "I think that these groups really aren't tapping the political potential of the larger movement. They tend to be skeletal organizations, made up of mailing lists. There's no hard membership core."

The Christian Right organizations also face theological and personal differences among themselves. Although all stress their nonsectarian nature, observers have found that their memberships tend to follow splits within the larger evangelical movement. Many of the leaders of the old Moral Majority, for example, were members along with Falwell in the Baptist Bible Fellowship denomination, representing the theologically conservative fundamentalist wing of the faith that adheres strictly to a literal reading of the Bible. The Freedom Council has special appeal to people like Robertson, who are part of the "charismatic" wing of evangelicism, some of whose members are thought to have special powers of healing and communicating after being infused with the Holy Spirit. In addition, the groups are divided by the strong personalities of their leaders. "This religion has been built around very dramatic personal leaders; these people tend to compete with each other," said Brookings Institution scholar A. James Reichley. Falwell was backing Bush, not Robertson, for president in 1988.

In spite of the obstacles facing the national Christian Right organizations, grass-roots activism appears to be increasing among evangelicals. Activists are recruited through television ministries, such as Robertson's, and local churches. Kenneth D. Wald, a University of Florida political scientist who studied church political involvement in the Gainesville area, said: "Something appears to happen in the evangelical churches that is not overtly political, but enables them to mobilize politically," he said. "People in the evangelical churches don't see their involvement as political — they see it as acting out their religious beliefs."

In several instances in 1986, conservative evangelical forces were able to take control of the party organs that run the GOP at the local and state level.

Comments like those of Rep. Mark D. Siljander, who was defeated in Michigan's GOP primary after implying that his opponent Fred Upton was backed by the devil — or Robertson's controversial June 30 claim that Christians "maybe feel more strongly than others do" about patriotism and love of family — fuel the anxiety that many people feel about the mixture of politics and religion. Polls show that many people are disturbed by candidates who suggest, even indirectly, that God is on their side. A July *Wall Street Journal*/NBC News survey found that nearly 80 percent of the public oppose politicians who claim to be acting on divine instructions. Robertson and other religiously affiliated candidates are likely to be vulnerable to the criticism that they are trying to impose their faith on the political system. Bush workers in Michigan distributed leaflets to primary voters urging them to "help keep religion out of politics."

Concern over the role of the Christian Right is evident within evangelical circles, too. "For Christians to step across the line and try to assume for the church a role of being power brokers or a power bloc is not only being untruthful to the faith, but it invites a backlash," Sen. Armstrong, an evangelical, has said. "They should never, never, never give the impression that . . . they are somehow speaking with authority of scripture or church or God." The NAE's Dugan expressed a similar view: "We are committed to urging Christian involvement in politics, but in the right way. I'm chagrined at seeing some of the things evangelicals are doing. Robertson has not had a lot of wisdom in some of the things he has said. When he tells the National Religious Broadcasters 'we're going to take over,' it scares people to death."

As several of the GOP primary contests have shown this year, Christian activists are coming into increasingly sharp conflict with other elements of the party. Many veteran GOP officials at the local level feel threatened by the influx of evangelical activists, whom they see as trying to take over a party they have only recently joined. The struggle for control of the local party machinery is exacerbated by social and cultural differences between traditional party leaders — frequently described as being dominated by an upper-class "country-club set" — and the religious activists, whose roots are often in the middle and lower-middle classes. "At the local level, these county chairmen want to protect their little fiefdoms," Jarmin of Christian Voice observed. "The establishment types just don't understand or mix well with our people. You have three-martini Episcopalians and teetotaling Baptists — socially, culturally and religiously they just don't mix."

Abiding Conflict

Throughout the history of the American evangelical movement, there have been conflicting strands of opinion about how believers should relate to the rest of society. One tendency, still evident today, has been to avoid politics and other efforts to change society, in favor of concentrating on religious conversion and awaiting the impending return of Jesus Christ to the world. The Christian Right represents a modern manifestation of a different stance: that Christians should seek to use politics and government to improve the moral and religious condition of society.

The origins of evangelicalism as a separate tradition within American Protestantism go back to the second half of the 19th century. Around 1870, the leadership of some Protestant denominations began to develop relatively liberal theological doctrines on issues such as the literal truth of the Bible. That led to a split that created two separate wings of Protestantism — the liberal wing, which allowed for a looser reading of the Bible, and the orthodox wing, which held to a stricter reading. Another major cause of the fracture was liberal advocacy of the "Social Gospel" — the belief that Christians had a responsibility to reform and improve society. In contrast, the orthodox group put its stress on personal salvation.

By 1920, the orthodox Protestant movement had come to be known as "fundamentalism." Combining a strict adherence to biblical doctrines with an insistence on separation from all those with different beliefs, the movement pulled further and further away from the liberalism that held sway in most denominations. At the same time, however, the fundamentalists also became increasingly willing to become involved in movements to change society. Their chief goal was to resist secular trends they disapproved of. They were a leading force in the anti-alcohol movement that culminated in 1919 with Prohibition. Outraged by the scientific attack on the biblical account of creation, they also pushed state laws barring the teaching of the theory of evolution in schools.

By the 1940s some theological conservatives had become dissatisfied with fundamentalism's rigidity. The critics argued that the movement had to become more open to working with other Christians and encourage intellectual development. The formation of the NAE in 1942 signaled the birth of moderate evangelicalism, which today represents the centrist element of the movement. To the theological right are both the fundamentalists and charismatics, whose views conflict in many respects.

The most important representative of moderate evangelicalism is Rev. Billy Graham, whose touring revivals and televised sermons have made him the best-known religious figure in American life since World War II. In the decades following the war, Graham and others spearheaded the rapid growth of evangelicalism. While the mainline Protestant denominations, such as the Presbyterian, Episcopalian and Methodist churches, have experienced steady declines in membership, many evangelical churches have grown rapidly. The evangelical Southern Baptist Convention, for example, grew by 17 percent, to 14.5 million, between 1973 and 1985.

Tie to Changing Society

It has only been within the past decade that the evangelical movement has turned to politics. Fifteen years ago, the conservative religious political movement was limited to a small group of zealots. Today, the Christian Right is capable of mounting a politically significant campaign for the presidency.

The growth of the Christian Right is all the more remarkable in light of the strong theological objections that the evangelical movement — particularly its fundamentalist wing — traditionally had to politics. A religion that believes in the individual nature of salvation and the impending end of history would not appear to provide fertile ground for growing political militants. The traditional attitude of many fundamentalists was typified by Falwell in a 1965 sermon: "We have few ties to this earth. We pay our taxes, cast votes as a responsibility of citizenship, obey the laws of the land and other things demanded of us by the society in which we live. But, at the same time, we are cognizant that our only purpose on this earth is to know Christ and to make Him known." Contrast that thought with this current-day statement by Tim LaHaye, ACTV president, of whose executive board Falwell is a member: "At this crucial time in history, every Christian should do one or the other — run for office or help someone else run."

Academic observers of the Christian Right and the activists themselves attribute the increasing political involvement by evangelicals to deep social changes in American society since 1960. Seeing a world where abortion was legalized, homosexuality and promiscuity were tolerated and school prayer was banned, many evangelicals began to feel that their traditional, family-oriented lifestyle was profoundly threatened. According to Seymour Martin Lipset and other political sociologists, groups that have experienced such social alienation are prime candidates for conservative political movements.

Evangelicals had come to feel that their values were being challenged," said Reichley. "The political side of it was something they could get their hands on. When some of the television preachers began urging them to get into politics, it provided them with a release. A lot of them realize that the world won't change that much, but at least it's something they can do."

Christian activists say they moved into politics to protect themselves from secularization imposed by the rest of society. "People try to portray us as the intolerant oppressors, who want to go out and ram our values down their throats," said Jarmin. "The opposite is true — we are the ones who feel oppressed. Christians look around at the culture and feel like aliens. The whole culture is against them. We feel that we are the majority tyrannized by the minority."

However, not all evangelicals have accepted the idea that political involvement is a Christian imperative, or that the Christian Right is the correct way to become involved. Rev. Bob Jones, head of fundamentalist Bob Jones University in South Carolina, has repeatedly warned that politics will entangle Christians in worldly affairs, distracting them from spiritual life. Rev. Graham, on the other hand, has evolved in a different direction politically. In the early 1970s, he was a prominent ally of President Nixon. Disillusioned by the Watergate scandal, however, he moved away from close identification with politicians and has since kept his distance from the organized Christian Right. Most of his political pronouncements in recent years have stressed the need for world peace and an end to the nuclear competition between the United States and the Soviet Union.

Televangelism

Robertson and his fellow televangelists have played a key role in the growth of the Christian Right. The conservative political message that they have pushed with increasing frequency and fervor in recent years has encouraged many evangelical viewers to become committed political activists.

The impressive growth of televangelism in recent decades has been linked to changes in the broadcast industry, particularly the development of cable systems and the proliferation of small, independent stations. With little prospect of getting air time from the networks or major local stations — which favored religious programming provided by the established Protestant denominations — evangelical preachers began during the 1960s to purchase blocks of time from independent stations. With that air time, they were able to raise increasing amounts of money by asking viewers for contributions. Soon, they began buying some of the small stations, as did Robertson, who purchased the Virginia Beach station that became the foundation of his Christian Broadcasting Network (CBN) for $37,000 in 1961. The development of cable systems in the 1970s allowed the tel-evangelists to reach even larger audiences.

Today, religious broadcasters — most of them conservative evangelicals — are a major force in the television and radio industry. There are about 200 religious television stations, as well as more than 1,000 religious radio stations. There are several networks that offer broadcast and cable programming from an evangelical point of view, including CBN, the Trinity and PTL (Praise the Lord) networks. CBN alone has an annual budget of $250 million. In addition, evangelical preachers such as Falwell, Jimmy Swaggart and Oral Roberts regularly purchase air time on hundreds of independent television stations around the country.

Recent surveys have shown that the televangelists are reaching a sizable audience. A 1985 study by the A. C. Nielsen Co. found that 61 million people watched at least one of 10 major religious programs during the course of one month. The survey, commissioned by CBN, also found that one or more of the shows was watched on a weekly basis in 21 percent of the 86 million American households with a television set.

The most popular religious television show was CBN's flagship program, "The 700 Club," which reaches a monthly audience of nearly 29 million people. A combination of talk show, news program and old-fashioned revival, "The 700 Club" features Robertson and co-hosts Ben Kinchlow and Danuta Soderman. A typical show may include a documentary presenting the politically conservative viewpoint on some current event, an interview with a guest whose life was changed by accepting Jesus, appeals for contributions and sessions in which Robertson seeks to use prayer to heal viewers with physical ailments.

The televangelists are not without their problems, however. Dependent on viewer contributions, which may vary greatly over time, they frequently are faced with financial crises because of the high cost of air time. Even CBN, the giant of the industry, was forced earlier this year to cancel its experiment with a nightly news program, while other religious broadcasters have had to lay off employees to stay afloat. A basic difficulty for the networks is that most people, no matter how strong their beliefs, do not want to watch religious instruction exclusively. CBN greatly expanded its audience in 1981 when it began adding other types of shows — including old movies and reruns of family-oriented television series from the 1950s and 1960s — to its religious programming.

Some of the televangelists avoid discussion of political issues. Among those that do discuss politics, though, the viewpoint is almost exclusively conservative. The styles vary — from Swaggart, with his fiery denunciations of modern immorality, to Robertson, with a detailed analysis of Federal Reserve Board monetary policy, for example. But the common message is that America has gone far down the wrong road and only Christians can put it back in the right direction.

The audience the televangelists are reaching is receptive to their appeals. In a 1984 study of evangelical voters, Stuart Rothenberg and Frank Newport found that frequent viewers of religious programs were strongly inclined to base their political opinions on their religion, suggesting that "there is a potential for these religious programs to be a significant and potent political force in this country." Observers think that many of the Christian activists around the nation were first inspired and recruited by the televangelists. "Television is clearly the catalyst that is used to energize and mobilize people," said Hadden of the University of Virginia. "You don't have to watch 'The 700 Club' very long before the political aspect becomes clear." ∎

POLITICS

Elections '86:
In Congress, An All-Democratic Show

After six uneasy years in the minority, Democrats were set to retake control of the Senate in 1987 — with all of the committee chairmanships, agenda-setting privileges and other advantages that flow from majority power. Their margin of Senate control in the 100th Congress, 55-45, was slightly greater than the 53-47 advantage Republicans held the previous two years.

In the House, Democrats boosted their already sizable edge by an apparent net gain of five seats, to 258-177.

The 1986 election outcome tilted the balance of political power for the last two years of Ronald Reagan's presidency, giving him a Congress entirely controlled by the opposition party for the first time since he took office.

Those two years would test the ability of Senate and House Democrats to overcome internal divisions and develop coherent strategies and alternatives to Reagan policies they oppose.

"What are we going to do now that we've got to set policy?" Rep. Charles B. Rangel, D-N.Y., asked a colleague, only half in jest, after it became clear that Democrats had regained control of the Senate.

In the immediate flush of victory, however, Democrats went to great lengths to emphasize their desire to seek bipartisan solutions to national problems and to compromise with the White House.

"Democrats want to cooperate," said Senate Democratic leader Robert C. Byrd of West Virginia. "We will work toward meeting the president halfway."

These changes in the congressional power balance came at a time of transition for the Democatic leadership. The House was facing a wholesale shake-up of its leaders as a result of the retirement of Speaker Thomas P. O'Neill Jr., D-Mass. In the Senate, J. Bennett Johnston of Louisiana dropped a short-lived campaign to wrest the majority leader's position from Byrd, who reportedly was telling colleagues that the 1987-89 term would be his last as Democratic leader.

After the 1986 elections Senate Democrats' new majority, while wider than expected, was narrower than the 59-41 margin they enjoyed before losing control of the Senate in 1980.

Seasoned Hands at Helm

The changing of the guard in the Senate brought massive turnover in staff and other perquisites of majority power, but the transition appeared to be somewhat less tumultuous than when Republicans took control six years earlier after being in the minority for 26 years. That catapulted into positions of power a team of GOP committee chairmen and leaders unaccustomed to calling the shots.

Eight of the 15 Republicans who rose to chairmanships of standing committees in 1981 had served in the Senate for less than two terms.

By contrast, all but one of the Democrats in line after the 1986 elections to lead the Senate committees had been in office at least three terms, and all had chaired a committee or subcommittee.

The team of Democratic chairmen waiting in the wings included several Southern moderates and conservatives who were not much more liberal — some even less so — than their Republican predecessors.

For example, few changes were expected at the Budget Committee under Lawton Chiles, D-Fla., who had worked closely with his GOP counterpart, Pete V. Domenici, N.M., in crafting middle-of-the-road budgets.

At Appropriations there would be, if anything, a shift to the right when John C. Stennis, D-Miss., took over the chair from liberal Republican Mark O. Hatfield of Oregon.

The Armed Services chairmanship fell to Sam Nunn, D-Ga., a defense expert who had earned wide respect but had frustrated Democratic liberals with his hawkish views.

However, more marked ideological shifts to the left were expected from the chairmanship changes at two committees central to the liberal agenda — the Judiciary Committee and the Labor and Human Resources Committee — which had been headed by two of the Senate's staunchest conservative Republicans.

Edward M. Kennedy, D-Mass., had the seniority rights to chair either panel but he reportedly chose to chair Labor, taking over from Orrin G. Hatch, R-Utah. The Judiciary chairmanship was expected to fall to Joseph R. Biden Jr., D-Del., succeeding Strom Thurmond, R-S.C. Liberal maverick Howard M. Metzenbaum, D-Ohio, had been in line to chair the Labor panel if Kennedy passed it up.

Balancing Power in Committee

Democrats gained not only the chairmanships of Senate committees but also additional seats on each panel, as committee ratios were adjusted to reflect the new party balance in the Senate as a whole.

In the 99th Congress, when the Republicans outnumbered Democrats 53-47, they worked with only a one- or two-seat advantage in committees. That left some chairmen without working majorities on panels where moderate Republicans were inclined to cross party lines. On the Labor Committee, for example, the GOP's 9-7 majority was neutralized on many issues by the threat of defections by Robert T. Stafford, R-Vt., and Lowell P. Weicker Jr., R-Conn.

Similarly, a Democratic-dominated Judiciary Committee with a narrow majority would be in danger of losing effective control if Republicans voted in lock step and were consistently joined by conservative Democrats such as Dennis DeConcini of Arizona or Howell Heflin of Alabama.

With their 55-45 Senate majority in the 100th Congress, Democrats were likely to claim at least a two-seat majority on all committees. Byrd said that some panels could have margins as wide as three seats, but that the ratios would stay in line with the makeup of Congress.

Control of the committees gave Democrats the power not only to set the legislative agenda but also to launch investigations and stage hearings — important congressional vehicles for criticizing the administration or capturing media attention.

The minority party, by contrast, often has to resort to other public relations tools. For example, Senate Democrats in their first year in the minority found themselves powerless to call a hearing on controversial administration regulations allowing smaller and less-nutritious meals to be served in the federal school lunch program. In a well-covered media extravaganza, Democrats served themselves a meager lunch they said would be typical under the new regulations, which were subsequently withdrawn.

Limits of Democratic Control

Despite their control of the floor schedule and of committees, Democrats would have to build bipartisan coalitions to pass legislation in the Senate, where relatively few roll-call votes split strictly along party lines.

Democrats' ability to enact a party program would be limited by other forces, including Reagan's continued power to veto bills he opposes. Democrats had comfortable margins in both chambers, but not the two-thirds majority needed to override a veto.

And many members of both parties continued to give high priority to reducing the federal deficit and obeying the strictures of the Gramm-Rudman-Hollings budget law (PL 99-177).

"We don't have the option to go into a lot of new initiatives," said Johnston before he abandoned his bid for the job of Senate leader. "We're operating within narrow tolerances, and have our work cut out for us."

Nonetheless, with majority control of both chambers, the Democrats would be under pressure to come up with a positive program rather than simply sniping at administration and Republican initiatives.

"Sometimes it's easy to be irresponsible and complain," said Rangel. "Now we have to put together a program and get it through."

"One thing is clear: The Democratic waiting game is over," said a Senate GOP leadership aide. "They sat around waiting for us to lay out our proposals and took potshots from the sidelines," the aide said, citing House Democrats' strategy in recent years of waiting for the Senate to act on a budget resolution before drafting its own.

Congress vs. White House

A political landscape with the White House in Republican hands and the Congress dominated by Democrats, while new to the Reagan administration, was by no means uncharted territory. The same balance of political power existed under the administrations of Dwight D. Eisenhower, Richard Nixon and Gerald R. Ford.

"It's a return to the normal situation," said Thomas S. Foley, D-Wash., who was expected to be House majority leader in the 100th Congress. "Looking at those past presidencies, there was effective cooperation between the two branches of government, because each knew it had to accommodate the other."

White House officials sought to counter the suggestion that a Democratic-controlled Congress would paralyze Reagan in his last two years.

"He has a history of being able to work with the opposition party," said Larry Speakes, the White House spokesman. "It will result in a change of tactics which would, of course, be coalition-building within the various elements of the Senate or the House on specific issues."

For their part, Democrats in post-election comments denied an interest in confrontation with the White House, calling for cooperation, particularly on the politically thankless task of reducing the budget deficit.

But while making those conciliatory gestures, Democrats put at the top of their legislative agenda trade legislation, which could provoke an early confrontation with a White House opposed to measures it considered protectionist.

"It reflects a political schizophrenia — Democrats will go back and forth between confrontation and caution," said Thomas E. Mann, executive director of the American Political Science Association.

Two Country Mice?

Democrats were hopeful that coordination between their forces in the two chambers would improve in the face of Reagan's unmatched political popularity. "That's going to drive House and Senate Democrats into closer collaboration," said Richard P. Conlon, executive director of the House Democratic Study Group.

Some members complained that the lines of communication between House and Senate Democrats had not always been clear in recent years, partly as a result of institutional rivalries and stylistic differences between Speaker O'Neill and Byrd — "the city mouse and the country mouse," as one aide described them.

There were some early indications of improved communications between Byrd and Jim Wright, D-Texas, who was unopposed in his bid to succeed O'Neill as Speaker. Byrd said the two had agreed to meet every two weeks to "coordinate our strengths and ideas."

However, one participant in similar House-Senate meetings in the past said they tended to be "very ritualistic" and of limited utility.

Readjustment for GOP

It remained to be seen as of Nov. 6, 1986, what role Republicans would play once they readjusted to their once-familiar status as the minority party in the Senate.

On the other side of the Capitol, the Senate takeover could give some small consolation to House Republicans, who had complained about being taken for granted by White House strategists, who had focused on the Senate GOP leaders as their power brokers on Capitol Hill.

"House Republicans in a sense become more of an integral player in administration strategy," said J. David Hoppe, executive director of the House Republican Conference, the organization of all House GOP members. "Not that they ignored House Republicans, but when you hold [the majority in one chamber of Congress] you tend to emphasize efforts there."

Voters Restore Democrats to Senate Control

Boosted by farm-state turmoil and a partial resurgence of traditional voting habits in the South, Democrats Nov. 4, 1986, laid to rest the specter of the GOP's stunning 1980 Senate sweep.

Six Republicans who won their seats that year were defeated in their bids for re-election, as Democrats captured a total of nine GOP seats and lost only one of their own to take a 55-45 Senate majority. Their net pickup of eight seats is the party's largest since 1958. In all, Democrats won 20 of the 34 Senate contests at stake.

The results also give them their largest class of freshman senators since 1958; of the 13 new senators elected, 11 are Democrats. *(State-by-state returns, 1986 CQ Weekly Report p. 2864)*

The party's most significant set of victories came in the South, where Democrats won every Senate contest but one. Republican freshmen Paula Hawkins of Florida, Mack Mattingly of Georgia and Jeremiah Denton of Alabama all lost. In North Carolina, Republican James T. Broyhill, who was appointed to the Senate earlier in 1986 after fellow Republican John P. East's suicide, was also defeated.

In addition, Democratic Rep. John B. Breaux overcame an early lead by GOP Rep. W. Henson Moore to hold onto the Louisiana seat of retiring Democratic Sen. Russell B. Long. Only Oklahoma Sen. Don Nickles managed to stave off the Democratic tide in the region.

Democrats' gains elsewhere were sprinkled across the map. In the Midwest, farm unrest cost two GOP members of the class of 1980 their seats: Mark Andrews of North Dakota lost to state Tax Commissioner Kent Conrad, and James Abdnor of South Dakota fell to Rep. Thomas A. Daschle.

In Washington state, controversy over the possible siting of a high-level nuclear-waste site in Hanford helped unseat Republican Slade Gorton.

The Democrats' other gains came in Maryland, where Rep. Barbara A. Mikulski easily won the seat of retiring GOP Sen. Charles McC. Mathias Jr., and in Nevada, where Rep. Harry

U.S. Senate		
99th Congress	**100th Congress**	
Democrats 47	Democrats 55	
Republicans 53	Republicans 45	
Democrats		
Freshmen		11
Incumbents re-elected		9
Incumbents defeated		0
Republicans		
Freshmen		2
Incumbents re-elected		12
Incumbents defeated		7
(Jeremiah Denton, Ala.; Paula Hawkins, Fla.; Mack Mattingly, Ga.; James T. Broyhill, N.C.; Mark Andrews, N.D.; James Abdnor, S.D.; Slade Gorton, Wash.)		

Reid defeated former Rep. Jim Santini for the right to succeed retiring GOP Sen. Paul Laxalt.

The sole Republican pickup was in Missouri. There, former Gov. Christopher S. "Kit" Bond defeated Lt. Gov. Harriett Woods to win the seat held by retiring Democratic veteran Thomas F. Eagleton.

Using the Democrats' overpowering Senate performance to draw conclusions about the two parties' relative

standing is chancy, given the GOP's strong showing in governors' races and the virtual standoff in House elections. But the Senate campaign does deserve special notice for what it says about the state of electioneering in the latter half of the 1980s.

Most spectacularly, it laid to rest a theory that took hold in 1980 — that the GOP's superior financial resources give it an infallible ability to win close contests. The notion gained widespread currency in 1982, when the GOP's high-tech campaign techniques and last-minute infusions of money saved several endangered Republican candidates. That year, the GOP won five of the six contests in which the winner took 52 percent or less.

But in 1986, of the 11 races won by 52 percent or less, nine went to Democrats. That achievement came in spite of daunting obstacles: the National Republican Senatorial Committee's nearly 8-to-1 funding advantage over its Democratic counterpart, a $10 million nationwide GOP get-out-the-vote effort, and an army of consultants, pollsters, media advisers and GOP field staff at the disposal of Republican candidates.

The difference lay in what each side did with the resources at its disposal. In many contests, Democrats latched onto issues — of substance

Democrat Wyche Fowler Jr. celebrates his Senate victory in Georgia.

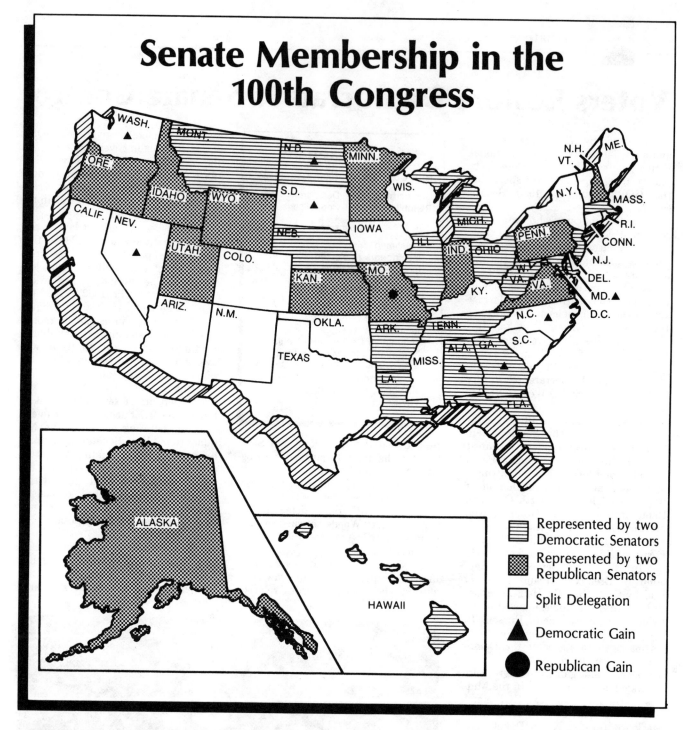

Senate Membership in the 100th Congress

Represented by two Democratic Senators

Represented by two Republican Senators

Split Delegation

▲ Democratic Gain

● Republican Gain

and of personality — that by Election Day were helping them frame the terms of the debate.

Even more important, while the GOP was spending much of its money on TV advertising and on a technology-driven voter mobilization effort, Democrats built on their strength at the grass roots. They developed extensive local organizations and — especially in the South — reawakened old party apparatuses and alliances.

Not every potentially close election broke the Democrats' way. In Oklahoma and Pennsylvania, Democratic Reps. James R. Jones and Bob Edgar tried to turn local economic troubles to their advantage. Neither, however, could arouse the core Democratic constituency in the western half of their states. Nickles and Pennsylvania Republican Arlen Specter both won handily. And in Idaho, Democratic Gov. John V. Evans failed to

capitalize on the state's "triple recession" in mining, timber and farming; he lost to conservative Republican Steven D. Symms.

But in a year when there were so many close contests, the Republicans' lack of organizational depth hurt them, particularly in states where Democrats latched onto local issues that seemed more compelling to voters than national Republican pleas to keep the Senate in GOP hands.

Not even President Reagan's help could overcome the Democrats' advantages — of the 16 states to which Reagan traveled after Labor Day, Republican Senate candidates won only four; and only in Idaho could Reagan's presence be said to have boosted his candidate over the top.

'The North Carolina Way'

The most striking examples of the Democrats' ability to out-campaign their opponents came in the South. Each Democrat there used a variation on a single theme — that he was a home-grown state patriot, while his opponent was a national Republican with little interest in local affairs. And each used his state's traditional Democratic base to surmount better-financed Republican efforts.

In North Carolina, for example, Democrat Terry Sanford stressed his longstanding ties to the state, as governor from 1961-65, and later as president of Duke University, while painting Broyhill as a captive of the Washington establishment.

He spent much of the campaign traveling the state, touching base with local Democratic leaders and getting acquainted with the generation of reporters and editors that had come into their jobs since he last held office. When he came under fire for spending his time in such low-profile work while Broyhill was constantly on TV, Sanford responded that he was running the "North Carolina way."

His efforts paid off. Where former Democratic Gov. James Hunt relied extensively on his personal organization in his unsuccessful 1984 Senate bid, Sanford tied in with conservative Democratic officials. They gave his campaign vital credibility, especially in the eastern part of the state, where conservative Democrats form a base of support for GOP Sen. Jesse Helms. Sanford ran far ahead of Broyhill in the east, and he also cut deeply into Broyhill's strength in the moderately Republican counties of central North Carolina's Piedmont region.

In Alabama, Rep. Richard C. Shelby lashed out at Denton as more interested in his personal agenda of "family" and social issues than in helping Alabama's economy. Late in the campaign, he issued a series of hard-hitting attacks that accused Denton of voting to cut Social Security benefits. The approach enabled the conservative Shelby to develop links to his state's well-organized labor and black communities — groups he had largely avoided during his House career.

Moore Blunders, Breaux Wins

The most persuasive examples of the power of the Democrats' localized approach came in Louisiana and Georgia, where both Breaux and Democratic Rep. Wyche Fowler Jr. used it to overcome strong Republican leads.

From the start, Breaux hammered away at Moore as a representative of Republican policies that were hurting Louisiana's farmers and its oil and gas industry. Moore, Breaux said over and over, owed his allegiance to the national GOP and not to Louisiana — a point the Democrat summed up in his slogan, "Louisiana First."

With Louisiana's economy in a deep slump, and the state ranking first in the nation in unemployment, Breaux's message was bound to get a sympathetic hearing. But several miscalculations by the Republicans also helped Breaux score his victory.

Moore initially had pegged his campaign to a parochial appeal. He maintained that the state's scandal-ridden Democratic administration and faltering economy called out for new leadership. The Republicans, Moore contended, were the only ones capable of getting the state back to work.

As long as he stuck with that approach, Moore remained in front. But as the nonpartisan September primary approached and the GOP mounted an all-out push to win more than 50 percent of the vote — and so avoid a runoff — he faltered. His campaign shifted its emphasis towards attacking Breaux, while the national GOP launched a program to purge ineligible voters from the rolls in black precincts, which angered black voters.

The result was that Moore ran worse than expected in the primary, while Breaux did better. Though Moore tried to recoup by shifting back to his original tack, the damage had been done. Many voters had been turned off by his attacks on Breaux, and Democrats who had ignored the campaign or sided with Moore began to shift to Breaux. Working hard to mobilize both the Democratic base in New Orleans and white Democratic parish officials in southern Louisiana, Breaux overtook Moore.

Fowler's Flair Prevails

In Georgia, Fowler ran an almost picture-perfect campaign. Mattingly won in 1980 largely because Democratic Sen. Herman E. Talmadge had

---

Senate Switched Seats, Newcomers, Losers

State	99th	100th	Winner	Loser	Incumbent
Alabama	R	D	Richard C. Shelby (D)	Jeremiah Denton (R)	Denton
Arizona	R	R	John McCain (R)	Richard Kimball (D)	Barry Goldwater (R) *
Colorado	D	D	Timothy E. Wirth (D)	Ken Kramer (R)	Gary Hart (D) *
Florida	R	D	Bob Graham (D)	Paula Hawkins (R)	Hawkins
Georgia	R	D	Wyche Fowler Jr. (D)	Mack Mattingly (R)	Mattingly
Louisiana	D	D	John B. Breaux (D)	W. Henson Moore (R)	Russell B. Long (D) *
Maryland	R	D	Barbara A. Mikulski (D)	Linda Chavez (R)	Charles McC. Mathias Jr. (R) *
Missouri	D	R	Christopher S. "Kit" Bond (R)	Harriett Woods (D)	Thomas F. Eagleton (D) *
Nevada	R	D	Harry Reid (D)	Jim Santini (R)	Paul Laxalt (R) *
North Carolina	R	D	Terry Sanford (D)	James T. Broyhill (R)	Broyhill
North Dakota	R	D	Kent Conrad (D)	Mark Andrews (R)	Andrews
South Dakota	R	D	Thomas A. Daschle (D)	James Abdnor (R)	Abdnor
Washington	R	D	Brock Adams (D)	Slade Gorton (R)	Gorton

* Retired

been badly tarnished by misconduct charges. In 1986, Mattingly's greatest strength was his conservatism; Fowler, who has represented Atlanta since 1977, was the Georgia delegation's most liberal member.

But Mattingly had a serious weakness — he had not built a political base. Without it, he had to rely heavily on media advertising.

Fowler, on the other hand, is an accomplished stump campaigner who — despite his urban base — showed an actor's deft touch at setting conservative rural Georgians at ease. While Mattingly based his campaign on television attacks that accused Fowler of being too liberal and missing votes in the House, Fowler traveled the state, lining up "courthouse crowds."

The thrust of Fowler's campaign was to paint Mattingly as a captive of GOP policies that were doing harm to his state. "Republican policies are threatening family farms, small business and the rural way of life," ran one Fowler ad. "What has Republican Mack Mattingly done to help?" He coupled that approach with a series of populist attacks on the GOP as the party of the affluent. Mattingly, he said, "votes to protect the wealthy and powerful."

Despite Georgia's huge size, which makes a media-dominated campaign almost a necessity, Fowler's travels paid off. Like Sanford, he brought local Democratic officials to his side, and they helped him undercut rural voters' suspicion of his Atlanta background. His attacks on Mattingly mobilized his Atlanta base and voters in the state's smaller, less cosmopolitan areas. Fowler carried just under two-thirds of the state's 159 counties.

The Dakotas Revolt

Other Democrats elsewhere in the country also proved adept at finding issues that helped them cut into Republican strength. Both Conrad and Daschle, for example, jumped on the farm crisis at the start of their campaigns and never let go.

In South Dakota's cold economic climate, with farmers worrying about bankruptcy and normally Republican small businessmen feeling the pinch of hard times on the farm, Daschle's vigorous attacks on Republican farm policies put Abdnor on the defensive. Abdnor also had to deal with widespread sentiment that Daschle would be a more aggressive and eloquent

spokesman for the state in Washington. Toward the end of the campaign, the avuncular Abdnor tried to make the most of his rather ineloquent manner, airing an enormously successful ad playing on his likability. "So I'm not a great speaker," he told viewers. "Heck, I'm not a great dancer, either."

The ad helped Abdnor make up ground, but not enough. Helped by a massive effort to get farmers to the polls, Daschle turned out a strong vote in the state's rural counties.

Conrad Paints a Bleak Picture

In North Dakota, Conrad carefully crafted a campaign to take advantage both of the state's farm problems and of Andrews' personal difficulties. Although Andrews had stood up against the administration's farm policies — especially its effort to cut wheat target prices — Conrad questioned the Republican's ability to deliver for his state.

He painted a bleak picture of the economic prosperity enjoyed by the East and West coasts while North Dakota suffered. "We need someone who will fight for us, for our way of life," one of his ads commented.

The issue was enough to bring Conrad within striking distance, but several other factors helped him. A longstanding legal battle between Andrews and his family physicians grated on some voters, and the senator also was dogged by a feeling among some voters that he had lost touch with North Dakota as his stature had grown in Washington.

Moreover, as Conrad continued to hammer at Andrews and began to draw almost even in the polls, Andrews was mired in Washington as the congressional session dragged on into mid-October. When Congress finally adjourned and Andrews started campaigning full time, he tried to arouse suspicion of Conrad by calling him "a favorite of the East Coast limousine liberals." The tack did not succeed. With help from the political network of Democratic Rep. Byron L. Dorgan, Conrad won by about 2,000 votes.

Paths to Power

Though the Democrats' ability to blend grass-roots organizing with innovative campaign tactics was crucial to their success, it was not a prerequisite everywhere. In some states, one or the other sufficed on its own.

In Colorado, for example, Democratic Rep. Timothy E. Wirth was

never able to gain the upper hand against GOP Rep. Ken Kramer on the issues alone. Kramer's support for the strategic defense initiative and his dedication to a balanced budget proved popular in Colorado, and his ad declaring, "I'm not slick, just good," helped him stay even with Wirth in the public relations battle.

The difference was provided by the two candidates' organizations. Wirth's was extensive, sophisticated and smoothly run, while Kramer's was inefficient and limited. On Election Day, Wirth's was able to deliver its vote. Kramer, who relied extensively on help from the state GOP and from the national party's computerized get-out-the-vote program, fell short.

In Washington state, former Transportation Secretary Brock Adams rode into office on the strength of the Hanford issue. He ran ads pledging to "stop this nuclear garbage dead in its tracks," and repeatedly questioned Gorton's ability to stop the administration from choosing the site.

Gorton, who never managed to build much of a personal following as senator, could not dodge the issue. He tried to deflect it by following the national GOP script and challenging Adams' attendance record as a House member from 1965-77. He also tried to convince voters he was working hard to see that Hanford would not be chosen. But the president undercut Gorton by traveling to the state on his behalf and not giving any indication he would rule out a waste facility at Hanford.

Democrats also dominated the two states where media ads played a crucial role, California and Florida. In Florida, Democratic Gov. Bob Graham, a popular moderate, put Hawkins on the defensive by portraying her as a Senate lightweight with a narrow focus. Hawkins sought to turn her emphasis on anti-drug legislation and children's issues into an advantage, but wound up with only 45 percent — the worst showing of any Senate incumbent.

In California, Democratic Sen. Alan Cranston ran a masterly campaign that for much of its length kept Rep. Ed Zschau's legislative record in the spotlight and prevented the Republican from focusing on Cranston's performance. Zschau's hard-hitting effort to label Cranston as soft on drugs and terrorism helped him gain considerable ground late in the campaign, but he fell short of his goal.

Senate Membership in the 100th Congress

Democrats - 55   Republicans - 45
Freshman senators - 13

Seats switched D to R - 1   Seats switched R to D - 9

Senators elected in 1986 are *italicized*

 # Freshman senators
✔ Seat switched parties

ALABAMA
Howell Heflin (D)
✔ *Richard C. Shelby (D)#*

ALASKA
Frank H. Murkowski (R)
Ted Stevens (R)

ARIZONA
Dennis DeConcini (D)
John McCain (R)#

ARKANSAS
Dale Bumpers (D)
David Pryor (D)

CALIFORNIA
Alan Cranston (D)
Pete Wilson (R)

COLORADO
William L. Armstrong (R)
Timothy E. Wirth (D)#

CONNECTICUT
Christopher J. Dodd (D)
Lowell P. Weicker Jr. (R)

DELAWARE
Joseph R. Biden Jr. (D)
William V. Roth Jr. (R)

FLORIDA
Lawton Chiles (D)
✔ *Bob Graham (D)#*

GEORGIA
✔ *Wyche Fowler Jr. (D)#*
Sam Nunn (D)

HAWAII
Daniel K. Inouye (D)
Spark M. Matsunaga (D)

IDAHO
James A. McClure (R)
Steven D. Symms (R)

ILLINOIS
Alan J. Dixon (D)
Paul Simon (D)

INDIANA
Richard G. Lugar (R)
Dan Quayle (R)

IOWA
Charles E. Grassley (R)
Tom Harkin (D)

KANSAS
Robert Dole (R)
Nancy Landon Kassebaum (R)

KENTUCKY
Wendell H. Ford (D)
Mitch McConnell (R)

LOUISIANA
John B. Breaux (D)#
J. Bennett Johnston (D)

MAINE
George J. Mitchell (D)
William S. Cohen (R)

MARYLAND
✔ *Barbara A. Mikulski (D)#*
Paul S. Sarbanes (D)

MASSACHUSETTS
Edward M. Kennedy (D)
John Kerry (D)

MICHIGAN
Carl Levin (D)
Donald W. Riegle Jr. (D)

MINNESOTA
Rudy Boschwitz (R)
Dave Durenberger (R)

MISSISSIPPI
John C. Stennis (D)
Thad Cochran (R)

MISSOURI
✔ *Christopher S. "Kit" Bond (R)#*
John C. Danforth (R)

MONTANA
Max Baucus (D)
John Melcher (D)

NEBRASKA
J. James Exon (D)
Edward Zorinsky (D)

NEVADA
✔ *Harry Reid (D)#*
Chic Hecht (R)

NEW HAMPSHIRE
Gordon J. Humphrey (R)
Warren B. Rudman (R)

NEW JERSEY
Bill Bradley (D)
Frank R. Lautenberg (D)

NEW MEXICO
Jeff Bingaman (D)
Pete V. Domenici (R)

NEW YORK
Alfonse M. D'Amato (R)
Daniel Patrick Moynihan (D)

NORTH CAROLINA
Jesse Helms (R)
✔ *Terry Sanford (D)#*

NORTH DAKOTA
Quentin N. Burdick (D)
✔ *Kent Conrad (D)#*

OHIO
John Glenn (D)
Howard M. Metzenbaum (D)

OKLAHOMA
David L. Boren (D)
Don Nickles (R)

OREGON
Mark O. Hatfield (R)
Bob Packwood (R)

PENNSYLVANIA
John Heinz (R)
Arlen Specter (R)

RHODE ISLAND
John H. Chafee (R)
Claiborne Pell (D)

SOUTH CAROLINA
Ernest F. Hollings (D)
Strom Thurmond (R)

SOUTH DAKOTA
✔ *Thomas A. Daschle (D)#*
Larry Pressler (R)

TENNESSEE
Albert Gore Jr. (D)
Jim Sasser (D)

TEXAS
Lloyd Bentsen (D)
Phil Gramm (R)

UTAH
Jake Garn (R)
Orrin G. Hatch (R)

VERMONT
Patrick J. Leahy (D)
Robert T. Stafford (R)

VIRGINIA
Paul S. Trible Jr. (R)
John W. Warner (R)

WASHINGTON
✔ *Brock Adams (D)#*
Daniel J. Evans (R)

WEST VIRGINIA
Robert C. Byrd (D)
John D. Rockefeller IV (D)

WISCONSIN
Bob Kasten (R)
William Proxmire (D)

WYOMING
Alan K. Simpson (R)
Malcolm Wallop (R)

Failed Campaign Cost Republicans the Senate

The 1986 Senate elections were a Republican disaster that need not have happened.

It is always possible in the aftermath of a result such as the one that cost the GOP eight seats and a majority to argue that it carried a silver lining, or that it was a statistical fluke, or that it was inevitable, or some combination of the three.

After all, Republicans point out, they gained eight governorships and avoided serious erosion in the House.

Even on the Senate side, they can argue, Republicans would have preserved their majority if they picked up no more than 55,000 votes in five states. And in any case, they were struggling against history — they had to keep their losses to three seats to maintain control, and no party holding the White House has ever lost that few at its six-year point in power.

Those defenses are easy to erect; they are even easier to knock down.

Any set of competitive Senate contests produces quite a few that turn on a small number of votes. An additional 42,000 would have kept the Senate Democratic in the Reagan landslide of 1980. If another 55,000 votes would have saved the Republican majority this year, 150,000 in the other direction would have given Democrats a majority of 58-42.

The argument from history presents similar problems. All of the other midterm Senate debacles of modern times occurred against the backdrop of serious problems in the country — a national recession in 1958, the Vietnam War in 1966, the Watergate scandal in 1974. No such problem existed for the Republicans in 1986.

And while the GOP can draw legitimate consolation from their gubernatorial showing and their single-digit losses in the House, those successes simply underscore the only lesson one can fairly draw from the day's voting. There was no landslide, no "six-year itch," not even a discernible national trend against voting Republican.

The only valid explanation for the Republicans' poor electoral performance was a failed Republican Senate campaign.

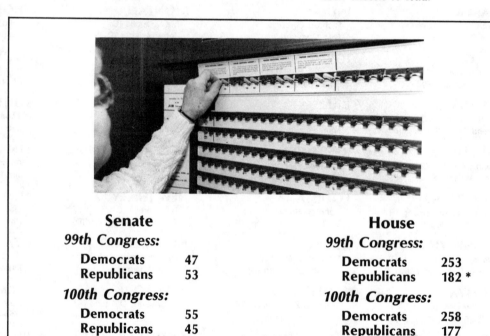

Senate		House	
99th Congress:		**99th Congress:**	
Democrats	47	Democrats	253
Republicans	53	Republicans	182 *
100th Congress:		**100th Congress:**	
Democrats	55	Democrats	258
Republicans	45	Republicans	177
Based on apparent winners as of Nov. 7.		** Including two vacancies.*	

It is possible to glean some of the reasons for that failure in the transcripts of the speeches President Reagan gave as he barnstormed the country in an effort to boost his party's candidates the week before the election.

His speech for Sen. James T. Broyhill in North Carolina on Oct. 28 is a fairly typical example.

"It's wonderful to be here in North Carolina," the president began. "You probably know I couldn't do this much traveling when Congress was in session.... That's because some of those folks need watching."

He went on to describe himself and Broyhill as part of the "1980 cleanup crew."

Ever since Reagan took office, his critics have marveled at his ability, as head of the national government, to ridicule that government, hold himself apart from it and ask the electorate to help him protect them from the absurdities of the political system he has been chosen to lead.

On Nov. 4, Reagan and the Republican Senate paid the price for their ability to distance themselves from government. After six years in power, they appealed to the country one more time as the opposition, and it was one time too many.

When a house is messy, its residents welcome a cleanup crew. When the place is clean again, they thank the crew, pay them, and let them leave. If the crew wants to stay, it has to offer reasons why it is still needed.

Republicans campaigned for the Senate in 1986 somewhat in the manner that former Minnesota Sen. Eugene J. McCarthy campaigned for the White House in 1968. Asked if he really wanted to be president, Democrat McCarthy took a moment to consider the question and then said simply he was "willing to be president."

By and large, this year's Republicans offered themselves as the party willing to perform the unpleasant chore of governing the country in order to prevent the Democratic villains of the 1970s from returning to power and making a mess again.

To be fair, the president and his allies did spend some time talking about the economic successes of the past few years and the importance of the Reagan military buildup. But these issues were not offered consistently or clearly enough to drown out the trivia that dominated the campaign on both sides.

The absence of a national theme in the 1986 Senate election has been cited all year as a curiosity of modern campaign strategy or a function of ideological lethargy in the closing years of the Reagan era. With the benefit of hindsight, it is possible to see this themelessness for what it was — an important Republican miscalculation.

It is perfectly true that the Democrats offered no theme either, but they did not need one. The theme of any opposition party is opposition. It is the vehicle for whatever protests voters may choose to make against the party perceived as holding power. It is

the job of those representing the party in power to offer a coherent rationale for their re-election. Few Republicans did that.

In Georgia in 1986, after Democrat Wyche Fowler Jr. won his party's Senate nomination, Republican incumbent Mack Mattingly launched his own campaign with a blistering attack on Fowler's attendance as a member of the House. It seemed to work: Fowler's poll numbers plummeted.

But after the initial impact wore

With the benefit of hindsight, it is possible to see the lack of a national campaign theme for what it was — an important Republican miscalculation.

---

off, the tactic allowed Fowler to suggest to voters that after six years in office, the incumbent could think of nothing better to run on than his challenger's attendance record.

Meanwhile, in South Dakota, Republican Sen. James Abdnor was fighting to hold off Democrat Thomas A. Daschle with commercials charging that Daschle was friendly with Jane Fonda, the liberal actress. Again, Daschle sustained some damage. After a few weeks, though, it began to seem that Abdnor was running a challenger-style campaign.

For an incumbent senator, and an incumbent party, to run full blast against the people trying to unseat them, is indeed a novel tactic. Perhaps it worked in 1986 in some places. In general, though, it is not what voters expect, and it is not what they reward.

Penalizing the Leaders

The irony of the Republican failure to campaign forthrightly as the governing party was that it most penalizes those who tried hardest to govern — the party's leaders in the Senate.

The split Congress established by the 1980 election generated one set of legislators — Senate Republicans — who had every reason to govern responsibly and a special reason to fear failure. As the majority in their chamber, they were the president's agents in Congress, and also the spokesmen for Congress in negotiating with the president.

If voters became dissatisfied, these Republicans would be the obvious scapegoats no matter which institution seemed to be at fault.

Republican leader Robert Dole of Kansas and such chairmen as Bob Packwood of Oregon at Finance, Pete V. Domenici of New Mexico at Budget, and Richard G. Lugar of Indiana at Foreign Relations proved they were more than competent as the governing party, and they showed no signs of embarrassment at having to govern.

Theirs was a case that Republican senators might have made all over the country in 1986, and if they had, the result might have been different. ∎

Lively Contests Fail to Attract Many Voters to the Ballot Box

Maybe it was the absence of riveting national issues; maybe it was the extensive negative campaigning. But when all the ballots are counted, the Nov. 4, 1986, voter turnout rate may be the lowest since World War II.

Voters did not rush to the ballot box in spite of a vigorous battle for control of the U.S. Senate. In only three of the 34 states holding Senate contests in 1986 did a majority of the voting-age population turn out; in the vast majority, turnout rates were lower than in 1982, the last midterm election. And that year, only three out of every eight who were eligible voted in congressional races. The lowest-turnout year since World War II was 1978, when only 34.9 percent voted. *(Chart, 1986 CQ Weekly Report, p. 2805)*

Republican officials particularly felt the effects of low turnout in 1986, noting that a total of some 55,000 more GOP votes in five states — Alabama, Colorado, Nevada and the Dakotas — would have let the GOP keep control of the Senate. "People almost believe that the president is so strong and popular that he can do anything," lamented John Heinz, National Republican Senatorial Committee chairman. "People took this election somewhat for granted."

Ticket-Splitting

Clearly, a tight Senate race was not enough to lure voters. In the close contest in Georgia between GOP Sen. Mack Mattingly and Democratic Rep. Wyche Fowler Jr., which the Democrat won with just 51 percent, barely one out of four eligible persons voted. The turnout rate was not much higher in many of the other contests that returned Senate control to the Democrats.

Basically, it took lively governors' races to help draw voters to the polls. Of the 10 states with Senate contests where turnout rose, all but two — North Carolina and North Dakota — had high-voltage gubernatorial races.

Most of the turnout increases were concentrated in states where freshman Republican senators faced aggressive Democratic challenges — among them Alabama, Florida, Idaho, North Carolina, North Dakota and South Dakota. GOP Sen. Steven D. Symms held his seat in Idaho, but Republicans were ousted in the other states, often by narrow margins.

Yet even in the states where Democrats regained Senate seats that they had lost when Republicans rode in on Ronald Reagan's 1980 coattails, the Democratic ticket did not necessarily sweep the state. Each race tended to stand on its own.

A strong tide in favor of one party seemed to have been replaced by a more muted "time-for-a-change" mood that hurt Republicans in Senate races and Democrats in gubernatorial contests. Such voting schizophrenia apparently did not hurt turnout.

In Florida, for instance, voters replaced freshman GOP Sen. Paula Hawkins with Democrat Bob Graham but gave the governor's chair to Republican Bob Martinez — only the second time since Reconstruction that a Republican has won that Statehouse.

In Alabama, Democratic Rep. Richard C. Shelby unseated Republican Sen. Jeremiah Denton — another member of the class of 1980. But Guy Hunt won the governorship that Democrat George C. Wallace was vacating and will become Alabama's first Republican governor since Reconstruction.

Altogether, Democrats picked up nine previously Republican Senate seats and three governorships, while Republicans won from Democrats 11 governorships and one Senate seat.

When there are large, strongly partisan turnouts, the economy has usually been a driving force. That was the case in 1958, 1974 and even 1982, when recessions during Republican presidencies helped galvanize Democrats while dampening Republicans' enthusiasm. But in 1986, economic factors were felt more by region than nationwide, tending to produce more apathy than an angry rush to the polls.

That was true in the black Democratic precincts of Chicago as well as the affluent Republican neighborhoods of Southern California.

In 1982, Democrats used the recession to construct a "have-not" coalition of minorities, blue-collar workers and the unemployed, and nowhere was the black element more conspicuous than in Chicago. That year, nearly 500,000 voters in the predominantly black 1st, 2nd and 7th districts turned out, helping Adlai E. Stevenson III come within 5,100 votes of upsetting Republican Gov. James R. Thompson.

In 1986, with the economy looking better and area unemployment at just 7.4 percent, barely 300,000 voted in the three majority-black districts. Stevenson was handily beaten.

But Republicans had problems of their own. In California, for instance, the suburbs of Los Angeles, Orange and San Diego counties usually turn out well for GOP candidates. Yet a fairly rosy economic climate there this year failed to stir voter passions. In 1982, three of these suburban GOP districts cast more than 200,000 votes; in 1986, none did. That did not matter in the governor's race, which GOP incumbent George Deukmejian won easily, but it was costly to Republican Rep. Ed Zschau, who lost his Senate challenge to Democratic incumbent Alan Cranston by barely 100,000 votes. ∎

Apathy at the polls: Turnout often dropped, compared with the last midterm election.

A Year of Little Turmoil in House Elections

Voters in the Nov. 4 , 1986, House elections flaunted the widely heralded "six-year-itch" theory by not scratching. Any frustration they felt with the Republicans' six-year reign in the White House was vented in Senate contests. House GOP incumbents had remarkably little trouble on Election Day.

With the outcome of a handful of close contests still to be determined, Democrats appear to have registered a net gain of five seats in the House, giving the party a 258-177 edge over the GOP for the 100th Congress, which convenes in January. While celebrating their 81-seat advantage, House Democratic leaders cannot claim to have kept pace with the rhythms of recent House election history.

In the last four elections held during a party's second term in control of the White House — 1938, 1958, 1966 and 1974 — the party in power has lost an average of 52 House seats. Given that track record, the GOP's five-seat setback in 1986 hardly qualifies as a resounding repudiation. One has to go back to 1902 to find a sixth-year midterm election in which the party in power fared better.

The 'Ins' Stay In

Actually, it was an extraordinarily good election for incumbents of both parties. Only five Republican House members went down to defeat: Reps. Mike Strang of Colorado; Webb Franklin of Mississippi; Fred J. Eckert of New York; and Bill Cobey and Bill Hendon, both of North Carolina. The Democrats, meanwhile, suffered only one incumbent casualty: Rep. Robert A. Young of Missouri. *(State-by-state returns, 1986 CQ Weekly Report, p. 2864)*

As of Nov. 6, the fates of four other House GOP incumbents were still unclear. They are: Reps. John Hiler of Indiana's 3rd District and George C. Wortley of New York's 27th, both members of the House class of 1980; eight-year veteran Rep. Arlan Stangeland of Minnesota's 7th District; and Howard Coble, a freshman representing the North Carolina 6th.

Most GOP Incumbents Avoid the 'Itch'

Even if all four of those undecided races fall to the Democratic challengers, the number of incumbents defeated in the 1986 House elections still would be the lowest in postwar history. Although only nine incumbents lost in the 1968 general election, four lost in primaries, for a total of 13 incumbents defeated. In 1986, only two incumbents lost in primaries.

The small number of House incumbents defeated is particularly remarkable when compared with the outcome in the Senate elections; six Senate incumbents were defeated in this year's balloting.

Open Seats a Wash

There was little partisan turbulence in the 44 districts left open by House incumbents who died, retired, lost in primaries or ran for other offices. Democrats picked up eight seats previously occupied by Republicans, but the GOP responded by wrenching away seven seats that had been in the Democratic column. The result — a net Democratic gain of one open seat — was essentially a partisan wash.

The combination of open-seat outcomes and challenger victories yielded a freshman House class of 1986 of 50 members, which included 23 Republicans and 27 Democrats. That was larger than the 43-member freshman class of 1984, but was much smaller than the 74-member GOP-dominated class of 1980 and the Democrat-heavy, 80-member contingent elected in 1982.

What the 1986 freshman House class lacks in numbers, however, it makes up for in sheer diversity. Its membership ranges from Republican Fred Grandy of Iowa's 6th District — an actor best-known for his portrayal of the hapless "Gopher" on the television sitcom "The Love Boat" — to Democrat Floyd H. Flake of New York's 6th District, an African Methodist Episcopal minister given to sharp, tailored suits and the captivating, oratorical cadences of the black church.

Competing Theories

There is no shortage of theories to explain the limited turnover in the 1986 House elections.

Democrat Mike Espy is Mississippi's first black U.S. House member since 1883.

Actor-turned-politician Fred Grandy won Iowa's 6th District for the Republicans.

Republicans like to argue that they were able to thwart the six-year itch theory in 1986 because of the presence of a popular president, relative economic prosperity and the absence of any major political blunders — such as Watergate, which dragged House Republicans down in the six-year midterm election of 1974.

Democrats, for their part, cite their ability to play good defense during Reagan's 1984 presidential landslide. By limiting their losses in that election to 14 seats, they argue, the party did not have to go back in 1986 and recover a great deal of lost ground.

As Tony Coelho, the Democrat from California who chaired the Democratic Congressional Campaign Committee, never tired of saying in 1986, "We can't win back seats we didn't lose."

There is truth to both those arguments. But there is also another, institutional factor that has helped shrink the window of vulnerability for incumbents of both parties.

Crafty cartographers, through the redistricting process, have significantly reduced the number of competitive House districts by increasing the number of safe constituencies that are enjoyed by Democrats and Republicans alike.

Challengers must necessarily temper their expectations in an era in which roughly three-quarters of all House members routinely win re-election with 60 percent of the vote or more.

Revisiting North Carolina

Of the five victories Democrats registered by defeating GOP incumbents, perhaps none were sweeter for the party's national leadership than the two seats captured in North Carolina.

Coelho and other national strategists resented Republican advances made in 1984 in the traditionally Democratic Tarheel State; buoyed by the top-of-the-ticket presence of Reagan and Sen. Jesse Helms, the Republicans gained three House seats that year. National Democrats regarded 1986 as an important opportunity for revenge.

They got it in the central North Carolina-based 4th District by capitalizing on a GOP-created opening. Republican Cobey had an aura of vulnerability entering the 1986 election, stemming from two factors: his mixed record of political success (Cobey lost a 1980 bid for lieutenant governor and a 1982 bid for the 4th before finally winning election in 1984), and the

U.S. House Members Defeated

	Terms
Mike Strang, R-Colo.	1
Webb Franklin, R-Miss.	2
Robert A. Young, D-Mo.	5
Fred J. Eckert, R-N.Y.	1
Bill Cobey, R-N.C.	1
Bill Hendon, R-N.C.	2

Democratic nature of the district, which is anchored by college communities and a pool of state government employees in Raleigh.

But if those factors placed Cobey in tight competition with Democratic challenger David E. Price, it was a Cobey blunder that helped put Price over the edge. In mid-September, Cobey created a controversy by mailing out a campaign letter — under the heading, "Dear Christian Friend" — that urged fundamentalists to support him "so that our voice will not be silenced and then replaced by someone who is not willing to take a strong stance for the principles outlined in the word of God."

Price, a political science professor with a Yale divinity school degree, complained that the letter impugned his piety. With other Democrats and the news media loath to let voters forget the letter's remarks, Price was able to win easily. He posted a 56-44 percentage-point victory.

The other measure of Democratic revenge came in North Carolina's 11th District, where James McClure Clarke has been engaged in a political pas de deux with Republican Hendon for the last three House elections.

Bolstered by protest over the recession-racked economy, Clarke turned Hendon out of office in 1982, only to return the district to the Republican amidst the GOP tide that washed over mountainous western North Carolina two years later.

In 1986, Clarke came back, defying predictions that at 69, he was too old to make an effective challenger. He took advantage of concern about the possibility of a nuclear-waste dump site being located in the 11th to establish a 51 to 49 percent edge.

Landmark Win in the Delta

Another Democratic triumph in the South came in Mississippi's 2nd District, where two-term Republican Franklin was defeated by Mike Espy, a former assistant state attorney general. Espy's victory makes him the first black person Mississippi voters have sent to the House since Republican John R. Lynch left the chamber in 1883.

Members of the Delta-based 2nd District's black community had dreams of making that breakthrough in both 1982 and 1984, when Franklin faced off against a veteran civil rights leader, state Rep. Robert G. Clark. But Franklin managed to carve out narrow victories by capitalizing on a

1987 House Makeup, Party Gains and Losses *

	Seats	99th Congress Dem.	99th Congress Rep.	100th Congress Dem.	100th Congress Rep.	Gain/ Loss		Seats	99th Congress Dem.	99th Congress Rep.	100th Congress Dem.	100th Congress Rep.	Gain/ Loss
Ala.	7	5	2	5	2		Neb.	3	0	3	0	3	
Alaska	1	0	1	0	1		Nev.	2	1	1	1	1	
Ariz.	5	1	4	1	4		N.H.	2	0	2	0	2	
Ark.	4	3	1	3	1		N.J.	14	8	6	8	6	
Calif.	45	27	18	27	18		N.M.	3	1	2	1	2	
Colo.	6	2	4	3	3	+1D/-1R	N.Y.	34	19	15	20	14	+1D/-1R
Conn.	6	3	3	3	3		N.C.	11	6	5	8	3	+2D/-2R
Del.	1	1	0	1	0		N.D.	1	1	0	1	0	
Fla.	19	12	7	12	7		Ohio	21	11	10	11	10	
Ga.	10	8	2	8	2		Okla.	6	5	1	4	2	-1D/+1R
Hawaii	2	2	0	1	1	-1D/+1R	Ore.	5	3	2	3	2	
Idaho	2	1	1	1	1		Pa.	23	13	10	12	11	-1D/+1R
Ill.	22	13	9	13	9		R.I.	2	1	1	1	1	
Ind.	10	5	5	6	4	+1D/-1R	S.C.	6	3	3	4	2	+1D/-1R
Iowa	6	2	4	2	4		S.D.	1	1	0	1	0	
Kan.	5	2	3	2	3		Tenn.	9	6	3	6	3	
Ky.	7	4	3	4	3		Texas	27	17	10	17	10	
La.	8	6	2	5	3	-1D/+1R	Utah	3	0	3	1	2	+1D/-1R
Maine	2	0	2	1	1	+1D/-1R	Vt.	1	0	1	0	1	
Md.	8	6	2	6	2		Va.	10	4	6	5	5	+1D/-1R
Mass.	11	10	1	10	1		Wash.	8	5	3	5	3	
Mich.	18	11	7	11	7		W.Va.	4	4	0	4	0	
Minn.	8	5	3	5	3		Wis.	9	5	4	5	4	
Miss.	5	3	2	4	1	+1D/-1R	Wyo.	1	0	1	0	1	
Mo.	9	6	3	5	4	-1D/+1R	**TOTALS**	435	253	182	258	177	+5D/-5R
Mont.	2	1	1	1	1								

* As of Nov. 6.

slight turnout advantage among white voters.

Espy managed to overcome Franklin by developing a sophisticated grass-roots organization that targeted previously untapped black voters, and by making a bolder bid than Clark had made for white votes. The Democrat benefited further from feelings that Republican policies were not reviving the wilting agricultural economy.

GOP Breakthrough

In Louisiana's 8th District, the site of another contest between a black Democrat and a conservative white Republican, fortune smiled on the GOP.

Nursery owner Clyde Holloway, who had fallen short in two previous bids for this central Louisiana-based House seat, edged out black teacher and attorney Faye Williams. The contest — held to replace retiring Democratic Rep. Cathy (Mrs. Gillis) Long — forced many of the district's white Democrats to choose between race and party.

There are a total of 23 black members of the House in the 100th Congress, including Walter E. Faunt-

roy, the non-voting delegate from the District of Columbia. *(Characteristics of Congress, 1986 CQ Weekly Report, p. 2861)*

Beating the Odds

In Colorado's 3rd District, GOP freshman Strang's re-election race had been billed as a cowboys-and-Indians contest, a reference to Strang's white Stetson hat and the North Cheyenne ancestry of Ben Nighthorse Campbell, his Democratic opponent.

For once, the Indian won. By emphasizing issues such as local water rights and farmers' needs, Campbell was able to hold down Strang's margin among voters along the conservative Western Slope and to emerge with an upset victory.

In New York's 30th District, the central issue was freshman Republican Eckert's personality. An aggressive, sometimes abrasive conservative, Eckert had trouble shoring up support even among some members of his own party, who were more accustomed to the gentler style and moderate Republicanism practiced by former GOP Rep. Barber B. Conable Jr., Eckert's predecessor in the 30th.

Democrat Louise Slaughter, a

two-term state assemblywoman who was born in Kentucky and projects a soft-spoken Southern charm, was well-positioned to take advantage of voter dissatisfaction with Eckert's manner. She picked up enough crossover support to secure a 2,900-vote margin of victory.

Time Ran Out on Young

The surprising thing about the Democrats' lone incumbent casualty — Young of suburban St. Louis, Missouri — was the timing.

National Republican strategists have long been predicting that demographics would eventually catch up to the craggy, five-term incumbent. The GOP maintained that changes in the 2nd District's composition had cut into Young's blue-collar base and enhanced the political power of more affluent GOP suburbanites.

But Young's ability to fend off former state Rep. Jack Buechner in 1984 — despite the top-of-the-ticket presence of President Reagan — left doubts in the minds of even some Missouri Republicans about Buechner's chances in the 1986 rematch.

Buechner organized and raised money earlier than he had in his 1984

House Switched Seats, Newcomers and Losers

State	District	Old	New	Winner	Loser	Incumbent
Alabama	7	D	D	Claude Harris (D)	Bill McFarland (R)	Richard C. Shelby (D) [1]
Arizona	1	R	R	John J. Rhodes III (R)	Harry Braun III (D)	John McCain (R) [1]
	4	R	R	Jon Kyl (R)	Philip R. Davis (D)	Eldon Rudd (R) [2]
California	2	R	R	Wally Herger (R)	Stephen C. Swendiman (D)	Gene Chappie (R) [2]
	12	R	R	Ernest L. Konnyu (R)	Lance T. Weil (D)	Ed Zschau (R) [1]
	21	R	R	Elton Gallegly (R)	Gilbert R. Saldana (D)	Bobbi Fiedler (R) [3]
Colorado	2	D	D	David Skaggs (D)	Michael J. Norton (R)	Timothy E. Wirth (D) [1]
	3	R	D	Ben Nighthorse Campbell (D)	Mike Strang (R)	Strang
	5	R	R	Joel Hefley (R)	Bill Story (D)	Ken Kramer (R) [1]
Florida	2	D	D	Bill Grant (D)	unopposed	Don Fuqua (D) [2]
Georgia	5	D	D	John Lewis (D)	Portia A. Scott (R)	Wyche Fowler Jr. (D) [1]
Hawaii	1	D	R	Patricia Saiki (R)	Mufi Hannemann (D)	Neil Abercrombie (D) [4]
Illinois	4	R	R	Jack Davis (R)	Shawn Collins (D)	George M. O'Brien (R) [5]
	14	R	R	J. Dennis Hastert (R)	Mary Lou Kearns (D)	John E. Grotberg (R) [2]
Indiana	5	R	D	Jim Jontz (D)	James R. Butcher (R)	Elwood Hillis (R) [2]
Iowa	3	R	D	David R. Nagle (D)	John McIntee (R)	Cooper Evans (R) [2]
	6	D	R	Fred Grandy (R)	Clayton Hodgson (D)	Berkley Bedell (D) [2]
Kentucky	4	R	R	Jim Bunning (R)	Terry L. Mann (D)	Gene Snyder (R) [2]
Louisiana	6	R	R	Richard Baker (R)	unopposed	W. Henson Moore (R) [1]
	7	D	D	Jimmy Hayes (D)	Margaret Lowenthal (D)	John B. Breaux (D) [1]
	8	D	R	Clyde Holloway (R)	Faye Williams (D)	Cathy (Mrs. Gillis) Long (D) [2]
Maine	1	R	D	Joseph E. Brennan (D)	H. Rollin Ives (R)	John R. McKernan Jr. (R) [6]
Maryland	3	D	D	Benjamin L. Cardin (D)	Ross Z. Pierpont (R)	Barbara A. Mikulski (D) [1]
	4	R	D	Thomas McMillen (D)	Robert R. Neall (R)	Marjorie S. Holt (R) [2]
	7	D	D	Kweisi Mfume (D)	Saint George I. B. Crosse III (R)	Parren J. Mitchell (D) [7]
	8	D	R	Constance A. Morella (R)	Stewart Bainum Jr. (D)	Michael D. Barnes (D) [3]
Massachusetts	8	D	D	Joseph P. Kennedy II (D)	Clark C. Abt (R)	Thomas P. O'Neill Jr. (D) [2]
Michigan	4	R	R	Fred Upton (R)	Dan Roche (D)	Mark D. Siljander (R) [4]
Mississippi	2	R	D	Mike Espy (D)	Webb Franklin (R)	Franklin
Missouri	2	D	R	Jack Buechner (R)	Robert A. Young (D)	Young
Nevada	1	D	D	James H. Bilbray (D)	Bob Ryan (R)	Harry Reid (D) [1]
New York	1	R	D	George J. Hochbrueckner (D)	Gregory J. Blass (R)	William Carney (R) [2]
	6	D	D	Floyd H. Flake (D)	Richard Dietl (R)	Alton R. Waldon Jr. (D) [4]
	30	R	D	Louise Slaughter (D)	Fred J. Eckert (R)	Eckert
	34	D	R	Amory Houghton Jr. (R)	Larry M. Himelein (D)	Stan Lundine (D) [7]
North Carolina	3	D	D	Martin Lancaster (D)	Gerald B. Hurst (R)	Charles Whitley (D) [2]
	4	R	D	David E. Price (D)	Bill Cobey (R)	Cobey
	10	R	R	Cass Ballenger (R)	Lester D. Roark (D)	James T. Broyhill (R) [1]
	11	R	D	James McClure Clarke (D)	Bill Hendon (R)	Hendon
Ohio	8	R	R	Donald E. "Buz" Lukens (R)	John W. Griffin (D)	Thomas N. Kindness (R) [1]
	14	D	D	Thomas C. Sawyer (D)	Lynn Slaby (R)	John F. Seiberling (D) [2]
Oklahoma	1	D	R	James M. Inhofe (R)	Gary D. Allison (D)	James R. Jones (D) [1]
Oregon	4	D	D	Peter A. DeFazio (D)	Bruce Long (R)	James Weaver (D) [2]
Pennsylvania	7	D	R	Curt Weldon (R)	Bill Spingler (D)	Bob Edgar (D) [1]
South Carolina	1	R	R	Arthur Ravenel Jr. (R)	Jimmy Stuckey (D)	Thomas F. Hartnett (R) [7]
	4	R	D	Elizabeth Patterson (D)	William D. Workman III (R)	Carroll A. Campbell Jr. (R) [6]
South Dakota	AL	D	D	Tim Johnson (D)	Dale Bell (R)	Thomas A. Daschle (D) [1]
Texas	21	R	R	Lamar Smith (R)	Pete Snelson (D)	Tom Loeffler (R) [8]
Utah	2	R	D	Wayne Owens (D)	Tom Shimizu (R)	David S. Monson (R) [2]
Virginia	2	R	D	Owen B. Pickett (D)	A. J. "Joe" Canada Jr. (R)	G. William Whitehurst (R) [2]

[1] *Ran for Senate.*
[2] *Retired.*
[3] *Defeated in Senate primary.*
[4] *Defeated in primary.*

[5] *Died July 17, 1986.*
[6] *Ran for governor.*
[7] *Ran for lieutenant governor.*
[8] *Defeated in gubernatorial primary.*

campaign, but ultimately, the amiable Republican may have Democratic Senate nominee Harriett Woods to thank for his victory.

Buechner had never been on the best terms with hard-core conservatives in St. Louis County, largely because of the moderate-to-liberal reputation he had built during his tenure in the Missouri Legislature. But local conservatives were eager for the opportunity to come out to vote against Woods — whom they deride as an unabashed liberal. Having cast that vote, many conservatives in the 2nd District stayed on the GOP ballot and chose Buechner.

Farm Belt Vote a Mixed Bag

Anyone searching for signs of a significant rural revolt in the 1986 House contests will find mixed results. Democrats had hoped that farmers throughout the Midwest would blame the Republican Party for their economic woes. Some didn't; some did.

Democrat Tim Johnson capitalized on farm discontent to register a stronger-than-expected victory in the race for South Dakota's at-large House seat, left vacant due to Democrat Thomas A. Daschle's successful Senate candidacy. And in Iowa, farm fury contributed at least in part to Democrat Dave Nagle's triumph in the 3rd District, vacant because of GOP Rep. Cooper Evans' retirement.

But elsewhere in Iowa, there were no signs of the storm. Republican Reps. Tom Tauke and Jim Lightfoot both held off farm protest candidates; in the open 6th District, vacated by retiring Democratic Rep. Berkley Bedell, corn and soybean grower Clayton Hodgson lost out to television actor — and Republican — Fred Grandy. Similarly, Republican Reps. E. Thomas Coleman and Bill Emerson of Missouri turned back challenges from farmers.

The Unexpected

Nonetheless, Democrats did enjoy

U.S. House

99th Congress		100th Congress	
Democrats	253	Democrats	258 *
Republicans	182	Republicans	177 *

Democrats

Net Gain	5
Freshmen	27
Incumbents re-elected	231
Incumbents defeated	1

Republicans

Net Loss	5
Freshmen	23
Incumbents re-elected	154
Incumbents defeated	5

* Based on results as of Nov. 6.

---

some surprises. In South Carolina, state Sen. Elizabeth Patterson took the 4th District seat vacated by GOP Rep. Carroll A. Campbell Jr., who was elected governor. Patterson had been considered an underdog against Greenville Mayor William D. Workman.

In Indiana, Democrats took advantage of the retirement of 5th District Republican Rep. Elwood Hillis to steal away a traditionally GOP seat. State Sen. Jim Jontz, an astute politician whose career reflects his ability to buck the electoral odds, won the seat for the Democrats.

The GOP was not without its own surprises, however. Republican Pat Saiki became the first person of her party ever to win a House seat in Hawaii. She defeated Democrat Mufi Hannemann for the right to represent the Honolulu-based 1st District.

Republicans also derived satisfaction from capturing two districts vacated by Democrats who ran unsuccessfully for the Senate. Even as Pennsylvania's Bob Edgar and Oklahoma's James R. Jones were losing, Republicans Curt Weldon and James M. Inhofe were winning House seats.

Republican Rep.-elect Cass Ballenger of North Carolina will enjoy one advantage over his 1986 colleagues: seniority. Ballenger also won a special election Nov. 4 to fill out GOP Rep. James T. Broyhill's term.

In complete, unofficial returns, Ballenger had 82,823 votes (57.5 percent) to Democratic nominee Lester D. Roark's 61,208 votes (42.5 percent).

House Membership in 100th Congress . . .

ALABAMA
1. Sonny Callahan (R)
2. William L. Dickinson (R)
3. Bill Nichols (D)
4. Tom Bevill (D)
5. Ronnie G. Flippo (D)
6. Ben Erdreich (D)
7. Claude Harris (D) #

ALASKA
AL Don Young (R)

ARIZONA
1. John J. Rhodes III (R) #
2. Morris K. Udall (D)
3. Bob Stump (R)
4. Jon Kyl (R) #
5. Jim Kolbe (R)

ARKANSAS
1. Bill Alexander (D)
2. Tommy F. Robinson (D)
3. John Paul Hammerschmidt (R)
4. Beryl Anthony Jr. (D)

CALIFORNIA
1. Douglas H. Bosco (D)
2. Wally Herger (R) #
3. Robert T. Matsui (D)
4. Vic Fazio (D)
5. Sala Burton (D)
6. Barbara Boxer (D)
7. George Miller (D)
8. Ronald V. Dellums (D)
9. Fortney H. "Pete" Stark (D)
10. Don Edwards (D)
11. Tom Lantos (D)
12. Ernest L. Konnyu (R) #
13. Norman Y. Mineta (D)
14. Norman D. Shumway (R)
15. Tony Coelho (D)
16. Leon E. Panetta (D)
17. Charles Pashayan Jr. (R)
18. Richard H. Lehman (D)
19. Robert J. Lagomarsino (R)
20. William M. Thomas (R)
21. Elton Gallegly (R) #
22. Carlos J. Moorhead (R)
23. Anthony C. Beilenson (D)
24. Henry A. Waxman (D)
25. Edward R. Roybal (D)
26. Howard L. Berman (D)
27. Mel Levine (D)
28. Julian C. Dixon (D)
29. Augustus F. Hawkins (D)
30. Matthew G. Martinez (D)
31. Mervyn M. Dymally (D)
32. Glenn M. Anderson (D)
33. David Dreier (R)
34. Esteban Edward Torres (D)
35. Jerry Lewis (R)
36. George E. Brown Jr. (D)
37. Al McCandless (R)
38. Bob Dornan (R)
39. William E. Dannemeyer (R)
40. Robert E. Badham (R)
41. Bill Lowery (R)
42. Dan Lungren (R)
43. Ron Packard (R)

44. Jim Bates (D)
45. Duncan L. Hunter (R)

COLORADO
1. Patricia Schroeder (D)
2. David Skaggs (D) #
3. Ben Nighthorse Campbell (D) #
4. Hank Brown (R)
5. Joel Hefley (R) #
6. Daniel L. Schaefer (R)

CONNECTICUT
1. Barbara B. Kennelly (D)
2. Sam Gejdenson (D)
3. Bruce A. Morrison (D)
4. Stewart B. McKinney (R)
5. John G. Rowland (R)
6. Nancy L. Johnson (R)

DELAWARE
AL Thomas R. Carper (D)

FLORIDA
1. Earl Hutto (D)
2. Bill Grant (D) #
3. Charles E. Bennett (D)
4. Bill Chappell Jr. (D)
5. Bill McCollum (R)
6. Buddy MacKay (D)
7. Sam Gibbons (D)
8. C.W. Bill Young (R)
9. Michael Bilirakis (R)
10. Andy Ireland (R)
11. Bill Nelson (D)
12. Tom Lewis (R)
13. Connie Mack (R)
14. Daniel A. Mica (D)
15. E. Clay Shaw Jr. (R)
16. Larry Smith (D)
17. William Lehman (D)
18. Claude Pepper (D)
19. Dante B. Fascell (D)

GEORGIA
1. Robert Lindsay Thomas (D)
2. Charles Hatcher (D)
3. Richard Ray (D)
4. Pat Swindall (R)
5. John Lewis (D) #
6. Newt Gingrich (R)
7. George "Buddy" Darden (D)
8. J. Roy Rowland (D)
9. Ed Jenkins (D)
10. Doug Barnard Jr. (D)

HAWAII
1. Patricia Saiki (R) #
2. Daniel K. Akaka (D)

House Lineup

Democrats 258

Freshman Democrats - 27
\# Freshman Representative

Republicans 177

Freshman Republicans - 23
† Former Representative

Based on apparent winners as of Nov. 6.   Seats in doubt marked by an (✳)

IDAHO
1. Larry E. Craig (R)
2. Richard H. Stallings (D)

ILLINOIS
1. Charles A. Hayes (D)
2. Gus Savage (D)
3. Marty Russo (D)
4. Jack Davis (R) #
5. William O. Lipinski (D)
6. Henry J. Hyde (R)
7. Cardiss Collins (D)
8. Dan Rostenkowski (D)
9. Sidney R. Yates (D)
10. John Edward Porter (R)
11. Frank Annunzio (D)
12. Philip M. Crane (R)
13. Harris W. Fawell (R)
14. J. Dennis Hastert (R) #
15. Edward R. Madigan (R)
16. Lynn Martin (R)
17. Lane Evans (D)
18. Robert H. Michel (R)
19. Terry L. Bruce (D)
20. Richard J. Durbin (D)
21. Melvin Price (D)
22. Kenneth J. Gray (D)

INDIANA
1. Peter J. Visclosky (D)
2. Philip R. Sharp (D)
3. John Hiler (R) ✳
4. Dan Coats (R)
5. Jim Jontz (D) #
6. Dan Burton (R)
7. John T. Myers (R)
8. Frank McCloskey (D)
9. Lee H. Hamilton (D)
10. Andrew Jacobs Jr. (D)

IOWA
1. Jim Leach (R)
2. Tom Tauke (R)
3. Dave R. Nagle (D) #
4. Neal Smith (D)
5. Jim Lightfoot (R)
6. Fred Grandy (R) #

KANSAS
1. Pat Roberts (R)
2. Jim Slattery (D)
3. Jan Meyers (R)
4. Dan Glickman (D)
5. Bob Whittaker (R)

KENTUCKY
1. Carroll Hubbard Jr. (D)
2. William H. Natcher (D)
3. Romano L. Mazzoli (D)

4. Jim Bunning (R) #
5. Harold Rogers (R)
6. Larry J. Hopkins (R)
7. Carl C. Perkins (D)

LOUISIANA
1. Bob Livingston (R)
2. Lindy (Mrs. Hale) Boggs (D)
3. W. J. "Billy" Tauzin (D)
4. Buddy Roemer (D)
5. Jerry Huckaby (D)
6. Richard Baker (R) #
7. Jimmy Hayes (D) #
8. Clyde Holloway (R) #

MAINE
1. Joseph E. Brennan (D) #
2. Olympia J. Snowe (R)

MARYLAND
1. Roy Dyson (D)
2. Helen Delich Bentley (R)
3. Benjamin L. Cardin (D) #
4. Thomas McMillen (D) #
5. Steny H. Hoyer (D)
6. Beverly B. Byron (D)
7. Kweisi Mfume (D) #
8. Constance A. Morella (R) #

MASSACHUSETTS
1. Silvio O. Conte (R)
2. Edward P. Boland (D)
3. Joseph D. Early (D)
4. Barney Frank (D)
5. Chester G. Atkins (D)
6. Nicholas Mavroules (D)
7. Edward J. Markey (D)
8. Joseph P. Kennedy II (D) #
9. Joe Moakley (D)
10. Gerry E. Studds (D)
11. Brian J. Donnelly (D)

MICHIGAN
1. John Conyers Jr. (D)
2. Carl D. Pursell (R)
3. Howard Wolpe (D)
4. Fred Upton (R) #
5. Paul B. Henry (R)
6. Bob Carr (D)
7. Dale E. Kildee (D)
8. Bob Traxler (D)
9. Guy Vander Jagt (R)
10. Bill Schuette (R)
11. Robert W. Davis (R)
12. David E. Bonior (D)
13. George W. Crockett Jr. (D)
14. Dennis M. Hertel (D)
15. William D. Ford (D)
16. John D. Dingell (D)
17. Sander M. Levin (D)
18. William S. Broomfield (R)

MINNESOTA
1. Timothy J. Penny (D)
2. Vin Weber (R)
3. Bill Frenzel (R)
4. Bruce F. Vento (D)
5. Martin Olav Sabo (D)
6. Gerry Sikorski (D)

...Reflects Strong Showing by Incumbents

7. Arlan Stangeland (R) *
8. James L. Oberstar (D)

MISSISSIPPI
1. Jamie L. Whitten (D)
2. Mike Espy (D) #
3. G. V. ''Sonny'' Montgomery (D)
4. Wayne Dowdy (D)
5. Trent Lott (R)

MISSOURI
1. William L. Clay (D)
2. Jack Buechner (R) #
3. Richard A. Gephardt (D)
4. Ike Skelton (D)
5. Alan Wheat (D)
6. E. Thomas Coleman (R)
7. Gene Taylor (R)
8. Bill Emerson (R)
9. Harold L. Volkmer (D)

MONTANA
1. Pat Williams (D)
2. Ron Marlenee (R)

NEBRASKA
1. Doug Bereuter (R)
2. Hal Daub (R)
3. Virginia Smith (R)

NEVADA
1. James H. Bilbray (D) #
2. Barbara F. Vucanovich (R)

NEW HAMPSHIRE
1. Robert C. Smith (R)
2. Judd Gregg (R)

NEW JERSEY
1. James J. Florio (D)
2. William J. Hughes (D)
3. James J. Howard (D)
4. Christopher H. Smith (R)
5. Marge Roukema (R)
6. Bernard J. Dwyer (D)
7. Matthew J. Rinaldo (R)
8. Robert A. Roe (D)
9. Robert G. Torricelli (D)
10. Peter W. Rodino Jr. (D)
11. Dean A. Gallo (R)
12. Jim Courter (R)
13. H. James Saxton (R)
14. Frank J. Guarini (D)

NEW MEXICO
1. Manuel Lujan Jr. (R)
2. Joe Skeen (R)
3. Bill Richardson (D)

NEW YORK
1. George J. Hochbrueckner (D) #
2. Thomas J. Downey (D)
3. Robert J. Mrazek (D)
4. Norman F. Lent (R)
5. Raymond J. McGrath (R)
6. Floyd H. Flake (D) #
7. Gary L. Ackerman (D)
8. James H. Scheuer (D)
9. Thomas J. Manton (D)

10. Charles E. Schumer (D)
11. Edolphus Towns (D)
12. Major R. Owens (D)
13. Stephen J. Solarz (D)
14. Guy V. Molinari (R)
15. Bill Green (R)
16. Charles B. Rangel (D)
17. Ted Weiss (D)
18. Robert Garcia (D)
19. Mario Biaggi (D)
20. Joseph J. DioGuardi (R)
21. Hamilton Fish Jr. (R)
22. Benjamin A. Gilman (R)
23. Samuel S. Stratton (D)
24. Gerald B. H. Solomon (R)
25. Sherwood L. Boehlert (R)
26. David O'B. Martin (R)
27. George C. Wortley (R) *
28. Matthew F. McHugh (D)
29. Frank Horton (R)
30. Louise M. Slaughter (D) #
31. Jack F. Kemp (R)
32. John J. LaFalce (D)
33. Henry J. Nowak (D)
34. Amory Houghton Jr. (R) #

NORTH CAROLINA
1. Walter B. Jones (D)
2. Tim Valentine (D)
3. Martin Lancaster (D) #
4. David E. Price (D) #
5. Stephen L. Neal (D)
6. Howard Coble (R) *
7. Charlie Rose (D)
8. W. G. ''Bill'' Hefner (D)
9. J. Alex McMillan (R)
10. Cass Ballenger (R) #
11. James McClure Clarke (D)† #

NORTH DAKOTA
AL Byron L. Dorgan (D)

OHIO
1. Thomas A. Luken (D)
2. Bill Gradison (R)
3. Tony P. Hall (D)
4. Michael G. Oxley (R)
5. Delbert L. Latta (R)
6. Bob McEwen (R)
7. Michael DeWine (R)
8. Donald E. ''Buz'' Lukens (R)† #
9. Marcy Kaptur (D)
10. Clarence E. Miller (R)
11. Dennis E. Eckart (D)
12. John R. Kasich (R)
13. Don J. Pease (D)
14. Tom Sawyer (D) #
15. Chalmers P. Wylie (R)
16. Ralph Regula (R)
17. James A. Traficant Jr. (D)
18. Douglas Applegate (D)
19. Edward F. Feighan (D)
20. Mary Rose Oakar (D)
21. Louis Stokes (D)

OKLAHOMA
1. James M. Inhofe (R) #
2. Mike Synar (D)
3. Wes Watkins (D)

4. Dave McCurdy (D)
5. Mickey Edwards (R)
6. Glenn English (D)

OREGON
1. Les AuCoin (D)
2. Robert F. Smith (R)
3. Ron Wyden (D)
4. Peter A. DeFazio (D) #
5. Denny Smith (R)

PENNSYLVANIA
1. Thomas M. Foglietta (D)
2. William H. Gray III (D)
3. Robert A. Borski (D)
4. Joe Kolter (D)
5. Richard T. Schulze (R)
6. Gus Yatron (D)
7. Curt Weldon (R) #
8. Peter H. Kostmayer (D)
9. Bud Shuster (R)
10. Joseph M. McDade (R)
11. Paul E. Kanjorski (D)
12. John P. Murtha (D)
13. Lawrence Coughlin (R)
14. William J. Coyne (D)
15. Don Ritter (R)
16. Robert S. Walker (R)
17. George W. Gekas (R)
18. Doug Walgren (D)
19. Bill Goodling (R)
20. Joseph M. Gaydos (D)
21. Tom Ridge (R)
22. Austin J. Murphy (D)
23. William F. Clinger Jr. (R)

RHODE ISLAND
1. Fernand J. St Germain (D)
2. Claudine Schneider (R)

SOUTH CAROLINA
1. Arthur Ravenel Jr. (R) #
2. Floyd Spence (R)
3. Butler Derrick (D)
4. Elizabeth J. Patterson (D) #
5. John M. Spratt Jr. (D)
6. Robin Tallon (D)

SOUTH DAKOTA
AL Tim Johnson (D) #

TENNESSEE
1. James H. Quillen (R)
2. John J. Duncan (R)
3. Marilyn Lloyd (D)
4. Jim Cooper (D)
5. Bill Boner (D)
6. Bart Gordon (D)
7. Don Sundquist (R)
8. Ed Jones (D)
9. Harold E. Ford (D)

TEXAS
1. Jim Chapman (D)
2. Charles Wilson (D)
3. Steve Bartlett (R)
4. Ralph M. Hall (D)
5. John Bryant (D)
6. Joe L. Barton (R)
7. Bill Archer (R)

8. Jack Fields (R)
9. Jack Brooks (D)
10. J. J. Pickle (D)
11. Marvin Leath (D)
12. Jim Wright (D)
13. Beau Boulter (R)
14. Mac Sweeney (R)
15. E. ''Kika'' de la Garza (D)
16. Ronald D. Coleman (D)
17. Charles W. Stenholm (D)
18. Mickey Leland (D)
19. Larry Combest (R)
20. Henry B. Gonzalez (D)
21. Lamar Smith (R) #
22. Thomas D. DeLay (R)
23. Albert G. Bustamante (D)
24. Martin Frost (D)
25. Michael A. Andrews (D)
26. Dick Armey (R)
27. Solomon P. Ortiz (D)

UTAH
1. James V. Hansen (R)
2. Wayne Owens (D)† #
3. Howard C. Nielson (R)

VERMONT
AL James M. Jeffords (R)

VIRGINIA
1. Herbert H. Bateman (R)
2. Owen B. Pickett (D) #
3. Thomas J. Bliley Jr. (R)
4. Norman Sisisky (D)
5. Dan Daniel (D)
6. James R. Olin (D)
7. D. French Slaughter Jr. (R)
8. Stan Parris (R)
9. Frederick C. Boucher (D)
10. Frank R. Wolf (R)

WASHINGTON
1. John R. Miller (R)
2. Al Swift (D)
3. Don Bonker (D)
4. Sid Morrison (R)
5. Thomas S. Foley (D)
6. Norman D. Dicks (D)
7. Mike Lowry (D)
8. Rod Chandler (R)

WEST VIRGINIA
1. Alan B. Mollohan (D)
2. Harley O. Staggers Jr. (D)
3. Bob Wise (D)
4. Nick J. Rahall II (D)

WISCONSIN
1. Les Aspin (D)
2. Robert W. Kastenmeier (D)
3. Steve Gunderson (R)
4. Gerald D. Kleczka (D)
5. Jim Moody (D)
6. Thomas E. Petri (R)
7. David R. Obey (D)
8. Toby Roth (R)
9. F. James Sensenbrenner Jr. (R)

WYOMING
AL Dick Cheney (R)

Democrats Have Their Own Priorities:

Reagan Policies Face Stiff Challenges on Hill

Policy shifts would be expected now that Democrats have retaken the Senate, but President Reagan's campaign-trail pitch that a vote for Republicans was a vote for his policies has allowed his triumphant opponents to claim a mandate for change.

"It was President Reagan who sought to make this a referendum on his program, and he did not get the mandate he was looking for," Senate Democratic leader Robert C. Byrd of West Virginia said Nov. 5, 1986, a day after his party gained a net of eight Senate seats, for a 55-45 majority.

The new guard takes over Jan. 6, 1987, the start of the 100th Congress. For the first time, Reagan is confronted with a Congress in which both chambers are dominated by the opposition party. That means new directions not only in policy, but also in overall relations between the legislative and executive branches.

Though both sides have pledged cooperation, signs of trouble ahead are plenty. An emboldened Congress is likely to press Reagan early to accept initiatives on trade, agriculture and arms control. The Senate will confirm the president's nominees for federal judgeships only after exhaustive scrutiny.

And Reagan's annual budgets will be relevant on Capitol Hill only for the political hay that Democrats choose to make of them. Even with a Republican-controlled Senate, Reagan had seen Congress block his massive defense spending buildup and annual bids for deep domestic program cuts. Now the conflict over spending priorities is sure to escalate.

But despite what the Democrats see as evidence that voters repudiated Reagan's policies, they are not likely to do the same to the issues that top his rather limited agenda.

Reagan's opposition to higher taxes and his promotion of the strategic defense initiative (SDI), popularly known as "star wars," were incorporated in Byrd's post-election preview of the coming Senate agenda. But the Democratic Congress is likely to limit severely both the cost and concept of SDI. Similarly, it is unlikely that Congress will give Reagan full backing for his campaign against the government of Nicaragua.

Both Byrd and his only declared challenger for the majority leader post, J. Bennett Johnston of Louisiana, agreed that a Democratic Senate will join the House in making trade legislation a top priority. So did Lloyd Bentsen, D-Texas, who will chair the Senate Finance Committee with jurisdiction over trade matters.

A bill to encourage exports and curtail imports from countries deemed to trade unfairly is the Democrats' way of both addressing and drawing attention to the record-high trade deficits of the Reagan years. House Democrats made trade an issue for the 1986 elections.

And while evidence is slight that the issue hurt Republicans, Democrats nonetheless want to deliver on past campaign promises and to position

Democrats say President Reagan gambled and lost when he turned the 1986 Senate elections into a referendum on his policies.

themselves for 1988, a presidential election year.

In May 1986, the House passed a trade package (HR 4800), but the Senate took no action and the bill died when the 99th Congress adjourned Oct. 18.

Reagan repeatedly has condemned such legislation as protectionist and vowed to veto trade bills. And while Senate Democrats will have a 10-vote majority, they are far shy of the two-thirds needed to override a veto.

House Democrats, with an even wider margin of control, were unable in August to override Reagan's December 1985 veto of a trade bill (HR 1562) limiting textile and apparel imports. *(1986 CQ Weekly Report p. 2666)*

Despite the president's opposition, Senate Republican leader Robert Dole, Kan., joined Byrd's call for a

trade bill during a joint election-night television appearance. Dole said a bill could be drafted that would allay Reagan's fears of protectionism.

Budget and Taxes

The president's threats to veto any tax increase is taken more seriously. Senate Democrats say that they, like House leaders, will refuse Reagan's bait to "Make my day" by sending him a bill to veto.

"I see no need to increase taxes to reduce the deficit," Byrd said.

"If there is to be a tax increase to deal with the deficit, it will have to initiate with President Reagan," added George J. Mitchell, D-Maine, a member of the tax-writing Senate Finance Committee.

Mitchell echoed what had been House policy under Speaker Thomas P. O'Neill Jr., D-Mass. No change is expected when Majority Leader Jim Wright of Texas succeeds O'Neill, even though Wright has argued that deficits cannot be reduced without new taxes.

Likewise, the chairmen of both tax-writing committees, Bentsen and Dan Rostenkowski of Illinois at House Ways and Means, have taken the no-taxes-without-Reagan pledge.

But in 1987-88 both Reagan and the Democrats face the perhaps insurmountable challenge of holding the fiscal 1988 budget deficit to $108 billion — the target set by the 1985 Gramm-Rudman-Hollings anti-deficit law (PL 99-177). That could require cuts of more than $70 billion, given estimates that the current fiscal 1987 deficit will be about $180 billion.

In the past, Senate Republicans took responsibility for making the first budget moves. Now that Democrats control both chambers, the tough choices shift to them.

By all accounts, their budgets will resemble those of recent years — freezing or cutting most defense and domestic programs. Added funding is expected to be shifted to programs on the domestic side, specifically for education and scientific research.

But austerity without higher taxes probably will not allow them to meet the $108 billion target. Byrd's preliminary answer was to move the target — to make it "more flexible."

Such a move would invite hoots from Republicans, but it would have support from leading economists who argue that taking $70 billion in federal outlays out of circulation would have a wrenching effect on the economy.

Generally, the Democrats' Senate takeover was greeted as ominous news for deficit reduction. When Senate Republicans were in charge, what incremental reductions were achieved — through restrained Pentagon budgets and minimal revenue hikes — were all but forced on Reagan by Senate Republican leaders.

"The ball is in the Democrats' court," said Sen. John Heinz, R-Pa.

"They're going to have to show what they can do about the budget deficit, taxes and all the promises they've made during this election."

Democrats counter that they will fail at deficit reduction only if Reagan refuses to compromise. Lawton Chiles of Florida, the next head of the Senate Budget Committee, is banking that Reagan will negotiate rather than leave office with a legacy of record deficits and federal debt.

If he is wrong, Chiles said, Democrats should be "bold enough to put together a meaningful plan."

In a televised speech to his staff Nov. 5, 1986, Reagan outlined an agenda that included budget-process reform, power to veto individual items in appropriations bills and a constitutional amendment for a balanced budget. The line-item veto and balanced-budget amendment both failed in the past two years when Republicans controlled the Senate. *(Text, 1986 Weekly Report p. 2872; pp. 34, 2756)*

That Reagan has revived the two unpopular ideas is further indication of the conflicts ahead between him and Congress. But it also illustrates how much he and Congress need to cooperate. Just as Congress needs Reagan's support to avert vetoes of its bills, as on trade, he needs Congress to approve the remaining elements of his second-term program.

Democratic Foreign Policy

One such Reagan initiative is his offensive against Nicaragua's government. After the election, Senate Democratic leaders predicted Reagan's current aid program for the "contra" guerrillas would continue. That reflects political realities: The elections gave contra-aid foes a net gain of just two Senate votes — not enough to overcome the six-vote margin by which the Senate endorsed Reagan's $100 million aid package in 1986.

But requests for future aid face tougher scrutiny. Foes on the Senate Foreign Relations Committee, like John Kerry, D-Mass., will be free to conduct well-publicized hearings into the rebels' alleged human-rights abuses and financial improprieties.

Byrd, criticizing Reagan's reliance on military might, promised instead an approach that combined economic, diplomatic *and* military options.

In another foreign policy area, a Democratic Senate will be vigilant in seeing that Reagan carries out Congress' 1986 mandate to impose sanctions against South Africa's white-minority government. While the Foreign Relations panel under Chairman Richard G. Lugar, R-Ind., probably would have given Reagan time to reverse his formerly supportive policies, Democrats are likely to prod him.

Arms Control and SDI

In campaigning for Republican candidates, Reagan foresaw the end of SDI in a Democratic Congress. But victorious Democrats say it's not so.

"Democrats support SDI," Byrd said. Nevertheless, that support is likely to be limited to research in space technology, rather than testing and production. Also, the concept of the space defense is likely to be altered, from Reagan's vision of a celestial Astrodome protecting the entire population to a scaled-down plan for protecting only military sites.

Even the Republican Senate agreed to a fiscal 1987 budget that pared Reagan's SDI request by more than a third. The prospect of deeper cuts in a Democratic Senate is clear from an Aug. 5, 1986, vote: An amendment slashing total SDI funding by 40 percent failed by a single vote. *(1986 Weekly Report p. 2759)*

Reagan's concept of SDI would have been in trouble even if Republicans had kept the Senate, given some members' anger that Reagan forfeited an arms-control agreement rather than give in on SDI during his October meeting in Iceland with Soviet leader Mikhail S. Gorbachev.

But given the Democrats' sensitivity to Reagan's charges that they do not support a strong defense, SDI is not likely to be killed. "It doesn't have to be that controversial," said Kirk O'Donnell, director of the Democratic-leaning Center for National Policy. "What's wrong with research?"

On arms control, meanwhile, Democrats in both chambers will be eager to push proposals they shelved, at Reagan's urging, on the eve of the Iceland summit. But now they face reluctance on the Democratic right from Sen. Sam Nunn of Georgia, the next Armed Services Committee head.

Nevertheless, action is possible on measures to ban some nuclear-weapons tests, assuming the Soviets do the same, and to bar production of chemical weapons. In 1986, a Democratic amendment blocking manufacture of the "Bigeye" chemical bomb failed on a 51-50 vote. Vice President George Bush broke the tie, as he did twice in 1983 on chemical-weapons votes.

"I don't think there are going to be automatic changes," said arms-control lobbyist David Cohen. "But we're in a better position to wage battles."

Cohen sees new support specifically from two House Democrats moving to the Senate — Timothy E. Wirth of Colorado and Thomas A. Daschle of South Dakota.

Judging the Potential Judges

Dole said the biggest difference in a Senate run by Democrats would be a colder reception for Reagan's judicial nominees. In the six years of his administration, 299 nominees have been confirmed. Democrats demanded roll-call votes on just eight of those, and none was rejected on the floor.

Democrat Mitchell, a former federal judge, said Senate Democrats will be on guard against incompetent or ideological appointees. But "the greatest effect," he said, "will be on the internal selection process of the administration itself."

For, as Byrd warned, "a Manion won't get through this Senate now."

The reference was to Daniel A. Manion of Indiana, a conservative whom Democrats opposed as unqualified for the bench. He was confirmed after Democrats failed by a single vote, 49-50, to win reconsideration of a controversial 48-46 vote on June 26. ∎

Republicans Take Solace in Governors' Races

Democratic efforts to portray the 1986 elections as a repudiation of the Republican Party were mitigated by the strong GOP showing in gubernatorial contests. Republicans made an apparent net gain of eight governorships.

The Democrats, who entered the election holding 34 of the 50 governorships, saw their advantage drop to 26-24. The GOP count is the largest since 1970, when the party last held a majority of the governorships. *(State-by-state returns, 1986 CQ Weekly Report, p. 2864)*

Despite the overall Republican success in the gubernatorial elections, the party lost three of its open seats: Oregon, Pennsylvania and Tennessee. But these defeats were offset by the unseating of Democratic incumbents in Texas and Wisconsin, and by GOP victories in nine Democratic open seats — including upset wins in Alabama and Arizona and a solid victory in megastate Florida.

Republicans benefited from Democratic self-destruction in several states, particularly Alabama and Illinois. Democrats also suffered from the problem of "exposure." They defended 27 governorships, the GOP only 9. Democrats won a majority of the 36 seats at stake, but that was not enough to avoid losing ground to the GOP.

An Eye on the Future

The Republican success could put the party in a more favorable position to influence congressional redistricting in the early 1990s. If, for instance, GOP governors in fast-growing Texas and Florida seek and win re-election in 1990, they may be able to see that the GOP reaps some of the new seats those states are sure to gain. Similarly, if GOP Gov. James R. Thompson wins another term in 1990, he could work to protect his party's interests in Illinois, which is likely to lose seats.

But there was also disappointment for Republicans seeking more influence in redistricting: The GOP failed to dent Democratic domination of the state legislatures. Democrats claimed to have picked up at least 150 legislative seats and to have gained

Wins in South Include Texas and Florida

control of four more state chambers.

A more immediate result of the GOP gubernatorial gains is that the party's 1988 presidential nominee will find more helping hands in state capitals across the country.

The base of the Republican success on Nov. 4 was a small core of popular incumbents. California's George Deukmejian defeated Los Angeles Mayor Tom Bradley by less than 1 percentage point in 1982, but as the state deficit he inherited turned into a surplus, his political stock rose. Bradley campaigned aggressively in 1986, accusing the incumbent of failing to deal with toxic wastes. But Deukmejian maintained his image as a competent fiscal manager and won easily.

GOP incumbents in New England won re-election: Rhode Island Gov. Edward DiPrete swamped Democratic businessman Bruce G. Sundlun by 2-to-1, while New Hampshire's John H. Sununu won more modestly, with 54

Governorships

Current lineup		1987	
Democrats	34	Democrats	26 †
Republicans	16	Republicans	24

Democrats	
Net loss	8
Incumbents re-elected	10 †
Incumbents defeated	2
(Anthony S. Earl, Wis.; Mark White, Texas)	

Republicans	
Net Gain	8
Incumbents re-elected	5
Incumbents defeated	0

† *Madeleine M. Kunin, D-Vt., the incumbent, received a plurality of the vote and is included as a Democratic win. However, because Vermont law requires a governor to be elected by a majority of the vote, the state Legislature will choose the governor in January.*

percent, over Democrat Paul McEachern. Also in New England, the GOP picked up Maine, where Democratic Gov. Joseph E. Brennan ran successfully for the House seat of GOP Rep. John R. McKernan Jr. McKernan won the governorship, taking 39 percent in a four-candidate race.

Unpopularity of Democratic incumbents helped produce GOP victories in Wisconsin and Texas. Democratic Gov. Anthony S. Earl never lived down the "Tony the Taxer" label he received after pushing through Wisconsin tax increases in 1983, and he lost to state House Minority Leader Tommy G. Thompson. In Texas, a budget shortfall resulting from the state's energy and farm recessions forced Democratic Gov. Mark White to propose a tax increase during the 1986 campaign. He also had antagonized several key groups, including teachers, who opposed his push for competency testing. White lost to the man he had ousted from office in 1982, Republican William Clements.

GOP Progress in the South

Despite the GOP's poor showing in Senate elections in the South, Republicans looking for evidence of realignment can point out that the party made its greatest gubernatorial gains in that region. A big plum was Florida, where Tampa Mayor Bob Martinez, a former Democrat, will succeed Democratic Sen.-elect Bob Graham.

Martinez' pledge to support Reagan administration priorities helped him overcome doubts of conservative Republicans, who were skeptical about his recent party switch and his former support for President Carter. Martinez also appealed to conservative Democrats who disliked their party's liberal nominee, former state Rep. Steve Pajcic, and he won the backing of many Cuban-Americans, although he is of Spanish, not Cuban, descent.

Oklahoma voters endorsed the political comeback attempt of Henry Bellmon, a former GOP governor and senator. The economic stagnation that made the outgoing Democratic administration unpopular also made Bellmon a strong favorite. But a vigorous

Governors for 1987

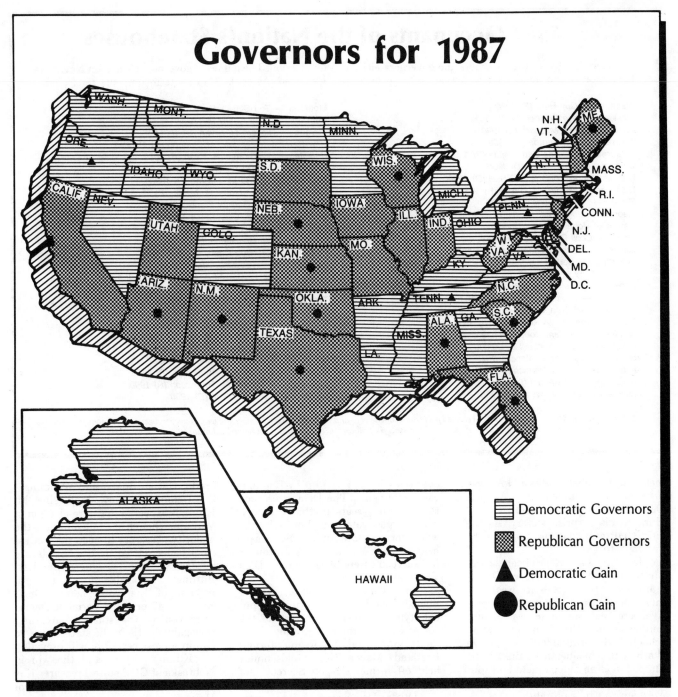

Legend:
- Democratic Governors
- Republican Governors
- ▲ Democratic Gain
- ● Republican Gain

campaign by conservative Democratic businessman David Walters, an upset primary winner, held Bellmon to a slimmer-than-expected victory.

The farm crisis that helped oust at least two Republican senators did not hurt most of the party's gubernatorial nominees. Iowa incumbent Terry E. Branstad won narrowly, as did GOP candidates for open governorships in South Dakota, Nebraska and Kansas. Their victories gave the GOP a strong hold on the breadbasket. Minnesota incumbent Rudy

Perpich was the only Democrat to win in a Midwestern state where agriculture was a major issue.

Self-Destruction

In several states, Democrats were their own worst enemies. Alabama Democratic Gov. George C. Wallace's retirement sparked a fierce squabble over the Democratic nomination that helped Guy Hunt become the state's first Republican governor since Reconstruction.

The state Democratic Party's re-

versal of conservative state Attorney General Charles Graddick's apparent runoff win over Lt. Gov. William J. Baxley (because of illegal Republican crossover votes for Graddick) led to court challenges that lasted long into the campaign. Graddick dropped a threatened write-in campaign just before the election, but blasted Baxley, a moderate with support from blacks and labor, as the candidate of "special interests."

Baxley did not offset conservative animosity by portraying Hunt, a for

1987 Occupants of the Nation's Statehouses

Here is a list of the governors and governors-elect of the 50 states, and the years in which each office is next up for election. The names of governors elected on Nov. 4 are *italicized*. Asterisks (*) denote incumbents re-elected.

Alabama — *Guy Hunt (R) 1990*	Montana — Ted Schwinden (D) 1988
Alaska — *Steve Cowper (D) 1990*	Nebraska — *Kay A. Orr (R) 1990*
Arizona — *Evan Mecham (R) 1990*	Nevada — *Richard H. Bryan (D) 1990**
Arkansas — *Bill Clinton (D) 1990**	New Hampshire — *John H. Sununu (R) 1988**
California — *George Deukmejian (R) 1990**	New Jersey — Thomas H. Kean (R) 1989
Colorado — *Roy Romer (D) 1990*	New Mexico — *Garrey E. Carruthers (R) 1990*
Connecticut — *William A. O'Neill (D) 1990**	New York — *Mario M. Cuomo (D) 1990**
Delaware — Michael N. Castle (R) 1988	North Carolina — James G. Martin (R) 1988
Florida — *Bob Martinez (R) 1990*	North Dakota — George Sinner (D) 1988
Georgia — *Joe Frank Harris (D) 1990**	Ohio — *Richard F. Celeste (D) 1990**
Hawaii — *John Waihee (D) 1990*	Oklahoma — Henry Bellmon (R) 1990
Idaho — Cecil D. Andrus (D) 1990	Oregon — *Neil Goldschmidt (D) 1990*
Illinois — *James R. Thompson (R) 1990**	Pennsylvania — *Bob Casey (D) 1990*
Indiana — Robert D. Orr (R) 1988	Rhode Island — *Edward DiPrete (R) 1988**
Iowa — *Terry E. Branstad (R) 1990**	South Carolina — *Carroll A. Campbell Jr. (R) 1990*
Kansas — Mike Hayden (R) 1990	South Dakota — *George S. Mickelson (R) 1990*
Kentucky — Martha Layne Collins (D) 1987	Tennessee — *Ned McWherter (D) 1990*
Louisiana — Edwin W. Edwards (D) 1987	Texas — *Bill Clements (R) 1990*
Maine — *John R. McKernan Jr. (R) 1990*	Utah — Norman H. Bangerter (R) 1988
Maryland — *William Donald Schaefer (D) 1990*	Vermont — *Madeleine M. Kunin (D) 1988**†
Massachusetts — *Michael S. Dukakis (D) 1990**	Virginia — Gerald L. Baliles (D) 1989
Michigan — *James J. Blanchard (D) 1990**	Washington — Booth Gardner (D) 1988
Minnesota — *Rudy Perpich (D) 1990**	West Virginia — Arch A. Moore Jr. (R) 1988
Mississippi — Bill Allain (D) 1987	Wisconsin — *Tommy G. Thompson (R) 1990*
Missouri — John Ashcroft (R) 1988	Wyoming — *Mike Sullivan (D) 1990*

† *Madeleine M. Kunin, the incumbent, received a plurality of the vote and is included as a Democratic win. However, because Vermont law requires a governor to be elected by a majority of the vote, the state Legislature will choose the governor in January.*

mer county probate judge and Amway distributor, as unqualified. A huge Democratic crossover vote boosted Hunt to his surprise victory. As the 1978 GOP gubernatorial nominee, he lost by 3-to-1.

In Arizona, Republican Evan Mecham's victory to succeed Democratic Gov. Bruce Babbitt was even more surprising. Mecham, a conservative perennial candidate, was an underdog against the Democratic state school Superintendent Carolyn Warner. But businessman Bill Schulz jumped in as an independent and split the Democratic vote, enabling Mecham to win a plurality.

At one time, Illinois' Thompson was viewed as vulnerable to Democrat Adlai E. Stevenson III, whom he narrowly beat in 1982. But Stevenson's challenge fizzled when two associates of Lyndon H. LaRouche Jr. won Democratic primaries for state office. Stevenson disowned the pair and renounced his Democratic nomination, but his independent bid fell far short.

Democrats Pick Off GOP Seats

The biggest accomplishment for Democrats was their success at taking over seats being given up by Republican incumbents. The Democrats took three of four seats in that category. Their largest catch was Pennsylvania, where former state Auditor Bob Casey beat Lt. Gov. William W. Scranton III to succeed Republican Gov. Dick Thornburgh.

In Tennessee, state House Speaker Ned Ray McWherter, a populist-style Democrat, thwarted the comeback of former GOP Gov. Winfield Dunn. And in Oregon, former Portland Mayor Neil Goldschmidt held off former Oregon Secretary of State Norma Paulus.

Other Democratic bright spots were the landslide victories of two incumbents often mentioned as possible Democratic presidential contenders — New York's Mario M. Cuomo and Massachusetts' Michael S. Dukakis. Economic comebacks in the "Rust Belt" helped Democrats James J. Blanchard of Michigan and Richard F. Celeste of Ohio score easy wins.

As expected, Baltimore Mayor William Donald Schaefer took Maryland's open seat by a huge margin. Democrats maintained control in tighter open-seat races in Alaska, Col-orado, Hawaii, Idaho and Wyoming.

Democratic Gov. Madeleine M. Kunin is expected to win re-election in Vermont, though she failed to take the majority necessary to keep the contest from being settled by the Legislature in January 1987. Bernard Sanders, Burlington's socialist mayor, took 15 percent of the vote, helping hold Kunin to 47 percent. Vermont Democrats control the state Senate, and they gained a tie in the state House so Kunin almost certainly will prevail.

Kunin's victory and the win in Nebraska of GOP state Treasurer Kay A. Orr over former Lincoln Mayor Helen Boosalis increase the number of women governors to three (Kentucky Democrat Martha Layne Collins is the third). But other women running as major-party nominees lost in Arizona, Connecticut, Oregon and Nevada.

Two major-party black candidates also fell short — Bradley in California, and Wayne County Executive William Lucas in Michigan. The landslide loss of Lucas, who switched from the Democratic Party to the GOP in 1985, underlined the difficulty of persuading Republican voters to support black candidates. ∎

Glossary of Congressional Terms

Act—The term for legislation once it has passed both houses of Congress and has been signed by the president or passed over his veto, thus becoming law. *(See below.)* Also used in parliamentary terminology for a bill that has been passed by one house and engrossed. *(See Engrossed Bill.)*

Adjournment Sine Die—Adjournment without definitely fixing a day for reconvening; literally "adjournment without a day." Usually used to connote the final adjournment of a session of Congress. A session can continue until noon, Jan. 3, of the following year, when, under the 20th Amendment to the Constitution, it automatically terminates. Both houses must agree to a concurrent resolution for either house to adjourn for more than three days.

Adjournment to a Day Certain—Adjournment under a motion or resolution that fixes the next time of meeting. Under the Constitution, neither house can adjourn for more than three days without the concurrence of the other. A session of Congress is not ended by adjournment to a day certain.

Amendment—A proposal of a member of Congress to alter the language, provisions or stipulations in a bill or in another amendment. An amendment usually is printed, debated and voted upon in the same manner as a bill.

Amendment in the Nature of a Substitute—Usually an amendment that seeks to replace the entire text of a bill. Passage of this type of amendment strikes out everything after the enacting clause and inserts a new version of the bill. An amendment in the nature of a substitute also can refer to an amendment that replaces a large portion of the text of a bill.

Appeal—A member's challenge of a ruling or decision made by the presiding officer of the chamber. In the Senate, the senator appeals to members of the chamber to override the decision. If carried by a majority vote, the appeal nullifies the chair's ruling. In the House, the decision of the Speaker traditionally has been final; seldom are there appeals to the members to reverse the Speaker's stand. To appeal a ruling is considered an attack on the Speaker.

Appropriations Bill—A bill that gives legal authority to spend or obligate money from the Treasury. The Constitution disallows money to be drawn from the Treasury "but in Consequence of Appropriations made by Law."

By congressional custom, an appropriations bill originates in the House, and it is not supposed to be considered by the full House or Senate until a related measure authorizing the funding is enacted; appropriations bills need not provide the full amount permissible under the authorization measures. Under the 1985 Gramm-Rudman-Hollings law, the House is supposed to pass by June 30 the last regular appropriations bill for the fiscal year starting the following Oct. 1. *(See also Authorization, Budget Process.)*

In addition to general appropriations bills, there are two specialized types. *(See Continuing Resolution, Supplemental Appropriations Bill.)*

Authorization—Basic, substantive legislation that establishes or continues the legal operation of a federal program or agency, either indefinitely or for a specific period of time, or which sanctions a particular type of obligation or expenditure. An authorization normally is a prerequisite for an appropriation or other kind of budget authority. Under the rules of both houses, the appropriation for a program or agency may not be considered until its authorization has been considered. An authorization also may limit the amount of budget authority to be provided or may authorize the appropriation of "such sums as may be necessary." *(See also Backdoor Spending.)*

Backdoor Spending—Budget authority provided in legislation outside the normal appropriations process. The most common forms of backdoor spending are borrowing authority, contract authority and entitlements. *(See below.)*

In some cases, such as interest on the public debt, a permanent appropriation is provided that becomes available without further action by Congress.

Bills—Most legislative proposals before Congress are in the form of bills and are designated by HR in the House of Representatives or S in the Senate, according to the house in which they originate, and by a number assigned in the order in which they are introduced during the two-year period of a congressional term. "Public bills" deal with general questions and become public laws if approved by Congress and signed by the president. "Private bills" deal with individual matters such as claims against the government, immigration and naturalization cases, land titles, etc., and become private laws if approved and signed. *(See also Concurrent Resolution, Joint Resolution, Resolution.)*

Bills Introduced—In both the House and Senate, any number of members may join in introducing a single bill or resolution. The first member listed is the sponsor of the bill, and all members' names following his are the bill's cosponsors.

Many bills are committee bills and are introduced under the name of the chairman of the committee or subcommittee. All appropriations bills fall into this category. A committee frequently holds hearings on a number of related bills and may agree to one of them or to an entirely new bill. *(See also Report, Clean Bill, By Request.)*

Bills Referred—When introduced, a bill is referred to the committee or committees that have jurisdiction over the subject with which the bill is concerned. Under the standing rules of the House and Senate, bills are referred by the Speaker in the House and by the presiding officer in the Senate. In practice, the House and Senate parliamentarians act for these officials and refer the vast majority of bills.

Borrowing Authority—Statutory authority that permits a federal agency to incur obligations and make payments for specified purposes with borrowed money.

Budget—The document sent to Congress by the president early each year estimating government revenue and expenditures for the ensuing fiscal year.

Budget Authority—Authority to enter into obligations that will result in immediate or future outlays involving federal funds. The basic forms of budget authority are appropriations, contract authority and borrowing authority. Budget authority may be classified by (1) the period of availability (one-year, multiple-year or without a time limitation), (2) the timing of congressional action (current or permanent), or (3) the manner of determining the amount available (definite or indefinite).

Budget Process—Congress in 1985 attempted to strengthen its 11-year-old budget process with the goal of balancing the federal budget by October 1980. The law, known as Gramm-Rudman-Hollings for its congressional sponsors, established annual maximum deficit targets and mandated across-the-board automatic cuts if the deficit goals were not achieved through regular budget and appropriations action.

The 1985 law also established an accelerated timetable for presidential submission of budgets and for congressional approval of budget resolutions and reconciliation bills, two mechanisms created by the Congressional Budget and Impoundment Control Act of 1974. Budget resolutions, due by April 15 annually, set guidelines for congressional action on spending and tax measures; they are adopted by the House and Senate but are not signed by the president and do not have the force of law. Reconciliation bills, due by June 15, actually make changes in existing law to meet budget resolution goals. *(See Budget Reconciliation)*

A special federal court found Gramm-Rudman's automatic spending cut mechanism to be unconstitutional. The mechanism was to be activated in mid-August each year if deficit re-estimates showed Congress and the president had not managed through conventional legislation to hold deficits below targets set by the statute. Absent the automatic device, the cuts necessitated by those estimates would take effect only if approved by Congress and the president. The Supreme Court July 7, 1986, upheld the lower court ruling that the automatic mechanism violated the separation-of-powers doctrine, because it assigned executive-type responsibilities to the General Accounting Office, which the court found to be a legislative branch entity. Under the remaining procedure deficit re-estimates will be made, but Congress and the president must approve any spending cuts.

Budget Reconciliation—The 1974 budget act provides for a "reconciliation" procedure for bringing existing tax and spending laws into conformity with the congressional budget resolutions. Under the procedure, Congress instructs designated legislative committees to approve measures adjusting revenues and expenditures by a certain amount. The committees have a deadline by which they must report the legislation, but they have the discretion of deciding what changes are to be made. The recommendations of the various committees are consolidated without change by the Budget committees into an omnibus reconciliation bill, which then must be considered and approved by both houses of Congress.

By Request—A phrase used when a senator or representative introduces a bill at the request of an executive agency or private organization but does not necessarily endorse the legislation.

Calendar—An agenda or list of business awaiting possible action by each chamber. The House uses five legislative calendars. *(See Consent, Discharge, House, Private and Union Calendar.)*

In the Senate, all legislative matters reported from committee go on one calendar. They are listed there in the order in which committees report them or the Senate places them on the calendar, but may be called up out of order by the majority leader, either by obtaining unanimous consent of the Senate or by a motion to call up a bill. The Senate also uses one non-legislative calendar; this is used for treaties and nominations. *(See Executive Calendar.)*

Calendar Wednesday—In the House, committees, on Wednesdays, may be called in the order in which they appear in Rule X of the House, for the purpose of bringing up any of their bills from either the House or the Union Calendar, except bills that are privileged. General debate is limited to two hours. Bills called up from the Union Calendar are considered in Committee of the Whole. Calendar Wednesday is not observed during the last two weeks of a session and may be dispensed with at other times by a two-thirds vote. This procedure is rarely used and routinely is dispensed with by unanimous consent.

Call of the Calendar—Senate bills that are not brought up for debate by a motion, unanimous consent or a unanimous consent agreement are brought before the Senate for action when the calendar listing them is "called." Bills must be called in the order listed. Measures considered by this method usually are non-controversial, and debate is limited to a total of five minutes for each senator on the bill and any amendments proposed to it.

Chamber—The meeting place for the membership of either the House or the Senate; also the membership of the House or Senate meeting as such.

Clean Bill—Frequently after a committee has finished a major revision of a bill, one of the committee members, usually the chairman, will assemble the changes and what is left of the original bill into a new measure and introduce it as a "clean bill." The revised measure, which is given a new number, then is referred back to the committee, which reports it to the floor for consideration. This often is a timesaver, as committee-recommended changes in a clean bill do not have to be considered and voted on by the chamber. Reporting a clean bill also protects committee amendments that might be subject to points of order concerning germaneness.

Clerk of the House—Chief administrative officer of the House of Representatives, with duties corresponding to those of the secretary of the Senate. *(See also Secretary of the Senate.)*

Cloture—The process by which a filibuster can be ended in the Senate other than by unanimous consent. A motion for cloture can apply to any measure before the Senate, including a proposal to change the chamber's rules. A cloture motion requires the signatures of 16 senators to be introduced, and to end a filibuster the cloture motion must obtain the votes of three-fifths of the entire Senate membership (60 if there are no vacancies), except that to end a filibuster against a proposal to amend the standing rules of the Senate a two-thirds vote of senators present and voting is required. The cloture request is put to a roll-call vote one hour after the Senate meets on the second day following introduction of the motion. If approved, cloture limits each senator to one hour of debate. The bill or amendment in question comes to a final vote after 100 hours of consideration (including debate time and the time it takes to conduct roll calls, quorum calls and other procedural motions). *(See Filibuster.)*

Committee—A division of the House or Senate that prepares legislation for action by the parent chamber or makes investigations as directed by the parent chamber. There are several types of committees. *(See Standing and Select or Special Committees.)* Most standing committees are divided into subcommittees, which study legislation, hold hearings and report bills, with or without amendments, to the full committee. Only the full committee can report legislation for action by the House or Senate.

Committee of the Whole—The working title of what is formally "The Committee of the Whole House (of Representatives) on the State of the Union." The membership is comprised of all House members sitting as a committee. Any 100 members who are present on the floor of the chamber to consider legislation comprise a quorum of the committee. Any legislation, however, must first have passed through the regular legislative or Appropriations committee and have been placed on the calendar.

Technically, the Committee of the Whole considers only bills directly or indirectly appropriating money, authorizing appropriations or involving taxes or charges on the public. Because the Committee of the Whole need number only 100 representatives, a quorum is more readily attained, and legislative business is expedited. Before 1971, members' positions were not individually recorded on votes taken in Committee of the Whole. *(See Teller Vote.)*

When the full House resolves itself into the Committee of the Whole, it supplants the Speaker with a "chairman." A measure is debated and amendments may be proposed, with votes on amendments as needed. *(See Five-Minute Rule.)* When the committee completes its work on the measure, it dissolves itself by "rising." The Speaker returns, and the chairman of the Committee of the Whole reports to the House that the committee's work has been completed. At this time members may demand a roll-call vote on any amendment *adopted* in the Committee of the Whole. The final vote is on passage of the legislation.

Committee Veto—A requirement added to a few statutes directing that certain policy directives by an executive department or agency be reviewed by certain congressional committees before they are implemented. Under common practice, the government department or agency and the committees involved are expected to reach a consensus before the directives are carried out. *(See also Legislative Veto.)*

Concurrent Resolution—A concurrent resolution, designated H Con Res or S Con Res, must be adopted by both houses, but it is not sent to the president for his signature and therefore does not have the force of law. A concurrent resolution, for example, is used to fix the time for adjournment of a Congress. It also is used as the vehicle for expressing the sense of Congress on various foreign policy and domestic issues, and it serves as the vehicle for coordinated decisions on the federal budget under the 1974 Congressional Budget and Impoundment Control Act. *(See also Bills, Joint Resolution, Resolution.)*

Conference—A meeting between the representatives of the House and the Senate to reconcile differences between the two houses on provisions of a bill passed by both chambers. Members of the conference committee are appointed by the Speaker and the presiding officer of the Senate and are called "managers" for their respective chambers. A majority of the managers for each house must reach agreement on the provisions of the bill (often a compromise between the versions of the two chambers) before it can be considered by either chamber in the form of a "conference report." When the conference report goes to the floor, it cannot be amended, and, if it is not approved by both chambers, the bill may go back to conference under certain situations, or a new conference must be convened. Many rules and informal practices govern the conduct of conference committees.

Bills that are passed by both houses with only minor differences need not be sent to conference. Either chamber may "concur" in the other's amendments, completing action on the legislation. Sometimes leaders of the committees of jurisdiction work out an informal compromise instead of having a formal conference. *(See Custody of the Papers.)*

Confirmations—*(See Nominations.)*

Congressional Record—The daily, printed account of proceedings in both the House and Senate chambers, showing substantially verbatim debate, statements and a record of floor action. Highlights of legislative and committee action are embodied in a Daily Digest section of the Record, and members are entitled to have their extraneous remarks printed in an appendix known as "Extension of Remarks." Members may edit and revise remarks made on the floor during debate, and quotations from debate reported by the press are not always found in the Record.

The Record provides a way to distinguish remarks spoken on the floor of the House and Senate from undelivered speeches. In the Senate, all speeches, articles and other matter that members insert in the Record without actually reading them on the floor are set off by large black dots, or bullets. However, a loophole allows a member to avoid the bulleting if he delivers any portion of the speech in person. In the House, undelivered speeches and other material are printed in a distinctive typeface.

Congressional Terms of Office—Normally begin on Jan. 3 of the year following a general election and are two years for representatives and six years for senators. Representatives elected in special elections are sworn in for the remainder of a term. A person may be appointed to fill a Senate vacancy and serve until a successor is elected; the successor serves until the end of the term applying to the vacant seat.

Consent Calendar—Members of the House may place on this calendar most bills on the Union or House Calendar that are considered to be non-controversial. Bills on the Consent Calendar normally are called on the first and third Mondays of each month. On the first occasion that a bill is called in this manner, consideration may be blocked by the objection of any member. The second time, if there are three objections, the bill is stricken from the Consent Calendar. If fewer than three members object, the bill is given immediate consideration.

A bill on the Consent Calendar may be postponed in

another way. A member may ask that the measure be passed over "without prejudice." In that case, no objection is recorded against the bill, and its status on the Consent Calendar remains unchanged. A bill stricken from the Consent Calendar remains on the Union or House Calendar.

Cosponsor—(See Bills Introduced.)

Continuing Resolution—A joint resolution drafted by Congress "continuing appropriations" for specific ongoing activities of a government department or departments when a fiscal year begins and Congress has not yet enacted all of the regular appropriations bills for that year. The continuing resolution usually specifies a maximum rate at which the agency may incur obligations. This usually is based on the rate for the previous year, the president's budget request or an appropriation bill for that year passed by either or both houses of Congress, but not cleared.

Contract Authority—Budget authority contained in an authorization bill that permits the federal government to enter into contracts or other obligations for future payments from funds not yet appropriated by Congress. The assumption is that funds will be available for payment in a subsequent appropriation act.

Controllable Budget Items—In federal budgeting this refers to programs for which the budget authority or outlays during a fiscal year can be controlled without changing existing, substantive law. The concept "relatively uncontrollable under current law" includes outlays for open-ended programs and fixed costs such as interest on the public debt, Social Security benefits, veterans' benefits and outlays to liquidate prior-year obligations.

Correcting Recorded Votes—Rules prohibit members from changing their votes after the result has been announced. But, occasionally hours, days or months after a vote has been taken, a member may announce that he was "incorrectly recorded." In the Senate, a request to change one's vote almost always receives unanimous consent. In the House, members are prohibited from changing their votes if tallied by the electronic voting system installed in 1973. If taken by roll call, it is permissible if consent is granted.

Current Services Estimates—Estimated budget authority and outlays for federal programs and operations for the forthcoming fiscal year based on continuation of existing levels of service without policy changes. These estimates of budget authority and outlays, accompanied by the underlying economic and policy assumptions upon which they are based, are transmitted by the president to Congress when the budget is submitted.

Custody of the Papers—To reconcile differences between the House and Senate versions of a bill, a conference may be arranged. The chamber with "custody of the papers" — the engrossed bill, engrossed amendments, messages of transmittal — is the only body empowered to request the conference. By custom, the chamber that asks for a conference is the last to act on the conference report once agreement has been reached on the bill by the conferees. Custody of the papers sometimes is manipulated to ensure that a particular chamber acts either first or last on the conference report.

Deferral—Executive branch action to defer, or delay, the spending of appropriated money. The 1974 Congressional Budget and Impoundment Control Act requires a special message from the president to Congress reporting a proposed deferral of spending. Deferrals may not extend beyond the end of the fiscal year in which the message is transmitted. A federal district court in 1986 struck down the president's authority to defer spending for policy reasons; the Justice Department planned to appeal. (See also Rescission Bill.)

Dilatory Motion—A motion made for the purpose of killing time and preventing action on a bill or amendment. House rules outlaw dilatory motions, but enforcement is largely within the discretion of the Speaker or chairman of the Committee of the Whole. The Senate does not have a rule banning dilatory motions, except under cloture.

Discharge a Committee—Occasionally, attempts are made to relieve a committee from jurisdiction over a measure before it. This is attempted more often in the House than in the Senate, and the procedure rarely is successful.

In the House, if a committee does not report a bill within 30 days after the measure is referred to it, any member may file a discharge motion. Once offered, the motion is treated as a petition needing the signatures of 218 members (a majority of the House). After the required signatures have been obtained, there is a delay of seven days. Thereafter, on the second and fourth Mondays of each month, except during the last six days of a session, any member who has signed the petition must be recognized, if he so desires, to move that the committee be discharged. Debate on the motion to discharge is limited to 20 minutes, and, if the motion is carried, consideration of the bill becomes a matter of high privilege.

If a resolution to consider a bill is held up in the Rules Committee for more than seven legislative days, any member may enter a motion to discharge the committee. The motion is handled like any other discharge petition in the House.

Occasionally, to expedite non-controversial legislative business, a committee is discharged by unanimous consent of the House, and a petition is not required. (Senate procedure, see Discharge Resolution.)

Discharge Calendar—The House calendar to which motions to discharge committees are referred when they have the required number of signatures (218) and are awaiting floor action.

Discharge Petition—(See Discharge a Committee.)

Discharge Resolution—In the Senate, a special motion that any senator may introduce to relieve a committee from consideration of a bill before it. The resolution can be called up for Senate approval or disapproval in the same manner as any other Senate business. (House procedure, see Discharge a Committee.)

Division of a Question for Voting—A practice that is more common in the Senate but also used in the House, a member may demand a division of an amendment or a motion for purposes of voting. Where an amendment or motion can be divided, the individual parts are voted on separately when a member demands a division. This procedure occurs most often during the consideration of conference reports.

Division Vote—*(See Standing Vote.)*

Enacting Clause—Key phrase in bills beginning, "Be it enacted by the Senate and House of Representatives...." A successful motion to strike it from legislation kills the measure.

Engrossed Bill—The final copy of a bill as passed by one chamber, with the text as amended by floor action and certified by the clerk of the House or the secretary of the Senate.

Enrolled Bill—The final copy of a bill that has been passed in identical form by both chambers. It is certified by an officer of the house of origin (clerk of the House or secretary of the Senate) and then sent on for the signatures of the House Speaker, the Senate president pro tempore and the president of the United States. An enrolled bill is printed on parchment.

Entitlement Program—A federal program that guarantees a certain level of benefits to persons or other entities who meet requirements set by law, such as Social Security or unemployment benefits. It thus leaves no discretion with Congress on how much money to appropriate.

Executive Calendar—This is a non-legislative calendar in the Senate on which presidential documents such as treaties and nominations are listed.

Executive Document—A document, usually a treaty, sent to the Senate by the president for consideration or approval. Executive documents are identified for each session of Congress as Executive A, 97th Congress, 1st Session; Executive B, etc. They are referred to committee in the same manner as other measures. Unlike legislative documents, however, treaties do not die at the end of a Congress but remain "live" proposals until acted on by the Senate or withdrawn by the president.

Executive Session—A meeting of a Senate or House committee (or occasionally of either chamber) that only its members may attend. Witnesses regularly appear at committee meetings in executive session — for example, Defense Department officials during presentations of classified defense information. Other members of Congress may be invited, but the public and press are not allowed to attend.

Expenditures—The actual spending of money as distinguished from the appropriation of funds. Expenditures are made by the disbursing officers of the administration; appropriations are made only by Congress. The two are rarely identical in any fiscal year. In addition to some current budget authority, expenditures may represent budget authority made available one, two or more years earlier.

Filibuster—A time-delaying tactic associated with the Senate and used by a minority in an effort to prevent a vote on a bill or amendment that probably would pass if voted upon directly. The most common method is to take advantage of the Senate's rules permitting unlimited debate, but other forms of parliamentary maneuvering may be used. The stricter rules used by the House make filibusters more difficult, but delaying tactics are employed occasionally through various procedural devices allowed by House rules. *(Senate filibusters, see Cloture.)*

Fiscal Year—Financial operations of the government are carried out in a 12-month fiscal year, beginning on Oct. 1 and ending on Sept. 30. The fiscal year carries the date of the calendar year in which it ends. (From fiscal year 1844 to fiscal year 1976, the fiscal year began July 1 and ended the following June 30.)

Five-Minute Rule—A debate-limiting rule of the House that is invoked when the House sits as the Committee of the Whole. Under the rule, a member offering an amendment is allowed to speak five minutes in its favor, and an opponent of the amendment is allowed to speak five minutes in opposition. Debate is then closed. In practice, amendments regularly are debated more than 10 minutes, with members gaining the floor by offering pro forma amendments or obtaining unanimous consent to speak longer than five minutes. *(See Strike Out the Last Word.)*

Floor Manager—A member who has the task of steering legislation through floor debate and the amendment process to a final vote in the House or the Senate. Floor managers are usually chairmen or ranking members of the committee that reported the bill. Managers are responsible for apportioning the debate time granted supporters of the bill. The ranking minority member of the committee normally apportions time for the minority party's participation in the debate.

Frank—A member's facsimile signature, which is used on envelopes in lieu of stamps, for the member's official outgoing mail. The "franking privilege" is the right to send mail postage-free.

Germane—Pertaining to the subject matter of the measure at hand. All House amendments must be germane to the bill being considered. The Senate requires that amendments be germane when they are proposed to general appropriation bills, bills being considered once cloture has been adopted, or, frequently, when proceeding under a unanimous consent agreement placing a time limit on consideration of a bill. The 1974 budget act also requires that amendments to concurrent budget resolutions be germane. In the House, floor debate must be germane, and the first three hours of debate each day in the Senate must be germane to the pending business.

Grandfather Clause—A provision exempting persons or other entities already engaged in an activity from rules or legislation affecting that activity. Grandfather clauses sometimes are added to legislation in order to avoid antagonizing groups with established interests in the activities affected.

Grants-in-Aid—Payments by the federal government to states, local governments or individuals in support of specified programs, services or activities.

Guaranteed Loans—Loans to third parties for which the federal government in the event of default guarantees, in whole or in part, the repayment of principal or interest to a lender or holder of a security.

Hearings—Committee sessions for taking testimony from witnesses. At hearings on legislation, witnesses usually include specialists, government officials and spokesmen for persons or entities affected by the bill or bills under study. Hearings related to special investigations bring forth a variety of witnesses. Committees sometimes use their subpoena power to summon reluctant witnesses. The public and press may attend open hearings, but are barred from closed, or "executive," hearings. The vast majority of hearings are open to the public. (See Executive Session.)

Hold-Harmless Clause—A provision added to legislation to ensure that recipients of federal funds do not receive less in a future year than they did in the current year if a new formula for allocating funds authorized in the legislation would result in a reduction to the recipients. This clause has been used most frequently to soften the impact of sudden reductions in federal grants.

Hopper—Box on House clerk's desk where members deposit bills and resolutions to introduce them. (See also Bills Introduced.)

Hour Rule—A provision in the rules of the House that permits one hour of debate time for each member on amendments debated in the House of Representatives sitting as the House. Therefore, the House normally amends bills while sitting as the Committee of the Whole, where the five-minute rule on amendments operates. (See Committee of the Whole, Five-Minute Rule.)

House—The House of Representatives, as distinct from the Senate, although each body is a "house" of Congress.

House as in Committee of the Whole—A procedure that can be used to expedite consideration of certain measures such as continuing resolutions and, when there is debate, private bills. The procedure only can be invoked with the unanimous consent of the House or a rule from the Rules Committee and has procedural elements of both the House sitting as the House of Representatives, such as the Speaker presiding and the previous question motion being in order, and the House sitting as the Committee of the Whole, such as the five-minute rule pertaining.

House Calendar—A listing for action by the House of public bills that do not directly or indirectly appropriate money or raise revenue.

Immunity—The constitutional privilege of members of Congress to make verbal statements on the floor and in committee for which they cannot be sued or arrested for slander or libel. Also, freedom from arrest while traveling to or from sessions of Congress or on official business. Members in this status may be arrested only for treason, felonies or a breach of the peace, as defined by congressional manuals.

Impoundments—Any action taken by the executive branch that delays or precludes the obligation or expenditure of budget authority previously approved by Congress. (See also Deferral, Rescission Bill.)

Joint Committee—A committee composed of a specified number of members of both the House and Senate. A joint committee may be investigative or research-oriented, an example of the latter being the Joint Economic Committee. Others have housekeeping duties such as the joint committees on Printing and on the Library of Congress.

Joint Resolution—A joint resolution, designated H J Res or S J Res, requires the approval of both houses and the signature of the president, just as a bill does, and has the force of law if approved. There is no practical difference between a bill and a joint resolution. A joint resolution generally is used to deal with a limited matter such as a single appropriation.

Joint resolutions also are used to propose amendments to the Constitution in Congress. They do not require a presidential signature, but become a part of the Constitution when three-fourths of the states have ratified them.

Journal—The official record of the proceedings of the House and Senate. The *Journal* records the actions taken in each chamber, but, unlike the *Congressional Record*, it does not include the substantially verbatim report of speeches, debates, etc.

Law—An act of Congress that has been signed by the president or passed over his veto by Congress. Public bills, when signed, become public laws, and are cited by the letters PL and a hyphenated number. The two digits before the number correspond to the Congress, and the one or more digits after the hyphen refer to the numerical sequence in which the bills were signed by the president during that Congress. Private bills, when signed, become private laws. (See also Slip Laws, Statutes at Large, U.S. Code.)

Legislative Day—The "day" extending from the time either house meets after an adjournment until the time it next adjourns. Because the House normally adjourns from day to day, legislative days and calendar days usually coincide. But in the Senate, a legislative day may, and frequently does, extend over several calendar days. (See Recess.)

Legislative Veto—A procedure, no longer allowed, permitting either the House or Senate, or both chambers, to review proposed executive branch regulations or actions and to block or modify those with which they disagreed.

The specifics of the procedure varied, but Congress generally provided for a legislative veto by including in a bill a provision that administrative rules or action taken to implement the law were to go into effect at the end of a designated period of time unless blocked by either or both houses of Congress. Another version of the veto provided for congressional reconsideration and rejection of regulations already in effect.

The Supreme Court June 23, 1983, struck down the legislative veto as an unconstitutional violation of the law-making procedure provided in the Constitution.

Lobby—A group seeking to influence the passage or defeat of legislation. Originally the term referred to persons frequenting the lobbies or corridors of legislative chambers in order to speak to lawmakers.

The definition of a lobby and the activity of lobbying is a matter of differing interpretation. By some definitions, lobbying is limited to direct attempts to influence lawmakers through personal interviews and persuasion. Under other definitions, lobbying includes attempts at indirect, or "grass-roots," influence, such as persuading members of a group to write or visit their district's representative and state's senators or attempting to create a climate of opinion favorable to a desired legislative goal.

The right to attempt to influence legislation is based on the First Amendment to the Constitution, which says Congress shall make no law abridging the right of the people "to petition the government for a redress of grievances."

Majority Leader—The majority leader is elected by his party colleagues. In the Senate, in consultation with the minority leader and his colleagues, the majority leader directs the legislative schedule for the chamber. He also is his party's spokesman and chief strategist. In the House, the majority leader is second to the Speaker in the majority party's leadership and serves as his party's legislative strategist.

Majority Whip—In effect, the assistant majority leader, in either the House or Senate. His job is to help marshal majority forces in support of party strategy and legislation.

Manual—The official handbook in each house prescribing in detail its organization, procedures and operations.

Marking Up a Bill—Going through the contents of a piece of legislation in committee or subcommittee, considering its provisions in large and small portions, acting on amendments to provisions and proposed revisions to the language, inserting new sections and phraseology, etc. If the bill is extensively amended, the committee's version may be introduced as a separate bill, with a new number, before being considered by the full House or Senate. *(See Clean Bill.)*

Minority Leader—Floor leader for the minority party in each chamber. *(See also Majority Leader.)*

Minority Whip—Performs duties of whip for the minority party. *(See also Majority Whip.)*

Morning Hour—The time set aside at the beginning of each legislative day for the consideration of regular, routine business. The "hour" is of indefinite duration in the House, where it is rarely used.

In the Senate it is the first two hours of a session following an adjournment, as distinguished from a recess. The morning hour can be terminated earlier if the morning business has been completed.

Business includes such matters as messages from the president, communications from the heads of departments, messages from the House, the presentation of petitions, reports of standing and select committees and the introduction of bills and resolutions.

During the first hour of the morning hour in the Senate, no motion to proceed to the consideration of any bill on the calendar is in order except by unanimous consent. During the second hour, motions can be made but must be decided without debate. Senate committees may meet while the Senate conducts morning hour.

Motion—In the House or Senate chamber, a request by a member to institute any one of a wide array of parliamentary actions. He "moves" for a certain procedure, the consideration of a measure, etc. The precedence of motions, and whether they are debatable, is set forth in the House and Senate manuals. *(See some specific motions above and below.)*

Nominations—Presidential appointments to office subject to Senate confirmation. Although most nominations win quick Senate approval, some are controversial and become the topic of hearings and debate. Sometimes senators object to appointees for patronage reasons — for example, when a nomination to a local federal job is made without consulting the senators of the state concerned. In some situations a senator may object that the nominee is "personally obnoxious" to him. Usually other senators join in blocking such appointments out of courtesy to their colleagues. *(See Senatorial Courtesy.)*

One-Minute Speeches—Addresses by House members at the beginning of a legislative day. The speeches may cover any subject but are limited to one minute's duration.

Override a Veto—If the president disapproves a bill and sends it back to Congress with his objections, Congress may try to override his veto and enact the bill into law. Neither house is required to attempt to override a veto. The override of a veto requires a recorded vote with a two-thirds majority in each chamber. The question put to each house is: "Shall the bill pass, the objections of the president to the contrary notwithstanding?" *(See also Pocket Veto, Veto.)*

Oversight Committee—A congressional committee, or designated subcommittee of a committee, that is charged with general oversight of one or more federal agencies' programs and activities. Usually, the oversight panel for a particular agency also is the authorizing committee for that agency's programs and operations.

Pair—An voluntary arrangement between two lawmakers, usually on opposite sides of an issue. If passage of the measure requires a two-thirds majority vote, a pair would require two members favoring the action to one opposed to it. Pairs can take one of three forms — specific, general and live. The names of lawmakers pairing on a given vote and their stands, if known, are published in the *Congressional Record*.

The specific pair applies to one or more votes on the same subject. On special pairs, lawmakers usually specify how they would have voted.

A general pair in the Senate, now rarely used, applies to all votes on which the members pairing are on opposite sides. It usually does not specify the positions of the senators pairing. In a general pair in the House, no agreement is involved. A representative expecting to be absent may notify the House clerk he wishes to make a "general" pair. His name then is paired arbitrarily with that of another member desiring a pair, and the list is published in the *Congressional Record*. He may or may not be paired with a member taking the opposite position. General pairs in the House give no indication of how a member would have voted.

A live pair involves two members, one present for the vote, the other absent. The member present casts his vote and then withdraws it and votes "present." He then announces that he has a live pair with a colleague, identifying how each would have voted on the question. A live pair subtracts the vote of the member in attendance from the final vote tabulation.

Petition—A request or plea sent to one or both chambers from an organization or private citizens' group asking support of particular legislation or favorable consideration of a matter not yet receiving congressional attention. Petitions are referred to appropriate committees.

Pocket Veto—The act of the president in withholding his approval of a bill after Congress has adjourned. When Congress is in session, a bill becomes law without the president's signature if he does not act upon it within 10 days, excluding Sundays, from the time he gets it. But if Congress adjourns sine die within that 10-day period, the bill will die even if the president does not formally veto it.

The Supreme Court in 1986 agreed to decide whether the president can pocket veto a bill during recesses and between sessions of the same Congress or only between Congresses, as a lower court had ruled. (See also Veto.)

Point of Order—An objection raised by a member that the chamber is departing from rules governing its conduct of business. The objector cites the rule violated, the chair sustaining his objection if correctly made. Order is restored by the chair's suspending proceedings of the chamber until it conforms to the prescribed "order of business."

President of the Senate—Under the Constitution, the vice president of the United States presides over the Senate. In his absence, the president pro tempore, or a senator designated by the president pro tempore, presides over the chamber.

President Pro Tempore—The chief officer of the Senate in the absence of the vice president; literally, but loosely, the president for a time. The president pro tempore is elected by his fellow senators, and the recent practice has been to elect the senator of the majority party with the longest period of continuous service.

Previous Question—A motion for the previous question, when carried, has the effect of cutting off all debate, preventing the offering of further amendments, and forcing a vote on the pending matter. In the House, the previous question is not permitted in the Committee of the Whole. The motion for the previous question is a debate-limiting device and is not in order in the Senate.

Printed Amendment—A House rule guarantees five minutes of floor debate in support and five minutes in opposition, and no other debate time, on amendments printed in the *Congressional Record* at least one day prior to the amendment's consideration in the Committee of the Whole.

In the Senate, while amendments may be submitted for printing, they have no parliamentary standing or status. An amendment submitted for printing in the Senate, however, may be called up by any senator.

Private Calendar—In the House, private bills dealing with individual matters such as claims against the government, immigration, land titles, etc., are put on this calendar. The private calendar must be called on the first Tuesday of each month, and the Speaker may call it on the third Tuesday of each month as well.

When a private bill is before the chamber, two members may block its consideration, which recommits the bill to committee. Backers of a recommitted private bill have recourse. The measure can be put into an "omnibus claims bill" — several private bills rolled into one. As with any bill, no part of an omnibus claims bill may be deleted without a vote. When the private bill goes back to the House floor in this form, it can be deleted from the omnibus bill only by majority vote.

Privilege—Privilege relates to the rights of members of Congress and to the relative priority of the motions and actions they may make in their respective chambers. The two are distinct. "Privileged questions" deal with legislative business. "Questions of privilege" concern legislators themselves.

Privileged Questions—The order in which bills, motions and other legislative measures are considered by Congress is governed by strict priorities. A motion to table, for instance, is more privileged than a motion to recommit. Thus, a motion to recommit can be superseded by a motion to table, and a vote would be forced on the latter motion only. A motion to adjourn, however, takes precedence over a tabling motion and thus is considered of the "highest privilege." (See also Questions of Privilege.)

Pro Forma Amendment—(See Strike Out the Last Word.)

Public Laws—(See Law.)

Questions of Privilege—These are matters affecting members of Congress individually or collectively. Matters affecting the rights, safety, dignity and integrity of proceedings of the House or Senate as a whole are questions of privilege in both chambers.

Questions involving individual members are called questions of "personal privilege." A member rising to ask a question of personal privilege is given precedence over almost all other proceedings. An annotation in the House rules points out that the privilege rests primarily on the Constitution, which gives him a conditional immunity from arrest and an unconditional freedom to speak in the House. (See also Privileged Questions.)

Quorum—The number of members whose presence is necessary for the transaction of business. In the Senate and House, it is a majority of the membership. A quorum is 100 in the Committee of the Whole House. If a point of order is made that a quorum is not present, the only business that is in order is either a motion to adjourn or a motion to direct the sergeant-at-arms to request the attendance of absentees.

Readings of Bills—Traditional parliamentary procedure required bills to be read three times before they were passed. This custom is of little modern significance. Normally a bill is considered to have its first reading when it is introduced and printed, by title, in the *Congressional Record*. In the House, its second reading comes when floor consideration begins. (This is the most likely point at which there is an actual reading of the bill, if there is any.) The second reading in the Senate is supposed to occur on the legislative day after the measure is introduced, but before it is referred to committee. The third reading (again, usually by title) takes place when floor action has been completed on amendments.

Recess—Distinguished from adjournment *(see above)* in that a recess does not end a legislative day and therefore does not interrupt unfinished business. The rules in each house set forth certain matters to be taken up and disposed of at the beginning of each legislative day. The House usually adjourns from day to day. The Senate often recesses, thus meeting on the same legislative day for several calendar days or even weeks at a time.

Recognition—The power of recognition of a member is lodged in the Speaker of the House and the presiding officer of the Senate. The presiding officer names the member who will speak first when two or more members simultaneously request recognition.

Recommit to Committee—A motion, made on the floor after a bill has been debated, to return it to the committee that reported it. If approved, recommittal usually is considered a death blow to the bill. In the House, a motion to recommit can be made only by a member opposed to the bill, and, in recognizing a member to make the motion, the Speaker gives preference to members of the minority party over majority party members.

A motion to recommit may include instructions to the committee to report the bill again with specific amendments or by a certain date. Or, the instructions may direct that a particular study be made, with no definite deadline given for further action.

If the recommittal motion includes instructions to "report the bill back forthwith" and the motion is adopted, floor action on the bill continues; the committee does not actually reconsider the legislation.

Reconciliation—*(See Budget Reconciliation.)*

Reconsider a Vote—A motion to reconsider the vote by which an action was taken has, until it is disposed of, the effect of putting the action in abeyance. In the Senate, the motion can be made only by a member who voted on the prevailing side of the original question or by a member who did not vote at all. In the House, it can be made only by a member on the prevailing side.

A common practice in the Senate after close votes on an issue is a motion to reconsider, followed by a motion to table the motion to reconsider. On this motion to table, senators vote as they voted on the original question, which allows the motion to table to prevail, assuming there are no switches. The matter then is finally closed and further motions to reconsider are not entertained. In the House, as a routine precaution, a motion to reconsider usually is made every time a measure is passed. Such a motion almost always is tabled immediately, thus shutting off the possibility of future reconsideration, except by unanimous consent.

Motions to reconsider must be entered in the Senate within the next two days of actual session after the original vote has been taken. In the House they must be entered either on the same day or on the next succeeding day the House is in session.

Recorded Vote—A vote upon which each member's stand is individually made known. In the Senate, this is accomplished through a roll call of the entire membership, to which each senator on the floor must answer "yea," "nay" or, if he does not wish to vote, "present." Since January 1973, the House has used an electronic voting system for recorded votes, including yea-and-nay votes formerly taken by roll calls.

When not required by the Constitution, a recorded vote can be obtained on questions in the House on the demand of one-fifth (44 members) of a quorum or one-fourth (25) of a quorum in the Committee of the Whole. *(See Yeas and Nays.)*

Report—Both a verb and a noun as a congressional term. A committee that has been examining a bill referred to it by the parent chamber "reports" its findings and recommendations to the chamber when it completes consideration and returns the measure. The process is called "reporting" a bill.

A "report" is the document setting forth the committee's explanation of its action. Senate and House reports are numbered separately and are designated S Rept or H Rept. When a committee report is not unanimous, the dissenting committee members may file a statement of their views, called minority views and referred to as a minority report. Members in disagreement with some provisions of a bill may file additional or supplementary views. Sometimes a bill is reported without a committee recommendation.

Adverse reports occasionally are submitted by legislative committees. However, when a committee is opposed to a bill, it usually fails to report the bill at all. Some laws require that committee reports — favorable or adverse — be made.

Rescission Bill—A bill rescinding or canceling budget authority previously made available by Congress. The president may request a rescission to reduce spending or because the budget authority no longer is needed. Under the 1974 budget act, however, unless Congress approves a rescission bill within 45 days of continuous session after receipt of the proposal, the funds must be made available for obligation. *(See also Deferral.)*

Resolution—A "simple" resolution, designated H Res or S Res, deals with matters entirely within the prerogatives of one house or the other. It requires neither passage by the other chamber nor approval by the president, and it does not have the force of law. Most resolutions deal with the rules or procedures of one house. They also are used to express the sentiments of a single house such as condolences to the family of a deceased member or to comment on foreign policy or executive business. A simple resolution is the vehicle for a "rule" from the House Rules Committee. *(See also Concurrent and Joint Resolutions, Rules.)*

Rider—An amendment, usually not germane, that its sponsor hopes to get through more easily by including it in other legislation. Riders become law if the bills embodying them are enacted. Amendments providing legislative directives in appropriations bills are outstanding examples of riders, though technically legislation is banned from appropriations bills.

The House, unlike the Senate, has a strict germaneness rule; thus, riders usually are Senate devices to get legislation enacted quickly or to bypass lengthy House consideration and, possibly, opposition.

Rules—The term has two specific congressional meanings. A rule may be a standing order governing the conduct of House or Senate business and listed among the permanent rules of either chamber. The rules deal with duties of officers, the order of business, admission to the floor, parliamentary procedures on handling amendments and voting, jurisdictions of committees, etc.

In the House, a rule also may be a resolution reported by its Rules Committee to govern the handling of a particular bill on the floor. The committee may report a "rule," also called a "special order," in the form of a simple resolution. If the resolution is adopted by the House, the temporary rule becomes as valid as any standing rule and lapses only after action has been completed on the measure to which it pertains. A rule sets the time limit on general debate. It also may waive points of order against provisions of the bill in question such as non-germane language or against certain amendments intended to be proposed to the bill from the floor. It may even forbid all amendments or all amendments except those proposed by the legislative committee that handled the bill. In this instance, it is known as a "closed" or "gag" rule as opposed to an "open" rule, which puts no limitation on floor amendments, thus leaving the bill completely open to alteration by the adoption of germane amendments.

Secretary of the Senate—Chief administrative officer of the Senate, responsible for overseeing the duties of Senate employees, educating Senate pages, administering oaths, handling the registration of lobbyists, and handling other tasks necessary for the continuing operation of the Senate. *(See also Clerk of the House.)*

Select or Special Committee—A committee set up for a special purpose and, usually, for a limited time by resolution of either the House or Senate. Most special committees are investigative and lack legislative authority — legislation is not referred to them and they cannot report bills to their parent chamber. *(See also Standing Committees.)*

Senatorial Courtesy—Sometimes referred to as "the courtesy of the Senate," it is a general practice — with no written rule — applied to consideration of executive nominations. Generally, it means that nominations from a state are not to be confirmed unless they have been approved by the senators of the president's party of that state, with other senators following their colleagues' lead in the attitude they take toward consideration of such nominations. *(See Nominations.)*

Sequester Order—The Gramm-Rudman-Hollings law of 1985 established an automatic budget-cutting procedure that the Supreme Court declared unconstitutional a year later. Under that procedure, the Congressional Budget Office (CBO) and the Office of Management and Budget (OMB) must separately calculate deficits for an upcoming fiscal year and the across-the-board cuts that would be needed to meet the deficit fixed by the statute. The General Accounting Office (GAO) would review, and could revise, the CBO-OMB numbers. GAO would then submit the final figures to the president, who must issue a "sequester order" making the cuts. Although the Supreme Court invalidated the automatic feature, another section of the law provided that the cuts would take effect if the president and Congress approved them. *(See Budget Process.)*

Sine Die—*(See Adjournment Sine Die.)*

Slip Laws—The first official publication of a bill that has been enacted and signed into law. Each is published separately in unbound single-sheet or pamphlet form. *(See also Law, Statutes at Large, U.S. Code.)*

Speaker—The presiding officer of the House of Representatives, selected by the caucus of the party to which he belongs and formally elected by the whole House.

Special Session—A session of Congress after it has adjourned sine die, completing its regular session. Special sessions are convened by the president.

Spending Authority—The 1974 budget act defines spending authority as borrowing authority, contract authority and entitlement authority *(see above)*, for which budget authority is not provided by appropriation acts.

Sponsor—*(See Bills Introduced.)*

Standing Committees—Committees permanently established by House and Senate rules. The standing committees of the House were last reorganized by the committee reorganization of 1974. The last major realignment of Senate committees was in the committee system reorganization of 1977. The standing committees are legislative committees — legislation may be referred to them and they may report bills and resolutions to their parent chambers. *(See also Select or Special Committees.)*

Standing Vote—A non-recorded vote used in both the House and Senate. (A standing vote also is called a division vote.) Members in favor of a proposal stand and are counted by the presiding officer. Then members opposed stand and are counted. There is no record of how individual members voted.

Statutes at Large—A chronological arrangement of the laws enacted in each session of Congress. Though indexed, the laws are not arranged by subject matter, and there is not an indication of how they changed previously enacted laws. *(See also Law, Slip Laws, U.S. Code.)*

Strike From the Record—Remarks made on the House floor may offend some member, who moves that the offending words be "taken down" for the Speaker's cognizance, and then expunged from the debate as published in the *Congressional Record.*

Strike Out the Last Word—A motion whereby a House member is entitled to speak for five minutes on an amendment then being debated by the chamber. A member gains recognition from the chair by moving to "strike out the last word" of the amendment or section of the bill under consideration. The motion is pro forma, requires no vote and does not change the amendment being debated.

How a Bill Becomes Law

Note: Parliamentary terms used below are defined in the Glossary.

Introduction of Bills

A House member (including the resident commissioner of Puerto Rico and non-voting delegates of the District of Columbia, Guam, the Virgin Islands, and American Samoa) may introduce any one of several types of bills and resolutions by handing it to the clerk of the House or placing it in a box called the hopper. A senator first gains recognition of the presiding officer to announce the introduction of a bill. If objection is offered by any senator the introduction of the bill is postponed until the following day.

As the next step in either the House or Senate, the bill is numbered, referred to the appropriate committee, labeled with the sponsor's name, and sent to the Government Printing Office so that copies can be made for subsequent study and action. Senate bills may be jointly sponsored and carry several senators' names. Until 1978, the House limited the number of members who could co-sponsor any one bill; the ceiling was eliminated at the beginning of the 96th Congress. A bill written in the Executive Branch and proposed as an administration measure usually is introduced by the chairman of the congressional committee which has jurisdiction.

Bills—Prefixed with "HR" in the House, "S" in the Senate, followed by a number. Used as the form for most legislation, whether general or special, public or private.

Joint Resolutions—Designated H J Res or S J Res. Subject to the same procedure as bills, with the exception of a joint resolution proposing an amendment to the Constitution. The latter must be approved by two-thirds of both houses and is thereupon sent directly to the administrator of general services for submission to the states for ratification rather than being presented to the president for his approval.

Concurrent Resolutions—Designated H Con Res or S Con Res. Used for matters affecting the operations of both houses. These resolutions do not become law.

Resolutions—Designated H Res or S Res. Used for a matter concerning the operation of either house alone and adopted only by the chamber in which it originates.

Committee Action

A bill is referred to the appropriate committee by a House parliamentarian on the Speaker's order, or by the Senate president. Sponsors may indicate their preferences for referral, although custom and chamber rule generally govern. An exception is the referral of private bills, which are sent to whatever group is designated by their sponsors. Bills are technically considered "read for the first time" when referred to House committees.

When a bill reaches a committee it is placed upon the group's calendar. At that time it comes under the sharpest congressional focus. Its chances for passage are quickly determined — and the great majority of bills fall by the legislative roadside. Failure of a committee to act on a bill is equivalent to killing it; the measure can be withdrawn from the group's purview only by a discharge petition signed by a majority of the House membership on House bills, or by adoption of a special resolution in the Senate. Discharge attempts rarely succeed.

The first committee action taken on a bill usually is a request for comment on it by interested agencies of the government. The committee chairman may assign the bill to a subcommittee for study and hearings, or it may be considered by the full committee. Hearings may be public, closed (executive session), or both. A subcommittee, after considering a bill, reports to the full committee its recommendations for action and any proposed amendments.

The full committee then votes on its recommendation to the House or Senate. This procedure is called "ordering a bill reported." Occasionally a committee may order a bill reported unfavorably; most of the time a report, submitted by the chairman of the committee to the House or Senate, calls for favorable action on the measure since the committee can effectively "kill" a bill by simply failing to take any action.

When a committee sends a bill to the chamber floor, it explains its reasons in a written statement, called a report, which accompanies the bill. Often committee members opposing a measure issue dissenting minority statements which are included in the report.

Usually, the committee "marks up" or proposes amendments to the bill. If they are substantial and the measure is complicated, the committee may order a "clean bill" introduced, which will embody the proposed amendments. The original bill then is put aside and the "clean bill," with a new number, is reported to the floor.

The chamber must approve, alter, or reject the committee amendments before the bill itself can be put to a vote.

Floor Action

After a bill is reported back to the house where it originated, it is placed on the calendar.

There are five legislative calendars in the House, issued in one cumulative calendar titled *Calendars of the United States House of Representatives and History of Legislation.* The House calendars are:

The Union Calendar to which are referred bills raising revenues, general appropriation bills and any measures directly or indirectly appropriating money or property. It is the Calendar of the Committee of the Whole House on the State of the Union.

The House Calendar to which are referred bills of a public character not raising revenue or appropriating money or property.

The Consent Calendar to which are referred bills of a non-controversial nature that are passed without debate when the Consent Calendar is called on the first and third Mondays of each month.

The Private Calendar to which are referred bills for relief in the nature of claims against the United States or private immigration bills that are passed without debate when the Private Calendar is called the first and third Tuesdays of each month.

The Discharge Calendar to which are referred motions to discharge committees when the necessary signatures are signed to a discharge petition.

There is only one legislative calendar in the Senate and one "executive calendar" for treaties and nominations

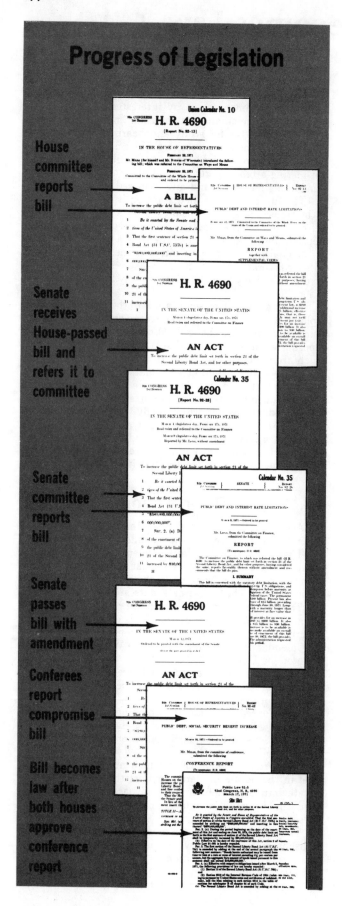

Progress of Legislation

House committee reports bill

Senate receives House-passed bill and refers it to committee

Senate committee reports bill

Senate passes bill with amendment

Conferees report compromise bill

Bill becomes law after both houses approve conference report

submitted to the Senate When the Senate Calendar is called, each senator is limited to five minutes debate on each bill.

DEBATE. A bill is brought to debate by varying procedures. If a routine measure, it may await the call of the calendar. If it is urgent or important, it can be taken up in the Senate either by unanimous consent or by a majority vote. The policy committee of the majority party in the Senate schedules the bills that it wants taken up for debate.

In the House, precedence is granted if a special rule is obtained from the Rules Committee. A request for a special rule is usually made by the chairman of the committee that favorably reported the bill, supported by the bill's sponsor and other committee members. The request, considered by the Rules Committee in the same fashion that other committees consider legislative measures, is in the form of a resolution providing for immediate consideration of the bill. The Rules Committee reports the resolution to the House where it is debated and voted upon in the same fashion as regular bills. If the Rules Committee should fail to report a rule requested by a committee, there are several ways to bring the bill to the House floor — under suspension of the rules, on Calendar Wednesday or by a discharge motion.

The resolutions providing special rules are important because they specify how long the bill may be debated and whether it may be amended from the floor. If floor amendments are banned, the bill is considered under a "closed rule," which permits only members of the committee that first reported the measure to the House to alter its language, subject to chamber acceptance.

When a bill is debated under an "open rule," amendments may be offered from the floor. Committee amendments are always taken up first, but may be changed, as may all amendments up to the second degree, i.e., an amendment to an amendment to an amendment is not in order.

Duration of debate in the House depends on whether the bill is under discussion by the House proper or before the House when it is sitting as the Committee of the Whole House on the State of the Union. In the former, the amount of time for debate is determined either by special rule or is allocated with an hour for each member if the measure is under consideration without a rule. In the Committee of the Whole the amount of time agreed on for general debate is equally divided between proponents and opponents. At the end of general discussion, the bill is read section by section for amendment. Debate on an amendment is limited to five minutes for each side.

Senate debate is usually unlimited. It can be halted only by unanimous consent by "cloture," which requires a three-fifths majority of the entire Senate except for proposed changes in the Senate rules. The latter requires a two-thirds vote.

The House sits as the Committee of the Whole when it considers any tax measure or bill dealing with public appropriations. It can also resolve itself into the Committee of the Whole if a member moves to do so and the motion is carried. The Speaker appoints a member to serve as the chairman. The rules of the House permit the Committee of the Whole to meet with any 100 members on the floor, and to amend and act on bills with a quorum of the 100, within the time limitations mentioned previously. When the Committee of the Whole has acted, it "rises," the Speaker returns as the presiding officer of the House and the member appointed chairman of the Committee of the Whole reports the action of the committee and its recommendations (amendments adopted).

VOTES. Voting on bills may occur repeatedly before they are finally approved or rejected. The House votes on the rule for the bill and on various amendments to the bill. Voting on amendments often is a more illuminating test of a bill's support than is the final tally. Sometimes members approve final passage of bills after vigorously supporting amendments which, if adopted, would have scuttled the legislation.

The Senate has three different methods of voting: an untabulated voice vote, a standing vote (called a division) and a recorded roll call to which members answer "yea" or "nay" when their names are called. The House also employs voice and standing votes, but since January 1973 yeas and nays have been recorded by an electronic voting device, eliminating the need for time-consuming roll calls.

Another method of voting, used in the House only, is the teller vote. Traditionally, members filed up the center aisle past counters; only vote totals were announced. Since 1971, one-fifth of a quorum can demand that the votes of individual members be recorded, thereby forcing them to take a public position on amendments to key bills. Electronic voting now is commonly used for this purpose.

After amendments to a bill have been voted upon, a vote may be taken on a motion to recommit the bill to committee. If carried, this vote removes the bill from the chamber's calendar. If the motion is unsuccessful, the bill then is "read for the third time." An actual reading usually is dispensed with. Until 1965, an opponent of a bill could delay this move by objecting and asking for a full reading of an engrossed (certified in final form) copy of the bill. After the "third reading," the vote on final passage is taken.

The final vote may be followed by a motion to reconsider, and this motion itself may be followed by a move to lay the motion on the table. Usually, those voting for the bill's passage vote for the tabling motion, thus safeguarding the final passage action. With that, the bill has been formally passed by the chamber. While a motion to reconsider a Senate vote is pending on a bill, the measure cannot be sent to the House.

Action in Second House

After a bill is passed it is sent to the other chamber. This body may then take one of several steps. It may pass the bill as is — accepting the other chamber's language. It may send the bill to committee for scrutiny or alteration, or reject the entire bill, advising the other house of its actions. Or it may simply ignore the bill submitted while it continues work on its own version of the proposed legislation. Frequently, one chamber may approve a version of a bill that is greatly at variance with the version already passed by the other house, and then substitute its amendments for the language of the other, retaining only the latter's bill designation.

A provision of the Legislative Reorganization Act of 1970 permits a separate House vote on any non-germane amendment added by the Senate to a House-passed bill and requires a majority vote to retain the amendment. Previously the House was forced to act on the bill as a whole; the only way to defeat the non-germane amendment was to reject the entire bill.

Often the second chamber makes only minor changes.

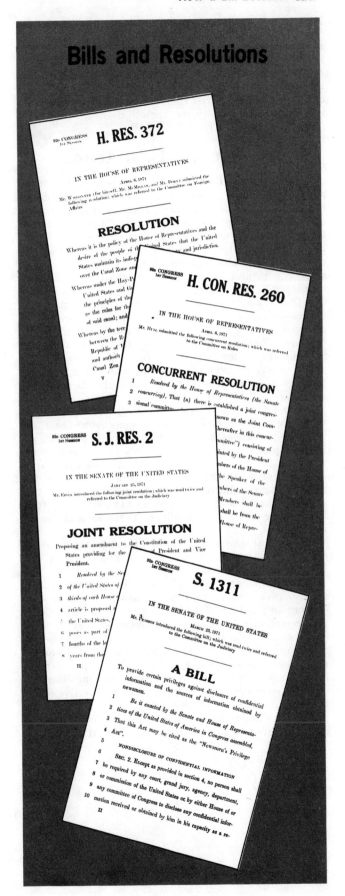

Bills and Resolutions

If these are readily agreed to by the other house, the bill then is routed to the White House for signing. However, if the opposite chamber basically alters the bill submitted to it, the measure usually is "sent to conference." The chamber that has possession of the "papers" (engrossed bill, engrossed amendments, messages of transmittal) requests a conference and the other chamber must agree to it. If the second house does not agree, the bill dies.

Conference, Final Action

CONFERENCE. A conference undertakes to harmonize conflicting House and Senate versions of a legislative bill. The conference is usually staffed by senior members (conferees), appointed by the presiding officers of the two houses, from the committees that managed the bills. Under this arrangement the conferees of one house have the duty of trying to maintain their chamber's position in the face of amending actions by the conferees (also referred to as "managers") of the other house.

The number of conferees from each chamber may vary, the range usually being from three to nine members in each group, depending upon the length or complexity of the bill involved. There may be five representatives and three senators on the conference committee, or the reverse. But a majority vote controls the action of each group so that a larger representation does not give one chamber a voting advantage over the other chamber's conferees.

Theoretically, conferees are not allowed to write new legislation in reconciling the two versions before them, but this curb sometimes is bypassed. Many bills have been put into acceptable compromise form only after new language was provided by the conferees. The 1970 Reorganization Act attempted to tighten restrictions on conferees by forbidding them to introduce any language on a topic that neither chamber sent to conference or to modify any topic beyond the scope of the different House and Senate versions.

Frequently the ironing out of difficulties takes days or even weeks. Conferences on involved appropriation bills sometimes are particularly drawn out.

As a conference proceeds, conferees reconcile differences between the versions, but generally they grant concessions only insofar as they remain sure that the chamber they represent will accept the compromises. Occasionally, uncertainty over how either house will react, or the positive refusal of a chamber to back down on a disputed amendment, results in an impasse, and the bills die in conference even though each was approved by its sponsoring chamber.

Conferees sometimes go back to their respective chambers for further instructions, when they report certain portions in disagreement. Then the chamber concerned can either "recede and concur" in the amendment of the other house, or "insist on its amendment."

When the conferees have reached agreement, they prepare a conference report embodying their recommendations (compromises). The reports, in document form, must be submitted to each house.

The conference report must be approved by each house. Consequently, approval of the report is approval of the compromise bill. In the order of voting on conference reports, the chamber which asked for a conference yields to the other chamber the opportunity to vote first.

FINAL STEPS. After a bill has been passed by both the House and Senate in identical form, all of the original papers are sent to the enrolling clerk of the chamber in which the bill originated. He then prepares an enrolled bill which is printed on parchment paper. When this bill has been certified as correct by the secretary of the Senate or the clerk of the House, depending on which chamber originated the bill, it is signed first (no matter whether it originated in the Senate or House) by the Speaker of the House and then by the president of the Senate. It is next sent to the White House to await action.

If the president approves the bill he signs it, dates it and usually writes the word "approved" on the document. If he does not sign it within 10 days (Sundays excepted) and Congress is in session, the bill becomes law without his signature.

However, should Congress adjourn before the 10 days expire, and the president has failed to sign the measure, it does not become law. This procedure is called the pocket veto.

A president vetoes a bill by refusing to sign it and before the 10-day period expires, returning it to Congress with a message stating his reasons. The message is sent to the chamber which originated the bill. If no action is taken there on the message, the bill dies. Congress, however, can attempt to override the president's veto and enact the bill, "the objections of the president to the contrary notwithstanding." Overriding of a veto requires a two-thirds vote of those present, who must number a quorum and vote by roll call.

Debate can precede this vote, with motions permitted to lay the message on the table, postpone action on it, or refer it to committee. If the president's veto is overridden by a two-thirds vote in both houses, the bill becomes law. Otherwise it is dead.

When bills are passed finally and signed, or passed over a veto, they are given law numbers in numerical order as they become law. There are two series of numbers, one for public and one for private laws, starting at the number "1" for each two-year term of Congress. They are then identified by law number and by Congress — i.e., Private Law 21, 97th Congress; Public Law 250, 97th Congress (or PL 97-250).

How a Bill Becomes Law

This graphic shows the most typical way in which proposed legislation is enacted into law. There are more complicated, as well as simpler, routes, and most bills never become law. The process is illustrated with two hypothetical bills, House bill No. 1 (HR 1) and Senate bill No. 2 (S 2). Bills must be passed by both houses in identical form before they can be sent to the president. The path of HR 1 is traced by a solid line, that of S 2 by a broken line. In practice most bills begins as similar proposals in both houses.

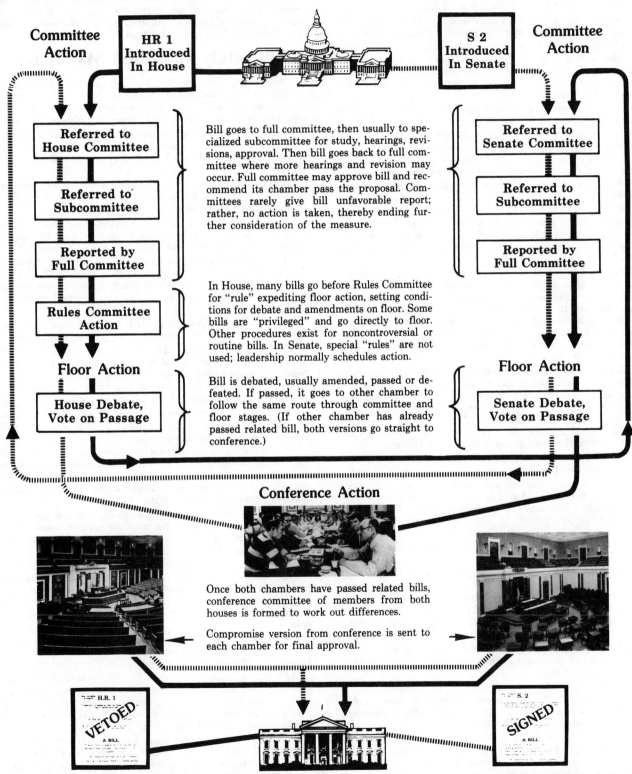

Committee Action

HR 1 Introduced In House

S 2 Introduced In Senate

Committee Action

Referred to House Committee

Referred to Subcommittee

Reported by Full Committee

Rules Committee Action

Floor Action

House Debate, Vote on Passage

Bill goes to full committee, then usually to specialized subcommittee for study, hearings, revisions, approval. Then bill goes back to full committee where more hearings and revision may occur. Full committee may approve bill and recommend its chamber pass the proposal. Committees rarely give bill unfavorable report; rather, no action is taken, thereby ending further consideration of the measure.

In House, many bills go before Rules Committee for "rule" expediting floor action, setting conditions for debate and amendments on floor. Some bills are "privileged" and go directly to floor. Other procedures exist for noncontroversial or routine bills. In Senate, special "rules" are not used; leadership normally schedules action.

Bill is debated, usually amended, passed or defeated. If passed, it goes to other chamber to follow the same route through committee and floor stages. (If other chamber has already passed related bill, both versions go straight to conference.)

Referred to Senate Committee

Referred to Subcommittee

Reported by Full Committee

Floor Action

Senate Debate, Vote on Passage

Conference Action

Once both chambers have passed related bills, conference committee of members from both houses is formed to work out differences.

Compromise version from conference is sent to each chamber for final approval.

H.R. 1 **VETOED** A BILL

S. 2 **SIGNED** A BILL

Compromise bill approved by both houses is sent to the president, who can sign it into law or veto it and return it to Congress. Congress may override veto by a two-thirds majority vote in both houses; bill then becomes law without president's signature.

REFERENCE GUIDE TO CONGRESS AND LEGISLATION

Current Government Documents

Bills and Resolutions—All legislation is printed daily after it is introduced. (Available from members of Congress)

Biographical Directory of the American Congress 1774-1971 — Data on all members who have served in Congress. (GPO)

Calendars of the House of Representatives—Published daily, the calendar lists all bills — Senate and House — which have been reported: gives report numbers, dates of passage in each chamber, dates of enactments, etc. Cumulative. Indexed on Mondays only. (Clerk of the House)

Cannon's Procedure in the House of Representatives—This volume condenses the eleven volumes of Hinds' and Cannon's Precedents of the House of Representatives. (GPO)

Committee Prints—These documents are usually committee staff studies and research papers issued by committees; they range from compilation of laws on particular subjects to studies of foreign policy problems. (Generally available from the issuing committee)

Committee Reports—A report accompanies each piece of legislation when it goes to the floor. It generally analyzes the bill, describes its purposes, and states the views of the members of the committee as to the desirability of enactment. (Available from committees)

Congressional Directory—Published each year, it contains brief biographical sketches of each member, lists committee memberships, committee assignments by member, maps of all congressional districts. It also lists major executives of all government agencies, members of the diplomatic corps, and members of the press accredited to the press galleries. A pocket edition of the Directory contains pictures of each member of Congress. (Available from GPO).

Congressional Record (Bound)—Since 1789, the proceedings of Congress have appeared under four different titles: *Annals of Congress*, 1789-1824; *The Register of Debates*, 1824-1837; *Congressional Globe*, 1833-1873; *The Congressional Record* has been published since 1873. The bound sets consist of 15 to 20 parts per year, including separate index and (since 1947) *Daily Digest* volumes. (Available from government Printing Office)

Constitution, Jefferson's Manual and Rules of the House of Representatives—The House's rules and regulations. (GPO)

Digest of Public General Bills and Resolutions—A compilation giving a brief description of each public bill introduced during the session. It is cumulative, in approximately five issues per year. Indexed by subject. (GPO)

Hearings—Copies of all testimony taken by committees in open session are printed by the GPO and made available by the issuing committee.

Hinds' and Cannon's Precedents of the House of Representatives Including References to Provisions of the Constitution, the Laws and Decisions of the United States Senate—Eleven-volume set contains the constitutional provisions, established rules and procedures, with explanation and documentation, governing the House of Representatives. (GPO)

Public and Private Laws—Copies of all laws enacted are printed with citations to the statutes that are amended or deleted by the legislation. (GPO)

Report of the Clerk of the House of Representatives—Semiannual report includes salaries of representatives, staffs, committee staffs, officers and employees of the House; statement of expenditures and allowances. (GPO)

Report of the Secretary of the Senate—Contains salaries of senators, staffs, committee staff members, officers and employees of the Senate; statements of expenditures and gross salaries of senators; issued semiannually. (GPO)

Senate Manual—The Manual contains "standing rules, orders, laws and regulations . . ." of the Senate. (GPO)

United States Code—The 50 titles of the code include all the general and permanent laws of the U.S. The Code is published every six years, with annual supplements until the next publication. (Available from GPO, 14 volumes and supplements)

Privately Published Materials

Almanac of American Politics—Contains biographies, group ratings, committee assignments, voting records and lobby interests of members, and political, demographic and economic makeup of congressmen's state or district. (Published by National Journal)

CIS Index—A monthly, quarterly, and annual index to hearings, reports, documents and other congressional papers by subject, committee and witness. (Published by Congressional Information Service)

CIS Microfiche Library—Complete texts of congressional hearings, reports and documents in microform; issued monthly. (Published by Congressional Information Service)

Commerce Clearing House Congressional Index—This weekly, loose-leaf index is a guide to all legislation by subject, author and bill number. (Published by C.C.H., Chicago, Ill.)

Congress and the Nation, Vol. I (1945-46), *Vol. II* (1965-68), *Vol. III* (1969-72), *Vol. IV* (1973-76) *Vol. V* (1977-80), *Vol. VI* (1981-84), Congressional Quarterly. The 6,600-page-six-volume set documents legislative actions and national political campaigns 1945-84.

Congressional Digest—Monthly coverage of major legislative issues in pro-con format. (Published by Congressional Digest)

Congressional Monitor—Daily report on congressional committee and floor actions, including advance schedule of committee hearings, weekly listing of status of major legislation and documents. (Published by Congressional Quarterly)

Congressional Quarterly Almanac—Published each year since 1945, the Almanac presents a thorough review of legislative and political activity for each session of Congress. (Available separately and with regular CQ service)

Congressional Quarterly Weekly Report—A weekly report of major congressional actions on the House and Senate floors and in committees. The Report contains roll-call votes and weekly political coverage. Carries rosters, updated committee and subcommittee assignments, presidential texts, etc.

Congressional Quarterly's Guide to Congress—A 1,000-page volume documenting the origins, development and operations of the U.S. Congress. Explains how Congress works, its powers and the pressures upon it.

Congressional Staff Directory—Published annually, the Directory contains biographical sketches of many members of congressmen's staffs; lists employees of members and committees; lists all cities of 1,500 or more population by congressional districts. (Available from Congressional Staff Directory, Alexandria, Va.)

National Journal—Weekly report of congressional and executive actions and programs, and reports on issues. (Published by Government Research Corporation)

Politics in America—Profiles of all members of Congress, including biographical data, committee assignments, campaign finances, election returns, key votes and interest group ratings. Also provides maps and detailed descriptions of each state and congressional district. (Published by CQ Press)

United States Code Congressional and Administrative News—This monthly service of the West Publishing Co., St. Paul, gives the full text of all public laws, and, in many cases, includes committee reports on the legislation.

CONSTITUTION OF THE UNITED STATES

We the People of the United States, in Order to form a more perfect Union, establish Justice, insure domestic Tranquility, provide for the common defence, promote the general Welfare, and secure the Blessings of Liberty to ourselves and our Posterity, do ordain and establish this Constitution for the United States of America.

ARTICLE I

Section 1. All legislative Powers herein granted shall be vested in a Congress of the United States, which shall consist of a Senate and House of Representatives.

Section 2. The House of Representatives shall be composed of Members chosen every second Year by the People of the several States, and the Electors in each State shall have the Qualifications requisite for Electors of the most numerous Branch of the State Legislature.

No Person shall be a Representative who shall not have attained to the age of twenty five Years, and been seven Years a Citizen of the United States, and who shall not, when elected, be an Inhabitant of that State in which he shall be chosen.

[Representatives and direct Taxes shall be apportioned among the several States which may be included within this Union, according to their respective Numbers, which shall be determined by adding to the whole Number of free Persons, including those bound to Service for a Term of Years, and excluding Indians not taxed, three fifths of all other Persons.][1] The actual Enumeration shall be made within three Years after the first Meeting of the Congress of the United States, and within every subsequent Term of ten Years, in such Manner as they shall by Law direct. The Number of Representatives shall not exceed one for every thirty Thousand, but each State shall have at Least one Representative; and until such enumeration shall be made, the State of New Hampshire shall be entitled to chuse three, Massachusetts eight, Rhode-Island and Providence Plantations one, Connecticut five, New-York six, New Jersey four, Pennsylvania eight, Delaware one, Maryland six, Virginia ten, North Carolina five, South Carolina five, and Georgia three.

When vacancies happen in the Representation from any State, the Executive Authority thereof shall issue Writs of Election to fill such Vacancies.

The House of Representatives shall chuse their Speaker and other Officers; and shall have the sole Power of Impeachment.

Section 3. The Senate of the United States shall be composed of two Senators from each State, [chosen by the Legislature thereof,][2] for six Years; and each Senator shall have one Vote.

Immediately after they shall be assembled in Consequence of the first Election, they shall be divided as equally as may be into three Classes. The Seats of the Senators of the first Class shall be vacated at the Expiration of the second Year, of the second Class at the Expiration of the fourth Year, and of the third Class at the Expiration of the sixth Year, so that one third may be chosen every second Year; [and if Vacancies happen by Resignation, or otherwise, during the Recess of the Legislature of any State, the Executive thereof may make temporary Appointments until the next Meeting of the Legislature, which shall then fill such Vacancies.][3]

No Person shall be a Senator who shall not have attained to the Age of thirty Years, and been nine Years a Citizen of the United States, and who shall not, when elected, be an Inhabitant of that State for which he shall be chosen.

The Vice President of the United States shall be President of the Senate, but shall have no Vote, unless they be equally divided.

The Senate shall chuse their other Officers, and also a President pro tempore, in the Absence of the Vice President, or when he shall exercise the Office of President of the United States.

The Senate shall have the sole Power to try all Impeachments. When sitting for that Purpose, they shall be on Oath or Affirmation. When the President of the United States is tried the Chief Justice shall preside: And no Person shall be convicted without the Concurrence of two thirds of the Members present.

Judgment in Cases of Impeachment shall not extend further than to removal from Office, and disqualification to hold and enjoy any Office of honor, Trust or Profit under the United States: but the Party convicted shall nevertheless be liable and subject to Indictment, Trial, Judgment and Punishment, according to Law.

Section 4. The Times, Places and Manner of holding Elections for Senators and Representatives, shall be prescribed in each State by the Legislature thereof; but the Congress may at any time by Law make or alter such Regulations, except as to the Places of chusing Senators.

The Congress shall assemble at least once in every Year, and such Meeting shall [be on the first Monday in December],[4] unless they shall by Law appoint a different Day.

Section 5. Each House shall be the Judge of the Elections, Returns and Qualifications of its own Members, and a Majority of each shall constitute a Quorum to do Business; but a smaller Number may adjourn from day to day, and may be authorized to compel the Attendance of absent Members, in such Manner, and under such Penalties as each House may provide.

Each House may determine the Rules of its Proceedings, punish its Members for disorderly Behaviour, and, with the Concurrence of two thirds, expel a Member.

Each House shall keep a Journal of its Proceedings, and from time to time publish the same, excepting such Parts as may in their Judgment require Secrecy; and the Yeas and Nays of the Members of either House on any question shall, at the Desire of one fifth of those Present, be entered on the Journal.

Neither House, during the Session of Congress, shall, without the Consent of the other, adjourn for more than three days, nor to any other Place than that in which the two Houses shall be sitting.

Section 6. The Senators and Representatives shall receive a Compensation for their Services, to be ascertained by Law, and paid out of the Treasury of the United States. They shall in all Cases, except Treason, Felony and Breach of the Peace, be privileged from Arrest during their Attendance at the Session of their respective Houses, and in going to and returning from the same; and for any Speech or Debate in either House, they shall not be questioned in any other Place.

No Senator or Representative shall, during the Time for which he was elected, be appointed to any civil Office under the Authority of the United States, which shall have been created, or the Emoluments whereof shall have been encreased during such time; and no Person holding any Office under the United States, shall be a Member of either House during his Continuance in Office.

Section 7. All Bills for raising Revenue shall originate in the House of Representatives; but the Senate may propose or concur with amendments as on other Bills.

Every Bill which shall have passed the House of Representatives and the Senate, shall, before it become a Law, be presented to the President of the United States; If he approve he shall sign it, but if not he shall return it, with his Objections to that House in which it shall have originated, who shall enter the Objections at large on their Journal, and proceed to reconsider it. If after such Reconsideration two thirds of that House shall agree to pass the Bill, it shall be sent, together with the Objections, to the other House, by which it shall likewise be reconsidered, and if approved by two thirds of that House, it shall become a Law. But in all such Cases the Votes of both Houses shall be determined by yeas and Nays, and the Names of the Persons voting for and against the Bill shall be entered on the Journal of each House respectively. If any Bill shall not be returned by the President within ten Days (Sunday excepted) after it shall have been presented to him, the Same shall be a Law, in like Manner as if he had signed it, unless the Congress by their Adjournment prevent its Return, in which Case it shall not be a Law.

Every Order, Resolution, or Vote to which the Concurrence of the Senate and House of Representatives may be necessary (except on a question of Adjournment) shall be presented to the President of the United States; and before the Same shall take Effect, shall be approved by him, or being disapproved by him, shall be repassed by two thirds of the Senate and House of Representatives, according to the Rules and Limitations prescribed in the Case of a Bill.

Section 8. The Congress shall have Power To lay and collect Taxes, Duties, Imposts and Excises, to pay the Debts and provide for the common Defence and general Welfare of the United States; but all Duties, Imposts and Excises shall be uniform throughout the United States;

To borrow Money on the credit of the United States;

To regulate Commerce with foreign Nations, and among the several States, and with the Indian Tribes;

To establish an uniform Rule of Naturalization, and uniform Laws on the subject of Bankruptcies throughout the United States;

To coin Money, regulate the Value thereof, and of foreign Coin, and fix the Standard of Weights and Measures;

To provide for the Punishment of counterfeiting the Securities and current Coin of the United States;

To establish Post Offices and post Roads;

To promote the Progress of Science and useful Arts, by securing for limited Times to Authors and Inventors the exclusive Right to their respective Writings and Discoveries;

To constitute Tribunals inferior to the supreme Court;

To define and punish Piracies and Felonies committed on the high Seas, and Offences against the Law of Nations;

To declare War, grant Letters of Marque and Reprisal, and make Rules concerning Captures on Land and Water;

To raise and support Armies, but no Appropriation of Money to that Use shall be for a longer Term than two Years;

To provide and maintain a Navy;

To make Rules for the Government and Regulation of the land and naval Forces;

To provide for calling forth the Militia to execute the Laws of the Union, suppress Insurrections and repel Invasions;

To provide for organizing, arming, and disciplining, the Militia, and for governing such Part of them as may be employed in the Service of the United States, reserving to the States respectively, the Appointment of the Officers, and the Authority of training the Militia according to the discipline prescribed by Congress;

To exercise exclusive Legislation in all Cases whatsoever, over such District (not exceeding ten Miles square) as may, by Cession of Particular States, and the Acceptance of Congress, become the Seat of the Government of the United States, and to exercise like Authority over all Places purchased by the Consent of the Legislature of the State in which the Same shall be, for the Erection of Forts, Magazines, Arsenals, dock-Yards, and other needful Buildings; — And

To make all Laws which shall be necessary and proper for carrying into Execution the foregoing Powers, and all other Powers vested by this Constitution in the Government of the United States, or in any Department or Officer thereof.

Section 9. The Migration or Importation of such Persons as any of the States now existing shall think proper to admit, shall not be prohibited by the Congress prior to the Year one thousand eight hundred and eight, but a Tax or duty may be imposed on such Importation, not exceeding ten dollars for each Person.

The Privilege of the Writ of Habeas Corpus shall not be suspended, unless when in Cases of Rebellion or Invasion the public Safety may require it.

No Bill of Attainder or ex post facto Law shall be passed.

No capitation, or other direct, Tax shall be laid, unless in Proportion to the Census of Enumeration herein before directed to be taken.[5]

No Tax or Duty shall be laid on Articles exported from any State.

No Preference shall be given by any Regulation of Commerce or Revenue to the Ports of one State over those of another; nor shall Vessels bound to, or from, one State, be obliged to enter, clear or pay Duties in another.

No Money shall be drawn from the Treasury, but in Consequence of Appropriations made by Law; and a regular Statement and Account of the Receipts and Expenditures of all public Money shall be published from time to time.

No Title of Nobility shall be granted by the United States: And no Person holding any Office of Profit or Trust under them, shall, without the Consent of the Congress, accept of any present, Emolument, Office, or Title, of any kind whatever, from any King, Prince or foreign State.

Section 10. No State shall enter into any Treaty, Alliance, or Confederation; grant Letters of Marque and Reprisal; coin Money; emit Bills of Credit; make any Thing but gold and silver Coin a Tender in Payment of Debts; pass any Bill of Attainder, ex post facto Law, or Law impairing the Obligation of Contracts, or grant any Title of Nobility.

No State shall, without the Consent of the Congress, lay any Imposts or Duties on Imports or Exports, except what may be absolutely necessary for executing it's inspection Laws: and the net Produce of all Duties and Imposts, laid by any State on Imports or Exports, shall be for the Use of the Treasury of the United States; and all such Laws shall be subject to the Revision and Controul of the Congress.

No State shall, without the Consent of Congress, lay any Duty of Tonnage, keep Troops, or Ships of War in time of Peace, enter into any Agreement or Compact with another State, or with a foreign Power, or engage in War, unless actually invaded, or in such imminent Danger as will not admit of delay.

ARTICLE II

Section 1. The executive Power shall be vested in a President of the United States of America. He shall hold his Office during the Term of four Years, and, together with the Vice President, chosen for the same Term, be elected, as follows.

Each State shall appoint, in such Manner as the Legislature thereof may direct, a Number of Electors, equal to the whole Number of Senators and Representatives to which the State may be entitled in the Congress: but no Senator or Representative, or Person holding an Office of Trust or Profit under the United States, shall be appointed an Elector.

[The Electors shall meet in their respective States, and vote by Ballot for two Persons, of whom one at least shall not be an Inhabitant of the same State with themselves. And they shall make a List of all the Persons voted for, and of the Number of Votes for each; which List they shall sign and certify, and transmit sealed to the Seat of the Government of the United States, directed to the President of the Senate. The President of the Senate shall, in the Presence of the Senate and House of Representatives, open all the Certificates, and the Votes shall then be counted. The Person having the greatest Number of Votes shall be the President, if such Number be a Majority of the whole Number of Electors appointed; and if there be more than one who have such Majority, and have an equal Number of Votes, then the House of Representatives shall immediately chuse by Ballot one of them for President; and if no Person have a Majority, then from the five highest on the list the said House shall in like Manner chuse the President. But in chusing the President, the Votes shall be taken by States, the Representation from each State having one Vote; a quorum for this Purpose shall consist of a Member or Members from two thirds of the States, and a Majority of all the States shall be necessary to a Choice. In every Case, after the Choice of the President, the Person having the greatest Number of Votes of the Electors shall be the Vice President. But if there should remain two or more who have equal Votes, the Senate shall chuse from them by Ballot the Vice President.][6]

The Congress may determine the Time of chusing the Electors, and the Day on which they shall give their Votes; which Day shall be the same throughout the United States.

No Person except a natural born Citizen, or a Citizen of the United States, at the time of the Adoption of this Constitution, shall be eligible to the Office of President; neither shall any Person be eligible to that Office who shall not have attained to the Age of thirty five Years, and been fourteen Years a Resident within the United States.

In Case of the Removal of the President from Office, or of his Death, Resignation, or Inability to discharge the Powers and Duties of the said Office,[7] the Same shall devolve on the Vice President, and the Congress may by Law provide for the Case of Removal, Death, Resignation or Inability, both of the President and Vice President, declaring what Officer shall then act as President, and such Officer shall act accordingly, until the Disability be removed, or a President shall be elected.

The President shall, at stated Times, receive for his Services, a Compensation, which shall neither be increased nor diminished during the Period for which he shall have been elected, and he shall not receive within that Period any other Emolument from the United States, or any of them.

Before he enter on the Execution of his Office, he shall take the following Oath or Affirmation: — "I do solemnly swear (or affirm) that I will faithfully execute the Office of President of the United States, and will to the best of my Ability, preserve, protect and defend the Constitution of the United States."

Section 2. The President shall be Commander in Chief of the Army and Navy of the United States, and of the Militia of the several States, when called into the actual Service of the United States; he may require the Opinion, in writing, of the principal Officer in each of the executive Departments, upon any Subject relating to the Duties of their respective Offices, and he shall have Power to grant Reprieves and Pardons for Offenses against the United States, except in Cases of Impeachment.

He shall have Power, by and with the Advice and Consent of the Senate, to make Treaties, provided two thirds of the Senators present concur; and he shall nominate, and by and with the Advice and Consent of the Senate, shall appoint Ambassadors, other public Ministers and Consuls, Judges of the supreme Court, and all other Officers of the United States, whose Appointments are not herein otherwise provided for, and which shall be established by Law: but the Congress may by Law vest the Appointment of such inferior Officers, as they think proper, in the President alone, in the Courts of Law, or in the Heads of Departments.

The President shall have Power to fill up all Vacancies that may happen during the Recess of the Senate, by granting Commissions which shall expire at the End of their next Session.

Section 3. He shall from time to time give to the Congress Information of the State of the Union, and recommend to their Consideration such Measures as he shall judge necessary and expedient; he may, on extraordinary Occasions, convene both Houses, or either of them, and in Case of Disagreement between them, with Respect to the Time of Adjournment, he may adjourn them to such Time as he shall think proper; he shall receive Ambassadors and other public Ministers; he shall take Care that the Laws be faithfully executed, and shall Commission all the Officers of the United States.

Section 4. The President, Vice President and all Civil Officers of the United States, shall be removed from office on Impeachment for, and Conviction of, Treason, Bribery, or other high Crimes and Misdemeanors.

ARTICLE III

Section 1. The judicial Power of the United States, shall be vested in one supreme Court, and in such inferior Courts as the Congress may from time to time ordain and establish. The Judges, both of the supreme and inferior Courts, shall hold their Offices during good Behaviour, and shall, at stated Times, receive for their Services, a Compensation, which shall not be diminished during their Continuance in Office.

Section 2. The judicial Power shall extend to all Cases, in Law and Equity, arising under this Constitution, the Laws of the United States, and Treaties made, or which shall be made, under their Authority; — to all Cases affecting Ambassadors, other public Ministers and Consuls; — to all Cases of admiralty and maritime Jurisdiction; — to Controversies to which the United States shall be a Party; — to Controversies between two or more States; — between a State and Citizens of another State;[8] — between Citizens of different States; — between Citizens of the same State claiming Lands under Grants of different States, and between a State, or the Citizens thereof, and foreign States, Citizens or Subjects.[8]

In all Cases affecting Ambassadors, other public Ministers and Consuls, and those in which a State shall be Party, the supreme Court shall have original Jurisdiction. In all the other Cases before mentioned, the supreme Court shall have appellate Jurisdiction, both as to Law and Fact, with such Exceptions, and under such Regulations as the Congress shall make.

The Trial of all Crimes, except in cases of Impeachment, shall be by Jury; and such Trial shall be held in the State where the said Crimes shall have been committed; but when not committed within any State, the Trial shall be at such Place or Places as the Congress may by Law have directed.

Section 3. Treason against the United States, shall consist only in levying War against them, or in adhering to their Enemies, giving them Aid and Comfort. No Person shall be convicted of Treason unless on the Testimony of two Witnesses to the same overt Act, or on Confession in open Court.

The Congress shall have Power to declare the Punishment of Treason, but no Attainder of Treason shall work Corruption of Blood, or Forfeiture except during the Life of the Person attainted.

ARTICLE IV

Section 1. Full Faith and Credit shall be given in each State to the public Acts, Records, and judicial Proceedings of every other State. And the Congress may by general Laws prescribe the Manner in which such Acts, Records and Proceedings shall be proved, and the Effect thereof.

Section 2. The Citizens of each State shall be entitled to all Privileges and Immunities of Citizens in the several States.

A Person charged in any State with Treason, Felony, or other Crime, who shall flee from Justice, and be found in another State, shall on Demand of the executive Authority of the State from which he fled, be delivered up, to be removed to the State having Jurisdiction of the Crime.

[No Person held to Service or Labour in one State, under the Laws thereof, escaping into another, shall, in Consequence of any Law or Regulation therein, be discharged from such Service or Labour, but shall be delivered up on Claim of the Party to whom such Service or Labour may be due.][9]

Section 3. New States may be admitted by the Congress into this Union; but no new State shall be formed or erected within the Jurisdiction of any other State; nor any State be formed by the Junction of two or more States, or Parts of States, without the Consent of the Legislatures of the States concerned as well as of the Congress.

The Congress shall have Power to dispose of and make all needful Rules and Regulations respecting the Territory or other Property belonging to the United States; and nothing in this Constitution shall be so construed as to Prejudice any Claims of the United States, or of any particular State.

Section 4. The United States shall guarantee to every State in this Union a Republican Form of Government, and shall protect each of them against Invasion; and on Application of the Legislature, or of the Executive (when the Legislature cannot be convened) against domestic Violence.

ARTICLE V

The Congress, whenever two thirds of both Houses shall deem it necessary, shall propose Amendments to this Constitution, or, on the Application of the Legislatures of two thirds of the several States, shall call a Convention for proposing Amendments, which, in either Case, shall be valid to all Intents and Purposes, as Part of this Constitution, when ratified by the Legislatures of three fourths of the several States, or by Conventions in three fourths thereof, as the one or the other Mode of Ratification may be proposed by the Congress; Provided [that no Amendment which may be made prior to the Year One thousand eight hundred and eight shall in any Manner affect the first and fourth Clauses in the Ninth Section of the first Article; and][10] that no State, without its Consent, shall be deprived of its equal Suffrage in the Senate.

ARTICLE VI

All Debts contracted and Engagements entered into, before the Adoption of this Constitution, shall be as valid against the United States under this Constitution, as under the Confederation.

This Constitution, and the Laws of the United States which shall be made in Pursuance thereof; and all Treaties made, or which shall be made, under the Authority of the United States, shall be the supreme Law of the Land; and the Judges in every State shall be bound thereby, any Thing in the Constitution or Laws of any State to the Contrary notwithstanding.

The Senators and Representatives before mentioned, and the Members of the several State Legislatures, and all executive and judicial Officers, both of the United States and of the several States, shall be bound by Oath or Affirmation, to support this Constitution; but no religious Test shall ever be required as a Qualification to any Office or public Trust under the United States.

ARTICLE VII

The Ratification of the Conventions of nine States, shall be sufficient for the Establishment of this Constitution between the States so ratifying the Same. Done in Convention by the Unanimous Consent of the States present the Seventeenth Day of September in the Year of our Lord one thousand seven hundred and Eighty seven and of the Independence of the United States of America the Twelfth. In witness whereof We have hereunto subscribed our Names, George Washington, President and deputy from Virginia.

New Hampshire:	John Langdon, Nicholas Gilman.
Massachusetts:	Nathaniel Gorham, Rufus King.
Connecticut:	William Samuel Johnson, Roger Sherman.
New York:	Alexander Hamilton
New Jersey:	William Livingston, David Brearley, William Paterson, Jonathan Dayton.
Pennsylvania:	Benjamin Franklin, Thomas Mifflin, Robert Morris, George Clymer, Thomas FitzSimons, Jared Ingersoll, James Wilson, Gouverneur Morris.
Delaware:	George Read, Gunning Bedford Jr., John Dickinson, Richard Bassett, Jacob Broom.
Maryland:	James McHenry, Daniel of St. Thomas Jenifer, Daniel Carroll.
Virginia:	John Blair, James Madison Jr.
North Carolina:	William Blount, Richard Dobbs Spaight, Hugh Williamson.
South Carolina:	John Rutledge, Charles Cotesworth Pinckney, Charles Pinckney, Pierce Butler.
Georgia:	William Few, Abraham Baldwin.

[The language of the original Constitution, not including the Amendments, was adopted by a convention of the states on Sept. 17, 1787, and was subsequently ratified by the states on the following dates: Delaware, Dec. 7, 1787; Pennsylvania, Dec. 12, 1787; New Jersey, Dec. 18, 1787; Georgia, Jan. 2, 1788; Connecticut, Jan. 9, 1788; Massachusetts, Feb. 6, 1788; Maryland, April 28, 1788; South Carolina, May 23, 1788; New Hampshire, June 21, 1788.

Ratification was completed on June 21, 1788.

The Constitution subsequently was ratified by Virginia, June 25, 1788; New York, July 26, 1788; North Carolina, Nov. 21, 1789; Rhode Island, May 29, 1790; and Vermont, Jan. 10, 1791.]

AMENDMENTS

Amendment I

(First ten amendments ratified Dec. 15, 1791.)

Congress shall make no law respecting an establishment of religion, or prohibiting the free exercise thereof; or abridging the freedom of speech, or of the press; or the right of the people peaceably to assemble, and to petition the Government for a redress of grievances.

Amendment II

A well regulated Militia, being necessary to the security of a free State, the right of the people to keep and bear Arms, shall not be infringed.

Amendment III

No Soldier shall, in time of peace be quartered in any house, without the consent of the Owner, nor in time of war, but in a manner to be prescribed by law.

Amendment IV

The right of the people to be secure in their persons, houses, papers, and effects, against unreasonable searches and seizures, shall not be violated, and no Warrants shall issue, but upon probable cause, supported by Oath or affirmation, and particularly describing the place to be searched, and the persons or things to be seized.

Amendment V

No person shall be held to answer for a capital, or otherwise infamous crime, unless on a presentment or indictment of a Grand Jury, except in cases arising in the land or naval forces, or in the Militia, when in actual service in time of War or public danger; nor shall any person be subject for the same offence to be twice put in jeopardy of life or limb; nor shall be compelled in any criminal case to be a witness against himself, nor be deprived of life, liberty, or property, without due process of law; nor shall private property be taken for public use, without just compensation.

Amendment VI

In all criminal prosecutions, the accused shall enjoy the right to a speedy and public trial, by an impartial jury of the State and district wherein the crime shall have been committed, which district shall have been previously ascertained by law, and to be informed of the nature and cause of the accusation; to be confronted with the witnesses against him; to have compulsory process for obtaining witnesses in his favor, and to have the Assistance of Counsel for his defence.

Amendment VII

In Suits at common law, where the value in controversy shall exceed twenty dollars, the right of trial by jury shall be preserved, and no fact tried by a jury, shall be otherwise re-examined in any Court of the United States, than according to the rules of the common law.

Amendment VIII

Excessive bail shall not be required, nor excessive fines imposed, nor cruel and unusual punishments inflicted.

Amendment IX

The enumeration in the Constitution, of certain rights, shall not be construed to deny or disparage others retained by the people.

Amendment X

The powers not delegated to the United States by the Constitution, nor prohibited by it to the States, are reserved to the States respectively, or to the people.

Amendment XI *(Ratified Feb. 7, 1795)*

The Judicial power of the United States shall not be construed to extend to any suit in law or equity, commenced or prosecuted against one of the United States by Citizens of another State, or by Citizens or Subjects of any Foreign State.

Amendment XII *(Ratified June 15, 1804)*

The Electors shall meet in their respective states and vote by ballot for President and Vice-President, one of whom, at least, shall not be an inhabitant of the same state with themselves; they shall name in their ballots the person voted for as President, and in distinct ballots the person voted for as Vice-President, and they shall make distinct lists of all persons voted for as President, and of all persons voted for as Vice-President, and of the number of votes for each, which lists they shall sign and certify, and transmit sealed to the seat of the government of the United States, directed to the President of the Senate; — The President of the Senate shall, in the presence of the Senate and House of Representatives, open all the certificates and the votes shall then be counted; — The person having the greatest number of votes for President, shall be the President, if such number be a majority of the whole number of Electors appointed; and if no person have such majority, then from the persons having the highest numbers not exceeding three on the list of those voted for as President, the House of Representatives shall choose immediately, by ballot, the President. But in choosing the President, the votes shall be taken by states, the representation from each state having one vote; a quorum for this purpose shall consist of a member or members from two-thirds of the states, and a majority of all the states shall be necessary to a choice. [And if the House of Representatives shall not choose a President whenever the right of choice shall devolve upon them, before the fourth day of March next following, then the Vice-President shall act as President, as in the case of the death or other constitutional disability of the President —][11] The person having the greatest number of votes as Vice-President, shall be the Vice-President, if such number be a majority of the whole number of Electors appointed, and if no person have a majority, then from the two highest numbers on the list, the Senate shall choose the Vice-President; a quorum for the purpose shall consist of two-thirds of the whole number of Senators, and a majority of the whole number shall be necessary to a choice. But no person constitutionally ineligible to the office of President shall be eligible to that of Vice-President of the United States.

Amendment XIII *(Ratified Dec. 6, 1865)*

Section 1. Neither slavery nor involuntary servitude, except as a punishment for crime whereof the party shall have been duly convicted, shall exist within the United States, or any place subject to their jurisdiction.

Section 2. Congress shall have power to enforce this article by appropriate legislation.

Amendment XIV *(Ratified July 9, 1868)*

Section 1. All persons born or naturalized in the United States and subject to the jurisdiction thereof, are citizens of the United States and of the State wherein they reside. No State shall make or enforce any law which shall abridge the privileges or immunities of citizens of the United States; nor shall any State deprive any person of life, liberty, or property, without due process of law; nor deny to any person within its jurisdiction the equal protection of the laws.

Section 2. Representatives shall be apportioned among the several States according to their respective numbers, counting the whole number of persons in each State, excluding Indians not taxed. But when the right to vote at any election for the choice of electors for President and Vice President of the United States, Representatives in Congress, the Executive and Judicial officers of a State, or the members of the Legislature thereof, is denied to any of the male inhabitants of such State, being twenty-one years of age,[12] and citizens of the United States, or in any way abridged, except for participation in rebellion, or other crime, the basis of representation therein shall be reduced in the proportion which the number of such male citizens shall bear to the whole number of male citizens twenty-one years of age in such State.

Section 3. No person shall be a Senator or Representative in Congress, or elector of President and Vice President, or hold any office, civil or military, under the United States, or under any State, who, having previously taken an oath, as a member of Congress, or as an officer of the United States, or as a member of any State legislature, or as an executive or judicial officer of any State, to support the Constitution of the United States, shall have engaged in insurrection or rebellion against the same, or given aid or comfort to the enemies thereof. But Congress may by a vote of two-thirds of each House, remove such disability.

Section 4. The validity of the public debt of the United States, authorized by law, including debts incurred for payment of pensions and bounties for services in suppressing insurrection or rebellion, shall not be questioned. But neither the United States nor any State shall assume or pay any debt or obligation incurred in aid of insurrection or rebellion against the United States, or any claim for the loss or emancipation of any slave; but all such debts, obligations and claims shall be held illegal and void.

Section 5. The Congress shall have power to enforce, by appropriate legislation, the provisions of this article.

Amendment XV *(Ratified Feb. 3, 1870)*

Section 1. The right of citizens of the United States to vote shall not be denied or abridged by the United States or by any State on account of race, color, or previous condition of servitude.

Section 2. The Congress shall have power to enforce this article by appropriate legislation.

Amendment XVI *(Ratified Feb. 3, 1913)*

The Congress shall have power to lay and collect taxes on incomes, from whatever source derived, without apportionment among the several States, and without regard to any census or enumeration.

Amendment XVII *(Ratified April 8, 1913)*

The Senate of the United States shall be composed of two Senators from each State, elected by the people thereof, for six years; and each Senator shall have one vote. The electors in each State shall have the qualifications requisite for electors of the most numerous branch of the State legislatures.

When vacancies happen in the representation of any State in the Senate, the executive authority of such State shall issue writs of election to fill such vacancies: *Provided,* That the legislature of any State may empower the executive thereof to make temporary appointments until the people fill the vacancies by election as the legislature may direct.

This amendment shall not be so construed as to affect the election or term of any Senator chosen before it becomes valid as part of the Constitution.

Amendment XVIII *(Ratified Jan. 16, 1919)*

Section 1. After one year from the ratification of this article the manufacture, sale, or transportation of intoxicating liquors within, the importation thereof into, or the exportation thereof from the United States and all territory subject to the jurisdiction thereof for beverage purposes is hereby prohibited.

Section 2. The Congress and the several States shall have concurrent power to enforce this article by appropriate legislation.

Section 3. This article shall be inoperative unless it shall have been ratified as an amendment to the Constitution by the legislatures of the several States, as provided in the Constitution, within seven years from the date of the submission hereof to the States by the Congress.][13]

Amendment XIX *(Ratified Aug. 18, 1920)*

The right of citizens of the United States to vote shall not be denied or abridged by the United States or by any State on account of sex.

Congress shall have power to enforce this article by appropriate legislation.

Amendment XX *(Ratified Jan. 23, 1933)*

Section 1. The terms of the President and Vice President shall end at noon on the 20th day of January, and the terms of Senators and Representatives at noon on the 3d day of January, of the years in which such terms would have ended if this article had not been ratified; and the terms of their successors shall then begin.

Section 2. The Congress shall assemble at least once in every year, and such meeting shall begin at noon on the 3d day of January, unless they shall by law appoint a different day.

Section 3.[14] If, at the time fixed for the beginning of the term of the President, the President elect shall have died, the Vice President elect shall become President. If a President shall not have been chosen before the time fixed for the beginning of his term, or if the President elect shall have failed to qualify, then the Vice President elect shall act as President until a President shall have qualified; and the Congress may by law provide for the case wherein neither a President elect nor a Vice President elect shall have qualified, declaring who shall then act as President, or the manner in which one who is to act shall be selected, and such person shall act accordingly until a President or Vice President shall have qualified.

Section 4. The Congress may by law provide for the case of the death of any of the persons from whom the House of Representatives may choose a President when-

ever the right of choice shall have devolved upon them, and for the case of the death of any of the persons from whom the Senate may choose a Vice President whenever the right of choice shall have devolved upon them.

Section 5. Sections 1 and 2 shall take effect on the 15th day of October following the ratification of this article.

Section 6. This article shall be inoperative unless it shall have been ratified as an amendment to the Constitution by the legislatures of three-fourths of the several States within seven years from the date of its submission.

Amendment XXI *(Ratified Dec. 5, 1933)*

Section 1. The eighteenth article of amendment to the Constitution of the United States is hereby repealed.

Section 2. The transportation or importation into any State, Territory or possession of the United States for delivery or use therein of intoxicating liquors, in violation of the laws thereof, is hereby prohibited.

Section 3. This article shall be inoperative unless it shall have been ratified as an amendment to the Constitution by conventions in the several States, as provided in the Constitution, within seven years from the date of the submission hereof to the States by the Congress.

Amendment XXII *(Ratified Feb. 27, 1951)*

Section 1. No person shall be elected to the office of the President more than twice, and no person who has held the office of President, or acted as President, for more than two years of a term to which some other person was elected President shall be elected to the office of the President more than once. But this Article shall not apply to any person holding the office of President when this Article was proposed by the Congress, and shall not prevent any person who may be holding the office of President, or acting as President, during the term within which this Article become operative from holding the office of President or acting as President during the remainder of such term.

Section 2. This Article shall be inoperative unless it shall have been ratified as an amendment to the Constitution by the legislatures of three-fourths of the several States within seven years from the date of its submission to the States by the Congress.

Amendment XXIII *(Ratified March 29, 1961)*

Section 1. The District constituting the seat of Government of the United States shall appoint in such manner as the Congress may direct:

A number of electors of President and Vice President equal to the whole number of Senators and Representatives in Congress to which the District would be entitled if it were a State, but in no event more than the least populous State; they shall be in addition to those appointed by the States, but they shall be considered, for the purposes of the election of President and Vice President, to be electors appointed by a State; and they shall meet in the District and perform such duties as provided by the twelfth article of amendment.

Section 2. The Congress shall have power to enforce this article by appropriate legislation.

Amendment XXIV *(Ratified Jan. 23, 1964)*

Section 1. The right of citizens of the United States to vote in any primary or other election for President or

Vice President, for electors for President or Vice President, or for Senator or Representative in Congress, shall not be denied or abridged by the United States or any State by reason of failure to pay any poll tax or other tax.

Section 2. The Congress shall have power to enforce this article by appropriate legislation.

Amendment XXV *(Ratified Feb. 10, 1967)*

Section 1. In case of the removal of the President from office or of his death or resignation, the Vice President shall become President.

Section 2. Whenever there is a vacancy in the office of the Vice President, the President shall nominate a Vice President who shall take office upon confirmation by a majority vote of both Houses of Congress.

Section 3. Whenever the President transmits to the President pro tempore of the Senate and the Speaker of the House of Representatives his written declaration that he is unable to discharge the powers and duties of his office, and until he transmits to them a written declaration to the contrary, such powers and duties shall be discharged by the Vice President as Acting President.

Section 4. Whenever the Vice President and a majority of either the principal officers of the executive departments or of such other body as Congress may by law provide, transmit to the President pro tempore of the Senate and the Speaker of the House of Representatives their written declaration that the President is unable to discharge the powers and duties of his office, the Vice President shall immediately assume the powers and duties of the office as Acting President.

Thereafter, when the President transmits to the President pro tempore of the Senate and the Speaker of the House of Representatives his written declaration that no inability exists, he shall resume the powers and duties of his office unless the Vice President and a majority of either the principal officers of the executive department or of such other body as Congress may by law provide, transmit within four days to the President pro tempore of the Senate and the Speaker of the House of Representatives their written declaration that the President is unable to dis-charge the powers and duties of his office. Thereupon Congress shall decide the issue, assembling within forty-eight hours for that purpose if not in session. If the Congress, within twenty-one days after receipt of the latter written declaration, or, if Congress is not in session, within twenty-one days after Congress is required to assemble, determines by two-thirds vote of both houses that the President is unable to discharge the powers and duties of his office, the Vice President shall continue to discharge the same as Acting President; otherwise, the President shall resume the powers and duties of his office.

Amendment XXVI *(Ratified July 1, 1971)*

Section 1. The right of citizens of the United States, who are eighteen years of age or older, to vote shall not be denied or abridged by the United States or by any State on account of age.

Section 2. The Congress shall have power to enforce this article by appropriate legislation.

Footnotes

1. The part in brackets was changed by section 2 of the Fourteenth Amendment.
2. The part in brackets was changed by section 1 of the Seventeenth Amendment.
3. The part in brackets was changed by the second paragraph of the Seventeenth Amendment.
4. The part in brackets was changed by section 2 of the Twentieth Amendment.
5. The Sixteenth Amendment gave Congress the power to tax incomes.
6. The material in brackets has been superseded by the Twelfth Amendment.
7. This provision has been affected by the Twenty-fifth Amendment.
8. These clauses were affected by the Eleventh Amendment.
9. This paragraph has been superseded by the Thirteenth Amendment.
10. Obsolete.
11. The part in brackets has been superseded by section 3 of the Twentieth Amendment.
12. See the Twenty-sixth Amendment.
13. This Amendment was repealed by section 1 of the Twenty-first Amendment.
14. See the Twenty-fifth Amendment.

Source: U.S. Congress, House, Committee on the Judiciary, *The Constitution of the United States of America, As Amended Through July 1971,* H. Doc. 93-215, 93rd Cong., 2nd sess., 1974.

INDEX

Index